"Kapic is not only an able guide to England's greatest theologian; he has also restored Owen's remarkable exposition of communion with God to its central place. Here is a study that understands and underlines the Puritan conviction that all truly biblical theology is profoundly pastoral."

Sinclair B. Ferguson, Chancellor's Professor of Systematic Theology, Reformed Theological Seminary

"This well-rounded research will be of interest to anyone concerned with the development of Reformed theology from a historical or systematic perspective. Kapic's analysis is clear and well constructed, solidly grounded in an excellent grasp of recent writing on Owen and with a sure sense of where its own distinctive contribution lies. Kapic has produced a meticulous piece of scholarship that brings a sophisticated and nuanced approach to the exploration of crucial themes in Owen's theology."

Susan Hardman Moore, School of Divinity, University of Edinburgh (emeritus)

"Kelly Kapic has carefully mined the theological riches of John Owen and has presented them for our study and edification. This welcome work provides the theological foundation for understanding the spiritual hunger and needs of our contemporary church and points us in the proper direction for addressing them. We are greatly in debt to Kapic for this reminder of the transforming message of John Owen for today."

Tom Schwanda, associate professor of Christian formation and ministry emeritus, Wheaton College

"This book, which draws from an impressive array of sources, is a marvelously rich, full, and systematic treatment of Owen's focus on communion with God. It will enhance our understanding and appreciation of Owen and, most importantly, of personal communion with the Triune God."

Joel R. Beeke, Puritan Reformed Theological Seminary

COMMUNION
WITH
GOD

The Divine
and the Human in the Theology of
John Owen

KELLY M. KAPIC

WITH A NEW PREFACE

Baker Academic
a division of Baker Publishing Group
Grand Rapids, Michigan

Published by Baker Academic
a division of Baker Publishing Group
P.O. Box 6287, Grand Rapids, MI 49516-6287
www.bakeracademic.com

Repackaged with a new preface in 2024

Printed in the United States of America

Library of Congress Cataloging-in-Publication Data
Kapic, Kelly M., 1972–
    Communion with God : the divine and the human in the theology of John Owen
/ Kelly M. Kapic.
        p.   cm.
    Includes bibliographical references and index.
    ISBN 10: 0-8010-3144-3 (pbk.)
    ISBN 978-0-8010-3144-1 (pbk.)
    1. Owen, John, 1616–1683. 2. Theology—Early works to 1800. I. Title.
BX5207.O88K37 2007
230'.59092—dc22   2006034025

Scripture quotations are from the King James Version of the Bible.

Chapter five of this volume appears in much abbreviated form in *The Devoted Life*, edited by Kelly M. Kapic and Randall C. Gleason. Used with permission of InterVarsity Press, P.O. Box 1400, Downers Grove, IL 60515. www.ivpress.com

Cover art: *Mullein*, by Jan Stanislawski (1887)

Baker Publishing Group publications use paper produced from sustainable forestry practices and postconsumer waste whenever possible.

In Memory of Colin E. Gunton
Scholar, Mentor, Friend

and

In Loving Appreciation of Tabitha Kapic
Beloved

To the Puritans, communion between God and man is the end to which both creation and redemption are the means; it is the goal to which both theology and preaching must ever point; it is the essence of true religion; it is, indeed, the definition of Christianity.

J. I. Packer, *A Quest for Godliness*

CONTENTS

CONTENTS

PREFACE

It is a joy and deep encouragement to have this volume reprinted just short of the 20th anniversary of its original publication. At the end of the last century, John Owen was beginning to capture the imagination of more people in the church and the academy. Out of this slowly growing stream my book surfaced.

Communion with God begins by surveying the "lingering shadow" of Owen up through roughly the year 2000; but since the book's publication, we have witnessed the continuing rise of scholarship on this "prince of Puritan theologians." A cottage industry of publications has included academic treatments of Owen's life, theology, and historical context as well as many more popular-level books and abridgments. Given that I have recently traced some of this literature and hinted at the directions in which I see future Owen studies pointing, I will not review that material again here.[1]

Instead of slowing down, interest seems to be ratcheting up even further with the advent of a new scholarly edition of the full works of John Owen, which is now slowly appearing. When complete, this new edition will contain forty volumes(!), including some never-before-published material and other work freshly translated. Clearly interest in Owen is not viewed as a passing trend but is worth continued careful attention by theologians, historians, pastors, and even the laity.

Many readers have encouraged the reprinting of this volume, suggesting that it serves as an especially helpful introduction and overview of some key contributions from Owen. Such encouragement has been

---

1. See Kelly M. Kapic, "Retrieving Owen," in *T&T Clark Handbook of John Owen*, ed. Crawford Gribben and John W. Tweeddale (London: T&T Clark, 2022), 489–516.

deeply meaningful, and I am hopeful they are right. I do believe that this book will give the reader a fair sense of Owen's overall theology and show why serious academics as well as those with a pastoral heart find Owen compelling.

This book lays out Owen's attempt at a holistic account of what it means to be human, framed around the idea that people were made for communion with God. To follow Owen's logic, this book progresses through the creation of humans in the image of God (chap. 2), the redemptive work of the incarnation (chap. 3), and the theme of reconciliation (especially justification; chap. 4). At the heart of the book and central to Owen's overall theology is an extended treatment of how he encourages communion with the distinct persons of the Trinity: Father, Son, and Spirit (chap. 5). I believe these are some of Owen's greatest contributions, both theologically and pastorally. We conclude with a fresh look at how the Lord's day and Lord's supper support the vision Owen has laid out for the life of the believer in communion with the living God (chap. 6).

It is my great hope and prayer that taking the time to study Owen's work—no matter how much of it one may agree with—will challenge you and bring you fresh thoughts and encouragement.

Kelly M. Kapic
Easter 2024

ACKNOWLEDGMENTS

Life is full of journeys, and those treks are enjoyable primarily because of the people with whom one walks. Although I remain responsible for all that follows—since it can only represent my limited perspective of the many things seen during my excursions—it must be said that if others had not helped me notice details in the landscape and pointed out distant vistas, my own record of the journey would be much less interesting. With this in mind, I would like briefly to thank those who have been so influential along the way.

It is appropriate for me to begin by thanking God for the late Colin E. Gunton. Like many others who studied under Colin, I find myself profoundly impacted by this man who unapologetically loved theology, his church, his family, and his garden. His investment in me has had a deep and lasting impact, and although it is painful to no longer hear Colin's laughter and see his smile as he fidgets with his tie or his pen, there is no doubt that aspects of his voice continue through the research, writing, and preaching of his former students.

Since this project has been in the works for many years, it is necessary to acknowledge some former teachers and friends who have been exceedingly helpful in shaping my own thinking about various aspects of this study, often offering invaluable feedback and encouragement: Mark A. Noll, Frank A. James III, J. I. Packer, Roger Nicole, Richard Gamble, Susan Hardman Moore, Ashley Null, Sinclair Ferguson, Paul Helm, Steve Holmes, Dave Horner, Daniel Hill, Randal Gleason, Charles MacKenzie, Paul Chang-Ha Lim, Carl Trueman, Graham McFarlane, Donald McKim, Jay Green, Jeff Morton, Jeff Hall, Justin Taylor, Ron Frost, Brian Brock, Randal Rauser, Babu Venkataraman, Eric Flett, and John Yates. While much of this book was presented at different academic conferences, I would like to express my particular debt to the

11

Research Institute of Systematic Theology, where members heard and commented on much of what follows. Finally, I have benefited from the grace of many former students who took the time to work carefully through the entire manuscript, including Cameron Moran, Andrea Long, Brian Hecker, Heidi Herberich, and Cole Hamilton. While I would prefer to write something particular about each individual mentioned in this paragraph, let me simply say a collective thank you, for without you this volume would be much weaker and my life far less rich.

Given that one cannot engage in this type of research without the help of some excellent research libraries, I would like to thank the following institutions and their exceptional staffs: King's College, the University of London, the British Library, Oxford University, Cambridge University, Dr. Williams Library, and Covenant College. Librarians Tad Mindeman and John Holberg deserve special mention.

Yet research requires more than the academy, and particular thanks goes out to a special group of family and friends, without whom this work could never have been accomplished. Since this work began as research for my doctoral dissertation, during our years overseas and since our return, Tabitha and I have found ourselves sustained through the prayers, words of encouragement, and strong support of others. Our parents and siblings have consistently demonstrated their love for us in remarkable ways. Thank you Gary and Linda Kapic, John and Lynne Malley, David and Jennifer Kapic, Ming and Jennifer Chiou, and Danny and Emily Kapic. A special thank you to Jim and Dayle Seneff for your tremendous support and guidance on so many different levels—your friendship is dear to us.

It is said that if you want to emphasize a point, you must either begin or end with it. Although it is common for authors to thank their spouses, and I am sure they mean it, I fear that this general practice may somehow take away from the abiding gratefulness I wish to express to Tabitha, my wife and most vigorous editor. Words cannot describe the joy I feel for being allowed to join you on this great journey over the last fourteen years of our marriage. Your sacrifices have been significant, your encouragement profound, your friendship steadfast, and your love unwavering. One of the best parts about the years of research and teaching has been those opportunities we have had, especially over long meals and coffee, to dream and hope together. Now with two little ones filling the house with the delightful sound of feet scampering across wood floors, our lives are fuller than we could have ever imagined. John Owen, quoting an earlier theologian, once said that, "The delight in love is that of the lover in the beloved. Love is the beat of the heart that delights itself in someone." Through being with you I believe that I have experienced hints of what Owen describes as the soul resting and delighting in another, and in this way you have pointed me to the very love of God.

ABBREVIATIONS

ANF	*Ante-Nicene Fathers*
BE	Owen, *Works,* Banner of Truth reprint edition
BQ	*The Baptist Quarterly*
BT	Owen, *Biblical Theology,* Westcott translation
CD	Barth, *Church Dogmatics*
CH	*Church History*
CTJ	*Calvin Theological Journal*
DA	Aristotle, *De anima*
DLGTT	Muller, *Dictionary of Latin and Greek Theological Terms*
DNB	*Dictionary of National Biography*
EN	Aristotle, *Ethica nicomachea*
EQ	*Evangelical Quarterly*
FR	*Fides reformata*
GC	Owen, Greater Catechism
HJ	*Historical Journal*
HTR	*Harvard Theological Review*
IJST	*International Journal of Systematic Theology*
JECS	*Journal of Early Christian Studies*
JEH	*Journal of Ecclesiastical History*
JHBS	*Journal of the History of the Behavioral Sciences*
JPP	*Journal of Pastoral Practice*
JTS	*Journal of Theological Studies*
KJV	King James (or Authorized) Version
KTR	*King's Theological Review*

LC	Owen, Lesser Catechism
NPNF[1]	*Nicene and Post-Nicene Fathers*, First Series
NPNF[2]	*Nicene and Post-Nicene Fathers*, Second Series
PL	Jacques Paul Migne, ed., Patrologiae . . . latina, 222 vols.
PRRD	Muller, *Post-Reformation Reformed Dogmatics*, vols. 1–4
RC	The Racovian Catechism
RD	Heppe, *Reformed Dogmatics*
RR	Johnson and Leith, eds., *Reformed Reader*, vol. 1
SBET	*The Scottish Bulletin of Evangelical Theology*
SC	Owen, A Short Catechism or A Brief Instruction in the Worship of God
SJT	*Scottish Journal of Theology*
ST	Aquinas, *Summa theologiae*
TB	*Tyndale Bulletin*
TR	*Theologia reformata*
TT	*Theology Today*
WCF	Westminster Confession of Faith
WLC	Westminster Larger Catechism
Works	Owen, *Works*, Goold Edition
WSC	Westminster Shorter Catechism
WTJ	*Westminster Theological Journal*

THE LINGERING SHADOW OF JOHN OWEN

Dr. John Owen was a man of no ordinary intellect.

Samuel Taylor Coleridge, *Notes on English Divines*

Some writer in the last century (Dr. James Hamilton, if I mistake not) declared that evangelical theology had been hitherto alluvial for the most part, and that its main element was a detritus from mount Owen.

James Moffatt, *The Golden Book of John Owen* (1904)

The Continuing Presence of a Theologian

Since many twenty-first-century Christians are not well-acquainted with John Owen (1616–83), it may surprise some to learn that the long shadow of this theological giant is still readily visible if one is paying attention. The streets of Liverpool, Belfast, or Edinburgh today pass by numerous book-shops bearing Owen's name.[1] Visiting the outskirts of London, one might also stumble across a nonconformist seminary that has recently opened the John Owen Theological Centre.[2] Moving from the streets of the city to

---

1. Wesley Owen Books and Music stores, which refer to John Wesley and John Owen, have over forty shops throughout the UK.
2. The London Theological Seminary opened this Centre in 1999. Students in their ThM program receive internationally accredited degrees through the Centre's partner, Westminster Theological Seminary, Philadelphia, USA.

the superhighway in cyberspace, one discovers numerous Web sites either dedicated solely to him, or including him as an authority.[3] Ages Software has even produced an entire CD-ROM that compiles most of Owen's writings in a searchable format.[4] A twenty-four volume edition of his *Works* remains in print,[5] and a recent translation of his major Latin treatise (with the Greek title ΘΕΟΛΟΓΟΥΜΕΝΑ ΠΑΝΤΟΔΑΠΑ—*Theologoumena pantodapa* [Theological Teachings of All Sorts]) on the discipline of theology has also recently appeared.[6] A revival has taken place in publishing abridged and "easy-to-read" versions of many of his key books.[7] Kris Lundgaard, although not exactly engaged in abridgment, openly confesses to having

3. Although countless Web sites either refer to Owen or use extensive quotations from his work, two particular examples demonstrate his popularity in this medium. The first is a recent Web site strictly dedicated to all things Owen: johnowen.org. This site includes a good and growing bibliography, some of Owen's works scanned for Internet reading, a gallery of quotations and images, an old biography, and so on. The second example shows how people continue to regard him as an authority able to persuade today's reader: "John Owen on the Jewish People," chaim.org/owen.htm. At this site one finds an appeal to Owen in order to convince contemporary Reformed congregations to minister particularly to Jewish people.

4. *The Works of John Owen* (Rio, WI: Ages Software, 2000). Although claiming to be the nineteenth-century edition, this is clearly a scanned copy of the Banner of Truth reprint mentioned below. Unfortunately, the CD is missing the Latin works, uses the Banner volume numbers, and has altogether new page numbers.

5. John Owen, *The Works of John Owen*, ed. William H. Goold, 24 vols. (Edinburgh & London: Johnstone & Hunter, 1850–55). Vols. 1–16 were reprinted in Edinburgh by Banner of Truth Trust, 1965. However, the Banner Edition (hereafter cited as BE) omitted all of Owen's Latin writings and orations, thus rearranging and combining vols. 16–17. The last seven volumes of the Goold set, containing Owen's Hebrews commentary, were also reprinted (Edinburgh: Banner of Truth, 1991). The BE of Hebrews does not follow the volume numbers of the Goold edition, being always one volume behind. E.g., BE's vol. 20 = Goold's vol. 21. Hereafter, *Works* (even without Owen's name) will refer to the original Goold 24-volume edition. Volume number and pages will always annotate references to Owen's *Works*. The frequent italics found in Owen's *Works* are not retained, since many times it is unclear, from the different seventeenth-century editions, whether the emphasis comes directly from Owen or from an excited printer.

6. John Owen, *Biblical Theology, or, The Nature, Origin, Development, and Study of Theological Truth, in Six Books*, trans. Stephen P. Westcott (Morgan, PA: Soli Deo Gloria, 1994); hereafter cited as *BT*. The original title of the translated work is ΘΕΟΛΟΓΟΥΜΕΝΑ ΠΑΝΤΟΔΑΠΑ, *sive, De natura, ortu, progressu, et studio, veræ theologiæ* . . . , 6 vols. (Oxoniæ [in Oxford]: Tho. Robinson, 1661), appearing in vol. 17 of the original Goold edition; it has been left out of the more recent BE publication.

7. E.g., The Treasures of John Owen for Today's Readers, a multivolume series printed by Banner of Truth Trust and edited by R. J. K. Law. See also James M. Houston's version of three of Owen's treatises, in *Sin and Temptation: The Challenge of Personal Godliness* (Minneapolis: Bethany House, 1996). Grace Publications also printed several abridgments of classic Owen treatises. Christian Focus Publishers (Fearn, Tain, UK) has just started new releases of nicely reformatted but unabridged paperback volumes of key Owen books, which were previously available only in the expensive hardbound *Works* edition.

"kidnapped Owen," using him as a sort of "co-author."[8] Lundgaard's book, in essence a modern version of Owen's thoughts on the believer's struggle with sin, has already sold over fifty-five thousand copies! These different adaptations have been well received, since even admirers of the learned Puritan fondly refer to his writing style as "Latinized English," which certainly does not make for easy reading.[9]

Beyond this popular literature and various reprintings, over the last thirty years there has been a steadily growing interest in scholarship on Owen, primarily concerned with his theology rather than his life. For the most part this revival has thus far taken the form of unpublished dissertations, with a few academic monographs now beginning to be available in print.[10] In all of these formats, this Puritan preacher shows his continued influence on clergy, laity, and scholars. Clearly Owen has cast a long shadow, and there is good reason for a new generation to rediscover him as a significant theological dialogue partner, worthy of serious study.

Before providing a brief sketch of the man who cast this shadow and outlining the focus of our study of Owen, it may prove interesting if we first hear a few examples of how Owen was viewed from the seventeenth through the early twentieth century. Again, the level of Owen's influence during this period is often surprising, and this quick survey helps make the case that Owen deserves a fresh hearing in the twenty-first century, for he has long been viewed as a first-rate spiritual theologian.

Signs of the Shadow through the Centuries

Little captures Owen's popularity during the seventeenth century better than a vicious letter sent to him by a Quaker sympathizer.[11] Apparently

8. Kris Lundgaard, *The Enemy Within: Straight Talk about the Power and Defeat of Sin* (Phillipsburg, NJ: P&R, 1998), 14. Lundgaard has also published another volume entitled *Through the Looking Glass: Reflections on Christ That Change Us* (Phillipsburg, NJ: P&R, 2000), which is likewise based on Owen's writings and has already sold over 8,000 copies.

9. J. I. Packer muses: "Owen's style is often stigmatised as cumbersome and tortuous. Actually it is a Latinized spoken style, fluent but stately and expansive, in the elaborate Ciceronian manner"; from *A Quest for Godliness: The Puritan Vision of the Christian Life* (Wheaton: Crossway, 1990), 194.

10. For a general review of the literature on John Owen over the last century, see Kelly M. Kapic, "Communion with God: Relations between the Divine and the Human in the Theology of John Owen" (PhD diss., King's College London, 2001), 12–48. An extensive bibliography of both primary and secondary literature is also included at the end of this book.

11. The original letter is found in the British Library, but Peter Toon, ed., has conveniently reprinted it in *The Correspondence of John Owen (1616–1683)* (Cambridge, UK:

"Thomas Truthsbye," in an effort to discover which "Clergy-men were famous, and notorious" in the eyes of the leaders of the "late revolutions in England," kept hearing Owen's name above the others.[12] Offering what appears to us to be a wonderful compliment of a theologian's accessibility—though never intended that way—he adds: "I can scarce visit a Tavern, or Country Ale-house, but forth comes some of the Learned Works of *John Owen*, a Servant, &c. as if you were cut out to entertain all sorts of Guests; if I send Tobacco, your Books are the inclosure of it, and there I finde your name stinking worse than that *Indian* Weed." This attack shows how influential Owen and his writings had become by the second half of the seventeenth century.

Owen's fame continued into the eighteenth century, though usually friends rather than foes remembered him. Judging by the testimony in David Clarkson's sermon at Owen's funeral and the two early biographies of Owen, the public clearly considered Owen a (if not *the*) leading British theologian of the seventeenth century.[13] As such, people often idealized him to represent the best of Puritan theology and practice, usually drawing attention away from his political involvement. This later generation's willingness to downplay Owen's participation in the political turmoil of the seventeenth century demonstrates the ongoing value placed upon his theological contributions. His writings continued to have a wide readership, giving rise to more than fifty printings in the eighteenth century of different works by Owen, many of which were translated into Dutch, Swedish, and Welsh.[14] Thus William Wilberforce (1759–1833), best known for his leading role in abolishing the slave trade in Britain, could highly recommend Owen to his readers in 1797, knowing that the books would be available to them.[15]

Nevertheless, it was the nineteenth century that witnessed a real explosion of interest. On average there was a book by Owen published every

James Clarke, 1970), 166–67, original emphasis. Toon suggests that "Thomas Truthsbye" is probably Thomas Taylor; cf. *DNB*.

12. Truthsbye writes: "Your [i.e., Owen's] Worship was cried up as high as Tyburn, as well known, and as little trusted; in my Travels Westward they calld [*sic*] you *Quaker*, Northward *Anabaptist*, in *Oxford* a State *Independent*, in *London* a *Jesuite*, beyond Seas a conscience-mender."

13. David Clarkson, Owen's successor at the Leadenhall Street church in London, preached Owen's funeral sermon. It is reprinted in Thomas Russell's 1826 edition of *The Works of John Owen*, 1:411–22. In 1720 an anonymous *Life of John Owen* was printed, followed by John Asty, "Memoirs of the Life of John Owen," in *A Complete Collection of the Sermons of John Owen*, ed. John Asty (London: John Clark, 1721).

14. See Oxford Libraries' Union Catalogue (OLIS) and WorldCAT.

15. William Wilberforce, *A Practical View of the Prevailing Religious System of Professed Christians, in the Higher and Middle Classes in This Country, Contrasted with Real Christianity*, 18th ed. (London: T. Cadell, 1830), 240–41.

year between 1800 and 1860.[16] In 1826 Thomas Russell made the first effort to publish Owen's complete works, although this early attempt left much to be desired.[17] Given the renewed zeal for Owen's writings and the inadequacies of the Russell edition, William H. Goold produced the definitive edition of Owen's works from 1850 to 1855.[18] Goold's final collection contained twenty-four volumes, including Owen's Latin speeches and writings. This edition grew out of and continued to encourage interest in Owen both for pastoral and academic purposes.

One need only look to the popular nineteenth-century Baptist minister C. H. Spurgeon (1834–92) to see that Owen's appeal in England remained strong. Spurgeon, influencing a whole generation of preachers through the Pastors' College, Metropolitan Tabernacle in London, clearly encourages his students to wrestle through Owen's writings. Commenting on Owen's exposition of Psalm 130, Spurgeon praises him:

> It is unnecessary to say that he is the prince of divines. To master his works is to be a profound theologian. Owen is said to be a prolix, but it would be truer to say that he is condensed. His style is heavy because he gives notes of what he might have said, and passes on without fully developing the great thoughts of his capacious mind. He requires hard study, and none of us ought to grudge it.[19]

While we may argue that Spurgeon is overly kind regarding Owen's prose style, his enthusiasm toward this Puritan remains representative of many at this time.

Abraham Kuyper (1837–1920) reminds us that Owen also had an international following. Kuyper was a renowned Dutch theologian and

16. Abridgments of Owen's writings testify to his popularity and wide readership during this time. E.g., W. Wilson, ed., *Selections from the Works of John Owen* (London, 1826).

17. Thomas Russell, ed., *The Works of John Owen*, 21 vols. (London: Richard Baynes, 1826), containing another biography by William Orme (1787–1830). This edition was criticized for numerous reasons. For example, Russell declined to correct the significant inaccuracies of earlier editions: these include mispointing of the Hebrew, incorrect Greek accents, and significant problems with quotations from the early Greek and Latin fathers. Russell's edition also omits such important works as *Exercitations concerning . . . a Day of Sacred Rest* and ΘΕΟΛΟΓΟΥΜΕΝΑ ΠΑΝΤΟΔΑΠΑ. Although in our study *Works* always refers to the later Goold edition, the reader must beware that even now some scholars persist in using the Russell edition, which has different volume and page numbers. E.g., Alister McGrath, *Iustitia Dei: A History of the Christian Doctrine of Justification*, 2nd ed. (Cambridge, UK: Cambridge University Press, 1998).

18. For more on Goold, see Nigel M. de S. Cameron, *Dictionary of Scottish Church History and Theology* (Downers Grove, IL: InterVarsity, 1993), 369.

19. Charles H. Spurgeon, *Commenting and Commentaries* (London: Passmore & Alabaster, 1876), 103. Cf. W. H. Goold, "John Owen," in *Evangelical Succession*, 3rd ser., printed lecture (Edinburgh: MacNiven & Wallace, 1883).

later prime minister of the Netherlands (1900–05). In the original Dutch edition to Kuyper's classic work *Het werk van den Heiligen Geest* (*The Work of the Holy Spirit*), he begins his tome by noting his debt to Owen, whom Kuyper even two centuries later considered the leading authority on the subject of the Holy Spirit.[20] After discussing Owen's important contribution, he lists for his readers many works of Owen—seventy-four volumes—many of which are available in Dutch translation. Kuyper's respect for Owen and the phenomenal number of Dutch translations demonstrates how Owen's books found an eager audience beyond Britain and the United States. Since their original appearance, Owen's books have been translated into a number of languages beyond Dutch, including Korean, Scottish Gaelic, Welsh, and Spanish. As recent studies of Owen published in Portuguese and Dutch clearly demonstrate, this international interest has not died.[21]

In the twentieth century the "Atlas of Independency"[22] remained a favorite among English conservative congregational ministers, providing an intellectual foundation for many of their distinct theological emphases in a changing world. Likewise, Owen's writings continued to elicit the occasional response from those who viewed his theology as unbiblical and dangerous. For example, in the early part of the twentieth century an anonymous author attacked Owen's classic statement on particular atonement, in *Under Calvin's Yoke: Dr. John Owen's Three Invincible Questions Answered by Bereana*.[23] Here the author tries to answer Owen's infamous syllogism, which countless Calvinists thought inevitably leads all reasonable Christians to conclude that Christ died only for the elect.[24]

---

20. Abraham Kuyper, *Het werk van den Heiligen Geest* (Amsterdam: J. A. Wormser, 1888). The material on Owen is in the *Voorrede* (prologue), which includes his listing of Owen's translated works. This listing of works is missing in the English translation of Kuyper's book. Cf. Abraham Kuyper, *The Work of the Holy Spirit*, trans. Henri de Vries (New York: Funk & Wagnalls, 1900).

21. E.g., Valdeci dos Santos, "O 'Crente Carnal' à Luz do ensino de John Owen sobre a Mortificação," *FR* 4, no. 1 (1999): 57–68; R. W. DeKoeyer, "Pneumatologia: Enkel aspecten van de leer van de heilige Geest bji de puritein John Owen," *TR* 34 (1991): 226–46, which is based on his thesis, "Pneumatologia: Een onderzoek naar de leer van de Heilige Geest bij de puritein John Owen (1616–1683)" (Utrecht, 1990). A recent thesis from the Philippines also testifies to Owen's remaining international appeal: D. J. McKinley, "John Owen's View of Illumination and Its Contemporary Relevance" (ThD diss., University of Santo Tomas, Manila, 1995).

22. This name given to Owen originated as a slur when used by George Vernon, *A Letter to a Friend* (London: printed by J. Redmayne, 1670), 36. He was discussing Owen's alleged role in bringing down Richard Cromwell. For a fuller discussion, see R. Tudor Jones, *Congregationalism in England, 1662–1962* (London: Independent Press, 1962), 71–72.

23. Anonymous, *Under Calvin's Yoke: Dr. John Owen's Three Invincible Questions Answered by Bereana* (London: Elliot Stock, 1930).

24. This syllogism is laid out and discussed in chap. 5 of this book.

While the argument in this brief book is of no direct concern to our study, what is of interest is that over two hundred years after Owen's death, Owen's arguments were still used by Calvinists, and Arminian theologians still found it necessary to interact with the long deceased spokesman of Puritan congregationalism. Clearly this anonymous author felt compelled to free those who, even after several centuries, remained not only under Calvin's influential yoke, but also Owen's!

The Life of John Owen, Who Cast This Shadow

We have given contemporary and historical examples of the high regard that people have shown to this Puritan divine, and now we turn our attention to the one who cast the shadow. Although we will not provide an extensive biography, a few highlights from Owen's life shed some light on our theological discussions.[25]

The year of Shakespeare's death, 1616, was also the year of John Owen's birth, and although Owen was no match for Shakespeare's eloquence, both men did share a remarkable ability to understand human nature.[26] Though Owen put his pen to treatises rather than plays and delivered sermons instead of poems, both men in their distinct ways were able to speak into the complexity of human nature: full of dignity and disease, deception and longing, pride and hope, fear and rest.

In the following chapters our theological interest will focus on Owen's view of humanity, which he distinctly frames in terms of relations with

25. For biographical material on Owen, Peter Toon's *God's Statesman: The Life and Work of John Owen; Pastor, Educator, Theologian* (Exeter: Paternoster, 1971) is a historically sensitive treatment and remains the most accessible point of entry into understanding the "historical Owen." Earlier Congregationalist historians tended to view Owen from an overtly partisan perspective and usually with an eye toward his theological writings. While Toon remains a bit too distant from Owen's theological writings, he presents the fullest and fairest biography of Owen readily available. To understand Owen's continuing popularity at the lay level, one should recognize that popular biographies were also written around this time. See, for example, Peter Barraclough, *John Owen, 1616–1683* (London: Independent Press, 1961); R. Glynne Lloyd, *John Owen—Commonwealth Puritan* (Liverpool: Modern Welsh Publications, 1972). Other academic treatments are found in Sarah Gibbard Cook, "A Political Biography of a Religious Independent: John Owen, 1616–83" (PhD diss., Harvard University, 1972); and Lloyd G. Williams, "'Digitus Dei': God and Nation in the Thought of John Owen; A Study in English Puritanism and Nonconformity, 1653–1683" (PhD diss., Drew University, 1981). See also the reissuing of Andrew Thomson's short biography of Owen, which was originally found in the first volume of the Goold edition in the nineteenth century: *The Life of Dr. Owen* (Edinburgh, 1850); repr. as *John Owen: Prince of Puritans*, History Makers (Fearn, Tain, UK: Christian Focus Publications, 2004).

26. For a provocative look at Shakespeare along these lines, see Harold Bloom, *Shakespeare: The Invention of the Human* (London: Fourth Estate, 1998).

God. Three principal sources guide Owen's reflections: the Scriptures, historical theology, and experience. Because novelty for novelty's sake has no strong appeal for this Puritan, the Scriptures and church history keep his reflections well within the paths of classical orthodox Christianity. Having said that, we should also avoid common stereotypes that continue to present Puritans like Owen as dry rationalists—such grievous misunderstandings appear to die hard. He is never content simply to repeat past theological formulations apart from pastoral application. As we will see throughout our study, Owen constantly moves from his received theology to experience, then back to theological reflection. By keeping this reciprocal relationship, with human experience informing theological reflection and theological reflection reforming experience, Owen provides fresh anthropological insights.

Geoffrey F. Nuttall ably argues that the seventeenth century was a time that put a great stress on experience, for this was

> the century which has Hamlet as its prototype and exemplar, and one could be only surprised if there were no corresponding emphasis in theology. At what other stage in philosophical development would it be argued *Cogito, ergo sum*? It is the age of diaries, often intensely introspective and finding in the slightest events God's personal dealings with the writer's souls; and of the earliest memoirs and autobiographies.[27]

Although there was debate about how to incorporate one's experience into one's theology, in seventeenth-century England it was not unusual to value learning from participation in daily life, and this is the context in which Owen was nurtured. Eventually this Puritan will carefully try to include the best aspects of this experiential emphasis within his own theology, while also trying to avoid some of what he will conclude are the extremes of his age. To know how Owen finds his own center, we turn to a rapid tour of his life.

Although we have some word of Owen's enjoyment of the flute, throwing the javelin, and even doing the long jump during his early years, from his youth he showed himself to be particularly zealous for study, sometimes averaging just four hours of sleep a night. While at Queen's College, Oxford, studying for his BA and MA degrees, Owen proved to be an able student in all manner of fields, including the classics, ancient languages, history, grammar, philosophy, and rhetoric. Growing ecclesi-

---

27. Geoffrey F. Nuttall, *The Holy Spirit in Puritan Faith and Experience*, 2nd ed. (1947; repr., Chicago: University of Chicago Press, 1992), 7; cf., Toon, *God's Statesman*, 166–67. Also see Gavin McGrath, "'But We Preach Christ Crucified': The Cross of Christ in the Pastoral Theology of John Owen, 1616–1683," St. Antholin's Lectureship Charity Lecture, 1994 (London: Latimer Trust, 1994).

astical and political tensions made it difficult for Puritans like Owen to stay at Oxford when the High Church William Laud was appointed to be Chancellor of Oxford (1630) and then Archbishop of Canterbury (1633). Leaving the university with his MA, Owen spent time as a private tutor, chaplain, author, and eventually as a pastor. During this period Owen had a noteworthy experience at Aldermanbury Chapel.

Since Owen was raised in a Puritan home with a father who was himself a pastor, he had long been familiar with the Scriptures and the doctrines of grace, but he longed for a personal experience that would help end his struggles with assurance. Although this young man had already served as a chaplain and tutor after leaving Oxford, Owen apparently did not yet find himself at peace about his spiritual state. According to an early biography, at the age of twenty-six those fears were done away with. He went to hear the celebrated Edmund Calamy preach at Aldermanbury Chapel, but instead a country preacher gave the sermon. Owen's cousin urged him to leave and hear another, more able minister elsewhere, but since Owen was weary he decided to stay. What he heard was a sermon on Matthew 8:26—"Why are ye fearful, O ye of little faith?" Through the homily of a man who always remained nameless to Owen, this young Puritan experienced the fullness of God's love and acceptance, and he was able to break his five-year melancholy. Sensitivity for those who struggle to feel God's gracious approval and delight never left Owen, as demonstrated by the endless pages he devoted to helping others come to believe the glory of the gospel message. Clearly Owen's view of human experience, under both sin and grace, was not merely theoretical, but also a reflection of his own journey and understanding.[28]

Shortly after this experience Owen began what would be a most prolific writing career. His first book, *A Display of Arminianism* (1643), is a zealous defense of his Reformed faith, which he believes is the only escape from the "modern blind patrons of human self-sufficiency."[29] Behind this early argument is a concern that those who diminish God's sovereignty and providence in the end remove the security promised to believers, for instead of focusing on the sufficiency of God in Christ, an Arminian (according to Owen) tends to focus on human attributes rather than on God's. Although rough at many points, this early work displays a basic theological framework from which Owen never fundamentally departed.

28. Although the story of Owen's experience is retold many times, early details come primarily from the anonymous *Life of Owen* (1720); and Asty, "Memoirs" (1721); more recently, see Toon, *God's Statesman*, 12–13.

29. For this early book, see Owen, *Works* 10:1–137, quotation from p. 11.

Demonstrating his growing place in the political and ecclesiastical arena, Owen preached before Parliament in 1646, when he was just thirty years old. During this period Owen began to work through numerous issues, including his early view of religious toleration and civil peace. Here his theology and political practice informed one another. Through his study of history, Owen concluded that ultimately when the church persecuted and punished heretics, it did not purify the church, but rather created tyranny. As Peter Toon rightly explains,

> Owen's own position was to the left of the Presbyterians and to the right of the Separatists and the Sectarians. He was firmly of the opinion that heretics as well as dissenters from the Established Church should not be punished merely because they were so, but only if they caused a public disturbance or were openly licentious. Their doctrinal errors should be countered by reasonable argument and spiritual weapons, not by the power of the sword.[30]

Here we encounter what will become Owen's common approach to a variety of issues: He studies the past experiences of the church to inform his view of present practice. He seeks to avoid the extremes. He believes in the Holy Spirit's activity as the only way to bring about true inner change in people, rather than depending upon external coercion. And he aims to allow freedom, but not chaos. Between the extremes Owen intends to be uncompromising in his view of God's sovereignty, while also strongly affirming human agency. These general principles will guide not only Owen's politics, but his fundamental theological methodology.

Proving to be a popular preacher and a man with influential relationships, Owen found himself preaching to the Commons several times in 1648–49. Two examples are noteworthy. First, Owen was present in London for the execution of King Charles I and was asked to preach the following day, wherein he gave an address entitled, "Righteous Zeal Encouraged by Divine Protection."[31] This sermon, which years later was condemned by Oxford University after Owen's death in 1683, draws some parallels between the prophet Jeremiah and the times in which Owen's contemporaries found themselves in England. Lest Owen be misunderstood, we must acknowledge that in the weeks after giving this sermon and before it went to print, he added "Of Toleration: and the Duty of the Magistrate about Religion," which, given the times, is a surprisingly liberal view of toleration.[32] In fact, there has even been some suggestion

30. Toon, *God's Statesman*, 24.
31. Owen, *Works* 8:127–62.
32. For this tract, see Owen, *Works* 8:163–206. L. G. Williams ("God and Nation," 153) concludes: "Owen's particular understanding of collective theology, especially his belief

that Owen's views of toleration eventually influenced John Locke, who later entered Oxford while Owen was dean at Christ Church and then vice-chancellor of Oxford University.[33]

Another sermon preached that year before the Commons was based on Hebrews 12:27: "Shaking and Translating of Heaven and Earth." For Owen, "heaven and earth" were not sky and dust; rather, using Old Testament examples he argues that these were clear references to all the proud national powers of the world (heavens) and the people who filled those nations (earth). He particularly had in mind the unfaithful political authorities, which he deemed as opposing the kingdom of Christ, tempting people to trust created powers rather than the Creator.[34] Listening to this eschatologically charged sermon was Oliver Cromwell, who was deeply impressed and afterward made himself known to the young preacher.

Cromwell and Owen were to have a long friendship, which in the end seems to parallel the tide of political affairs in the nation. After hearing Owen preach, Cromwell was adamant that this able minister must join him as a chaplain on an expedition to Ireland. This was to be the first of many times when Cromwell insisted on Owen's service, often against Owen's own desires. By 1650 he was an official preacher at Whitehall Chapel, and thus minister to the Council of State; consequently, Owen led prayers, Bible studies, and weekly preaching among those who were shaping the future of the Commonwealth.[35] His tremendous influence in seventeenth-century England is clearly shown by identifying some of those with whom he corresponded: Oliver and Richard Cromwell, leading Generals Charles Fleetwood and George Monk, members of Parliament, the governor of Massachusetts, Richard Baxter, and others.[36] Shortly after serving at Whitehall, Owen was appointed dean of Christ Church, Oxford (1651), and then vice-chancellor of Oxford University

---

in the toleration of dissent within a loose religious framework, aided in the development not of medieval conformity but of the greatest religious and social pluralism that England had ever seen till that time."

33. E.g., J. Wayne Baker, "Church, State, and Toleration: John Locke and Calvin's Heirs in England, 1644–1689," in *Later Calvinism: International Perspectives*, ed. W. Fred Graham (Kirksville, MO: Sixteenth Century Journal, 1994), 525–43, esp. 532; Cook, "Political Biography," 120–21. For Locke's writings, begin by reading his *First* and *Second Tract on Government* (1660 and 1662) and *An Essay on Toleration* (1667), in *Locke: Political Essays*, ed. Mark Goldie (Cambridge, UK: Cambridge University Press, 1997), 3–53, 54–78, 134–59, respectively.

34. Humanity, which suffers from "that deformity and dissimilitude to the divine nature" as a result of the fall, seeks now to "quiet and satiate his soul with restless movings towards changeable things [i.e., political powers]." The sermon (in a form longer than originally preached) can be found in Owen, *Works* 8:243–79; quotation from p. 247.

35. Toon, *God's Statesman*, 42.

36. See Toon, ed., *Correspondence of John Owen*.

(1652). Although personally feeling inadequate for the tasks of such appointments, he actually proved himself most able both academically and administratively. After these prestigious appointments, he was given the Doctor of Divinity degree in honor of his mastery of theological and philosophical learning. Nevertheless, Owen himself was no fan of titles, including being called "doctor" or "reverend." Of the latter label, he once exclaimed that he had no value for it, citing Luther's quip: "Religion is never put in danger except amongst the most reverend" (*nunquam periclatur religio nisi inter Reverendissimos*).[37] During these years at Oxford, Owen was able to produce numerous significant volumes, writing on topics from justification to schism, from divine justice to a defense of Hebrew vowel points, from mortification to perseverance. Many of these writings began as short sermons delivered to the challenging audience of young men at Christ Church; as a result, these works often prove to be not only intellectually rigorous, but also experientially sensitive and insightful.

After his time at Oxford, serving both as vice-chancellor of Oxford University and dean of Christ Church, Owen faced a difficult period of growing uncertainty about the spiritual and political state of England. Before 1650, when Owen was appointed preacher to the Council of State and a chaplain to Cromwell, the hopeful Puritan held a strong belief that the welfare of England as a nation was intertwined with the welfare of the saints and churches that were in the country. This belief was grounded in his strong Calvinistic understanding of providence. However, Owen and Cromwell alike were severely disillusioned by the failure of the Barebones Parliament.[38] Owen's previous optimism about the coming glory began to dwindle, and he started to view the end times as far in the future, rather than imminent, as he had once perceived.[39] According to Owen, human response to God influences eschatological realities, for although God maintains his sovereignty, he also responds to repentance (or to a lack thereof):

> Imperfect present and ideal future were, in Owen's mind, creatively accommodated to each other. The future would purify and fulfill the anomalous present; the present, with all its failings, could be utilized to prepare for the future. Incongruities in the present could be tolerated for they would eventually be removed in the future. Even if God should postpone

37. Toon, *God's Statesman*, 73.

38. L. G. Williams, "God and Nation," 21, 62. Cf. Christopher Hill, *God's Englishman: Oliver Cromwell and the English Revolution* (London: Weidenfeld & Nicholson, 1970), 141–43; idem, *The Experience of Defeat: Milton and Some Contemporaries* (London: Faber & Faber, 1984), 170–78.

39. Cf. L. G. Williams, "God and Nation," 69ff., 222.

the future because of human sin, it still remained "near" to the eye of
faith. It still retained its relevance. If the future were postponed Owen
would simply reassess the situation and do the work appropriate to that
generation.[40]

As realities on the ground changed, Owen was willing to rethink elements of his eschatological framework, since he allowed not simply for
theology to shape experience, but also for experience to have a role in
refining theological conclusions. In this way Owen proved a surprisingly
flexible thinker; he adapted to new situations by urging toleration and
social peace. For example, in 1657 the Puritan leader found himself in
opposition to his old friend Oliver Cromwell, who was entertaining the
idea of becoming king: it appears that the formerly strong friendship
between these two men suffered from then until Cromwell's death in
1658.[41] After Oliver's death and the fumbled leadership of his son Richard,
Charles II returned to England and was crowned in 1660.

Removed from his political and academic positions of leadership,
Owen henceforth doubled his efforts to push for religious toleration on
behalf of nonconformists, as well as spending considerable time pastor-
ing and writing. Demonstrating the high regard in which he was held in
New England, Owen was recruited during this time for positions at both
the First Church of Boston (John Cotton's former church), and later the
Third Church.[42] Owen did not accept either offer, deciding instead to
use his new freedom from academic administration to pour himself into
his studies and sermons. Already prolific, Owen produced a mountain
of learned theology and biblical exposition during the last twenty-five
years of his life, including the massive *Theologoumena pantodapa* and
his multivolume sets on the *Doctrine of the Holy Spirit* and the *Epistle to
the Hebrews*. One of the memorable endeavors Owen engaged in at this
time was helping John Bunyan find a publisher for *Pilgrim's Progress*. He
persuaded his own publisher, Nathaniel Ponder, thus making the volume
available to the populace. History has judged Owen's enthusiasm and
Ponder's risk as most justified.

This man who wore so many hats during his life, from army chaplain and country pastor to leading scholar and religious adviser to the
political authorities of his day, faced death with a quiet confidence in
1683. Although the practice of leaving property to women was not very

40. Ibid., 327.
41. For the best handling of this complex story, see Williams, "God and Nation,"
155–67.
42. Mark A. Peterson, *The Price of Redemption: The Spiritual Economy of Puritan New
England* (Stanford, CA: Stanford University Press, 1997), 31, 123; cf. Toon, *God's Statesman*, 124.

common, Owen left his estate to his wife: only after she died was it to be passed along to his brother Harry.[43] But more than his estate, this man had left his greatest legacy in his writings, which, as we saw at the beginning of this chapter, were consistently read and wrestled with from the seventeenth century unto our own.

Owen wrote to his friends Mr. and Mrs. Hartopp several years before his death, encouraging them—and himself—to find their true humanity, their meaning, in terms of their interaction with God, rather than merely in self-absorption: "Strive to love Christ more, to abide more with him, and to be less in our selves: He is our best friend and ere long will be our only friend. I pray God with all my heart that I may be weary of every thing else but converse and communion with him."[44] In his life Owen witnessed incredible social upheaval, the painful loss of numerous children, a first wife, and countless friends; hence, we should not dismiss his words as a simple devaluing of the physical world. Instead, here we find the thoughtful conclusion reached by a theologian nearing the end of his life. Our study will explore the theology behind Owen's conclusion.

Intellectual Context and the Direction of Our Examination

Because experiences shape the thinker, we cannot divorce Owen's thought from his life and the influences upon him. He struggled with pride, ambition, numerous painful family deaths, a disrupted academic and political career, and so on. Historical background provides some insight into the existential roots of Owen's anthropological reflections. What consistently emerges is a picture of a talented and influential man of his times who believed and proclaimed that communion with God defines who we are.

Owen self-consciously viewed himself as part of a generation of English Puritans seeking to continue the "unfinished reformation."[45] Defining "Puritan" is notoriously difficult because those who receive this label greatly differed in such key areas as theology, politics, and church government. However, the term in its broadest sense (as necessary if one is to include all identified with this label) includes some general characteristics, such as (1) an uncompromising commitment to the authority of the Bible as guiding *all* of life; (2) a heavy Augustinian ac-

43. Cook, "Political Biography," 382.

44. "Letter #86, To Sir John Hartopp," in *Correspondence of John Owen*, ed. Toon, 160.

45. Cf. his comment from 1655 in Owen, *Works* 12:595: "I have no singular opinion of my own, but embrace the common, known doctrine of the reformed churches."

cent on human sin and divine grace; (3) an intense focus on spirituality, especially communion with God; and (4) a persistent prominence given to the Spirit's role in the Christian's life.[46] These key concerns are, as one might expect, exemplified in Owen's thought.

Contrary to common stereotypes about the Puritans, Owen's intellectual formation is surprisingly broad. Owen's sizable library comprised a quite learned and diverse collection, containing a large number of writings by the early fathers, classic Greek literature and philosophy, philology, medieval scholastics, humanists, the leading Reformers, and obviously seventeenth-century authors.[47] Drawing from these various sources and his conservative education at Queen's College, Oxford, Owen tries to present a theological method that is biblical and ecclesiastical, appreciative yet discerning, intellectually rigorous while experientially oriented. Appreciating the various influences on Owen, Sebastian Rehnman concludes that he was "a typical Renaissance man."[48] The four main "contemporary currents of thought" that Rehnman finds in Owen are Augustinianism, Aristotelianism, scholasticism, and humanism. Reductionistic approaches have all too often simply dismissed Owen as Aristotelian or scholastic, rather than giving due credit to the fullness of his thought and expression.[49] Truly each of these four streams feeds into Owen's own theological formulations, but none so dominates him that it cancels out the others.

Carl R. Trueman similarly attributes a broad intellectual background to Owen's work, and his research makes several points relevant to our study.[50] Arguing against earlier dismissals of Owen's theology, particularly the assessment by Alan Clifford, Trueman warns against treating Owen in an historical vacuum. Clifford believes that Owen greatly distorted Calvin's theology by submitting more to Aristotelian sensitivities than biblical concerns, which in the end led him away from the Reformed heri-

46. For a much fuller discussion and detailed bibliography on the debate about unifying characteristics of Puritanism, see Kelly M. Kapic and Randall C. Gleason, "Who Were the Puritans?" in *The Devoted Life: An Invitation to the Puritan Classics*, ed. Kelly M. Kapic and Randall C. Gleason (Downers Grove, IL: InterVarsity, 2004), 15–37, esp. 23–32.

47. See *Bibliotheca Oweniana, sive, Catalogus librorum* (London: Edward Millington, 1684), which is an exhaustive list of Owen's books composed by the auctioneers who sold Owen's library after his death.

48. Sebastian Rehnman, *Divine Discourse: The Theological Methodology of John Owen*, Texts and Studies in Reformation and Post-Reformation Thought (Grand Rapids: Baker Academic, 2002), 25–46.

49. See Sebastian Rehnman, "John Owen: A Reformed Scholastic at Oxford," in *Reformation and Scholasticism: An Ecumenical Enterprise*, ed. W. J. van Asselt and E. Dekker (Grand Rapids: Baker Academic, 2001), 181–203.

50. Carl R. Trueman, *The Claims of Truth: John Owen's Trinitarian Theology* (Carlisle: Paternoster, 1998).

tage he claimed to represent.[51] Against such claims, Trueman forcefully argues that we should not take Owen's use of Aristotelian language and structure as significantly influencing his theology: this was the common method and language appropriated by seventeenth-century theologians no matter what their theological perspective.[52] Using the atonement as an example, Trueman, contra Clifford, claims that Owen used Aristotelian categories as a heuristic device rather than as the driving theological structure.[53] To illustrate the shared methodology and language of the day, Trueman consistently uses the theologically distinct Richard Baxter as a point of comparison, often arguing that Baxter embodies a more scholastic methodology than Owen.[54] For example, he briefly compares Baxter's faculty psychology with that of Owen, claiming that the former's plays a much greater role in his overall theology. Baxter's "faculty psychology is given a structural importance which is absent from the work of Owen."[55]

Though we will highlight Owen's use of faculty language later, Trueman is correct in claiming that Owen is not slavish to it. Our study demonstrates what Trueman seems to anticipate: the reason faculty psychology is significant for Owen has less to do with a dedication to Aristotle and more to do with Owen's attempt to find adequate language describing how humans may holistically respond to God. Trueman's research further contributes to our study as he lays out the structure of Owen's most systematic work, *Theologoumena pantodapa*, which has a historical framework organized around the covenants:

> Underlying this choice of organization is Owen's fundamental belief that theology *is relational*; that is, it depends upon the nature of the *relationship*

51. Alan C. Clifford, *Atonement and Justification: English Evangelical Theology, 1640–1790: An Evaluation* (Oxford: Clarendon, 1990), 98. Simply reporting one of Clifford's conclusions will demonstrate the gravity of his claims: "Whereas Owen seems quite oblivious to Calvin's theology of justification, Wesley derived his knowledge of Calvin via the Arminian Puritan John Goodwin's treatise *Imputatio fidei* (1642). Both Goodwin and Arminius claimed to concur with Calvin's sentiments. This would suggest that the Arminians rather than the scholastic Calvinists were the true heirs of Calvin, a thought which surely demands a redrawing of the theological map" (ibid., 179).

52. Cf. Trueman, *Claims of Truth*, 11, 38.

53. Ibid., 233–40.

54. E.g., ibid., 32. Cf. Trueman's later essay "A Small Step Towards Rationalism: The Impact of the Metaphysics of Tommaso Campanella on the Theology of Richard Baxter," in *Protestant Scholasticism: Essays in Reassessment*, ed. Carl R. Trueman and R. S. Clark (Carlisle: Paternoster, 1999), 181–95.

55. Trueman, *Claims of Truth*, 80. Here he is referring to Baxter's *Methodus theologiae christianae* (London, 1684). Trueman later concludes that "Baxter's break with the more traditional faculty psychology of Owen, both in reference to humans and to God, represents a fundamental difference in basic metaphysics" (*Claims of Truth*, 82).

that exists between God the revealer and the one revealed, and humans, the recipients of that revelation. In this context, the progressive nature of the covenant scheme serves to take account of the fact that *theology requires a divine-human relationship,* and that the biblical record shows that relationship has itself not been static but subject to historical movement, a movement which can be articulated by setting forth in order the key points at which God has explicitly defined his relationship with humanity: the various covenants which are found within the Bible.[56]

The relational emphasis is rightly highlighted here, since Owen's theology can never be divorced from his anthropology. Humanity's relationship to the God of Abraham, Isaac, and Jacob was a dynamic concern for Owen, not an irrelevant point of theological debate. How creation, the fall, and redemption have affected this relationship will be explored in our investigation of Owen's view of the *imago Dei.*

Finally, brief interaction with Dale A. Stover's research provides a bridge to our investigation. His slightly older study not only addresses anthropology, it also voices many misunderstandings that persist to this day. Concentrating upon Owen's view of the Holy Spirit, Stover examines how this Puritan divine handles the subjective/objective dimensions of the Christian faith.[57] His study leads him to the "revolutionary conclusion" that Owen and English Calvinists held "an anthropological theology," whereas Calvin clearly represented a christocentric theology.[58] Stover maintains that the extensive pneumatology and covenantal emphasis in Owen's theology inevitably leads him to become anthropocentric.[59] Additionally, Owen's trinitarian thought tended to emphasize the distinct role of each person of the Trinity to the neglect of a coherent unified Triune God christologically grounded.[60] Stover says that because Owen was concerned with how each person of the Trinity *distinctly related to the believer,* his theology was generated from an anthropocentric base. He claims that Owen "omitted the humanity of Christ," whereas Calvin emphasized "the body of Christ as the ground of the Spirit's relation to believers."[61] Likewise, he believed that Owen divorced the Spirit from his incarnational theology. This divorce wrought havoc on Owen's anthropology, according to Stover, leading to an "emphasis on the spiritual

56. Trueman, *Claims of Truth,* 49, emphasis added.
57. Dale Arden Stover currently is a professor at the University of Nebraska at Omaha, although his research interests have significantly changed since his original work: "The Pneumatology of John Owen: A Study of the Role of the Holy Spirit in Relation to the Shape of a Theology" (PhD diss., McGill University, Montreal, 1967), 10.
58. Ibid., 303, 46–49.
59. Ibid., 211, 301.
60. E.g., ibid., 304. Cf. 209, where the Spirit "has usurped the role of Christ."
61. Ibid., 304.

side of man's being—a stress on the soul at the expense of the body." For Stover, this ultimately leads to man's "dehumanization."[62] Throughout Stover's work one finds references to human faculties. He argues that sin primarily focuses on the will and affections, rather than the mind.[63] One particularly insightful comment that Stover contributes regarding human faculties is that they serve as the "locus" for the similarity that exists between man and God in Owen's theology, but Stover leaves the idea somewhat undeveloped.[64]

The anthropology in Stover's study is not without problems. Joel Beeke flatly and consciously contradicts Stover by arguing that Owen's theology is "theocentric" rather than anthropocentric.[65] Both authors may be closer than they realize, each acknowledging Owen's obvious concern for the human condition. They differ about what *drives* Owen's theology: is it an overriding concern for the glory of God or for the salvation and sanctification of humanity? Obviously the two ideas have tremendous overlap, and nuance becomes all the more important to avoid confusion. Suffice it to say, Stover has marked the importance of an anthropological perspective in Owen's work. Any study of Owen's anthropology must address Stover's concerns: human interaction with the Triune God, the humanity of Christ, humanity's supposed "dehumanization," and the leading role of human faculties.

This study seeks to demonstrate many conclusions that are directly opposed to Stover's analysis. Owen is not "anthropological" without being christocentric: rather, his robust Christology permeates every aspect of his thought, including his conception that we must understand being human primarily in terms of relations with God. Contrary to Stover's belief, Owen does not neglect the humanity of Christ; instead, he stands in awe of how the incarnation affirms Christ's true solidarity with the rest of humanity. Rather than dehumanizing humanity, we see Owen trying to arrange a holistic anthropology by using the intellectual furniture available to him in the seventeenth century. Furthermore, against the charge of Stover, Owen's trinitarian emphasis on the distinct roles of the three divine persons does not weaken his Christology, but actually may be understood as strengthening it. This will quickly become

62. Ibid., 305. Cf. William Ward Bass, "Platonic Influences on Seventeenth-Century English Puritan Theology as Expressed in the Thinking of John Owen, Richard Baxter, and John Howe" (PhD diss., University of Southern California, 1958), 117.

63. Stover, "Pneumatology of John Owen," 55. He has overestimated the Puritan value placed on reason when he later states, "It would seem that reason judged revelation more surely than revelation judged reason" (56); cf. his later more guarded statement (224).

64. Ibid., 246.

65. Joel Beeke, *Assurance of Faith: Calvin, English Puritanism, and the Dutch Second Reformation* (New York: Peter Lang, 1991), 221.

apparent in the emphasis he gives to communion with the Son in his book *Communion with God*.[66] Christ is the mediator between God and humanity, and only through him are relations between the divine and human secure.

Owen's Anthroposensitivity and an Outline of Our Study

Our investigation of the primary sources in chapters 2 through 6 demonstrates Owen's conception of human relations with God, seeking to provide a fresh analysis of his theological anthropology. The theologian we encounter here is somewhat different from the one commonly associated with the name John Owen: he is not a rationalist, nor a theologian simply interested in abstract speculations, nor is he easily labeled anthropocentric—since that term gives humanity a position that Owen consistently believes is reserved only for God. Instead, throughout our study we will observe Owen as an *anthroposensitive* theologian.

Since the following chapters—especially beginning in chapter 4—deal with this idea more fully, at this point we will simply define "anthroposensitive" as *a refusal to divorce theological considerations from practical human application, since theological reflections are always interwoven with anthropological concerns*. The combination of "anthropo-" (human; relating to human beings: from [Greek] *anthrōpos*) and "sensitive" is an attempt to avoid a simplistic classification of Owen as either theocentric *or* anthropocentric. If one had to choose between these options, Owen would be theocentric, but such a conclusion can be used to diminish the anthropological emphasis seen throughout Owen's corpus. Other common terms, such as "pastoral" or "experiential," often carry with them unnecessarily negative connotations or represent a notion of what is done *after* theological reflection, rather than informing that reflection. In other words, according to Owen's methodology, theological reflections must entail anthropological implications; otherwise there is something wrong with the theology that results.[67] For this reason we will see Owen consistently move between divine action and human response. Since humanity was created to commune with God, the theological enterprise

66. Owen, *Works* 2:5–274.
67. Cf. Owen's comments on the methodology of the author of Hebrews: "In the midst of his [the author's] reasonings and testimonies for the explanation or confirmation of what he delivers dogmatically, he lays hold on some occasion or other to press his exhortations unto faith, obedience, with constancy and perseverance in the profession of the gospel. . . . So insensibly passing from one thing unto another, that he might at the same time inform the minds and work upon the affections of them with whom he dealt" (*Works* 20:320; BE 19:320). We believe Owen, consciously or unconsciously, tries to follow this pattern himself.

must be primarily concerned with understanding humanity in its relation with God. As we see at the very end of our study, being made in God's image is primarily about loving Jesus Christ, who is the mediator between God and humanity. This unique relationship is ultimately what defines being in communion with God.

We begin the next chapter by exploring humanity as made in the image of God. Here we will focus on Owen's employment of what is commonly called faculty psychology, the grammar he uses to describe relations. Chapter 2 ends with a brief survey of humanity through history, providing a framework for fitting creation, fall, and redemption into Owen's conception of relations between God and humanity. In chapter 3 our attention turns from humanity in general to the God-man Jesus Christ in specific. Questions explored here include: Why the incarnation? How does the humiliation of the Son comfort struggling believers? Are there continuities and discontinuities between Christ's humanity and fallen humanity? After considering the incarnation, in chapter 4 our study next moves to the question of justification. Special attention will be given to Owen's anthroposensitive approach. We cover his understanding of faith, some important disagreements he has with his Roman Catholic opponents, and how he understands negative and positive imputation. Chapter 5 takes us to the core of our study: human communion with the Triune God. Here we discover Owen's creative attempt to view the Trinity within the context of worship. Owen describes in detail the Father's love, the Son's grace, and the Spirit's consolation. Finally, in chapter 6 we conclude our study by looking at the Lord's day and Lord's supper. In these two examples we find Owen pointing toward signs, the experience of which fosters the human interface with God as realized in Jesus Christ, who is the Lord of the day and Lord of the supper. Throughout the entire study we will observe Owen's consistent movement between theology and anthropology, made possible and based in his Christology.

CREATED TO COMMUNE WITH GOD

Owen's Formulation of the Imago Dei

And thou shalt love the Lord thy God with all thy heart, and with all thy soul, and with all thy mind, and with all thy strength: this is the first commandment.

Mark 12:30

Man's chief and highest end is to glorify God, and fully to enjoy him for ever.

Westminster Larger Catechism (1648)

The approaching unto God in his service is the chief exaltation of our nature above the beasts that perish.

John Owen, Greater Catechism (1645)

Introduction

As we turn our attention to John Owen's view of relations between God and humanity, we begin with Owen's formulation of the *imago Dei* in order to reveal the core issues informing Owen's view of humanity, and to lay the groundwork upon which the rest of the study builds. Since Owen uses basic Aristotelian faculty psychology in his development of the topic, we will highlight some of the similarities and dissimilarities between Owen's Christian conception and Aristotle's influential ideas throughout this chapter. The overall influence of Aristotle on Owen's thought remains a subject of much interest and debate,[1] but our discussion will avoid a general comparison of the two thinkers and focus instead on Owen's own theological maneuvering.

In this chapter we will first describe Owen's distinctions and terminology regarding the *imago*. Second, we will briefly highlight how he perceives Christ as the perfect image of God, although we more fully deal with this in chapter 3. Following this we will move to our third and primary concern, arguing that one cannot fully appreciate Owen's understanding of the *imago* without taking into account his conception and language of faculty psychology, and it is here that the discussion of Aristotle becomes most relevant. Thus drawing upon Aristotle serves primarily for illustrative purposes of comparison and contrast, but one should not take this as an unmediated correspondence between the two thinkers. Fourth, we will see that certain events in history have cosmic results concerning the *imago*: the creation, fall, regeneration, sanctification, and glorification of humans. Only when we consider faculty psychology and humanity's struggle with righteousness together can we fully understand Owen's position. These topics introduce Owen's anthropology as an early modern attempt to present a holistic conception of humanity as image bearers created to commune with the Creator. Because this chapter deals with themes so prevalent throughout Owen's writings, we shall concentrate upon his classic works, *ΠΝΕΥΜΑΤΟΛΟΓΙΑ*[2] and *ΧΡΙΣΤΟΛΟΓΙΑ* and *The Glory of Christ*.[3] In looking at these particular treatises, both in this chapter and in the following one, we will highlight

1. See James B. Torrance, "The Incarnation and 'Limited Atonement,'" *SBET* 2 (1984): 33, 37; and Clifford, *Atonement and Justification*, 96, 98, 104. Both argue that Owen's understanding of the atonement is negatively influenced by his Aristotelian presuppositions. On the other hand, see Michael W. Bobick, "Owen's Razor: The Role of Ramist Logic in the Covenant Theology of John Owen" (PhD diss., Drew University, 1996), 95–120; Carl R. Trueman, "John Owen's *Dissertation on Divine Justice*: An Exercise in Christocentric Scholasticism," *CTJ* 33 (1998): 103; idem, *Claims of Truth*, 38, 43, 227–40; and Rehnman, *Divine Discourse*, 25, 37–39, who while not denying the Aristotelian influence on Owen, nevertheless want to limit the speculations regarding its overall impact on the Puritan's theology.

2. This treatise of over 650 pages is found in vol. 3 of Owen's *Works*. Goold, making an editorial decision based upon Owen's own words, considers vols. 3–4 under the general heading *ΠΝΕΥΜΑΤΟΛΟΓΙΑ: A Discourse concerning the Holy Spirit*, even though the five treatises in vol. 4 were written at different times, and each was published later than vol. 3.

3. For *ΧΡΙΣΤΟΛΟΓΙΑ*, see *Works* 1:1–272; and *The Glory of Christ*, in *Works* 1:273–415, 419–61. These treatises, the first published in 1679 and the second in 1684, represent Owen's mature thought shortly before he died in 1683.

the connections Owen consistently makes between Christology, anthropology, and pneumatology.

Distinctions and Terminology

Owen's library gave him a broad background for the theological debates concerning the doctrine of the *imago Dei*.[4] He follows the tendency of some early church fathers in making a distinction between "image" and "likeness."[5] Although Owen occasionally interchanges these words, they normally are not treated simply as synonyms, but rather they appear to communicate complementary ideas. Although Irenaeus and others often (although not always consistently) utilize this distinction to communicate different attributes of man (e.g., reason and free will are distinguished from some supernatural endowment of the Spirit), Owen frames his discussion more in terms of righteousness.[6] Original righteousness is shorthand for right relations between God and humanity before the fall. Created good and upright, with all of their faculties properly oriented toward God (cf. image), Adam and Eve were righteous insofar as they were created to relate to their God and respond to him in obedience (cf. likeness).[7] Writing against John Biddle, the "father of English Socinianism," Owen carefully argues that "likeness" to God is not a reference to a "bodily shape," but points to a "kind of resemblance unto that holiness and righteousness which are in Him,

4. Owen's personal library had all of the major texts (e.g., Irenaeus, Athanasius) that discussed this issue, and he constantly interacts with them in his more academic works. The listing of Owen's library comes from the *Bibliotheca Oweniana*.

5. Cf. John of Damascus, *Exposition of the Orthodox Faith* 2.12, trans. S. D. F. Salmond, in *NPNF*[2] 9:31, with separate pagination (1899; repr., Peabody, MA: Hendrickson, 1994): "For the phrase 'after His image' clearly refers to the side of his nature which consists of mind and free will, whereas 'after His likeness' means likeness in virtue so far as that is possible."

6. J. N. D. Kelly, *Early Christian Doctrines*, rev. ed. (San Francisco: Harper & Row, 1978), 171. See also Karl Barth, *Church Dogmatics*, ed. G. W. Bromiley and T. F. Torrance, trans. T. H. L. Parker et al., 5 vols. in 14 (Edinburgh: T&T Clark, 1956–77), 3/1:192–93, hereafter cited as *CD*; James Barr, "The Image of God in the Book of Genesis—A Study in Terminology," *Bulletin of the John Rylands Library* 51 (1968–69): 11–26.

7. E.g., *Works* 12:156–58; 10:80; 22:158. Arguing against what he perceives as Arminius's innovations, Owen declares: "Hitherto we have thought that the original righteousness wherein Adam was created had comprehended the integrity and perfection of the whole man; not only that whereby the body was obedient unto the soul, and all the affections subservient to the rule of reason for the performance of all natural actions, but also a light, uprightness, and holiness of grace in the mind and will, whereby he was enabled to yield obedience unto God for the attaining of that supernatural end whereunto he was created" (*Works* 10:84).

Eph. iv. 23, 24, etc."[8] In this sense, to lose this righteousness is to lose their likeness to God.

So are humans still made in God's image even after the fall? One can retain the marks of the image of the Divinity while behaving in an unrighteous manner, which is completely unlike the Creator. In an analogy of parents and their children, Owen claims that "though all children do partake of the nature of their parents, yet they may be, and some of them are, very deformed, and bear very little likeness."[9] Such a deformity summarizes all of humanity. Humans "have the image of God in [their] hearts, and yet come short of that likeness unto him, in its degrees and improvement."[10] Therefore, "though the image of God may be in us, there is not much of his likeness upon us" even though the Christian profession and fundamental duty is to grow in this resemblance to God.[11]

This distinction between image and likeness raises a question: Was the image destroyed by the fall? Like Calvin, Owen does not answer this question definitively. Controversy has abounded as to whether Calvin believed that the *imago* was destroyed at the fall. This is a difficult question because, on the one hand, Calvin uses such phrases as "wiped out" (*Comm. on Ephesians* 4:24), "destroyed" (*Comm. on Gen.* 1:26), and "canceled" (*Comm. on 2 Cor.* 3:18) to refer to the *imago*, thus seeming to assert the end of the *imago* in humanity after the fall. Susan Schreiner, on the other hand, argues for a more balanced view of Calvin, claiming that "the fall, which was a 'confusion' of the natural order, effected a corresponding confusion in the order of knowing. Human beings no longer refer their excellence to God and consequently can no longer perceive God in nature. In short, the *relational character* of the *imago Dei* was destroyed."[12] How one defines the *imago* dictates what conclusion one will arrive at, and this applies not only to Calvin, but to Owen as well. If the image is purely relational, then yes, Calvin argues that it is destroyed as a result of the fall. If it is more than that, including different natural capacities, then Calvin argues that the *imago* remains but is severely marred. The tension within this view is that human faculties, for Calvin and Owen after him, are often viewed as the means that make our relationship with God possible. When the

8. Ibid., 12:100. We will see below the way Owen does try to incorporate some discussion of the body into his view of the *imago Dei*.

9. Ibid., 3:578–79.

10. Ibid., 3:579.

11. Ibid.

12. Susan Schreiner, *The Theater of His Glory: Nature and the Natural Order in the Thought of John Calvin* (Durham: Labyrinth, 1991), 66–67, emphasis added. Cf. Richard A. Muller, *Post-Reformation Reformed Dogmatics: The Rise and Development of Reformed Orthodoxy, ca. 1520 to ca. 1725*, 2nd ed., 4 vols. (Grand Rapids: Baker Academic, 2003), 1:275–76; hereafter cited as *PRRD*, followed by volume and page numbers.

faculties are not working properly, the possibility for unhindered fellowship with God suffers.[13]

Owen's language, like that of his contemporaries, may lend itself to the interpretation that he considers the image utterly lost after the fall. Hence, it is understandable that some Puritan preachers, less concerned with systematics, conclude without qualification that the image is completely destroyed. In his sermons and writings the Calvinist Scotsman Thomas Boston (1676–1732), for example, clearly and consistently asserts that the image was utterly annihilated with the fall. This pushes Boston "in the direction of seeing the natural man as something less than fully human."[14] While trying to avoid this conclusion, Owen often sounds similar to Boston. Owen affirms continuity between the first man and his progeny while at the same time asserting the relational devastation caused by the fall.

A few examples from Owen's writings, however, reveal the difficulty his interpreters have encountered at this point. The Oxford divine complains that few people consider the depravity "of their natures, that vileness which is come upon them by the loss of the image of God."[15] Elsewhere he makes a distinction between sinful man and the Messiah, who enjoys the fullness of grace: the image is "lost from our nature," impossible for people to comprehend, at least "until it was renewed and exemplified in the human nature of Christ,"[16] thus revealing the direct connection that he saw between Christology and anthropology. Finally, Owen makes the strong claim that with the loss of the image, humanity began to represent Satan rather than God.[17] In these examples, Owen's language points to the conclusion that humanity no longer bears the image after the fall.

In other places where Owen discusses the image of God, however, his comments reveal that he believes the image remains even after the fall. When considering Christ's roles as prophet, priest, and king, Owen recognizes that "the image of God in us was *defaced* by sin. The renovation

13. The question of physical handicaps and limitations is a different one, since here the concern for these thinkers is about whether or not one's faculties, no matter how limited, are directed toward God or toward self.

14. Philip Graham Ryken, *Thomas Boston as Preacher of the Fourfold State*, ed. David F. Wright and Donald Macleod, Rutherford Studies in Historical Theology (Edinburgh: published for Rutherford House by Paternoster, 1999), 143. Ryken goes on to accurately contrast Boston's views with Owen's more nuanced position. For a recent reprint of Boston's most important work, see Thomas Boston, *Human Nature in Its Fourfold State* (1720; repr., Edinburgh: Banner of Truth, 1997).

15. *Works* 3:450; cf. with 3:451, where he likewise declares that one should search the Bible to understand "the condition of our nature after the loss of the image of God."

16. Ibid., 1:171–72.

17. Ibid., 1:184.

or restoration hereof was one principle design of Christ in his coming."[18]
This language communicates the imagery of ruin, but not utter destruction. Sin appears to have shattered the once-reflective mirror; the mirror
remains, only in pieces instead of a perfect whole. Furthermore, Owen
discusses the entrance of sin and how it was humanity's righteousness
that was defaced and lost. He then explains that this righteousness "did
not depart from any one power, part, or faculty of our souls, but from
our whole nature." Owen goes on to describe how a "corruption . . .
ensued on our minds, wills, and affections, upon the loss of the image
of God."[19] To borrow more Greek philosophical language, human faculties remain, although they do not function as originally designed, thus
disrupting human nature.

Although it is clear that Owen believes the unblemished image is lost,
it is equally clear that he believes its vestiges remain.

> By the loss of the image of God, our nature lost its pre-eminence, and we
> were reduced into order amongst perishing beasts; for notwithstanding
> some *feeble relics of this image yet abiding with us*, we have really, with
> respect unto our proper end, in our lapsed condition, *more* of the bestial
> nature in us than of the divine. Wherefore, the restoration of this image
> in us by the grace of Jesus Christ . . . is the recovery of that pre-eminence
> and privilege of our nature which we had foolishly lost.[20]

What did Owen mean by this "loss of the image"? Certainly he acknowledged catastrophic consequences that resulted from sin's entrance into
the Garden of Eden,[21] but he also acknowledged the "feeble relics" of
God's image in humans. Yet we must see this image in the context of
relations with God.[22] By acknowledging this tension in Owen's wording, one may best conclude that Owen is referring to degrees along a
continuum rather than simply offering the two extremes as the only possible conclusions: the image perfectly remains *or* it is utterly destroyed.
Although sin brought chaos, disorder, and rebellion, in some respect
the defaced *imago* remains. A comment from Owen's massive treatise
on *The Saint's Perseverance* demonstrates his understanding. Discussing

18. Ibid., 3:629, emphasis added.
19. Ibid., 3:418; cf. 12:148.
20. Ibid., 3:580, emphasis added.
21. "Hereby we lost the image of God," which means that we "lost ourselves and our
souls" (ibid., 1:208).
22. For the Christian, "to be nigh unto God, and to be like unto him, are the same. To
be always with him, and perfectly like him, *according to the capacity of our nature*, is to
be eternally blessed. To live by faith in the contemplation of the glory of God in Christ,
is that initiation into both, whereof we are capable in this world" (ibid., 1:52, emphasis
added).

people who do not experience the indwelling of the Spirit, he writes: "Their minds remain; though depraved, destroyed, perverted, . . . yet the faculty remains still."[23] Somehow he finds it acceptable to talk about the mind as both destroyed and yet still remaining, and in maintaining this tension he follows many of his Reformed predecessors. It may be that "destroyed" doesn't mean "obliterated" but "ruined," like a town overrun and bombarded by a seventeenth-century army.

A brief review of how Owen uses the language of image and likeness will help us grasp this fundamental distinction in his anthropology. In Owen's view, likeness communicates righteousness. As a result of the fall, humanity becomes sinful and completely *unlike* God. Yet the image, though marred, remains because it is this aspect that allows for the relationship between the divine and human. Owen freely speaks of the image's "loss" because a person's natural ability to worship one's Creator has gone, while the faculties that allowed the original communion to occur between God and humanity remain. By retaining the faculties that make relations possible, he preserves some element of ontological continuity between pre-fall and fallen humanity. Although Owen will occasionally make the image more than merely human faculties, he does not make it less:[24] *the faculties are vital because they are what allow relations*, but since the fall humanity's faculties are no longer oriented toward God.[25] In this way, vestiges of the image remain (i.e., humans retain their faculties), yet the likeness is destroyed in that human persons were designed relationally, and this was disrupted as humanity turned from God to themselves.[26]

After the fall the shattered image must find renewal from another source, a second Adam. Owen approvingly quotes Ambrose's answer to humanity's predicament: "The image of God, that is, the Word of God, came unto him who was after the image of God, that is man. And this image of God seeks him who was after the image of God, that he might seal him with it again, and confirm him, because thou hadst lost that which thou hadst received."[27] Those who downplay the devastation caused by the fall inevitably present an "undervaluation of the love and

23. Ibid., 11:343.

24. Cf. ibid., 12:143.

25. See ibid., 19:387 (BE 18:387).

26. Cf. Heinrich Heppe, *Reformed Dogmatics: Set Out and Illustrated from the Sources*, trans. G. T. Thomson, ed. Ernst Bizer (Grand Rapids: Baker Academic, 1978), 313; hereafter cited as *RD*.

27. *Works* 1:26: "Imago [id est, Verbum Dei,] ad eum qui est ad imaginem, [hoc est, hominem,] venit, et quærit imago eum qui est ad similitudinem sui, ut iterum signet, ut iterum confirmet, quia amiseras quod accepisti" (Ambrose, *Expositio Psalmi 118*), PL 15, col. 1335C.

grace of Jesus Christ."[28] Sin destroyed good and right relations between humanity and the Creator, and thus the incarnation was essential to human renewal. Christ, therefore, as the perfect image of God, came to restore the lost relations and in so doing provided the way to everlasting communion between God and humanity.

Christ's Role as the Image of God

According to Owen, Christians ought to look to God in order to understand themselves, the world, and their Creator.[29] The contemplative person must then ask to whom or what do I look to see God most clearly? Owen focuses his answer upon Christ. In the preface to ΧΡΙΣΤΟΛΟΓΙΑ, he writes thus of Christ:

> In his divine person, as he was the only-begotten of the Father from eternity, he is the essential image of the Father, by the generation of his person, and the communication of the divine nature unto him therein. As he is incarnate, he is both in his own entire person God and man, and in the administration of his office, the image or representative of the nature and will of God unto us.[30]

Later he quotes from numerous early church fathers to show that Christ uniquely represents the image of the Father. For example, he mentions Eusebius's conclusion that since Jesus was begotten of the Father, he alone could perfectly bear the divine image. Christ alone "bears in himself the image of the ineffable and inconceivable Deity. Wherefore, he both is [God], and is called God, because of his being the character, similitude, or image of him who is the first."[31] In Owen's analysis of Scripture, he argues that Jesus Christ was the Son of God, the second Adam, and therefore he is the unblemished image to which the rest of humanity must look for restoration.[32] In the next chapter we will explore in far more detail Owen's conception of the humanity of Christ.

Basing much of his argument upon Ephesians 4:24 and Colossians 1:15, 17–18; 3:10, Owen reinforces his claim that we must consider Christ to be the perfect image of God.[33] This in turn leads Owen to understand

28. *Works* 19:347 (BE 18:347).

29. *Works* 2:80ff.

30. Ibid., 1:18.

31. Ibid., 1:19; from Eusebius, *Demonstratio evangelica* 4.2, translated by William Ferrar as *The Proof of the Gospel* (London: SPCK, 1920; repr., Grand Rapids: Baker Academic, 1981; Eugene, OR: Wipf & Stock, 2001).

32. Cf. *Works* 2:163–64; 5:323ff.; 10:391–92.

33. E.g., ibid., 3:478, 515, 573.

all of humanity in a christocentric fashion. When formulating the makeup of the *imago*, the theologian cannot exclusively study the first Adam. Following Greek thought, many previous Christian writers developed their understanding of the *imago* by comparing Adam with the animals.[34] In this they proved to be similar to ancient Greek philosophers like Aristotle, with his hierarchy of souls. Whatever was unique to Adam was declared the substance of the *image*. This method often led theologians to posit that reason encapsulated man's uniqueness, as Aristotle's rational soul was distinguished from the vegetative and sensitive lower souls.[35] Owen, however, following the lead of more christologically minded theologians, moves beyond this limited analysis by focusing upon Christ.

For example, Owen observes that God sent "his own Son to take our nature on him, and therein to represent unto us the perfect idea of that holiness and obedience which he requireth of us."[36] The above comment is taken from a section that describes how Christ is the moral example for believers. Before the incarnation, believers could only look to types and shadows to reveal the glory of God. In the incarnation, the glory and image of God manifested itself definitively. "Faith doth now clearly and distinctly view and consider Jesus Christ as he is represented unto us in the glass of the gospel; that is, the evidences of the presence of God in him and with him, in his work, purity, and holiness."[37] Looking to Christ is not an abstract concept for Puritan theologians, but rather the only way a person can view the unblemished image of God.[38] While Owen keeps some similarities to Aristotle's attempt at distinguishing the universal from what is unique to humanity through observation of the particulars, thus distinguishing the essential from the accidental in humans, there is also a significant difference.[39] Owen, unlike Aristotle, looks not to human beings haphazardly chosen as samples, but to *the* Man—Jesus Christ.

Only by being in Christ, who is the reconciler, may fallen humanity begin to resemble the image of God, for Christ is the one who brings God

34. David Cairns, *The Image of God in Man* (New York: Philosophical Library, 1953), 112.

35. Aristotle, *De anima (On the Soul)*, in *Introduction to Aristotle*, ed. Richard McKeon (New York: Modern Library, 1947), 414a–415a; hereafter cited as *DA*.

36. *Works* 3:511.

37. Ibid., 3:512.

38. Cf. William Ames, *The Marrow of Theology*, trans. John Dykstra Eusden (Boston: Pilgrim, 1968), 105: "In man the true basis for an image is found, but not a perfect one, for that is only in the son of God; Col. 1:15; Heb. 1:3. Yet the imperfection is the result not of deprival but of denial."

39. Cf. Samuel Enoch Stumpf, *Socrates to Sartre: A History of Philosophy*, 5th ed. (New York: McGraw-Hill, 1993), 84–91.

and humanity together.[40] By assuming a true human nature, Christ as the God-man is uniquely able to restore the broken communion between God and his creation through the restoration of a *relationship* in Christ, the true image. We will see this in more detail in chapters 3 and 4.

Owen builds a pneumatic understanding of Christ's humanity from the scriptural references to the Spirit's constant aid and help to the incarnate Lord. The great difference between Jesus's humanity and that of every other human being after the fall is related to the virgin birth: because the Holy Spirit formed the body of Jesus from his inception, the person of Christ was "pure": in fact, "there was no disposition or tendency in his constitution to the least deviation from perfect holiness in any kind."[41] Yet the Spirit's work in the life of Jesus does not end at the miraculous conception; instead, it continues throughout his earthly life. If Christ is the one to whom believers must look, then just as the Holy Spirit supernaturally worked in Jesus's life, securing his entire sanctification, so will the Spirit of Christ work in believers' lives.[42] Owen consistently emphasizes the relationship between Christ, the Spirit, and the believer. Christ is the perfect image while the Spirit functions as the one who is "communicating his grace, image, and likeness to the elect."[43] In other words, since the "source of [Christ and the believer's] sanctification is common, the image we bear is common, [and] thus we are brethren."[44] Again, relationship is the focus. Exploration of this union with Christ is another theme developed at greater length in the following chapters.

Christ provides the framework for understanding the *imago Dei*: he is the foundation, hope, and motive for every believer to seek restoration into the image.[45] The connection between the believer and Christ as the image is central to Owen's language of describing the believer "in" Christ. We will discuss the privileges associated with union with Christ in chapter 4. According to Owen, a believer's union with Christ confers not only benefits, but also tremendous responsibility. Renewal in the image of God only comes through identification with Christ as applied by the power of the Holy Spirit. Once "in" Christ, the believer is now "a

40. E.g., *Works* 1:16; 8:22. Most vividly in ibid., 22:25 (BE 21:25): "This was one principal end of the birth, life, death, and exaltation of Christ. His work in all these was to make peace and reconciliation between God and man. Hereunto belongeth the slaying, destruction, or removal of the enmity that was between them."

41. *Works* 3:167.

42. See ibid., 3:159–88, where Owen describes at length the role of the Spirit in the life of Christ.

43. Ibid., 3:62.

44. Alan J. Spence, "Christ's Humanity and Ours: John Owen," in *Persons, Divine and Human: King's College Essays in Theological Anthropology*, ed. C. Schwöbel and Colin E. Gunton (Edinburgh: T&T Clark, 1991), 85.

45. Cf. *Works* 3:570.

representation of him to the world."[46] The Christian acts as the physical representation of the incarnate Christ. Because each believer has this role, each must strive after holiness, the only way he or she can properly represent Christ. Having said that, true holiness is ultimately about one's relations with God, and this brings us back to Owen's underlying structure of the faculties and their importance for right relations.[47] The faculties are the created means for humanity to enjoy fellowship with God.

Human Faculties as Means to Relationship with God

Throughout Owen's writings the reader discovers a theologian trying to take into account the whole person. One of the ways he seeks to achieve this is by applying a basic Aristotelian psychology. Owen uses these ideas when helpful, but he also modifies and builds upon them to represent fairly (in his mind) the biblical account.

From the start we must recognize that "faculty psychology," though having its classic expression primarily in Aristotle, came to Owen in many forms.[48] Charles L. Cohen's masterful work *God's Caress: The Psychology of Puritan Religious Experience* provides arguably the best introduction to what he labels "Faculty-humor psychology."[49] His research covers roughly the period from the reign of Elizabeth to the early 1640s. Cohen's study neither reaches back into Aristotle's writings, which were popular among Protestant scholastics, nor does it extend to Owen's teaching; but it does show what psychological ideas were widely

46. Ibid., 3:589.

47. Ibid., 13:423–24.

48. One does find a rudimentary but similar psychology even in Plato, but Aristotle remains the most influential philosopher in this respect. For helpful background see Frederick Copleston, *Greece and Rome*, vol. 1, *A History of Philosophy* (New York: Image Books, 1985), 207–11, 266–378; Sir William David Ross, *Aristotle*, 6th ed. (New York: Routledge, 1995), 135–57, 195–239; T. H. Irwin, "The Metaphysical and Psychological Basis of Aristotle's Ethics," in *Essays on Aristotle's Ethics*, ed. Amélie Oksenberg Rorty (Berkeley: University of California Press, 1980): 35–53.

49. Charles L. Cohen, *God's Caress: The Psychology of Puritan Religious Experience* (New York: Oxford University Press, 1986), esp. 25–46. See also Norman Fiering, *Moral Philosophy at Seventeenth-Century Harvard* (Chapel Hill: University of North Carolina Press, 1981), 104–81; J. Rodney Fulcher, "Puritans and the Passions: The Faculty Psychology in American Puritanism," *JHBS* 9 (1973): 123–39; Robert Middlekauff, "Piety and Intellect in Puritanism," *William and Mary Quarterly*, 3rd ser., 2, no. 3 (July 1965): 457–70; James G. Blight, "Solomon Stoddard's *Safety of Appearing* and the Dissolution of the Puritan Faculty Psychology," *JHBS* 10 (1974): 238–50; Ruth L. Anderson, *Elizabethan Psychology and Shakespeare's Plays*, University of Iowa Humanistic Studies 3 (Iowa City: University of Iowa Press, 1927); Perry Miller, *The New England Mind: The Seventeenth Century* (Cambridge, MA: Harvard University Press, 1939), 230–79.

accepted in Owen's day. While we find the common source for many of these ideas in Greek philosophy, theologians throughout church history had already Christianized this understanding of human psychology well before Owen, who falls within this rich tradition.[50] Additionally, we must remember that Owen's approach to human faculties (e.g., mind, will, affections, body) resembles not only Aristotelian psychology, but also basic biblical spirit-flesh-heart language and psychology commonly assumed throughout the history of the church.

Turning our attention to Owen's vocabulary, we must recognize that he often uses the word "universal" as shorthand for the totality of a person's various faculties.[51] For example, in his Greater Catechism he asks his catechumens what holiness is required, to which he provides the answer: "That *universal*, sincere obedience to the whole will of God, *in our hearts, minds, wills, and actions*, whereby we are in some measure made conformable to Christ, our head."[52] Here the expression denotes what unifies the individual. Each of the faculties has a distinct role in enabling a person to honor God with his or her entire or universal being. Although Owen employs the language of "faculty" to refer to various human capacities (e.g., faith),[53] three seem to constitute his traditional faculty psychology: the mind, will, and affections. Taken together, these represent the natural capacities of the *imago*.[54] It is our contention that Owen maintains this classic formula in order to express how humanity was originally made to commune with God. Thus, when the relationship is ruptured, the faculties become entangled, and when the relationship is renewed, the faculties are positively affected. Discussing the various faculties and then tracing the image through redemptive history will demonstrate this in more detail.

The Importance of the Mind

Although it is true that Owen placed a great deal of emphasis upon each of the faculties that constitute the image, none receives more attention

50. Muller, *PRRD* 1:356 rightly observes that the Protestant scholastics adopted "without question the entire language of faculty psychology as one of the presuppositions of their discussions of human knowing."

51. E.g., *Works* 1:178; 2:101, 182, 265–66; 3:471, 509; 6:604–5; 7:420.

52. Ibid., 1:488, emphasis added; cf. GC 20.5.

53. E.g., *Works* 9:20; 20:524–25 (BE 19:524–25): here Owen connects faith with the faculties but does not seem to consider faith itself a faculty. See also *Works* 7:31, where even the stomach is considered a faculty.

54. Cf. T. F. Torrance, *Calvin's Doctrine of Man* (London: Lutterworth, 1949), 39. Among other things Torrance cites the Brief Confession of Faith: "I confess that man was created in the image of God, i.e., endued with full integrity of spirit, will, and all parts of the soul, faculties and senses." From Calvin, "Brief Confession of Faith," in *Treatises on the Sacraments*, ed. Henry Beveridge (repr., Grand Rapids: Reformation Heritage, 2002), 131.

than the "mind." Throughout Owen's life he wrestles with the status he should assign to reason. Different seasons of his life yield slightly different assessments of reason's role in the theological enterprise. As many readers will know from personal experience, the confidence placed in reason in theology can diminish, and occasionally rise again, throughout one's life. Aware of such phenomena, Sebastian Rehnman has seriously challenged the simplistic presupposition that Reformed scholasticism contained a disguised rationalism: using Owen as an example, he contends that Puritans highly valued reason for the theological enterprise, but they also recognized many potential dangers, especially in the form of pagan philosophy. According to Rehnman, early Owen contains a robust appreciation for the role of philosophical discourse, which later declined somewhat in his *Theologoumena pantodapa* (1661), only to reemerge near the end of his life as a possibly more "positive or balanced view."[55] Our focused study of Owen's later works (*ΠΝΕΥΜΑΤΟΛΟΓΙΑ* [1674], *ΧΡΙΣΤΟΛΟΓΙΑ* [1679], and *The Glory of Christ* [1684]) concurs with Rehnman's conclusions.

Playing a central role in "ruling" humanity, the mind allows us to function properly.[56] The mind "is that in us which looketh out after proper objects for the will and affections to receive and embrace."[57] It has supremacy over the other faculties, not necessarily in importance but surely in its role: "Light is received by the mind, applied by the understanding, used by the heart."[58] At its core, this is an example of Christianized Aristotelian epistemology.[59] The mind is the receptacle for images presented to it, using the other faculties to bring movement. Without each faculty working properly, and the mind coordinating them all, a person becomes dysfunctional.

Impotency of the mind is the result of the fall.[60] Owen claims that the "leading, conducting faculty of the soul is the mind or understanding. Now, this is corrupted and vitiated by the fall."[61] Humanity faces the consequences of the fall, but the believer's mind has opportunities to

55. Rehnman, *Divine Discourse*, 127.
56. Cf. Owen, *The Oxford Orations of Dr. John Owen*, ed. and trans. Peter Toon (Cornwall: Gospel Communication, 1971), 12–13.
57. *Works* 3:250.
58. Ibid., 3:252.
59. Cf. Aristotle, *DA* 3.4–5; Copleston, *Greece and Rome*, 328–31; Muller, *PRRD* 1:355–59.
60. *Works* 3:266. Cf. Muller, *PRRD* 1:108, observing: "Whereas the medieval doctors had assumed that the fall affected primarily the will and its affections and not the reason, the Reformers assumed also the fallenness of the rational faculty: a generalized or 'pagan' natural theology, according to the Reformers, was not merely limited to nonsaving knowledge of God—it was also bound in idolatry."
61. *Works* 3:330.

worship God in ways unavailable to the unbeliever. All who live outside the renewing work of the Spirit live in this corrupted state of mind. The mind cannot "receive spiritual things" because of its distorted orientation.[62] Original sin left the mind "filled with prejudices against the mystery of the gospel manner."[63] On its own, the mind will always reject the goodness and renewal of faith. When the mind is not working properly, the entire person becomes disoriented. Two of Owen's remarks illustrate this point of view and further demonstrate Owen's presupposition of Aristotelian psychological ordering:

1. Nothing in the soul, nor the will and affections, can will, desire, or cleave unto any good, but what is presented unto them by the mind, as it is presented. . . .
2. As the soul can no way, by any other of its faculties, receive, embrace, or adhere unto that good in a saving manner which the mind doth not savingly apprehend; so where the mind is practically deceived, or any way captivated under the power of prejudices, the will and the affections can no way free themselves from entertaining that evil which the mind hath perversely assented unto.[64]

The other faculties depend upon the mind to ensure good for the whole person. Once the mind goes astray, the other faculties inevitably turn from God and toward further degeneration. While Aristotle argues that this occurs primarily by not developing right habits through education and practice, Owen believes that all postlapsarian humanity suffers the consequences of a corrupted mind from birth to grave.[65] Yet for both

62. Ibid., 3:267.
63. Ibid., 3:277.
64. Ibid., 3:281.
65. Aristotle would say that people carry out improper actions because of irrationality rather than some inherited moral corruption. This is why he encourages raising a child in such a way that a proper "habit" is formed. Here Aristotle uses the Greek *hexis*, which is later translated into Latin as *habitus* and used extensively by the scholastics. Habits are crucial in forming our ability for virtuous actions: we become virtuous through actions, and thus through habits. This extends not simply to actions, but also to feelings and "appetites." A person's actions give rise to states of character, and these states of character will either enable or prohibit true virtue. Therefore, training of youth becomes all-important: "It makes no small difference, then, whether we form habits of one kind or of another from our very youth; it makes a very great difference, or rather *all* the difference." Aristotle, *Ethica nicomachea (Nicomachean Ethics)*, in *Introduction to Aristotle*, ed. Richard McKeon (New York: Modern Library, 1947), 1103b.24–25; cf. 1104b.9–14; hereafter cited as *EN*. Originally the child practices certain actions out of reverence and respect for the parents. Later in life one will learn, not simply to act rightly, but also to do the act from right motives for the action itself rather than for lesser reasons. See Susan Sauvé Meyer, "Responsibility for Character: Its Scope and Significance," in *Aristotle on Moral Responsibility: Character and Cause* (Oxford: Blackwell, 1993): 122–48.

thinkers, the mind is central in allowing or disallowing the human to live rightly. Once the mind is off track, the individual will live less and less rationally and thus less and less humanly. Focusing the mind on its proper end is all-important for both Aristotle and Owen: without the right object in mind, all efforts at moral improvement will be like arrows shot haphazardly into the air, completely missing the target.[66] Owen may disagree with Aristotle about *what* the end is, but he does not disagree that directing the mind toward a proper end is the necessary step toward that end.

According to Owen, Christians have the joy and responsibility of renewing their minds through communion with God. With regeneration, the Spirit works to transform a person's mind, eventually renovating his or her entire being. This is the process of the Spirit's "saving illumination" in the mind that reorients a believer's disposition.[67] Now the redeemed individual may look to the end for which humanity was created: to worship and enjoy God. This privilege of image renewal also carries consequences: "It is [the Christian's] duty to endeavour the improvement and enlargement of the light they have, in the daily exercise of the spiritual power they have received."[68] In this transformation of the mind, one seeks to renew the image and prepare for eternal communion with God. Owen argues, "Our minds by [love] will be changed into the image of what we contemplate, and we shall endeavour that our lives be conformed thereunto."[69] One must therefore turn the mind to Christ, so that through contemplation one will slowly become like Christ, who is the perfect image of God. Obviously the life and passion of Christ serve as the best examples of love.[70] Following a long theological tradition, Owen employs this insight to help believers grow closer to God.[71] Whereas Aristotle strongly encouraged contemplation of truth as vital in his view of the happy life, Owen's object of contemplation was not philosophical truth, but *the One* who is Truth.[72] Owen saw the object of contemplation as a person rather than an abstraction. In his classic work *The Grace and Duty of Being Spiritually Minded* (1681), Owen makes this very point:

66. Cf. Aristotle, *EN* 1094a.17–24.
67. *Works* 3:493.
68. Ibid., 3:494.
69. Ibid., 3:585.
70. Ibid., 3:564.
71. Cf. Simon K. H. Chan, "The Puritan Meditative Tradition, 1599–1691: A Study of Ascetical Piety" (PhD diss., University of Cambridge, 1986). Chan believes that Owen does at points present a "view of meditation which departs significantly from the orthodox position" (204–15, quotation from p. 6).
72. Cf. Aristotle, *EN* 1177a.14–24. See our discussion in chapter 3 on the "object of faith."

To be spiritually minded is, not to have the notion and knowledge of spiritual things in our minds; it is not to be constant, no, nor to abound, in the performance of duties: both which may be where there is no grace in the heart at all. It is to have our minds really exercised with delight about heavenly things, the things that are above, especially Christ himself as at the right hand of God.[73]

The Role of the Will

Before one can discuss the faculty of the will, a brief word about the fluidity of Owen's language is necessary. In his discussions of the faculties, Owen focuses less upon fixed distinctions and more upon the broader concepts communicated. Overlap between the discussions of the various faculties is common.[74] Some confusion regarding Owen's words may be avoided by remembering this overlap.

Owen believes that one may conceptualize the will in two ways. "First, as a rational, vital faculty of our souls; secondly, As a free principle, freedom being of its essence or nature."[75] A strong correlation exists between a person's will and his or her actions—between one's (in)ability to do certain things, and how these manifestations reveal one's disposition. Once regenerated, a new power enters the human and enables renewal of the image: it "consists in its liberty, freedom, and ability to consent unto, choose, and embrace spiritual things. Believers have free will unto that which is spiritually good; for they are freed from that bondage and slavery unto sin which they were under in the state of nature."[76] Here Owen follows Augustine's framework.[77] Before the fall, humanity lived in a state of *posse non peccare* (being able not to sin). After the fall natural humanity lives in the state of *non posse non peccare* (not being able

73. *Works* 7:344; for the entire treatise, see ibid., 7:261–497.

74. For example, William Ames and Jonathan Edwards, growing out of this Augustinian tradition, often speak of the affections and the will in an interchangeable manner (Fiering, *Moral Philosophy*, 138).

75. *Works* 3:334.

76. Ibid., 3:494. Owen elsewhere shows the relationship between the Spirit and a person's will. He argues that the Spirit in regeneration "offers no violence or compulsions unto the will. This faculty is not naturally capable to give admission unto. If it be compelled, it is destroyed. And the mention that is made in the Scripture of compelling ('Compel them to come in') respects the certainty of the event, not the manner of the operation on them. But whereas the will, in the depraved condition of fallen nature, is not only habitually filled and possessed with an aversion from that which is good spiritually . . . but also continually acts an opposition unto it, as being under the power of the 'carnal mind,' which is 'enmity against God'" (ibid., 3:319).

77. Augustine, *De correptione et gratia* (*Admonition and Grace*) 33, in PL 44 and in *NPNF*[1] 5:457–58; cf. idem, *Enchiridion* 118, in PL 40 and in *NPNF*[1] 3:275.

not to sin).[78] According to Owen, once regeneration occurs, a renewal of one's will takes place, and one's ability to honor and respond to God becomes a reality.[79] That is, each believer is able to sin and not to sin (*posse peccare et non peccare*).

Within this framework one can understand Owen's volunteerism, which Gavin McGrath fairly defines as "the prominence, but not the dominance, of the will's response to God's sovereign initiatives in the divine/human encounter."[80] Here the practical side of Owen's volunteerism is captured, for the Puritan divine consistently pushed for the significance of human response, arguing that the believer lives properly only when he freely—enabled by the Spirit—obeys God.[81] Unlike common stereotypes of Puritan theologians, Owen was not satisfied with a robotic presentation of humanity. Rather, he saw a dynamic relationship between the sovereign Creator and his living creation. Neglect of this insight would lead to a severe misunderstanding of Owen's anthropology.

So how is fallen humanity able to respond to God? The disposition of each believer changes when "grace and holiness" are "infused" into the elect (cf. *habitus infusus*).[82] This language echoes the debate between Protestants and Roman Catholics on the question of justification. Rome tended to speak of the "infusion" of righteousness in justification, while Protestants preferred the forensic language of "imputation" of righteousness.[83] We simply observe here that while Owen and other Reformed theologians rejected the idea of "infusion" for justification, they nevertheless commonly employed the language of infusion for sanc-

78. Cf. *Works* 3:494–95.

79. Owen maintains that even in this state of regeneration, the believer still relies upon the Spirit's activity to make his or her actions righteous and pleasing to God. Here one sees Owen's strong synergistic emphasis in the process of sanctification (*Works* 3:433, 535–36).

80. Gavin McGrath, "Puritans and the Human Will: Voluntarism within Mid-Seventeenth Century English Puritanism as Seen in the Works of Richard Baxter and John Owen" (PhD diss., University of Durham, 1989), 3. Here he is arguing against R. T. Kendall's (*Calvin and English Calvinism to 1649* [1979; repr., Carlisle: Paternoster, 1997]) problematic definition of volunteerism, which unnecessarily creates a chasm between faith in the mind and faith as an act of the will. Kendall's view is also ably questioned by Joel R. Beeke and Jan van Vliet, "*The Marrow of Theology* by William Ames (1576–1633)," in *The Devoted Life*, ed. Kapic and Gleason, 52–65.

81. Cf. McGrath, "Puritans and the Human Will," 194–95, 210, 283–84, 370, 388, 391.

82. Cf. *Works* 2:200, 206; 3:220; 4:437; 5:64; 11:97–98; 21:599–600 (BE 20:599–600). See Richard A. Muller, *Dictionary of Latin and Greek Theological Terms: Drawn Principally from Protestant Scholastic Theology* (Grand Rapids: Baker Academic, 1985), 134; hereafter cited as *DLGTT*.

83. E.g., "The Canons and Decrees of the Council of Trent," in Philip Schaff, *The Creeds of Christendom*, vol. 2, *The Greek and Latin Creeds*, 4th ed., rev. and enlarged (1877; repr., Grand Rapids: Baker Academic, 1990), 96: from session 6, chap. 7.

tification. Answer 77 of the Westminster Larger Catechism (based on the Westminster Confession) makes this point: "God in justification imputeth the righteousness of Christ; in sanctification his Spirit infuseth grace, and enableth to the exercise thereof."[84] Along these lines, Owen argues that by the Spirit "the will is freed, enlarged, and enabled to answer the commands of God for obedience, according to the tenor of the new covenant. This is that freedom, this is that power of the will, which the Scripture reveals and regards and which by all the promises and precepts of it we are obliged to use and exercise, and no other."[85]

With this understanding of infused grace, Owen grounds a person's moral actions in the will rather than in the intellect. At this point Owen shows the influence of Aristotle more openly than usual. He begins by quoting "the Philosopher" and then building upon him: "As Aristotle says, 'Virtue is a habit which maketh him that hath it good or virtuous, and his actions good.' Now all moral habits are seated in the will. Intellectual habits are not immediately effective of good or evil, but as the will is influenced by them. These habits do incline, dispose, and enable the will to act according to their nature."[86] The mind influences the will, but the will acts upon the information. Thomas Hooker, Owen's contemporary, similarly argues that "reason and understanding are the underlings, as it were, of inferior and lower ranck, and can but as servants and attendants offer and propound to the wil[l] and affections."[87]

According to Owen, a person's fallen nature and ungodly *habitus* inevitably cause the will to move toward inadequate ends instead of the ultimate end in Jesus Christ. Unlike some ancient philosophers, Owen believes that moral education is not enough for genuine righteousness, for the Spirit must free the will and capture a person's affections.[88] A supernatural change in the person is therefore necessary, and this always takes him back to the primacy of the Holy Spirit's action.[89] Owen's conception of the will is complex in that he thinks two aspects must come

84. *The Westminster Confession of Faith* (Glasgow: Free Presbyterian Publications, 1994), 169; hereafter cited as WCF.

85. *Works* 3:496.

86. Ibid., 3:502–3; cf. Aristotle, *EN* 1103a.14–25.

87. Thomas Hooker, *The Application of Redemption* . . . (London: printed by Peter Cole, 1657 [1656?]), 279.

88. Rejecting the Socratic idea that people do wrong out of ignorance, Aristotle also thinks the process is more complex. "The saying that 'no one is voluntarily wicked nor involuntarily happy' seems to be partly false and partly true; for no one is involuntarily happy, but wickedness is voluntary" (*EN* 1113b.14–16; cf. 1114b.1–9). He argues that there can be two senses of knowledge, one having it, the other using it (1147a.10–12). A person can know about something (i.e., the right thing to do), and yet not use that knowledge (i.e., act wrongly, though not ignorantly). But for Aristotle, this is to act irrationally.

89. See *Works* 3:244–82; 11:94–95.

under consideration: the action and the "end for which it is done."[90] An action may be good and result in the glory of God in Christ *only* by God's grace through the Spirit's movement.

In accordance with these external and internal guidelines, Owen in his ethics maintains a consistent emphasis upon the image of God in the human person as a whole, rather than simply the actions one performs. Owen's system moves beyond public "righteousness" and into private motivations. The renewal of the image changes both the actions and the reasons for performing them. Without this transformation, a person remains in a "natural state," in which one cannot hope for eternal communion with God.

The Struggle with the Affections

Owen's treatment of the affections is particularly interesting in light of his endeavor to recapture a theological justification for the prominent role of affections in defining what it means to be a human being.[91]

Owen's work teaches a clear coherence between experience and the affections. It is this aspect of Owen's treatise on the Holy Spirit that captured the attention of Geoffrey F. Nuttall. When beginning his treatise, Owen acknowledges that none before him have so fully discussed the "whole economy" of the Holy Spirit.[92] Nuttall argues that "what justifies Owen in his claim to be among the pioneers, is the place given in Puritan exposition to experience, and its acceptance as a primary authority. . . . The interest is primarily not dogmatic, at least not in any theoretic sense; it is experimental [experiential]. There is theology, but, in a way which has hardly been known since St. Augustine, it is a *theologia pectoris*."[93] Here Nuttall is hinting at what we have been calling Owen's anthroposensitivity: theological reflection informs and is informed by human experience. According to Owen, experience encompasses not just a person's past, but also his or her emotional response to the present. Owen emphasizes the importance of a person's holistic framework: one cannot understand the image without emphasizing the role of experiences and affections. Thus, Owen claims that the Spirit "doth not comfort us

90. Ibid., 3:503.
91. One reason why so many previous scholars have overlooked the vital role of the affections may be traced to Owen's own inconsistency and fluidity of language. Often he will not mention the affections, instead focusing upon the mind, will, understanding, and so on. The difficulty is that Owen will sometimes use these terms interchangeably, and then at other times in juxtaposition. For examples of Owen including the affections as part of the faculties, see ibid., 2:34, 172; 3:420, 437; etc.
92. Ibid., 3:7.
93. Geoffrey F. Nuttall, *The Holy Spirit in Puritan Faith and Experience*, 2nd ed. (1947; Chicago: University of Chicago Press, 1992), 7.

by words, but by things. . . . Give unto a soul an experience, a taste, of the love and grace of God in Christ Jesus, and be its condition what it will, it cannot refuse to be comforted."[94] One quickly notices how Owen freely mixes the language of experience with vivid emotive vocabulary. Again, Owen advocates a holistic understanding of the *imago*. How one feels can be as significant as how one thinks. However, as part of the image, the affections have also suffered from the fall.

Originally the affections were properly oriented toward God.[95] Humanity loved the Creator and experienced fellowship with God. The fall changed those affections, confusing and disorienting them.[96] Given this natural disruption, Aristotle's view that a person's desires will follow the guidance of his or her reason toward what is worthy of affection becomes impossible. Thus we have both continuity and discontinuity between Aristotle and Owen.

For Aristotle, the affections naturally tend toward disorder and therefore can create ethical and other problems. The Greek philosopher describes the conflict within the human soul with a vivid illustration: "For exactly as paralysed limbs when we intend to move them to the right turn on the contrary to the left, so is it with the soul; the impulses of incontinent people move in contrary directions."[97] He concludes that there must clearly be some other principle within the soul besides the rational, and it is this principle which causes disruption. So the soul of a human contains both a rational and an irrational principle, and the two often conflict. The irrational leads the soul in one direction, while the rational tries to steer it in the other. For Aristotle, the rational element of the soul must rule the untrustworthy irrational, and when this happens, there is order. Thus morality becomes possible for both the individual and the community. Aristotle contrasts the continent and incontinent man: the latter, "knowing that what he does is bad, does it as a result of passion"; the former, "knowing that his appetites are bad, refuses on account of his rational principle to follow them."[98]

Owen similarly believes that human affections have become corrupted and lead humans astray, but this is a tragic *consequence* of the fall rather than the original design. Here Owen displays a position closer to his contemporaries, as exemplified in William Fenner's classic treatment of the affections, than to that of Aristotle's basic schema. For Fenner, the affections are not intrinsically bad, but rather are the created means

94. *Works* 3:391.
95. Ibid., 17:39–42; John Owen, *BT*, 20–24.
96. *Works* 3:450; cf. 2:62–63: "As we are, so are all our affections. . . . We love one, one day, and hate him the next."
97. Aristotle, *EN* 1102b.18–22.
98. Ibid., 1145b.12–13.

through which a human responds to God and his grace.[99] Owen similarly believes that before the fall human affections faithfully pointed the heart toward the gracious Creator. Given the catastrophe of the original human rebellion, human affections *now* cannot be fully trusted: Owen's view of this state resembles Aristotle's view of the passions. Just as with the other aspects of the image, Owen argues that the Spirit provides the only hope for renewal of the affections.

As a Puritan theologian, Owen maintains that the Spirit uses different methods to shape and mold the believer's affections. Afflictions sometimes provide the impetus for the necessary reshaping of a person's affections.[100] Difficult experiences cause us to depend upon God, and this dependence deeply touches our affections. The Spirit also works

> by supplying believers with experiences of the truth, and reality, and excellency, of the things that are believed. Experience is the food of all grace, which it grows and thrives upon. Every taste that faith obtains of divine love and grace, or how gracious the Lord is, adds to its measure and stature.[101]

Grace is not simply a propositional truth to be perceived rationally: it is also a reality that we perceive with the affections. A change in disposition affects how one views the world and reacts to challenges. When the Spirit renews a person's affections, delight is found in the things of God. Christ, as the perfect image, again provides the ultimate example.

Owen argues that Christ had affections, and because his disposition remained uncorrupted by sin, his faculties worked perfectly. Christ demonstrates how one should have deep affections for God the Father and one's fellow humans. Christ showed tremendous compassion toward those around him in their state of sinfulness.[102] Such compassion was not a matter of willpower in which he persuaded himself to love those around him. Rather, it was the outworking of his disposition shaped by a deep affection for his heavenly Father. Owen believed what principally motivated Christ "in the whole was his unspeakable zeal for, and ardency of affection unto, the glory of God. These were the coals which with a vehement flame, as it were, consumed the sacrifice."[103] Christians who experience the renewing work of the Spirit become capable of an ap-

---

99. Cf. William Fenner, *A Treatise of the Affections* (1641; London: I. Rothwell, 1642), 63–66. Fenner's book is one of the most detailed and nuanced treatments of the affections produced in the seventeenth century.

100. *Works* 3:447–48.

101. Ibid., 3:390.

102. Ibid., 3:177.

103. Ibid., 3:177–78.

propriate love for God and their fellow humans, following the example
of Christ and empowered by the same Spirit that anointed him.

The Body as Part of the Image?

Having discussed the nonphysical aspects of the *imago*, we may now
turn our attention to the physical. Theologians have found it difficult to
understand the role of the body as part of the image of God. Augustine
argued that one's body prepares one to worship God in a way animals
cannot,[104] but because of his Neoplatonic tendencies, Augustine did
not emphasize the body as part of the image. Likewise, Calvin only
mentions the relationship between the image and the body in a passing
comment: "Although the primary seat of the divine image was in the
mind and heart, or in the soul and its powers, yet there was no part of
man, nor even the body itself, in which some sparks did not glow."[105]
Owen has received criticism for a similar neglect of the body. Some have
claimed that Owen's "concept of [humanity] . . . suggests the Platonic
depreciation of the physical."[106] Surprisingly, however, he developed a
stronger connection between the body and the image than many of his
orthodox predecessors. This may in part be the result of his Aristotelian education, although fairly standard among his predecessors, which
clearly emphasized the connection between the soul and body, between
form and matter. So, for example, Owen speaks of the link between the
body and soul as the "greatest, the nearest, the firmest" union that can
exist. Body and soul are not easily distinguished and separated. "The
soul and body are naturally and necessarily unwilling to fall into a state
of separation, wherein the one shall cease to be what it was, and the
other knows not clearly how it shall subsist. The body claspeth about
the soul, and the soul receiveth strange impressions from its embraces;
the entire nature, existing in the union of them both, being unalterably
averse unto a dissolution."[107]

104. Augustine claims that because man stands erect, he is elevated above the animals
and is therefore not to "seek earthly things as do the cattle, whose pleasure is entirely from
the earth, in consequence of which they are all inclined forward on their bellies and bend
downwards." In contradistinction, man's body was designed appropriately to fit his rational
soul "because of the fact that he stands erect, able to look up to heaven and gaze upon the
higher regions in the corporeal world"; from *The Literal Meaning of Genesis*, trans. and ed.
John Hammond Taylor, 2 vols., Ancient Christian Writers 41–42 (New York: Newman, 1982),
1:193 (6.12.22). Augustine also appears to have believed that the male body represents the
image, whereas the female body does not, cf. 1:98 (3.22.34); 2:26 (7.24.35).
105. John Calvin, *The Institutes of the Christian Religion*, trans. Ford Lewis Battles, ed.
John T. McNeill, 2 vols. (Philadelphia: Westminster, 1960), 1:188 (1.15.3).
106. Bass, "Platonic Influences," 117.
107. *Works* 1:281–82.

The body and the other aspects of the image must function together. When a person tries to describe the image without incorporating the body, this description is necessarily incomplete.

> *Our whole souls*, in the rectitude of all their faculties and powers, in order unto the life of God and his enjoyment, did *bear his image*. Nor was it confined unto the soul only; *the body also*, not as to its shape, figure, or natural use, but as an essential part of our nature, was interested in the image of God by a *participation* of original righteousness. Hence *the whole person* was a meet principle for the communication of this image of God unto others, by the means of *natural propagation, which is an act of the entire person*; for a person created and abiding in the image of God, begetting another in his own image and likeness, had, by virtue of the covenant of creation, begotten him in the image of God also,—that is, had communicated unto him a nature upright and pure.[108]

A strong element of mystery remains in Owen's words, resembling Calvin's ambiguous comment cited above, but Owen does stretch his conclusions as far as he thinks biblical.

The body was originally good, and therefore its design was oriented toward God. As with the other aspects of the image, it became corrupted by sin. In a fallen world the natural inclination of the body moves toward sin and "disorderly motions."[109] With regeneration, the Spirit's activity begins to transform the human "body." How this occurs remains a mystery. What is clear, according to Owen, is that "true sanctification reacheth unto the body" as well as the other faculties of the image.[110] Maintaining his language of hierarchy within a human, and sounding particularly Aristotelian, Owen argues: "Although our souls are the first proper subject of the infused habit or principle of holiness, yet our bodies, as essential parts of our natures, are partakers thereof."[111] Each Christian must seek holiness for his or her whole person. This includes specific warnings and exhortations regarding the particular sins against the body that the apostle Paul mentions.[112] Physical bodies are not necessarily evil, but they must be redirected toward God and disciplined to function again in an ordered fashion. Only regeneration sets the physical aspect of the *imago* back on the path toward God.

---

108. Ibid., 3:417–18, emphasis added.

109. Ibid., 3:420. Elsewhere Owen writes: "Our bodies were made vile by the entrance of sin; thence they became brothers to the worms, and sisters unto corruption" (1:245).

110. Ibid., 3:422.

111. Ibid., 3:420. On Aquinas's similar psychology, see Frederick Copleston, *Augustine to Scotus*, vol. 2, *A History of Philosophy* (New York: Image Books, 1985), esp. 375–85.

112. *Works* 3:426–27.

Tracing the Image through the History of Salvation

A brief diachronic tracing of humanity from Owen's perspective further reveals and reinforces his conception of the relationship between humanity's past, present, and future. Only by viewing the *imago* from these different angles can one fairly represent the fullness of Owen's thought. Beginning with humanity before the fall, we shall quickly trace the cosmic events that shape persons and lead to their eternal destiny.

According to Owen, before the fall Adam embodied humanity's communion with God, with the promise of unending life and fellowship with God if we would remain faithful to God's original design. Proper worship of God is the essence of humanity's uncorrupted nature, and this worship must engage each person's whole being.[113] The orientation of one's being is significant because it either allows or hinders the ability to worship. That is why Owen concentrates upon a person's disposition (cf. Aristotle's states of character), rather than his or her actions. In Adam's pre-fallen disposition, one sees the original concept of a person as the *imago*.

> In this image [Adam] was created, or it was con-created with him, as a perfection due to his nature in the condition wherein he was made. This gave him an habitual disposition unto all duties of that obedience that was required of him; it was the rectitude of all the faculties of his soul with respect unto his supernatural end.[114]

Before the fall, a right orientation to God allowed humanity to function properly. Each faculty of the *imago* (e.g., mind, will, affections) worked together and in submission to God. This placed humans in a situation where they could worship God naturally, since this ability for fellowship and communion with God lay "written into [humanity's] very constitution."[115] Yet, when temptation came and Adam and Eve responded inappropriately, sin brought chaos to what had once functioned in an orderly way.[116]

Owen compares three significant differences between the image before and after the fall.[117] First, before the fall, humans were distinct from the

113. Ibid., 1:48; cf. 1:206.
114. Ibid., 3:285.
115. Sinclair Ferguson, *John Owen on the Christian Life* (Edinburgh: Banner of Truth, 1987), 274.
116. *Works* 1:61. The contemporary philosopher Alvin Plantinga outlines and respectfully draws from a similar model of the faculties (he labels it as the Aquinas/Calvin Model, and Owen grows out of this tradition); see his *Warranted Christian Belief* (New York: Oxford University Press, 2000), esp. 204–16.
117. *Works* 1:182–85.

rest of creation in their unique representation of God's holiness and righ-teousness. Second, humanity was made in the image of God and thus was "a means of rendering actual glory unto him from all other parts of the creation."[118] In other words, all of creation depended upon humanity to voice their praise. Creation was "as an harmonious, well-tuned instru-ment, which gives no sound unless there be a skilful hand to move and act it."[119] Third, humanity was originally created to experience "eternal enjoyment" in relationship with the Creator. However, sin's entrance dra-matically altered these three points. Because of sin, there is nothing that distinctly and faithfully represents God's image on earth. Additionally, the rest of creation suffers from the fact that "man by sin did not only draw off himself from that relation unto God wherein he was made, but drew off the whole creation here below with himself into a uselessness unto his glory."[120] Fallen creation groans, since it now appears as a once "well-tuned instrument," yet with no one to properly play it. Finally, sin caused humans to lose their "power and ability" to enjoy their relationship with God for eternity. Owen uses these three points to show the consequences of original sin: humanity was no longer God's faithful display of righ-teousness among creation, creation was no longer able to worship God actively, and humanity's ability to enjoy God for eternity was lost.

A cosmic shift took place after the fall of humanity. Although sin now predisposes humanity to unrest, disorder, and rebellion, Owen acknowledges that there are certain external pressures that tend to set limits upon humans, restraining their tendencies to sin. These exter-nal actions are not Owen's vital concern; they are simply the outward manifestation of an inward reality. Unredeemed humanity remains in a sad condition: "The disease is uncured, the soul continues still in its disorder and in all inward confusion; for our original order, harmony, and rectitude consisted in the powers and inclinations of our minds, wills, and affections, unto regular actings towards God as our end and reward."[121] Sin changed humanity from the inside out. Humanity now acts like Aristotle's irrational and incontinent man: the psychological hierarchy has been replaced by unbridled passions, improperly directed actions, and tainted minds.[122]

118. Ibid., 1:183.
119. Ibid.
120. Ibid., 1:184.
121. Ibid., 3:643.
122. Cf. ibid., 1:401: "The stream of [fallen human affections] will cloud and darken the understanding, that it shall not be able clearly to discern any spiritual object,—least of all the greatest of them. There is nothing more acknowledged, even in things natural and moral, than that the disorder of the passions and affections will blind, darken, and deceive the mind in its operations."

No aspect of the *imago* remains unscathed by the intrusion of sin into the world. Owen views the destruction of sin in a holistic manner: he uses his categories for the *imago* to explain how sin affects the entire human being. After the fall humanity is "wholly defiled, polluted, and [in] every way unclean. There is a spiritual leprosy spread all over our natures, which renders us loathsome to God, and puts us in a state of separation from him."[123] The language of depravity only makes sense to Owen when viewed through the lens of the complete *imago*. All other attempts to explain the results of sin tend to emphasize one aspect of humanity to the neglect of another. For example, Owen combats those who see the fall as corrupting a person's will, but not the mind. This is the philosopher's (Aristotle's) mistake, which has made its way into the church via the heresies of the Pelagians and then the "Socinianized Arminians."[124] According to Owen, the Bible asserts that the whole person is corrupted—including the intellect.

Without a holistic view of humanity, regeneration through the Spirit would only renew certain aspects of a person rather than the whole human. Owen favors a position claiming that sin created confusion within the whole person, and redemption is the only possible hope for humanity to escape this chaos and despair.

At this point Owen's distinction between "confusion" and "rebellion" becomes relevant.[125] "Confusion" connotes the idea of a "state" wherein there is no rule or order. When a disposition is in a state of confusion, it cannot discern between what is righteous and what is evil, and thus is overwhelmed by chaos. "Rebellion" is different in that it communicates the idea of sporadic outbursts of "disturbance," but not an overall state of disorder. The Christian often wrestles with rebellion but is never in a state of confusion. Rebellion is not strong enough in the Christian to overthrow "the rule of grace," but it may nevertheless manifest itself in violent outbursts. Owen makes this point to allow for authentic Christian struggle while maintaining a distinction between the redeemed and the unconverted. Confusion is brought to all people by the fall, but through the death of Christ applied to the elect by the Spirit, there is now a positive change from a state of confusion to individual acts of rebellion.

123. Ibid., 3:449.
124. Ibid., 3:244–45. Cf. Gerard Reedy, "Socinians, John Toland, and the Anglican Rationalists," *HTR* 70 (1977): 285–304; see Robert K. M. Wright, "John Owen's Great High Priest: The Highpriesthood of Christ in the Theology of John Owen (1616–1683)" (PhD diss., Iliff School of Theology and University of Denver, 1989), 132–75 and 186–209 for his discussions regarding Owen and Socinianism; and 79–130 for his description of Owen's arguments against the rising tide of Arminianism.
125. See *Works* 3:645.

The change of orientation for the redeemed accompanies the next catastrophic event that occurs within humans. Since the fall our natural inclination turns us away from the Creator.[126] Movement away from God means a movement away from properly understanding ourselves, which creates a confusion of sorts within us.[127] For the redeemed, however, a process begins that directs humanity back to God and back to a right understanding of ourselves.

While a person's redemption is secured by the work of Christ, the application and actualization of redemption are only possible by the work of the Holy Spirit.[128] This theme undergirds Owen's entire treatise on the Holy Spirit. Owen spends a great deal of time exploring the role of the Spirit in restoring humanity to the image of God: "Now, this whole evil frame is cured by the effectual working of the Holy Ghost in the rectifying and renovation of our natures. He giveth a new understanding, a new heart, new affections, renewing the whole soul into the image of God."[129] However, the Spirit's role does not end with regeneration. The regenerate believer undergoes an essential and ongoing change in disposition as the Spirit engages him or her in the process of sanctification. Owen's emphasis upon the image of God in humanity provides the framework for understanding this process.

A definition of sanctification from Owen reveals the link between the *imago* and the work of the Spirit:

> Sanctification is an immediate work of the Spirit of God on the souls of believers, purifying and cleansing of their natures from the pollution and uncleanness of sin, renewing in them the image of God, and thereby enabling them, from a spiritual and habitual principle of grace, to yield obedience unto God, according unto the tenor and terms of the new covenant; by virtue of the life and death of Jesus Christ. Or more briefly:—It

126. Ibid., 3:430: "And this beauty originally consisted in the image of God in us, which contained the whole order, harmony, and symmetry of our natures, in all their faculties and actions, with respect unto God and our utmost end."

127. Cf. ibid., 3:266.

128. Cf. ibid., 3:299.

129. Ibid., 3:437. Owen is by no means unique in his use of faculty psychology when explaining human redemption. Matthew Barker, when discussing "union with Christ," also clearly uses it. Man's communion with God "consisteth of the Divine Operations of our Souls towards God, when the faculties of the Soul are tending towards him, and terminated upon him; when the Mind is exercised in the contemplation of him, the Will in chusing and embracing him, when the Affections are fixt upon him, and center in him, when by our Desires we pursue after him, by our Love we cleave to him, and by Delight we acquiesce and solace ourselves in him." From *A Continuation of Morning-Exercise* (1683), Sermon xix, 1022; cited by R. Tudor Jones, "Union with Christ: The Existential Nerve of Puritan Piety," *TB* 41, no. 2 (November 1990): 188.

is the universal renovation of our natures by the Holy Spirit into the image of God, through Jesus Christ.[130]

The goal of sanctification, according to Owen, is holiness, the renewing of the Christian in his or her whole being—mind, heart, will—into the image of Christ. Although Owen elsewhere makes it clear that "there is no faculty of our souls that is absolutely and perfectly renewed in this life," a process of real renewal takes place when a person moved by the Spirit turns from self to Christ, who is the perfect image of God.[131] Only the Spirit can change a person's disposition.

Although Owen often employs the term "disposition," he also uses the word "habit" to communicate the process of renewal in the *imago*.[132] These should not be viewed as different ideas, but rather as two terms communicating the same concept. Here Owen writes within the history of theological discourse that has used Aristotle's language of *hexis* (being in a certain state as produced by practice) and translated it as *habitus* in order to communicate the same idea, since habit and disposition can both be used as English translations of both terms. Aquinas serves as the classic example of a sophisticated theological handling of the idea of *habitus*.[133] Though Owen sometimes uses "habit" when simply referring to learned, reinforced, and repeated actions,[134] he also uses the term in a classical sense.[135] In full agreement with Aristotle,

130. *Works* 3:386. Elsewhere Owen describes sanctification as "the immediate work of God by his Spirit upon our whole nature, proceeding from the peace made for us by Jesus Christ, whereby, being changed into his likeness, we are kept entirely in peace with God, and are preserved unblamable, or in a state of gracious acceptance with him, according to the terms of the covenant, unto the end" (3:369).

131. Ibid., 4:231; 3:452.

132. E.g., ibid., 3:5, 102, 220, 252, etc.; cf. chap. 2, note 66.

133. See Thomas Aquinas, *Summa theologiae*, 61 vols. (London: Blackfriars, 1963–75, 1981), esp. 1a–2ae.49–55; cf. vol. 22, Appendix 2; hereafter cited as *ST*. For Protestant scholastic interaction with Aquinas on *habitus*, see Heppe, *RD*, 323–24. Note also the wide range of contexts in which the language of *habitus* may be understood, such as Ames, *Marrow of Theology*, 81, 112; esp. 224, 329; Francis Turretin, *Institutes of Elenctic Theology*, trans. George Musgrave Giger, ed. James T. Dennison Jr., 3 vols. (Phillipsburg, NJ: P&R, 1992), 1:18–20; Muller, *PRRD* 1:259, 355–59; Robert D. Preus, *The Theology of Post-Reformation Lutheranism*, vol. 1, *A Study of Theological Prolegomena* (Saint Louis: Concordia, 1970), 78–79, 155.

134. Cf. *Works* 3:475.

135. Etymologically the word "habit" comes from the Latin *habitus*, which was originally the past participle of the verb *habere*, "have." It was used as a noun to mean "how one is," and the connotation referred to a person's state, or condition. See John Ayto, *Dictionary of Word Origins: The Histories of More Than 8,000 English-Language Words* (New York: Arcade, 1990), 270. Previous theologians, especially the scholastics, used *habitus* to refer to a "spiritual capacity." According to Muller, *DLGTT*, 134, "The scholastics assumed that, in addition to defining the faculties of the soul, they also had to

Owen quotes his definition of a virtue as a habit.[136] The relationship between a person's will and a person's habit is indissoluble. As noted earlier, a person's actions, which are manifestations of the will, are the result of his or her habit or disposition.[137] Therefore, a fundamental transformation of a person's disposition best describes the process of sanctification.

A person's "habitual defilement" is removed by the cleansing of the Spirit, who applies the work of Christ to a new believer's life. Yet, not only does a negation occur; there is also the positive gift of "habitual grace," which opposes the natural lusts of fallen human nature.[138] This new habit applies naturally to his faculty schema: "In the understanding, it is light; in the will, obedience; in the affections, love; in all, faith."[139] At times this language sounds similar to Aristotle's emphasis on the role of training and education, although Owen grounds the renewal in the work of the Holy Spirit rather than human efforts. As the image is renewed, a person's habit or disposition is redirected toward God and holiness. On such theological grounds Owen would more accurately be understood as having digested a form of virtue ethics coming from Aquinas rather than directly from an unbaptized Aristotle.

Finally, Owen's treatises place relatively little emphasis upon the eschatological conclusion for humanity, putting it rather on the process of sanctification.[140] The eschatological emphasis that we do find, as we will see for example in chapter 6, is often centered on Christ's *accomplished* work, rather than on what is yet to come. Nevertheless, Owen provides enough material for the reader to know that the end

---

acknowledge the capacities or dispositions of those faculties. A faculty cannot receive a datum or act in a manner for which it has no capacity." Owen likewise uses "habit" to refer to a person's disposition.

136. *Works* 3:502–3.

137. The plural is often used in these contexts; thus theologians—including Owen—will speak of habits and dispositions (including habits of the will, of the mind, and so on). What harmonizes this plurality is the unity of the person, and for the sake of our concerns it is legitimate simply to use the singular. For example, Owen believes that one habit cannot be fallen or transformed without affecting the other habits, since a person's habits are ultimately interdependent and may be considered as a whole.

138. *Works* 2:172.

139. Ibid.

140. For an overview of Owen's eschatological views, often discussed in relationship to politics, see Ferguson, *John Owen*, esp. 275–79; Christopher Smith, "'Up and Be Doing'": The Pragmatic Puritan Eschatology of John Owen," *EQ* 61, no. 4 (1989): 335–49; Peter Toon, "A Message of Hope for the Rump Parliament," *EQ* 43 (1971): 82–96; idem, "Puritan Eschatology: 1600–1648," in *The Manifold Grace of God: Papers Read at the Puritan and Reformed Studies Conference, 1968* (London: Evangelical Magazine; Hartshill, Stoke-on-Trent: Tentmaker Publications, 1968), 49–60; L. G. Williams, "God and Nation," esp. 69ff.

for which he or she strives is perfect communion with the living God. Fellowship with God is the ultimate goal for the longing heart. This communion begins before glory, as it prepares the believer for a holy and eternal relationship with the Lord. Undefiled and continuous communion with God may only occur with a full renewal of the image in humanity.

This renewal includes the sanctification of each aspect of the *imago*. This is possible only by the work of the Holy Spirit, "whereby the mind is effectually renewed, the heart changed, the affections sanctified, all actually and effectually, or no deliverance will be wrought, obtained, or ensue, out of the estate" in which the unregenerate man finds himself.[141] The Christian lives in the process of sanctification, yet longing for the state of glorification. As Owen writes elsewhere, in heaven the glory of Christ is no longer a question of faith since it is "heightened into vision."[142] A person's nature will be perfected in glory, "especially in all the faculties, powers, and affections of our souls and all their operations."[143] In this consummate state there will be no sin or limitation to the enjoyment of being in the presence of God. Until then, every believer remains in the world of potential, awaiting the time when his or her sanctification becomes completely realized. Sanctification is "a great work in itself, that wherein the renovation of the image of God in us doth consist, yet is it not wrought in any but with respect unto a farther end in this world; and this end is, that we may live to God. We are made like unto God, that we may live unto God."[144]

We end this background with a brief anecdote. Believing that contemplating Christ as the image of God best prepares one for heaven, Owen was motivated to write his work *Meditations and Discourses on the Glory of Christ, in His Person, Office, and Grace: With the Differences Between Faith and Sight; Applied unto the Use of them that Believe.*[145] Yet when on his deathbed, having just found out that this book finally went to the press, Owen's recorded response characterizes his eschatological perspective. He was glad about the news, but replied, "The long-looked-for day is come at last, in which I shall see that glory in another manner than I have ever done yet, or was capable of doing in this world!"[146] He believed he would soon see the perfect image face to face, and thus he would be fully conformed to that image.

---

141. *Works* 3:315; cf. 1:405–6, where Owen claims that the "faculties of our souls shall then be made perfect."
142. Ibid., 7:339.
143. Ibid., 7:340.
144. Ibid., 3:482.
145. Ibid., 1:273–415.
146. Ibid., 1:274.

Conclusion

John Owen's formulation of the *imago Dei* provides a key to understanding his anthropology. He makes his formulation in a christocentric pattern, pointing to Jesus Christ as the incarnate and true image of God. Christ exhibits how the various aspects of the image should cooperate and enable the worship of God. Owen's holistic conception of the image includes a vibrant and interactive portrayal of the various faculties that make worshipping God possible. By following the history of salvation in his description, Owen not only describes how the image became defaced, but also how it may be restored. As the image, a human being is created in right communion with God, and only through Christ may the sinner enjoy renewed communion. Owen offers the hope that the Spirit of Christ faithfully renovates the whole person and prepares the believer for glorification.

Finally, Owen's work demonstrates both continuity and discontinuity with Aristotle. The ancient paradigm of faculty psychology pervades Owen's presuppositions and thus makes its way into the fabric of his theological discourse. We do not want to push the language of a "direct influence" from Aristotle too far, but clearly there is strong evidence for indirect influence that affects Owen's theology. Breathing the intellectual air of his day, Owen presupposes the fundamental accuracy of basic Aristotelian psychology. He employs faculty psychology as a scalpel for dissecting the *imago Dei* in order to display its parts and the work of the Spirit therein. At this point Owen represents a long theological heritage and also many of his Puritan contemporaries. What is most interesting is how his presentation aims to use this framework to offer a more holistic view of the human being.

Along with this continuity, Owen also significantly differs from his philosophical predecessor's fundamentally optimistic view of humanity. Here the radical nature of sin, a concept foreign to Aristotle, causes Owen to modify this primitive psychology to fit his theological conception of a fallen world. Owen only employs Aristotelian ideas to the degree that he thinks they accurately fit the biblical data and common human experience, and when Aristotle falls short of that criterion, Owen abandons his philosophy.

Knowing Owen's view of the image of God, informed not only by Greek thought, but also more strongly by biblical themes and human experience, we are also now better equipped to understand Owen's anthroposensitivity. From this point on, we will routinely see how his basic understanding of human nature guides his theological and pastoral reflections. Throughout the rest of our study, we will find his assumptions about faculty psychology, sin, and grace consistently surfacing, demonstrating a kind of reciprocal relationship between theology and practice, experience and doctrine. This relationship only makes sense in light of Owen's view of humanity made in God's image, fashioned to commune with the Creator and with other noble creatures.

Having this background, we are now prepared to observe how Owen seeks to answer the critical question of how reconciliation occurs between God and humanity. We now turn to Owen's Christology, paying particular attention to his view of the incarnation.

HUMANITY ACTUALIZED

*The Relationship between the Incarnation
and Fallen Humanity*

[The incarnation is the] most absurd conception that ever befell the minds of men.

John Owen (1677)

Had not God been thus mindful of man, and visited him in the person of his Son incarnate, every one partaker of that nature must have utterly perished in their lost condition.

John Owen (1668)

Introduction

A customary feature of systematic theology is the careful division of topics into various loci. This common practice can tremendously aid the student's understanding of biblical and historical questions. However, if these divisions become overly rigid and compartmentalized, then the different categories may appear unrelated.

John Owen seeks to avoid such a danger by fluidly moving between the various doctrines, consistently showing not only how they relate to one another, but also how they relate to common Christian experience. We hope to reflect Owen's approach in our study of his theological anthropology. While some might question the inclusion of christological and soteriological observations in the midst of an anthropological study, we contend that such detailed analysis is necessary for appreciating Owen's underlying anthroposensitivity. Accordingly, the next two chapters demonstrate how Christology and the doctrine of justification fit into Owen's overall anthropology. We begin with the former.

Given the vastness of Owen's extensive christological reflections, we must seriously restrict the discussion in this chapter.[1] We begin by exploring Owen's reasons for the necessity of the incarnation. Next we discuss Owen's strong emphasis on the Son of God's humiliation as providing the experiential grounds for spiritual comfort. Finally, we examine Owen's reflections concerning the true humanity of Jesus Christ. This final section argues that, according to Owen, only by maintaining the continuities and discontinuities between Jesus's human nature and fallen human nature can one preserve effective soteriology and a true affirmation of shared humanity. Through these observations we gain an insightful glimpse into how Owen's anthroposensitivity works itself out practically.

This chapter will concentrate on Owen's mature reflections on Christ, including his volumes ΧΡΙΣΤΟΛΟΓΙΑ (1679) and *The Glory of Christ* (1684), a revealing sermon preached in 1681, and a few key sections from his massive multivolume *Hebrews* commentary (1668–84). These will show how Owen, nearing the end of his life, pulls together his understanding of the relationship between anthropology and the incarnation.

Why the Incarnation?

Throughout our discussion of the *imago Dei* in chapter 2, we highlighted both the dignity of the original creation and the devastating implications of the human plunge into moral chaos. We now proceed to Owen's more specific discussions. Since this chapter discusses the person of Christ, we begin by asking, *Why was the incarnation necessary?* Only by starting with this question can the full gravity of Owen's discussion of the humanity of Jesus make sense.

1. For further studies of various aspects of Owen's Christology, see Richard W. Daniels, *The Christology of John Owen* (Grand Rapids: Reformation Heritage Books, 2004). Alan J. Spence, "Incarnation and Inspiration: John Owen and the Coherence of Christology" (PhD diss., King's College London, 1989); Trueman, *Claims of Truth*, 151–98; R. K. M. Wright, "Owen's Great High Priest." For brief reviews of these works refer to chap. 1 in Kapic, "Communion with God: Relations between the Divine and the Human in the Theology of John Owen" (PhD diss., King's College London, 2001).

The Human Debt

According to Owen, "religion" was originally pure, orderly, and beautiful.[2] In the original state humanity "was fit and able to glorify" God because of being made in God's image. Nevertheless, this should not be confused with the idea that God somehow made humanity partially divine. "Whatever perfection God had communicated" to human nature was susceptible to failure unless it was also uniquely united with God's self through a "personal union." Humanity was mutable and responsible; God remained immutable and sovereign. While in the garden, Adam and Eve communed with God freely until they chose to dishonor their Creator. One result of this tragedy was God's revelation that "no gracious relation between him and our nature could be stable and permanent, *unless our nature was assumed into personal union and subsistence with himself.*"[3] Fallen humanity now struggles to find rest and peace with God; relief in this new environment could only come through a unique mediator.[4]

Only a mediator who was both truly God and truly human could bring redemption. Such an assertion by Owen reflects not only a long tradition within Western theology going back to Chalcedon, but also the modifications of the sixteenth and seventeenth centuries, with their common theological emphasis on judicial satisfaction theory. In order that "human nature might be restored," it became necessary for a person to live in perfect obedience to God and divine law, and yet more than simple obedience was necessary. This unique person's obedience needed to be such that he "should give and bring more glory and *honour* unto [God's] holiness than there was dishonour reflected on it by the disobedience of us all."[5] Reflecting Anselm's emphasis on honor (which we will discuss below), Owen believes this equation preserves both God's glory and the reality of the sinful human disaster.

The theological problem remains: an ordinary person could not adequately fulfill this role. God's character demands both the perfect life of an individual and the necessary punishment of sin required by divine justice. Perfect obedience offered to God by a finite human would be sufficient for that person, but those actions could not benefit others; the obedient human was simply doing what was required of a creature responding faithfully to the Creator. For Owen, the person who offers this perfect obedience to God

2. See *Works* 1:48 for this discussion.
3. Ibid., emphasis added.
4. Cf. ibid., 1:52.
5. Ibid., 1:200, emphasis added. Here we find hints of Anselm's language of "honor" breaking through.

must be one who was not originally obliged thereunto, on his own account, or for himself. And this must be a divine person, and none other; for every mere creature is so obliged. And there is nothing more fundamental in Gospel principles, than that the Lord Christ, in his divine person, was *above the law*, and for himself owed no obedience thereunto; *but by his own condescension*, as he was "made of a woman" for us, so *he was "made under the law" for us*.[6]

Therefore, only the person who is "divine and infinite" could fulfill this requirement; for his obedience needed to be of "infinite value," which leads Owen to conclude that "he must be God."

This roughly resembles Anselm's argument in *Cur Deus homo*:[7] all of humanity has "dishonored" (i.e., sinned against) God. There are only two options for each person who so sins against God: either the honor taken from God must be repaid or punishment must follow. God cannot lose his honor; therefore, an individual may either freely be subject to God, or God will subject that person to himself by torment.[8] Anselm goes on to argue that although only God can make satisfaction, *no one ought to make it except man*; otherwise *humanity* does not make satisfaction. Since no one but God can make it, and no one but humanity ought to make it, "it is necessary for a God-man to make it."[9] The person to make satisfaction must be both "perfect God and perfect man, because none but true God can make it and none but true man owes it."[10] Owen's arguments show similarity to this traditional presentation, though at times

6. Ibid., 1:201, emphasis added; see also 1:208–9; 2:162. Cf. the patristic language and ideas as represented by Novatian, *The Trinity*, chap. 11, in The *Trinity* . . . , trans. Russell J. DeSimone, Fathers of the Church 67 (Washington, DC: Catholic University of America Press, 1974), 46–47 (cf. *ANF* 5:611–44); cited by Thomas C. Oden, *Systematic Theology*, vol. 2, *The Word of Life* (San Francisco: HarperSanFrancisco, 1989), 188: "And in the same manner that He [Christ], as Man, is made under the Law, so is He also, as God, declared to be the Lord of the Sabbath. . . . In the same manner that He, as Man, goes to the Father, so as a Son obedient to His Father shall he descend from the Father. . . . However, when you read both these truths, there is danger that you will believe not both of them but only one." Owen's contemporary William Sherlock, in *A Discourse Concerning the Knowledge of Jesus Christ, and our Union and Communion with him* . . . (London: Walter Kettilby, 1674), could not understand this distinction and considers it "to no purpose" (310). Owen answers him in *Works* 2:356–58.

7. See Anselm, *Cur Deus homo*, in *A Scholastic Miscellany: Anselm to Ockham*, ed. and trans. Eugene R. Fairweather, Library of Christian Classics 10 (Ichthus ed., 1956; repr., Philadelphia: Westminster, 1981), 100–183.

8. Ibid., 122, 123.

9. Ibid., 151. Cf. Owen speaking about Christ's obedience: "We were obliged unto [obedience], and could not perform it;—he was not obliged unto it any otherwise but by a free act of his own will, and did perform it. God gave him this honour, that he should obey for the whole church" (*Works* 1:339).

10. Anselm, *Cur Deus homo*, 152.

he reflects his seventeenth-century context by stressing the "wrath of God" more than the honor of God, the latter emphasis being far more Anselmian.[11]

From this we quickly learn that Owen's discussions of the humanity of Jesus naturally tend to take place under the umbrella of the *person* of Christ and thereby in conjunction with his divinity. Great error occurs, according to Owen, if the theologian does not always remember the two natures of the mediator and instead stresses one to the neglect of the other.

The Creator/Creature Distinction

Not only has sin caused a great chasm between God and humanity, but the Creator/creature distinction also presents problems. Human beings—and all other creatures—do not have the faculties to comprehend God's essence.[12] To argue otherwise inevitably results in either a heretical limiting of God or an improper exaltation of humanity. Owen demonstrates this idea by paraphrasing Eusebius's analogy of the sun and its rays.[13] The sun is a wonderful life-giving source for the world. Creation greatly benefits from the communication of the sun's heat, light, and refreshment, but only because the sun is mediated through its beams. If the actual sun were to descend unto the earth, the result would be destruction, for "nothing could bear its heat and luster, . . . and all things [would] be swallowed up and consumed by its greatness." Even so, the unmediated glory of the Father remains an unapproachable light. "We cannot bear the immediate approach of the Divine Being; but through him, as incarnate, are all things communicated unto us, in a way suited unto our reception and comprehension."[14] The Divine-human encounter and God's self-revelation must be viewed in light of the incarnation. Later in this study we will see more particularly how the *assumption* of human nature by the Son of God not only demonstrates God's loving initiative toward humanity,

11. Cf. Owen, *Works* 1:479, in the GC: "Q. Was it necessary that our Redeemer should be God? A. Yes; that he might be able to save to the uttermost, and to *satisfy the wrath* of his Father, which no creature could perform. . . . Q. Wherefore was our Redeemer to be man? A. That the nature which had offended might suffer, and make satisfaction, and so he might be every way a *fit and sufficient* Saviour for men" (emphasis added).

12. *Works* 1:66.

13. Ibid., 1:15–16. From Eusebius, *Demonstratio evangelica* 4.5–6. Book 4 deals with prophetic evidence of Christ's divinity, and book 3 tries to give such evidence for Christ's humanity. See Johannes Quasten, *Patrology*, vol. 3, *The Golden Age of Greek Patristic Literature from the Council of Nicaea to the Council of Chalcedon* (Westminster, MD: Newman, 1960), 331–32.

14. *Works* 1:16.

it also provides the only way of mediation and communion between God and humans.

Human limitations point to the need for the unique revelation of the incarnation. Although it is true that the "invisible things of God," which include "his eternal power and Godhead," are testified to in his creation, the creation can only point weakly to "divine excellencies" since creation is "all finite and limited, and so cannot properly represent that which is infinite and immense."[15] Confusion on this point can lead to idolatry: worshipping the creation rather than the Creator.

One reason that humanity tends toward idolatry grows from a deep internal yearning for a satisfying object of worship. Owen believes that all humanity has "always had a common apprehension that there was *a need of a nearer and more full representation of God unto them*," a need that no element of creation could satisfy.[16] Owen bases much of his argument on Romans 1. This longing feeds an inclination toward idolatry, which manifests itself in a desire to create representations of God fashioned after "birds, four-footed beasts, and creeping things."[17] Satan exploited this human desire to approach the Divine Being through earthy representations. This was Satan's common practice, argues Owen, in perverting the Gentiles, who so often devised ways to "bring God into human nature." Throughout history the God of Israel had consistently revealed that "this practice of making representations of him" was rebellious and consequently to be dealt with by serious punishment.

Why did God so stringently forbid carrying out the common human longing to make images that seem to bring God near? Owen's answer is twofold. First, God had made provision that "a glorious image and representation of himself, infinitely above what any created wisdom could find out," would come.[18] However, humanity must in good faith wait upon God's wisdom and timing, showing patience and trust in God. Such patience is scarce, as demonstrated by the Israelites' failure to wait for Moses's return from the mount after meeting with God. Instead of waiting for God's revelation, they built themselves an idol. Even so, many who impatiently plunged into idolatrous worship—trying to "bring God nearer" to themselves—ended by becoming "contemptibly foolish."

15. Ibid., 1:67; cf. 20:344 (BE 19:344): "These glorious works of God [i.e., creation] do indeed show the infinite glory of him that made them. This is the use that men should have made of their contemplation of them, and not have chosen them for their gods." In *Works* 20:344–50 (BE 19:344–50) he claims that creation reveals God's greatness, his infinite self-sufficiency, his infinite and eternal power, his wisdom, and his goodness. Cf. also *Works* 20:366 (BE 19:366).

16. *Works* 1:67, emphasis added.

17. Ibid., 1:68.

18. Ibid.

They "abased their nature" in such a way that the result was the "utmost distance from God, whom they sought to bring near unto them."[19]

Second, God had already provided some means of *limited* representations of his presence, "though not of his being."[20] These ordained temporary representations came through (1) God's works of creation and (2) "the visible institutions of his worship." While helpful, even these divine signs were insufficient to allow humans to worship God "in a due manner." Though much may be gained from these pointers to God, none "represent God as the complete object of all our affections, of all the actings of our souls in faith, trust, love, fear, obedience, in that way whereby he may be glorified, and we may be brought unto the everlasting fruition of him."[21] These signs alone were unable to completely satisfy every human faculty, although they *pointed* to One who could.

We should be clear that Owen does not see human longing as creating the need for the incarnation, but rather the divine promise of incarnation was what created the human longing. The human longing for a fuller representation of God was not completely satisfied through idolatry nor through the positive signs of God found in creation and the institutions of worship.[22] Consequently, Owen concludes that the incarnation, which does fully present God in the flesh, was necessary and always part of God's plan of redemption. Only in Jesus Christ are "the complete image and perfect representation of the Divine Being and excellencies" found.[23] To see Jesus is to see the Father in a way different from previous representations of God, for the Son is the self-revelation of the Father.

The Son Who Was Sent

Given God's commitment more fully to reveal himself and rescue humanity from their sin, which person of the Trinity should assume human flesh? Recognizing great mystery in discussing the divine counsel, Owen only provides a general answer. What he does believe is that there are "three

19. Ibid.
20. Ibid., 1:69.
21. Ibid.
22. Cf. ibid., 1:221: "Alas! the light of divine wisdom in the greatest works of nature holds not the proportion of the meanest star unto the sun in its full strength, unto that glory of it which shines in the mystery of God manifest in the flesh, and the work accomplished thereby!"
23. Ibid., 1:69. Cf. Owen, *Glory of Christ*, in *Works* 1:294: "Herein is [the Person of Christ] glorious, in that he is the great representative of the nature of God and his will unto us; which without him would have been eternally hid from us, or been invisible unto us; we should never have seen God at any time, here nor hereafter." He then declares that even the angels would not know the essential glory of the invisible God if it were not for the Son.

distinct persons in the holy Trinity," and for divine reason "it became the wisdom of God that the Son, the second person, should undertake this work, and be incarnate."[24] For Owen, the exact reasons for this decision remain outside finite speculation, and to look into such unrevealed matters does not edify or advance the faith. This anti-speculative mood prompts Owen to restrict his inquiry to what he believes the Scriptures clearly reveal, though one often hears in him more the echo of the sophisticated early fathers than merely the enigmatic statements of the New Testament.

While only the Second Person becomes incarnate, the incarnation remains the work of the Triune God. The best way to approach this mystery, according to Owen, is through the "order of the holy persons of the blessed Trinity in their operations; for their order herein doth follow that of their subsistence."[25] His language and formulation here represent a fairly orthodox understanding common in both patristic thought and Protestant scholasticism.[26] In Owen's thought, three crucial elements are required for the redemption of humanity: authority, love, and power, and all of these must be governed by "infinite wisdom."[27] These three characteristics "originally reside in the person of the Father, and the acting of them in [redemption] is constantly ascribed unto him."[28] Acting out of his sovereign authority the Father sends the Son and gives the Spirit. Second in the "order of subsistence" is the Son, who

24. *Works* 1:218.

25. Ibid. Owen's contemporary Francis Turretin, writing from the Academy of Geneva, likewise reasoned that "the order of operating follows the mode of subsisting. Hence, the Father operates from himself, but the Son from the Father" (*Elenctic Theology*, 1:281).

26. E.g., see John of Damascus, *Orthodox Faith* 3.15, for a discussion of the language of "operation" or "energy." He deals with both christological and trinitarian questions. Cf. Owen's use of ἐνέργεια in *Works* 2:51. For Protestant scholasticism, see Heppe, *RD*, 118–19, quoting J. Heinrich Heidegger (1633–98): "According then to the order of subsistence and action, just as the Father is *a se*, exists and operates through Son and H. Spirit, the Son exists and operates *a Patre* through the H. Spirit, the H. Spirit exists and operates *a Patre et Filio*. So, suitably to this order of subsistence and action *ad intra*, there is also assigned to the Father *ad extra* the inauguration of thing, or creation; to the Son their continuation, or redemption; to the H. Spirit their consummation, or sanctification and regeneration. Likewise, because of the goal of the action and of the habitude peculiar to the work of the fixed person whose operation shines out most in any *opus*, the incarnation, although the work of the entire Trinity, is referred singly to the Son" (Corpus theologiae Christiane . . . , 4:45). Johann Henrich Alsted (1588–1638): "The *opera deitatis ad extra* are common to the three persons—because they proceed from the essence. (But) as the essence is marked in the Father by a peculiar mode, and likewise in the Son and in the Spirit, so also the essential operations are distinct in the order and determination of the action" (Theologia Scholastica . . . , 125). Muller, *DLGTT*, correctly concludes: "The Reformed in particular prefer to say that the persons of the Trinity are distinguished, not merely *rationaliter* or *formaliter*, but *modaliter*, according to their distinct modes of subsistence" (195).

27. Cf. Ames, *Marrow of Theology*, 92.

28. *Works* 1:219.

in the "order of operation puts the whole authority, love, and power of the Father in execution."[29] The Son faithfully carries out the desires of the Father on behalf of his people. So, "whatever is in the person of the Father is in the person of the Son, and being all received from the Father, he is his essential image."[30] Moving on to the third order of subsistence of the Trinity, Owen believes that the Holy Spirit provides "a perfecting application of the whole unto all its proper ends."[31]

From this basic formulation Owen is able to deduce that "it became not [i.e., was not fitting for] the person of the Father to assume our nature," for this would wrongly reflect the Triune God's order of subsistence and operation.[32] Likewise, the Holy Spirit did not assume human nature since "in order of divine operation following that of his subsistence," his peculiar work was to complete the divine act of redemption by applying the work of Christ to the church. This argument, which moves between the immanent and the economic, allows Owen to reach a different conclusion from Aquinas. Whereas Aquinas seems to think that the Father *or* the Spirit, *instead of the Son,* could have become incarnate, Owen believes otherwise.[33] The conclusion Owen gleans from his meditations on the subsistence and order of the "Holy Persons" is that it remained uniquely for the Son to assume human nature.[34] Speculations beyond this general statement "must be referred unto another world."[35]

Christ as God's Revelation

On more practical grounds, Owen believes that the incarnate Son fulfills another unique role: all "spiritual truth" must ultimately find its

29. Ibid. Here Owen cites 1 Cor. 8:6: "To us there is but one God, the Father, of whom are all things, and we in him; and one Lord Jesus Christ, by whom are all things, and we by him."

30. Ibid., 1:218.

31. Ibid., 1:219.

32. Ibid., 1:220.

33. See Aquinas, *ST* 3a.3.5. Colin Gunton believes that Aquinas's view is the logical outcome of the inadequate trinitarian heritage that was first developed by Augustine; see Gunton, *The Promise of Trinitarian Theology* (Edinburgh: T&T Clark, 1991), 97, 102. Cf. Ralph Del Colle, "The Holy Spirit: Presence, Power, Person," *Theological Studies* 62 (2001): 322–40, esp. 335, arguing for a relationship between person and work, believing that the *distinct* mission of the Spirit is to "indwell the just person and the Church," for this "*proceeds* from the Spirit's presence and power and ultimately *from the Spirit's Person*" (emphasis added).

34. Cf. John of Damascus, *Orthodox Faith* 4.4: "The Father is Father and not Son: the Son is Son and not Father: the Holy Spirit is Spirit and not Father or Son. For the individuality is unchangeable. . . . Wherefore the Son of God became Son of Man in order that His individuality might endure."

35. *Works* 1:220. See also chap. 5 on "Communion with the Triune God."

source and connection in Christ. Employing familiar imagery, he claims that divine truth dislocated from Christ is like "a beam interrupted from its continuity unto the sun—it is immediately deprived of light."[36] All comprehension of divine truth comes only through revelation: "For in, by, and from [Christ] alone" are the truths of God "proposed unto us, that we are made partakers of them." To separate such truths from the person of Christ is to lose truth altogether. Emphatic on this point, Owen argues that Christ "is the life and soul" of all spiritual truth. Although these truths are attested to in "the Word," they "are but a dead letter, and . . . of such a character as is illegible unto us, as unto any real discovery of the grace and love of God."[37] Owen is making the point that *even Scripture*, God's special revelation to humanity, does not have efficacy without Christ. In this way he is also tightly weaving together his pneumatology and his Christology. He goes so far as to claim that the foundation of all biblical truth "was laid in the person of Christ," for Christ expresses God's attitude toward his people. All of God's action toward humanity only makes sense within the matrix of Christ, "who, as a living spirit diffused through the whole system [of divine revelation], both acts and animates it—all the treasures of truth, wisdom, and knowledge may be well said to be hid in him."[38] By closely tying all revelation to the person of Christ, Owen also reveals his belief that the incarnation implies a relational and epistemological necessity; for to truly *know* God or anything about him indicates some sort of relationship to Christ. Overlooking this relationship inevitably severs the beams from the sun.

Humiliation: Humanity Actualized and Redeemed in the Son

Having briefly sketched out the need for and importance of the incarnation, we can now move on to another question: What does the Bible mean when it claims that the Word was made flesh? Historically, the challenge has always been to maintain both the true humanity and true deity of Jesus Christ as first portrayed in the New Testament and early church.[39] As is commonly acknowledged, the church formulated its Christology by way of a slow development, normally spurred on by

36. Ibid., 1:81–82.

37. Ibid., 1:82; cf. *Works* 2:108, 120.

38. Ibid., 1:83. Owen, in his characteristic anthroposensitive manner, connects application with theology in this section by concluding that "much notional knowledge of the doctrines of the Scripture" is useless if not to "form Christ in the soul, and transform the whole person into his likeness and image. . . . It is learning the truth as it is in Jesus, which alone reneweth the image of God in us" (1:84). Note the relational emphasis here.

39. Kelly, *Early Christian Doctrines*, 138.

debates against early Christian heresies. Through this often painful and political process, the church was able to work out a basic christological framework: the result was the Council of Chalcedon (451), which offers the clearest ecumenical statement on the natures of Jesus Christ. In the brief Chalcedonian Creed the parameters for orthodox Christology are set: the guidelines require an acknowledgment that Jesus of Nazareth was "truly God and truly man."[40]

Since that time (and even more so before the creed), theological reflection has struggled to maintain both truths. Fleshing out this doctrine theologically and pastorally has never been easy; danger abounds for the theologian trying to trek through christological controversies. Since each era offers its own unique challenges and cultural biases, theologians have often emphasized one truth to the neglect of the other.[41] In this broader historical context, our investigation of Owen proves to be most rewarding.

Alan J. Spence has recently provided a stimulating attempt to recognize Owen's distinct contribution to the history of Christology, arguing that Owen helps to solve several contemporary christological problems.[42] According to Spence, the church has always struggled to hold together incarnational and inspirational Christology. The former tends to stress the *divinity of Christ*, whereas the latter emphasizes the *Spirit's inspiration* of

40. The creed more fully reads: Jesus is "truly God and truly man, of a reasonable soul and body; consubstantial with the Father according to the Godhead, and consubstantial with us according to the Manhood; in all things like unto us, without sin." It adds that Jesus must "be acknowledged in two natures, inconfusedly, unchangeably, indivisibly, inseparably; the distinction of natures being by no means taken away by the union, but rather the property of each nature being preserved, and concurring in one Person and one Subsistence, not parted or divided into two persons, but one and the same Son."

41. For example, the late nineteenth and early twentieth centuries saw both extremes emphasized to the neglect of the other. Late nineteenth-century "liberal" Protestant theologians often capitulated to the intellectual rules of the Enlightenment and thus tended to focus almost exclusively on the historical Jesus's ethics. In the process they often became vulnerable to the charge of virtually denying his divine nature (e.g., preexistence, ascension, and so on). Albrecht Ritschl (1822–89) is arguably such an example. Cf. Alister E. McGrath, *The Making of Modern German Christology: From the Enlightenment to Pannenberg* (Oxford: Blackwell, 1986), 55–58; Hans Schwarz, *Christology* (Grand Rapids: Eerdmans, 1998), 187–89. On the other hand, evangelicals eagerly engaged in apologetics to prove the deity of Jesus. In so doing they often neglected to emphasize the true humanity of Jesus. For recent critiques of this historical tendency, see Nigel M. de S. Cameron, *Complete in Christ: Rediscovering Jesus and Ourselves* (Carlisle: Paternoster, 1989; repr., 1997), esp. chap. 1; N. T. Wright, *The Challenge of Jesus: Rediscovering Who Jesus Was and Is* (Downers Grove, IL: InterVarsity, 1999), 24–25. Both overreactions risk failing to maintain the Chalcedonian dual emphasis.

42. Spence, "Incarnation and Inspiration." See also Alan J. Spence's shorter studies: "Inspiration and Incarnation: John Owen and the Coherence of Christology," *KTR* 12 (1989): 52–55; "John Owen and Trinitarian Agency," *SJT* 43 (1990): 157–73; and "Christ's Humanity and Ours," in *Persons, Divine and Human*, ed. Schwöbel and Gunton.

the Son. When those in the Alexandrian school stressed the incarnation of the Word to the neglect of inspiration, they inevitably diminished the "full humanity of the experiences of Jesus."[43] Those in the Antiochene school, who recognized Jesus's human nature as fully dependent upon the Spirit, also tended to diminish the orthodox understanding of the incarnation.[44] According to Spence, Owen tries anew to bring these two emphases together through "the integration of the concepts of Christ as the incarnate Word of God and as the Son inspired by the Spirit. . . . By incorporating them both, Owen's Christology brings a measure of theological stability to the Definition of Chalcedon and also serves as a pointer to the trinitarian direction modern Christology must take if its divisions are to be healed."[45] Spence's work serves as a springboard for our study regarding Owen's discussions of the person of Christ, the incarnate Son of God who hungered, thirsted, prayed, and wept.

We believe that there is no better test of a theologian's anthropological consistency than a close examination of his Christology. Does Owen paint a docetic Christ, who only *seemed* to be human, while really never partaking in the realities of human limitations, sufferings, and pain? Demonstrating his anthroposensitivity, Owen approaches this topic not only in light of the Scriptures, but also informed by common human experience in a fallen world. His view of the humanity of Christ both informs and is informed by his general anthropology. Finally, how does Owen hold together the truths of the divine and human natures in the person of Jesus Christ? Since our focus remains on Owen's anthropology, we will concentrate on his dealings with the humanity of Christ, but in so doing it will prove necessary to explore the divinity of Jesus, though with less detail.

The Assumption of Human Nature

Through the influence of the later fathers, the language of assumption (e.g., *assumptio carnis*) became a common way to speak of the mystery of the incarnation within Protestant scholasticism.[46] Self-consciously

---

43. Spence, "Incarnation and Inspiration," 26.

44. Ibid., 185–86.

45. Ibid., 211. Elsewhere, after sketching Owen's understanding of the Spirit's work in the life of Christ, Spence enthusiastically observes: "What is so interesting about Owen's exposition of the person of Christ in terms of the Spirit's inspiration, is that it took place within the context of an incarnational Christology. It appears to me that this was the first time since the brilliant defence of the Christian faith by Irenaeus in the second century, that a theologian with an 'orthodox' understanding of the incarnation had recognised so clearly what it meant for Christ as a man to be inspired by the Holy Spirit" (82).

46. E.g., Theodore Beza, *Epistolarum theologicarum Theodori Bezae Vezelii, liber unus: Secunda editio, ab ipso auctore recognita* (Geneva: apud Eustathium Vignon, 1575), 165; cf. Muller, *DLGTT*, 48, 152–53. Cf. the use by the Lutheran Martin Chemnitz, *De duabus*

falling within this tradition, Owen wants to maintain a clear distinction between the idea of assumption and union.

By assumption, Owen means the "divine constitution of the person of Christ as God and man."[47] Before the assumption, the Second Person of the Trinity did not have a human nature (cf. λόγος ἄσαρκος). In other words, God the Son does not change his "own nature or essence," nor is there a "transubstantiation of the divine nature into the human," nor should it be said that he ceased to be "what he was" before the incarnation.[48] Rather, the incarnation represents the Second Person of the Trinity becoming "what he was not, in taking our nature to his own, to be his own, whereby he dwelt among us" (cf. λόγος ἔνσαρκος).[49] Owen believed this truth is found in Scripture.

When the Bible refers to the *divine* nature in the person of Jesus Christ, it stresses the *activity* of the "nature assuming"; when it refers to the *human* nature—often *passively*—it stresses "the nature assumed."[50] Owen will later conclude that the Scriptures move freely between the two natures of the person of Christ, but all the while the focus is on his person.[51] While this freedom of movement is often confusing to the reader of the biblical texts, Owen offers four observations to help explain this difficulty.[52] Here he echoes the hermeneutical approach found throughout the fathers and exemplified in Leo's Tome.[53]

---

naturis in Christo: De hypostatica earum unione; De communicatione idiomatum, et aliis quaestionibus inde dependentibus libellus (Jena: typis Tobiae Steinmanni, 1591), 54.

47. *Works* 1:224.

48. Ibid., 1:46.

49. Ibid., 1:46–47. Cf. Gregory of Nazianzus, *Oration 29*, 19, in *NPNF²* 7:308: "What He was He continued to be; what He was not He took to Himself." Owen, *Works* 1:232, provides an almost word-for-word restatement of Gregory's sentence, though he does not use quote marks and cites no sources.

50. *Works* 1:224. Cf. Gregory of Nyssa on this point, who believed that "the flesh was the passive, the Logos the active" in the assumption (he speaks of "mingling," ἀνάκρασις); from Kelly, *Early Christian Doctrines*, 299. Owen's discussion here shows remarkable similarity to Gregory of Nyssa, who maintains that with the "historical Jesus" one can still distinguish the two natures. Here Kelly is summing up Gregory of Nyssa, *Adversus Eunomium* 3.3; 3.4. Cf. Theodore of Mopsuestia, in Kelly, *Early Christian Doctrines*, 306–7.

51. R. Glynne Lloyd has criticized Owen—and classical orthodoxy—for losing the personality of Jesus in these "abstractions"; see "The Life and Work of John Owen with Special Reference to the Socinian Controversies of the Seventeenth Century" (PhD diss., Edinburgh University, 1942), 220–21.

52. Cf. WCF, 8.7, which contains the core of Owen's presentation. Cf. Zwingli on this with his discussion of ἀλλοίωσις (i.e., transfer or exchange) in William Stacy Johnson and John H. Leith, eds., *Reformed Reader: A Sourcebook in Christian Theology*, vol. 1, *Classical Beginnings, 1519–1799* (Louisville: Westminster/John Knox, 1993), 204–5; hereafter cited as *RR*.

53. Pope Leo I, *Letter to Flavian of Constantinople*, in *The Christological Controversy: Sources of Early Christian Thought*, ed. Richard A. Norris (Philadelphia: Fortress, 1980), 145–55, esp. 150–52.

First, Scripture sometimes makes "enunciations" that are "verified with respect unto one nature only."[54] Examples he cites of this include John 1:1, "The Word was with God, and the Word was God"; 8:58, "Before Abraham was, I am"; and Hebrews 1:3, "Upholding all things by the word of his power." While all of these texts refer to the person of Christ, they "belong unto it on account of his divine nature." Other Scriptures speaking of the person of Christ are "verified in human nature only," and only by this means can we attribute them unto the person of Christ. Examples are Isaiah 9:6, "Unto us a child is born, unto us a son is given"; and 53:3, "A man of sorrows, and acquainted with grief."

Second, there are references in the Scriptures that concern the person of Christ yet belong "not distinctly and originally unto either nature" but refer to the hypostatic union of the two. In this category Owen includes all theological ideas of Christ as prophet, priest, king, and head of the church. He gives no biblical examples, apparently assuming that this would be an obvious deduction for his readers.[55]

Third, Owen believes that at places in Scripture when Christ's person is "denominated from one nature, the properties and act of the other are assigned unto it." In many ways this is similar to the first point, which becomes clearer when we observe Owen's scriptural illustrations. For example, when Scripture refers to those who "crucified the Lord of Glory," Owen believes Jesus's lordship is solely a result of his divine nature, although his crucifixion was only of the human nature. Likewise, he cites Acts 20:28, which he believes clearly demonstrates this biblical tendency to combine the two: "*God* purchased his church 'with *his own blood*.'"[56] Reflecting Cyril of Alexandria's understanding of the "communication of idioms" (i.e., *antidosis idiomatum*), Owen explains his meaning: "The denomination of the person is from the divine nature only—he is God; but the act ascribed unto it, or what he did by his own blood, was of the human nature only. But the purchase that was made thereby was the work of the *person* as both God and man."[57] As we will

54. For these four points, see *Works* 1:234–35.
55. Cf. WCF, 8.1 and WLC, Q&A #42, which similarly group these descriptions together to describe Christ as the Mediator.
56. *Works* 1:235, emphasis added; cf. 9:590. Wolfhart Pannenberg's discussion of Luther's treatment as expressed in the Formula of Concord provides interesting background; *Systematic Theology*, trans. Geoffrey W. Bromiley (Grand Rapids: Eerdmans, 1994), 2:388–89. Pannenberg, summarizing Luther, writes: "Scripture ascribes to the deity all that happens to the humanity and vice versa. If so, then we must say that the person suffers. But the person is true God; therefore we may rightly say that the Son of God suffers. For although the one part (if we may speak thus) does not suffer as deity, nevertheless the person, who is God, suffers in the other part as humanity."
57. *Works* 1:235, emphasis added. See Cyril of Alexandria, *On the Unity of Christ*, trans. John Anthony McGuckin (orig., 438; Crestwood, NY: St. Vladimir's Seminary Press, 1995), 44–45.

explain below, Owen can make these fine distinctions because he differentiates between assumption and union from the outset.

Finally, the Scriptures often speak of "the person denominated from one nature, that is ascribed unto it which is common unto both; or else being denominated from both, that which is proper unto one only is ascribed unto him."[58]

In his complex formulation Owen believes that he provides his readers with a synopsis not only of the biblical data, but also of the patristic understanding of these dilemmas.[59] For our purposes, we need simply to observe the shape of Owen's attempt to maintain the integrity of the two natures of Christ. Although the New Testament may at first seem to present conflicting data concerning Jesus Christ—sometimes referring to him as God, sometimes as human, sometimes as uniting the two, and so on—Owen believes that a robust theological conception of the *person* of Christ adequately allows for this flexibility. In fact, Owen explicitly argues that ultimately Christ's work should "not be considered as the act of this or that nature," because they are the actions of his "whole person."[60] Problems arise when theologians, such as Nestorius,[61] emphasize one element of the scriptural truth to the neglect of the other. Only by preserving the whole person of Jesus Christ can one maintain the proper distinctions and unity of the divine and human natures.

Returning to the more specific language of assumption, we see how Owen believes this language protects the distinction and unity of the two natures. Since the divine nature is immutable and impassible, Owen sees that the *assumption* proved to be the only way for the incarnation to occur; otherwise the divine would have to cease to be divine by becoming human. As a result, the Second Person of the Trinity, who was

58. His proof texts for this are Rom. 9:5 and Matt. 22:42. The meaning Owen intends his readers to glean from these texts is somewhat obscure.

59. Owen acknowledges that the fathers used different language, such as "alteration" (ἐναλλάψη), "permutation" (ἀλλοίωσις), "communion" (κοινότης), "the manner of mutual position" (τρόπος ἀντιδόσεως), and "the communication of properties" (κοινωνία ἰδιωμάτων); *Works* 1:235.

60. Ibid., 1:234.

61. For Owen's interaction with and responses to Nestorius's presumed position, see ibid., 1:231–32. According to modern scholarship, the traditional view that Nestorius rejected the two natures—a view started by the attacks of Cyril of Alexandria—is probably inaccurate. See Aloys Grillmeier, *Christ in Christian Tradition*, vol. 1, *From the Apostolic Age to Chalcedon (451)*, trans. John S. Bowden, 2nd and rev. ed. (London: Mowbray, 1975), 443–63. This reassessment has been spurred on by the discovery of *Book of Heracleides*, which current scholarship believes Nestorius wrote. In this book one finds a clear affirmation of the two natures of Christ in almost Chalcedonian terms. Obviously Owen was unaware of this text and so writes within the accepted tradition of his day.

not man, "was made flesh as man, in that he took our human nature to be his own."[62]

Developing the idea of the assumption again prompts Owen to return to his trinitarian conception. Because the incarnation was an outward act of the divine nature, it involved every person of the Trinity: The Father "as unto authoritative designation" acted by sending his Son. The Holy Spirit peculiarly acted "as unto the formation of the human nature." And the Son acted uniquely "as unto the term of the assumption," since he himself took on human nature.[63] Each divine person executes an action "peculiar" to that person. After giving this perspective, Owen instantly clarifies that *only in the assumption* is there an "immediate act of the divine on the human in the person of the Son." This proves to be an essential point in Owen's attempt at presenting a truly human Jesus rather than some divinized man—an alien to the realities of normal human suffering and temptations. Before further developing this discussion of Jesus's humanity, we must clarify Owen's distinction between assumption and union.

A chart may provide the most direct way to unpack the distinctions Owen makes:

Assumption	Hypostatic Union
"immediate act of divine nature"	*"mediate,* by virtue of that assumption"
"unto personality . . . the Son of God and our nature became one person"	*"act or relation* of natures *subsisting* in that one person"
"the *acting* of the divine and the *passion* of the human nature: the *one assumeth,* the other is *assumed."*	*"mutual relation* of the natures unto each other."*

* *Works* 1:225–26, emphasis added.

The importance here for Owen is that *initially* the action is entirely God's. There is no way in which humanity is said to become divine, no possibility of the divine nature "assumed as the human is."[64] This prevents any form of adoptionism from entering into Owen's Christology. God's great condescension comes in the incarnation. Hence, while Owen is diligent to maintain the true humanity of the person of Jesus Christ, he begins by claiming that Christ would have *no human nature*

62. *Works* 1:225.

63. Although he cites biblical texts to prove his points for the Father and Spirit, regarding the Son he cites the "Damascen" (i.e., John of Damascus), who likewise argued: "The other persons had no concurrence [in the assumption], but only κατά βούλησιν καὶ εὐδοκίαν—'by counsel and approbation'" (ibid., 1:225; also cited in 3:160). This reference to John of Damascus seems to come from his *Orthodox Faith* 3.11.

64. *Works* 1:226.

without divine assumption in the first place. Although theologians must be careful to protect the "mutual relation" that exists between the divine and human natures in the person of Christ, they must first appreciate the immediate divine action that took place in the assumption of the human nature.[65]

What Owen is arguing for here must be understood in light of an *anhypostasis-enhypostasis* christological framework. Although there has recently been tremendous debate about how often these actual terms are used (if at all) in the early church, there is a growing consensus that the idea was clearly there among some influential fathers.[66] In the early church there was a growing temptation to create two persons ("Sons" was the original language) in Jesus Christ, rather than one unified person; church historians normally associate this critiqued position with the label "Nestorian." In other words, if someone said that Jesus was truly God and truly man, others inevitably thought it sounded as though there were two *individual* people, one divine and one human. This meant two self-subsisting realities—two hypostases. To overcome this problem, theologians used the idea—and later the actual language—of anhypostasis.

Anhypostasis (no-hypostasis) simply conveys the idea that the human nature of Christ had no independent existence apart from its union to the Logos. Without the Son of God, there is no human nature of Christ, no time or existence apart from when the Son assumed this nature. *Enhypostasis* (in-hypostasis) expresses the complementary idea that the human nature of Christ does have its subsistence through or in union to the Logos. Nothing one can point to serves as the "human nature" of Christ apart from looking to the particularity of the incarnate Christ. Protestant scholastics built on this conceptual tradition with the use of the *anhypostasis-enhypostasis* distinction. In the twentieth century this

65. Cf. ibid., 20:367 (BE 19:367): The "hypostatical union could be no reward of obedience, being that which exceeds all the order of things and rules of remunerative justice. The assumption . . . of our nature . . . was an act of mere free, sovereign, unconceivable grace. And this is the foundation of all the following fruits of God's regard unto us. . . . Whatever God doth for us in and by Jesus Christ as made man for us . . . [must] be all of grace, because his being made man was so."

66. See B. E. Daley, "'A Richer Union': Leontius of Byzantium and the Relationship of Human and Divine in Christ," *Studia patristica* 24 (1993): 239–65; Ivor Davidson, "Theologizing the Human Jesus: An Ancient (and Modern) Approach to Christology Reassessed," *IJST* 3, no. 2 (2001): 129–53; M. Gockel, "A Dubious Christological Formula? Leontius of Byzantium and the Anhypostasis-Enhypostasis Theory," *JTS*, n.s., 51 (2000): 515–32; Aloys Grillmeier, *Christ in Christian Tradition*, vol. 2, *From the Council of Chalcedon (451) to Gregory the Great (590–604)*, part 1, *Reception and Contradiction*, trans. Pauline Allen and John Cawte (London: Mowbray, 1987), 181–229; U. M. Lang, "Anhypostatos-Enhypostatos: Church Fathers, Protestant Orthodoxy and Karl Barth," *JTS*, n.s., 49 (1998): 630–57; F. LeRon Shults, *Reforming Theological Anthropology: After the Philosophical Turn to Relationality* (Grand Rapids: Eerdmans, 2003), 140–60.

important idea has found a fresh audience, especially because of the creative and significant use Karl Barth gives to it.[67]

As already recognized, Owen believes that there is no self-existent human nature of Christ before the assumption. Although the actual term ἀνυπόστατος shows up only occasionally in Owen's writings, the idea is fairly prevalent. He does explicitly argue that Christ's human nature is "ἀνυπόστατος, or such as hath no personal subsistence of its own."[68] In fact, he clarifies his own position as he counters the accusation of William Sherlock (whom chapter 5 will discuss further). Sherlock seemed to believe that all actions were not ascribed to Christ's person, but only to his natures. Against this position, Owen builds on his "theandrical" view of Christ as mediator, believing that Sherlock does not understand the relationship between the natures and person of Christ. Writes Owen: "Although there be nothing in the person of Christ but his divine and human nature, yet the person of Christ is neither his divine nature nor his human; *for the human nature is, and ever was, of itself*, ἀνυπόστατος; and the divine, to the complete constitution of the person of the Mediator, in and unto its own hypostasis assumed the human."[69] This means that Christ's person is the "only agent" of the actions. In his commentary on *Hebrews*, Owen lays out eight points that he believes are fundamental to understanding the two natures in one person, and in so doing he consistently highlights the idea of anhypostasis.[70] Among his points is the conclusion that the eternally subsisting Logos assumed a human nature "into personal subsistence" with himself, "causing it to subsist in his own person." Consequently, there is no "multiplication of persons" in him, for "the human nature can have no personality of its own." By the assumption, these natures are brought into union "inseparably and for ever."

The Spirit and the Person of Christ

Since the eternal divine Son becomes man, this means that the incarnate Christ acts as the God-man, for there is no other way for him to operate. Rejecting the Apollinarian position of having the Logos substitute for a human soul or mind, which leaves Jesus less than fully human, Owen proposes a different route. Instead, in all of Christ's actions, by his "rational faculties and powers of soul, his understanding, will and

67. Bruce McCormack, *Karl Barth's Critically Realistic Dialectical Theology: Its Genesis and Development, 1909–1936* (Oxford: Oxford University Press, 1995), esp. 358–67.

68. *Works* 2:233; for other examples of ἀνυπόστατος, see 1:233–34; 2:329; cf. 24:6, 8 (BE 23:6, 8).

69. *Works* 2:329, emphasis added.

70. See ibid., 20:461–62 (BE 19:461–62).

affections," he "acted *as a man.*"[71] This line of argument is a classic way to express the orthodox doctrine of the incarnation, and when it is abandoned problems of pitting the natures against one another or "mixing" them often result. Recently Thomas Weinandy expressed the central concern, and in so doing he reflected a tradition going back to Cyril of Alexandria and upheld by Owen:

> Within the Incarnation the Son of God never does anything as God. If he did, he would be acting as God in a man. This the Incarnation will never permit. All that Jesus did as the Son of God was done as a man—whether it was eating carrots or raising someone from the dead. He may have raised Lazarus from the dead by his divine power or better, by the power of the Holy Spirit, but it was, nonetheless, as man that he did so. Similarly, the Son of God did not suffer as God in a man, for to do so would mean that he was not a man. The Son of God suffered as a man.[72]

Owen preserves the integrity of the natures and the unity of person by drawing heavily upon the work of the Spirit: Jesus acts as man, the God-man, empowered by the Spirit. Building upon his distinction between assumption and union, Owen argues that "all the voluntary communications of the divine nature unto the human nature were . . . by the Holy Spirit."[73] Although a more extended discussion of the Trinity will occur in chapter 5, a few words on the relationship between the Spirit and the person and work of Christ are necessary.

Based on the Augustinian principle—the actual words are not his—that the external "works of the Triune God are indivisible" (*opera Trinitatis ad extra sunt indivisa*), Owen sees the Spirit as essential to the incarnation. When God acts, he acts as Father, Son, and Spirit. Thus, while it was distinctly the Son's peculiar work to assume a human nature, "whatever the Son of God wrought in, by, or upon the human nature, he did by the Holy Ghost, who is his Spirit, as he is the Spirit of the Father."[74] Here Owen is carefully creating a way to preserve the full integrity of the human and divine natures of Christ, preserving this union by the Spirit. Thus, any divine "acts" in the incarnate Son come by the empowerment of the Spirit.

From conception to ascension, Owen highlights the work of the Spirit in the life of Christ. It is the Spirit, argues Owen, who creates the human nature assumed by the Son, and the relationship is such of "a creator and

71. Ibid., 3:169, emphasis added.
72. Thomas G. Weinandy, *Does God Suffer?* (Notre Dame, IN: University of Notre Dame Press, 2000), 205.
73. *Works* 3:175.
74. Ibid., 3:162.

a creature"![75] While the Spirit creates the human nature, the Son assumes it, although there is not time between the creation of the nature and its assumption. To prevent the mistaken inference that there was a human nature apart from the Son, Owen stresses that this was not "accomplished successively and in the process of time." His goal was to show that the incarnation was a triune act, although only the Son assumed the nature. Again affirming the anhypostatic quality of the human nature of Christ, he declares that "nothing of the human nature of Christ should exist of itself antecedently unto its union with the Son of God."[76]

From conception, the human nature of Christ was sanctified by the Spirit. Jesus had all of the "natural faculties" that every human has. Although his faculties were created free from sin, "pure, innocent, undefiled," even Jesus needed the Spirit to faithfully direct his faculties to the Father. In other words, Owen argues that all rational creatures, including even prelapsarian Adam and the incarnate Christ, require the Spirit to enable them to "live to God."[77] Jesus, like all other humans, made improvements by exercising these faculties: this does not mean, however, that he moves from sin to purity. Instead, this reflects Owen's unflinching affirmation (unpacked later in this chapter) that Jesus does grow in wisdom (cf. Luke 2:52) and learns obedience (Heb. 5:8), as he depends on the continuing work of the Spirit. Christ's wisdom and knowledge "objectively increased," and through trials and temptations he "experimentally [experientially] learned the new exercise of grace."[78]

Just as Owen highlights the authoritative sending of the Son by the Father, he argues similarly that the Spirit "sends" the Son by providing the "furniture . . . of gifts for his work and office."[79] Jesus's baptism is significant in this light. Owen speculates that before this time, Jesus could have privately done some extraordinary actions, but not until baptism did he receive the fullness of gifts by the Spirit, which enable him to turn to public ministry. Throughout his life, and especially during his final years on earth, Christ was led by the Spirit. By the Spirit Jesus was "guided, directed, comforted, supported" as he faced temptations and was faithful in obedience and sufferings.[80]

An interesting example of the Spirit's work in the life of Christ is found in Owen's handling of the wilderness temptations. Recognizing some differences between the Gospel accounts (cf. Matt. 4:1–11; Mark 1:12–13;

75. Ibid., 3:165.
76. Ibid.
77. Ibid., 3:168.
78. Ibid., 3:170.
79. Ibid., 3:173–74.
80. Ibid., 3:174.

Luke 4:1–13), it is Mark's rendering that appears the most ambiguous and potentially troubling, since it speaks of the Spirit *driving* (ἐκβάλλει) Jesus into the wilderness.[81] How Owen describes this driving force of the Spirit demonstrates his conception of the relationship of the Spirit's work in Christ's life, which stresses Jesus's continuity with the rest of humanity. After examining the passage, Owen concludes that Mark's word choice points to a common way the Spirit works in and through human nature. In this case, "no more is intended but the sending of him forth by a high and strong impression of the Holy Spirit *on his mind*."[82] Notice that Owen places the special work of the Spirit within the normal operation of human psychology: this is not supernatural lifting or pushing, in which Jesus doesn't know what he is doing or why and where he is going. Rather, the Spirit works through his created faculties to lead Christ. It does not escape Owen's attention that ἐκβάλλει is also used of other people led by the Spirit, such as when the Spirit drives laborers into the ready harvest (Matt. 9:38).[83]

The Spirit sustains Jesus throughout his life and into his death. Not only is the atoning work of Christ offered "through the eternal Spirit" (Heb. 9:14), but significantly the Spirit also sustains him through death. To explain the three days in the grave, Owen employs a creative pneumatological answer. Since in death Christ remained fully man, Owen argues that integrity must be maintained even as his soul goes to be with the Father and his body rests in the grave. While the Father preserved his soul, his body continued in the grave "under the especial care of the Spirit of God."[84] Here he echoes the Westminster Shorter Catechism, although in that context the focus was not on Christ, but on the benefits *believers* receive at their death: "The souls of believers are at their death made perfect in holiness, and do immediately pass into glory; and their bodies, being still *united to Christ*, do rest in their graves till the resurrection."[85] Union with Christ for believers is only through the Spirit, and in the intermediate state between death and resurrection, human integrity of body and soul is sustained in the power of the Spirit. Similarly, according to Owen, after the crucifixion it was the Spirit who sustained and reunited Jesus's "most holy soul and body" in the resurrection.[86] Furthermore, not only is Jesus raised in the power of the Spirit; it was also the Spirit who glorified his human nature, making "it every way meet for its eternal residence at the right

---

81. Luke instead uses ἤγετο, and Matthew has ἀνήχθη.
82. *Works* 3:175, emphasis added.
83. Ibid.
84. Ibid., 3:180.
85. WCF, 297–98 (WSC Q&A #37).
86. *Works* 3:182.

hand of God, and a pattern of the glorification of the bodies of them that believe on him."[87] Thus, just as the Spirit from conception made his human nature holy, now into eternity the same Spirit makes this nature glorious. In all of this not only does the incarnate Christ show himself as truly human; he also demonstrates his unbreakable relationship to the work of God's Spirit.

In summary, only by divine desire and activity does the Second Person of the Trinity become truly human and thus allow the renewal of the rest of humanity. Here Owen's theological method is clearly working "from above," but in so doing he seeks to preserve the true identification between Jesus and the rest of humankind.[88] He maintains that one cannot rightly understand the humanity of Jesus apart from the continuing work of the Spirit, who creates the human nature and sustains Christ from the wilderness to the grave, ultimately raising him to the right hand of God. This same Spirit, the Spirit of Christ, is now given to believers, and in the Spirit's power Christians find life, strength, and hope as they are united to their exalted Savior.

Preaching the Assumption

In 1681, just two years before his death, Owen preached a short sermon on Philippians 2:5–8, entitled "The Humiliation and Condescension of Christ."[89] Here he explained to his listeners both the mystery and application to be drawn from the divine assumption of human nature. The mature Owen reviews the ideas outlined above, expounding this profound and complex theology in order that his listeners might experience spiritual comfort. Although those discussing Owen's Christology often overlook this obscure sermon, it is an excellent illustration of Owen's anthroposensitivity: he moves easily from profound theological reflection to practical experiential application.

This sermon begins by asserting that fallen humanity could not save itself from sin. Yet, even God himself could not immediately be the mediator needed for the redemption and reconciliation of humanity, for "a

87. Ibid., 3:183.

88. Cf. John Macquarrie, "Christology without Incarnation? Some Critical Comments," in *The Truth of God Incarnate*, ed. Michael Green (London: Hodder & Stoughton, 1977), 143. Macquarrie lists three points essential to the idea of incarnation, revealing the continued relevance of Owen's orthodox reasoning: (1) "Initiative is from God and not from man." (2) "God is deeply involved in his creation." (3) "The centre of this initiative and involvement is Jesus Christ."

89. See *Works* 17:561–69 (BE 16:493–501). All quotes in this section come from this sermon, unless otherwise indicated. Preached in 1681, this sermon is extremely similar to chap. 4 of *The Glory of Christ*, on which Owen was working during this same time, though it was not published until 1684, after his death in 1683; see *Works* 1:322–33.

mediator must be a middle person, and God in his divine nature is one."[90] Again echoing an Anselmian argument, Owen believes that God is God from all eternity, and it was human sin that made a mediator necessary. So since humanity remained impotent in sin, and since the divine nature was unable to act as mediator, there was only one possibility left—*that perfect God should assume human nature unto himself, thus becoming the mediator*. This does not mean that God becomes more than "one," but simply that the Son assumes a human nature. Owen confesses that the mediator could not be a mere human exalted to divine status: "The most glorious exaltation that a creature can have brings him not one step nearer the essence of God than a worm; for between that which is infinite and that which is not infinite there is no proportion." God is completely self-sufficient in his own "blessedness and eternal satisfaction," and so the incarnation must primarily be viewed in terms of a loving divine act rather than an abstract metaphysical necessity.

By framing the dilemma and answer in this way, Owen again emphasizes the divine action behind the incarnation. Accordingly, the incarnation seems incredible in light "of that infinite distance which is between his nature, being, and essence, and the nature, being, and essence of any creature of any kind."[91] God alone may receive the title of an "infinite Being"; in comparison, all creation seems to be "nothing."[92] For some reason this Being who dwells in eternity and needs nothing takes action toward humanity. As we will see in chapter 5, one can explain the reason only by the Triune God's love.

God humbled himself from the realms of heaven to the realm of earth.[93] Although God is completely self-sufficient, humanity is completely dependent. All of creation depends ultimately on God. Showing how serious he is about the true humanity of Christ, Owen even claims that "the top of the creation, the flower, the glory of it, is the human nature of Christ; yet is it not self-sufficient. It *eternally lives in dependence* on God and *by communications* from the divine nature."[94] In this way, the assumption of human nature by the Second Person of the Trinity displays the ultimate condescension: the Son does not simply come down from the heavens to "look upon and behold us, and act kindly towards

90. Owen consistently draws upon 1 Tim. 2:5 and Gal. 3:20 for these arguments; cf. *Works* 1:323.

91. Cf. ibid., 12:286.

92. Here Owen's language of "nothing" (i.e., אִין) refers back to Isa. 40:17; cf. *Works* 1:324. Elsewhere he likewise describes humanity and creation as "nothing," fallen humanity is "miserable, . . . less than vanity, and nothing" (see *Works* 20:352–53 [BE 19:352–53]); cf. also Calvin, *Institutes*, 1:571 (3.2.25).

93. Cf. *Works* 12:286–87.

94. Ibid., 17:564 (BE 16:496), emphasis added; cf. 1:325.

us," but actually "took our nature upon him to be his own!" For Owen, this self-humiliation is the "centre, life, and soul, of religion, the main rock on which the church is built."

To speak more directly on what Owen believes about the human nature of Christ, we need to understand what he believes *does not* occur in the incarnation. In the condescension the Son does "not leave" nor does he "relinquish" or "forgo" his divine nature. More simply, "he did not cease to be God when he became man."[95] So strongly does Owen believe this and its practical significance that he allows himself to use difficult trinitarian language and ideas in his sermon to communicate the wonder of the incarnation. His trinitarian theology prevents him from setting up the three persons in opposition to one another or in levels of importance: "Though there is an order in the persons of the Trinity, there is no distinction or inequality in the nature of God. Every one who is partaker of that nature is equal in that nature, in dignity, power, and authority. This was the state of Christ."[96] Compromising on this point would inevitably jeopardize his doctrine of God with negative implications for various other doctrines (e.g., creation, providence).

Elsewhere in Owen's corpus he maintains this position through his teaching of what is commonly called *extra-Calvinisticum*.[97] He argues that Christ not only came "down from heaven," but that he also "still continued in heaven." To say otherwise proposes that there was a period of time when Christ was not holding the universe together.[98] But since Christ is always in the heavens in the "glory and essence of his divine nature," by assuming human nature "he alone is meet and able to be the prophet of the church in the revelation of the heavenly mysteries of the counsels of the will of God." This does not mean that Owen infuses divine attributes (omniscience, infinite wisdom, knowledge, and understanding) into the humanity of Christ. Rather, his human nature "was and is a creature, finite and limited"; in other words, it was incapable

95. Ibid.

96. *Works* 17:565 (BE 16:497).

97. The quotations for the rest of this paragraph come from *Works* 1:92–93. For historical background on *extra-Calvinisticum*, see Muller, *DLGTT*, 111. Muller rightly argues that for Reformed theologians, as against the Lutherans, "the Word is fully united to but never totally contained within the human nature and, therefore, even in incarnation [the Word also] is to be conceived of as beyond or outside of (extra) the human nature." For more background see David E. Willis, *Calvin's Catholic Christology: The Function of the So-Called Extra-Calvinisticum in Calvin's Theology* (Leiden: E. J. Brill, 1966).

98. Cf. Owen, *Summary of Doctrinal and Practical Observations, Drawn from the Exposition of the Epistle* [to the Hebrews], in *Works* 19:462 (BE 18:462). Commenting on Heb. 1:3, he writes: "Such is the nature and condition of the universe, that it could not subsist a moment, nor could any thing in it act regularly unto its appointed end, without the continual support, guidance, influence, and disposal, of the Son of God himself."

of "properties absolutely infinite and immense." This apparent christological difficulty is resolved by Owen's strong pneumatology; the Spirit unites the divine and human natures in the person of Christ, uniquely filling his human nature with the Spirit beyond measure, as "a fulness [*sic*] like that of light in the sun, or of water in the sea."[99] Without again developing a pneumatological discussion at this point, we must simply recognize that Owen's conception of the person of Christ allows him to maintain the initial and continued divine action of the Second Person of the Trinity while also preserving a realistic view of Jesus's humanity.[100]

Owen's sermon likewise claims that the incarnation should *not* be presented as the absorption or confusion of the two natures.[101] The divine does not absorb the human, for to do so would lead to a humanity that "is of no affinity and cognition unto us; not derived of Adam as we" are—an error Owen claims the Arians committed. Likewise, it is equally devastating to combine or confuse the two natures, an error commonly referred to as the *tertium quid* in the early church.[102] When this confusion of natures occurs, the result is a single nature that is "neither that divine nature that was originally and eternally, nor human nature, but another, a third nature, made in time." Owen wants to protect the essential continuity between the humanity of Jesus and that of his listeners—a goal that likewise protects him from several early christological heresies. Here again, his explanation of the person of Christ allows him to make these technical distinctions. For while the divine nature never hungered, thirsted, and wept, his human nature surely did so. In such instances the divine nature acts only in the "sustentation" of the human nature.[103]

Finally, in typical anthroposensitive form, Owen applies these weighty truths to the lives of his listeners. Contrary to common stereotypes, Jonathan Jong-Chun Won has rightly concluded that the Puritans in general "capitalized on the humanness of Christ" for the purpose of emphasizing that the incarnate one truly understood the believer's struggles and pain.[104] According to Owen, the Christian should receive

99. *Works* 2:61.
100. *Extra-Calvinisticum* was commonly agreed upon by Puritan theologians. Cf. Thomas Watson, *A Body of Practical Divinity* (London: Thomas Parkhurst, 1692); rev. ed. as *A Body of Divinity* (Edinburgh: Banner of Truth, 1983), 163: "Is God the Father omnipresent? So is Christ. 'The Son of Man which is in heaven.' John iii.13. Christ as God was then in heaven, when as man he was upon the earth."
101. We pick up his argument in *Works* 17:565–69 (BE 16:497–501).
102. See, e.g., Tertullian, *Against Praxeas* 27, in *ANF* 3:624. Cf. Owen, *Works* 1:229, where he charges Eutyches with promoting this misunderstanding.
103. *Works* 17:566 (BE 16:498).
104. Jonathan Jong-Chun Won, "Communion with Christ: An Exposition and Comparison of the Doctrine of Union and Communion with Christ in Calvin and the English Puritans" (PhD diss., Westminster Theological Seminary, 1989), 353.

the truths of this great condescension through admiration. Yet this is more than just praise from the believer's lips; the idea of the condescension of the Son assuming human nature should inspire comfort. Building from Isaiah 8:14, which prophesies of one who shall be a "sanctuary" to some and a cause for the "stumbling" of others, Owen moves to 1 Peter 2:6–8, which also refers to a sanctuary for believers and for the oppressed.[105] In both instances Owen thinks the reference is clearly pointing to Jesus, who through his humiliation became both a sanctuary and a "stone of stumbling." Believers are not those who stumble, but those who find in the incarnate one a sanctuary: "freedom from danger, deliverance out of trouble, and a supply of all their wants."[106] The only thing a believer must do is go to the sanctuary for such relief. To go to anyone or anywhere else besides Christ shows the believer's failure to grasp "his will and his power." The aged and experienced pastor-scholar pleads with his congregation and apparently even with himself:

> If he be willing and if he be able, you have no ground to question but you shall have relief. I know how it is with us all. We have all wants, we have all temptations, we have all fears, we have all inward conflicts and perplexities, more or less; and we all secretly groan to be delivered from all these things. Groaning is the best of our spiritual life,—to live in continual groaning. . . .
>
> Where shall we betake ourselves, then, for relief in all cases? If any one have will and power to relieve us, oh, that he would come in to our relief and help; thither would we go! But here is the loss of our souls and peace, here is that which keeps us at such a poor, low rate, and makes us scramble for the world,—because we neglect going unto Christ for relief in all our wants. How few of us live in the exercise of faith for this purpose! "But will he relieve me?" *Why, he hath humbled, emptied himself, and laid aside his glory, for this very end, that he might relieve us.* For my own part, I do verily believe that all coming short of gospel joy, strength, and power is for want of due application unto Jesus Christ for relief. . . . Why, can I give you greater encouragement than I do?[107]

The Son of God, who assumed human nature, has provided the ultimate sanctuary for a weak and weary humanity, and it is to this sanctuary that Owen points his flock. Owen's lifelong christological explorations

105. Cf. *Works* 1:330–33.

106. Ibid., 17:568 (BE 16:500).

107. *Works* 17:568 (BE 16:500), emphasis added. Elsewhere Owen describes "groaning" as "[the expression of] a vehement desire, mixed with sorrow, for the present want of what is desired. The desire hath sorrow, and that sorrow hath joy and refreshment in it" (*Works* 1:384).

only make sense to him in light of the comfort these ideas can bring to ordinary Christians. Though a difficult truth, understanding the complexity of the person of Jesus with two natures is essential, not simply for abstract theological reasons, but also for practical devotional living. These are not abstractions to be kept within the academy, but rather practical realities to be preached from the pulpit. This incarnate one proclaimed by Owen could bring relief to believers precisely because he assumed a true human nature, and as such, he became a sympathetic high priest.

In this final section we focus our attention on the continuities and discontinuities between Christ's humanity and that of the rest of humankind. According to Owen, communion with God is possible only because Jesus is the same ("truly man") and yet distinct ("without sin") from the rest of humanity.

Christ's Humanity and Our Humanity

Same Human Composition

From quite early in his career, Owen applied his basic formulation of the *imago Dei* to Jesus. As a young pastor at the parish of Fordham in Essex, Owen decided to write two Catechisms (1645), one for adults and the other for the instruction of children.[108] Our attention here is drawn specifically to chapter 10, question 5, of "The Greater [i.e., adult] Catechism," which tries to "prove" that Jesus was a "perfect man."[109] When Owen refers to Jesus as a "perfect man" in the catechism, we should understand "perfect" as meaning *whole* or *complete*, rather than simply sinless. In this context Owen's particular aim is to demonstrate Jesus's true humanity rather than his sinlessness. As we saw in our discussion of the *imago Dei*, Owen's default for speaking of a human being is to apply basic faculty psychology categories. True to form, Owen displays this again in his Christology.

Jesus has a body and a soul.[110] He meets the requirements of a "perfect man" because his soul has a will, affections, and "endowments." His proof text for the latter is Luke 2:52,[111] which preachers commonly used to point to Jesus's intellectual growth, and thus as a reference to his men-

---

108. See *Works* 1:465–94. For background on Owen's ministry during this period, see Toon, *God's Statesman*, 17–19.

109. For Owen's treatment of Jesus as "perfect man," see *Works* 1:479.

110. Ibid.

111. Luke 2:52: "Jesus increased in wisdom and stature, and in favour with God and man."

tal faculties.[112] Additionally, Owen has his catechumens memorize that Jesus's human nature was subject to "general infirmities of nature."[113] In sum, a human must have a body and soul, with the soul being the location of the mind, will, and affections. Just as we saw with the rest of humanity, Jesus must fit into these categories as well; otherwise his human nature is somehow alien, and thus he cannot be a "fit and sufficient Saviour for men."[114] Following this basic format, Owen believes he, in a great economy of words, has communicated to his congregation the simplest route to understanding the true humanity of Jesus.[115] Filling in the details of this thumbnail sketch requires interaction with the rest of Owen's corpus, to which we now turn.

A Sympathetic High Priest

Maintaining the true humanity of Christ proves essential in Owen's theology: he believes that to compromise here would cause devastating soteriological results. In the words of one of the early fathers, "only what was assumed can be healed."[116] We have already discussed Owen's view of assumption (above); here we simply draw attention to the degree to which Owen stresses the continuity between the incarnate Christ and the rest of humanity. An illustration of this comes in Owen's observation regarding those who encountered Jesus in first-century Israel. Not only did they fail to recognize Jesus as God; they also did not "look on him as a good man."[117] The reason for this was that Jesus was "no less a man

112. E.g., Calvin, *Institutes*, 1:483–84 (2.14.2).

113. Cf. *Works* 19:233 (BE 18:233).

114. *Works* 1:479; GC, 10.6. Owen counters those who claim only a "drop" of Christ's blood was needed for redemption. If that were the case, argues Owen, why is the "whole" in fact shed? See *Works* 20:403, 407 (BE 19:403, 407); cf. *Works* 2:97.

115. Here one sees an observable difference between Owen's GC (1645) and the Westminster Confession and Longer and Shorter Catechisms (completed in 1648). The WCF, WLC, and the WSC are much subtler in using faculty categories for describing the humanity of Jesus. Faculty language certainly appears in the Westminster standards, but never so tightly and as clearly as Owen phrases it in GC, 10.5. See the appendix, "Comparing Westminster Standards and John Owen on Humanity (Jesus's and Ours)." For more background see Ian Green, *The Christian's ABC: Catechisms and Catechizing in England c. 1530–1740* (Oxford: Clarendon, 1996).

116. See Gregory of Nazianzus, "To Cledonius the Priest against Apollinarius," *Epistolae* 101, in *NPNF*[2] 7:440: "For that which He has not assumed He has not healed; but that which is united to His Godhead is also saved. If only half Adam fell, then that which Christ assumes and saves may be half also; but if the whole of his nature fell, it must be united to the whole nature of Him that was begotten, and so be saved as a whole." Portions of this text are often used to support the idea that Jesus assumed *sinful* flesh or a *fallen* human nature, a debate we will take up below. How one defines "fallen" will determine if one reads Gregory as positing a fallen nature or not.

117. *Works* 17:566 (BE 16:498).

than any of themselves were." They so strongly believed in his humanity that they wanted to stone him because he, clearly a human, also claimed to be God.[118] Owen thus takes texts commonly used to prove the deity of Jesus—based on his self-disclosure—as testimony to Jesus's humanity!

In Jesus people saw a man just like themselves. Looking at this carpenter, they beheld someone whose experiences were similar to their own, even in his sufferings and temptations. For example, Owen writes of the incarnate Son, who "had the heart of a man, the affections of a man, and that in the highest degree of sense and tenderness. Whatever sufferings the soul of a man may be brought under, by grief, sorrow, shame, fear, pain, danger, loss, by any afflictive passions within or impressions of force from without, he underwent, he felt it all."[119] Jesus's sorrows were not only like those common to humanity, but also far more intense. He did not hide from difficulties and suffering, but "laid open his soul that they might soak into the inmost parts of it."[120] The result of this openness to human pain meant that Jesus "left nothing, in the whole nature of sorrow or suffering, that he tasted not and made experience of."[121] Owen wrote of Jesus:

> His participation of their nature was that which brought him into such a condition as wherein it was needful for him to put his trust in God, and to look for deliverance from him in a time of danger, . . . *which could not in any sense have been said of Christ had he not been partaker of that nature*, which is exposed unto all kinds of wants and troubles, with outward straits and oppositions, which the nature of angels is not.[122]

To be made "of the same nature" involves facing temptations, and this is the root of much of Jesus's sufferings.[123] Temptations in and of themselves are neutral, "of an indifferent nature," and thus to be tempted does not imply a moral evil.[124] But here we see the first difference between Christ's human nature and that of the rest of humanity,

118. *Works* 17:566 (BE 16:498). Here Owen is referring to John 8:58 and John 10:33. Cf. *Works* 20:357 (BE 19:357), where Owen argues that the Jews struggled to accept the Messiah in this "low and mean and despised condition."

119. *Works* 20:484 (BE 19:484). By "afflictive passions within," Owen *does not* mean sinful cravings stemming from a compromised human nature; otherwise his theology would be remarkably inconsistent. See below for further discussion.

120. *Works* 20:484 (BE 19:484). Later he adds, "All the advantage that he had above us by the excellency of his person, was only that the sorrows of his heart were enlarged thereby, and he was made capable of greater enduring without sin"; from *Works* 20:485 (BE 19:485).

121. *Works* 20:485 (BE 19:485).

122. *Works* 20:419 (BE 19:419), emphasis added.

123. Cf. *Works* 20:418 (BE 19:418); Jesus and believers "are of the same nature, of one mass, of one blood." Cf. *Works* 20:420 (BE 19:420).

124. *Works* 20:477 (BE 19:477).

according to Owen. Christ's various temptations "were all external, and by impressions from without," although Owen qualifies his statement by admitting that they do not all come from Satan.[125] Below we will discuss in greater detail why Owen must make this distinction between internal and external temptation. For now we need simply to observe that Owen believes Jesus faced *continual temptation*, especially during his years of ministry.

Four particular areas of temptations emerge.[126] First, Jesus's "state and condition in the world" meant that, although Jesus endured the continual temptation "cheerfully" for the sake of those whom he would save and preserve as their high priest, nevertheless his experiences were real and painful: he suffered "hunger, poverty, weariness, sorrow, reproach, shame, contempt; wherewith his holy soul was deeply affected."[127] Second, he faced particular temptations as a result of different relationships: His immediate family did not believe and thus rejected him. His common followers forsook his preaching. His close disciples left and denied him. His mother experienced "anguish" as a result of his sufferings. And his various enemies in one way or another worked against the gospel. Third, Satan tempted Jesus with a unique intensity. Fourth, "God's desertion of him was another temptation under which he suffered." Throughout his life Jesus exercised his faith as one relating rightly to God, even during the great temptation experienced on the cross, where he cried out as one forsaken: there was a "terrible conflict in the human nature," but the person of Christ faithfully trusted the Father throughout.[128] Enduring these and other difficulties was only possible for the Son, who assumed "the frail nature of man" by his constant looking to the Father for assistance, just as everyone else is called to do.[129]

Christ's temptations attest not simply to the true humanity of Jesus, but also to the relationship between him and those for whom he suffered. He underwent these things not only so that believers might be reconciled to God, but also that they might have strength in time of temptation.[130] Here again Owen's anthroposensitivity breaks through: Jesus faced temptations not simply to conform to an abstract criterion by which he can be considered truly human; instead, he faced temptations that he might

125. *Works* 20:478 (BE 19:478).
126. Owen discusses all these temptations in *Works* 20:478 (BE 19:478).
127. Cf. *Works* 2:135; Gregory of Nazianzus, *Oration 29*, 20, in *NPNF*² 7:308: "He was tempted as Man, but He conquered as God; yea, He bids us be of good cheer, for He has overcome the world."
128. See *Works* 9:530–34, 587.
129. *Works* 19:93–94 (BE 18:93–94).
130. *Works* 20:479 (BE 19:479).

overcome them and bring strength to his people.[131] Owen lists some of the horrific troubles and tribulations that believers may experience, and yet he draws his readers' attention away from their own struggles and on to the one who "comes in the midst of all this confusion and says, 'Surely these are my brethren, the children of my Father.' . . . And this is a stable foundation of comfort and supportment in every condition."[132] Our Lord's assumption of a human nature provides the foundation for comfort to the believer.

Yet without Sin . . .

Although Owen wholeheartedly argues that the Son incarnate was truly human, his human nature may be distinguished from the rest of fallen humanity. Owen maintains the corruption of human nature resulting from the fall, and yet the human nature of Jesus is free from this original sin; as such, there is "no small distance" between his human nature and that of the rest of humanity. "Human nature," he argues, "defiled with sin is farther distanced from the *same nature* as pure and holy, in worth and excellency, than the meanest worm is from the most glorious angel."[133] Yet, though Christ's human nature is uncorrupted by the fall, it is still "the same nature." Having a nature like his brothers, while on earth Jesus was "obnoxious [exposed to harm or liable] to sufferings and death itself;" yet Owen argues that this truth should always be held alongside the idea that Christ remains "holy, harmless, undefiled, and separate from sinners."[134] Jesus assumes an unblemished human nature in a fallen world, although he never boasts in or abuses this difference.[135]

At this point Jesus acts as the second Adam, the federal or covenant (*foedus*) head of those who would believe. Although the first Adam represents all of humankind, the second Adam represents believers.[136] According to Owen and common seventeenth-century Reformed theology, Jesus acts in a unique federal relationship to assume a full human nature while not

131. For the development of this line of his thinking, see *Works* 20:479–81 (BE 19:479–81).

132. *Works* 20:423–24 (BE 19:423–24).

133. *Works* 20:421 (BE 19:421), emphasis added.

134. *Works* 19:215 (BE 18:215); cf. Heb. 7:26. Owen later adds: "We are obnoxious unto these things on our own account, he only on ours."

135. Cf. *Works* 20:422 (BE 19:422): "He says not, with those proud hypocrites in the prophet, 'Stand farther off, I am holier than you'; but he comes unto us, and takes us by the hand in his love, to deliver us from this condition."

136. For comparisons between the first and second Adam, see, e.g., *Works* 5:323–29; 10:391–92; 22:390 (BE 21:390). For sample discussions of covenant (*foedus*), see *Works* 17:157–68 (*BT*, 205–22); 19:77–97 (BE 18:77–97).

having to assume a nature bound by original sin.[137] So, for example, when Owen argues elsewhere that the incarnate Christ is free from original sin, he describes two aspects of this reality as being (1) the "guilt of the first sin" and (2) the "derivation of a polluted, corrupted nature" coming from Adam.[138] Since Christ was never "federally in Adam," we cannot count him guilty, though the rest of humanity was guilty. Because all of humanity was in covenant with Adam as the first federal head, when he sinned all sinned (*omnes eramus unus ille homo*), yet Christ serves as the unique federal head for believers: thus, Adam's guilt does not apply to Jesus personally. Owen does not deny that Christ as mediator was made sin (cf. 2 Cor. 5:21), but he stresses that this was voluntary and not the legal imputation from Adam's covenant.[139] Distinguishing between being in Adam *naturally* (which he affirms of Christ's humanity) and *legally* (which he denies), Owen declares that the incarnate Christ, acting as a second Adam, singly fulfills the covenant of works, being victorious where Adam failed. Regarding the pollution of Christ's human nature, Owen follows the common Reformed understanding that the Spirit's role in Jesus's unique conception preserved him from any personal corruption.[140]

137. For classic representations of seventeenth-century federal theology, see Johannes Cocceius, *Summa doctrinæ de fœdere et testamentis Dei* (Lugduni Batavorum [Leiden]: Elseviriorum, 1648); and Herman Witsius, *The Oeconomy of the Covenants between God and Man*, trans. William Crookshank, 3 vols. (London: Edward Dilly, 1763). Among the vast literature—and debate about—the history of federal theology, see Barth, *CD* 4/1:50–66; Lyle D. Bierma, "Federal Theology in the Sixteenth Century: Two Traditions?" *WTJ* 45 (1983): 304–21; idem, "Law and Grace in Ursinus' Doctrine of the Natural Covenant: A Reappraisal," in *Protestant Scholasticism: Essays in Reassessment*, ed. Carl R. Trueman and R. S. Clark (Carlisle: Paternoster, 1999), 96–110; Bobick, "Owen's Razor"; A. T. B. McGowan, *The Federal Theology of Thomas Boston*, ed. David F. Wright and Donald Macleod, Rutherford Studies in Historical Theology (Edinburgh: published for Rutherford House by Paternoster, 1997); C. S. McCoy, "Johannes Cocceius: Federal Theologian," *SJT* 16 (1963): 352–70; Heinrich Heppe, "Die Föderaltheologie der reformierten Kirche," in *Geschichte des Pietismus und der Mystik in der reformierten Kirche namentlich der Niederlande* (Leiden: E. J. Brill, 1879), 204–40; Perry Miller, "The Marrow of Puritan Divinity," in *Errand into the Wilderness* (Cambridge, MA: Harvard University Press, Belknap, 1956), 48–98; Jens G. Møller, "The Beginnings of Puritan Covenant Theology," *JEH* 14 (1963): 46–67; Stephen Strehle, *Calvinism, Federalism, and Scholasticism: A Study of the Reformed Doctrine of Covenant*, Basler und Berner Studien zur historischen und systematischen Theologie 58 (Bern: Peter Lang, 1988); David N. J. Poole, *The Covenant Approach to the Ordo Salutis* (Lewiston, NY: Mellen, 1995); John von Rohr, *The Covenant of Grace in Puritan Thought*, AAR Studies in Religion 45 (Atlanta: Scholars Press, 1986); David A. Weir, *The Origins of the Federal Theology in Sixteenth-Century Reformation Thought* (Oxford: Clarendon, 1990); David Wai-Sing Wong, "The Covenant Theology of John Owen" (PhD diss., Westminster Theological Seminary, 1998).

138. *Works* 2:64.

139. Ibid., 2:65. For Owen's short discourse on 2 Cor. 5:21, see *Works* 9:521–23.

140. *Works* 2:65. See Kelly M. Kapic, "The Son's Assumption of a Human Nature: A Call for Clarity," *IJST* 3, no. 2 (2001): esp. 160–63.

Recent theological criticism of this older federal theology has argued that such a view inevitably portrays the Son as assuming a generic human nature. Such recent criticism not only tends to downplay federal theology, it also affirms that the Son assumed "fallen" or "sinful flesh."[141] In other words—the argument proceeds—if the Son does not assume a *fallen* human nature from the line of postlapsarian Adam, the nature assumed is not really like any other human nature since the first Adam, and thus the incarnate Christ would be unable to redeem humans. A significant problem arises when such terms as *fallen* and *unfallen* are employed, since even in recent debate there continues to be confusion over what exactly this vocabulary conveys, particularly when applied to Jesus. Even those who agree that the Son assumed a fallen nature do not agree as to what that designation includes and excludes. For example, some agree that Christ's human nature included concupiscence (an inner propensity to

141. "Sinful flesh" is biblical language (Rom. 8:3) and openly acknowledged by all; theologians have hotly debated whether the term implies a fallen or unfallen nature. This debate originally surfaced with the writings of Edward Irving (1792–1834), who used provocative language when he posited that Jesus took unto himself a fallen human nature. See his *The Doctrine of the Incarnation Opened in Six Sermons* (London, 1828); *The Orthodox and Catholic Doctrine of our Lord's Human Nature* (London, 1830); *The Opinions Circulating Concerning our Lord's Human Nature* (London, 1830); and *Christ's Holiness in Flesh* (Edinburgh, 1831)—all in *The Collected Writings of Edward Irving*, ed. G. Carlyle, 5 vols. (London: Alexander Strahan, 1865). Also see Graham W. P. McFarlane, *Christ and the Spirit: The Doctrine of the Incarnation according to Edward Irving* (Carlisle: Paternoster, 1996). Other prominent theologians to affirm a similar position include Barth, *CD* 1/2, esp. 147–59; cf. *CD* 2/1:397–98; J. B. Torrance, "The Vicarious Humanity of Christ," in *The Incarnation*, ed. T. F. Torrance (Edinburgh: Handsel, 1981), 141; idem, *Worship, Community, and the Triune God of Grace* (Downers Grove, IL: InterVarsity, 1996), 53, 56, 87, 105; T. F. Torrance, *The Trinitarian Faith: The Evangelical Theology of the Ancient Catholic Church* (Edinburgh: T&T Clark, 1988), 161–68. Two contemporary critics of the fallen view include Philip E. Hughes, *The True Image: The Origin and Destiny of Man in Christ* (Grand Rapids: Eerdmans, 1989), 125–35, 213–23; Donald Macleod, *The Person of Christ* (Downers Grove, IL: InterVarsity, 1998), esp. 221–30.

A recent work by a Catholic theologian, Thomas Weinandy, *In the Likeness of Sinful Flesh: An Essay on the Humanity of Christ* (Edinburgh: T&T Clark, 1993), tries to give both historical and biblical reasons for affirming that Jesus assumed "sinful flesh." In the preface the Protestant theologian Colin Gunton recommends the book for the most part, with an intriguing qualification: "A theologian of the Reformed tradition might well want to put some of this rather differently, and while welcoming the use made of the theology of the great Edward Irving—surely a modern pioneer of this approach—I would also point to its anticipation in the thought of the Puritan, John Owen" (x).

Though we do not have space to interact with this contemporary debate here, it seems clear that Owen's understanding and emphasis on the true humanity of Jesus Christ may offer both careful and creative insights into better appreciating this area of Christology. To date, the closest that Owen scholarship has approached this contemporary problem in light of Owen's thought comes from Spence, "Incarnation and Inspiration," though this is still several steps away from directly addressing this particular question.

sin); others reject the idea but still believe he assumed a fallen nature. Since we have dealt with this more contemporary debate elsewhere, our purpose here is to better understand Owen's conclusions by exploring his reasoning.[142]

Displaying concerns similar to both patristic and modern theologians, Owen boldly claims that "for a *sinning nature* to be saved, it was indispensably necessary that *it* should be assumed."[143] The question becomes, What does "it" refer to? By such a statement does Owen imply that Jesus assumed a fallen human nature, or should he be understood as claiming that "it" refers simply to human nature without the predicate "sinning"? Contextually, Owen is developing an Anselmian line of reasoning, arguing that the Son assumed a human rather than angelic nature; otherwise humanity would be unredeemable.[144] Stated another way, since the Son did not assume an angelic nature, the result was that those who "sinned in that [angelic] nature must perish for ever."[145] As recognized above, only by assuming a human nature—the same essential nature common to all humanity—could the Son accomplish his work. Those, like the Socinians, who believe that sinners could be saved any other way "but by satisfaction made in the nature that had sinned, seem not to have considered aright the nature of sin and the justice of God."[146] As a result, they undervalue the purity of the earthly Christ.[147] Following Owen's thought, the Son clearly needed to assume a true human nature as the federal head. Yet to suppose that therefore the Son assumes "fallen" nature is to misunderstand the virgin birth, the life of Christ, and most significantly, his death.

To summarize Owen's thought: through the Spirit's work in the extraordinary virgin birth, the Son assumes a sinless human nature,[148] lives a life of absolute faithfulness to God,[149] and uniquely through

142. See Kapic, "The Son's Assumption," 154–66. Since originally published, the following articles have furthered the discussion started in this essay: Oliver Crisp, "Did Christ Have a *Fallen* Human Nature?" *IJST* 6 (2004): 270–88; W. Ross Hastings, "'Honouring the Spirit': Analysis and Evaluation of Jonathan Edwards' Pneumatological Doctrine of the Incarnation," *IJST* 7, no. 3 (2005): 279–99, esp. 285–90.

143. *Works* 20:462 (BE 19:462), emphasis added.

144. Cf. Anselm, *Cur Deus homo*, 182.

145. *Works* 20:462 (BE 19:462).

146. *Works* 20:462 (BE 19:462). Cf. Alan W. Gomes, "*De Jesu Christo Servatore*: Faustus Socinus on the Satisfaction of Christ," *WTJ* 55 (1993): 209–31.

147. See *Works* 19:214–15 (BE 18:214–15).

148. E.g., *Works* 12:293: "'Whereas he was like men, namely, those first [i.e., Adam and Eve]; that is, without sin.' That Christ was without sin, that in his being made like to us there is an exception as to sin, is readily granted." McGowan, *Federal Theology*, 24–32, believes that Thomas Boston (1676–1732) reaches a conclusion similar to Owen's.

149. Cf. *Works* 19:153–54, 159 (BE 18:153–54, 159); again, the faithfulness is possible only by the communication of the Spirit.

his passion was able to completely take upon himself the sin of others. Unlike the rest of humanity, the Son assumed a nature uncorrupted by original sin and thus resembling a prelapsarian Adam.[150] Like the rest of humanity, the person of Jesus lived in a fallen world and thus faced extreme pain and temptation utterly unknown to the first Adam—which allows Owen to speak of him taking on our general infirmities.[151] Owen makes a distinction between *natural* infirmities (which open one up to temptations and sufferings) and *sinful* infirmities. The Son assumes the former, not the latter, since Jesus needed to be both *without sin* and also *tempted* in order to offer himself in the place of others.[152]

Thus we see not only continuity and discontinuity when comparing Jesus's human nature with others after the fall; there is also continuity and discontinuity with Adam's nature before original sin. It is a mistake of oversimplification to say either that (1) Jesus assumed a prelapsarian human nature, which is completely alien and oblivious to the painful realities of a fallen world, or that (2) he assumed a fallen human nature, just like every other human except that he never engaged in personal acts of sin. The Son's express purpose for his condescension was that he might come as the true and pure second Adam, able to redeem those who were lost.[153] As such, he could not avoid the pain of this world, but instead he voluntarily and graciously entered into suffering throughout his life, culminating in his death.[154]

Working within this system of federal theology, Owen might appear at odds with contemporary language that commonly describes the Son as assuming a *fallen* human nature. Yet, he inadvertently answers one of the main objections that such a position implies. In opposition to the objection that the Son assumed a generic human nature, Owen appears to maintain both the universality and particularity of the human nature Jesus assumes. A lengthy quotation from Owen is necessary to capture this dynamic of his thought. Jesus

150. *Works* 19:27 (BE 18:27): "The individual nature actually assumed into union was . . . considered as pure as in its first original and creation."

151. *Works* 19:466–67 (BE 18:466–67).

152. *Works* 19:234 (BE 18:234).

153. One may compare this element of Owen's theology to Irenaeus. As Gustaf Wingren keenly observes in his classic study *Man and the Incarnation: A Study of the Biblical Theology of Irenaeus*, trans. Ross Mackenzie (London: Oliver & Boyd, 1959), for Irenaeus "sin is never in itself anything human, but on the contrary destruction of man as God made him. It is no limitation of Christ's humanity that He has no sin, but on the contrary His very freedom from sin qualifies him for achieving the thing which is truly human, but which no other human being is capable of doing, for the whole of humanity is bound, captive, and unnatural" (86–87).

154. Cf. *Works* 20:430 (BE 19:430).

did take "upon" him (I use that word rather than take "unto him") the nature of man, into an individual subsistence in his own person, whereby he became *that* man; and what was done and acted in it by *that* man was done and acted *by the person of the Son of God*. . . .

We have all of us the same nature in general;—that is, the same specific human nature belongs unto us equally and unto all men in the world; *yet every man and woman hath this nature entire and absolutely unto himself, as if there were no other man or woman in the world*. And Adam was not more a single person when there was none in the world but himself, than every one of us is a single person now the world is full of men, as if there were but one man. And *every one comes into the world in his own individual subsistence unto himself*, whereby he becomes a man as much as any of us. *Here is the great act of self-denial in Christ.*[155]

The Son assumes a true human nature, both universal and particular. Owen completely excludes any idea of Jesus as some alien child who simply appeared from heaven: rather, he affirms that Christ has a traceable lineage (e.g., "seed of Abraham," Heb. 2:16),[156] acknowledging that Jesus was "a bud from the loins of sinful man."[157] Additionally, whereas those who are born by "ordinary generation" are "obnoxious unto all miseries" from their first breath, Jesus is not. Since he has not suffered from original sin, he is "just in himself, free from all, obnoxious to nothing that was grievous or irksome, no more than the angels in heaven or *Adam in paradise*."[158] This constitutes the most significant difference between Jesus's particular human nature and the rest of humanity: he assumes a sinless human nature within a fallen world.

While we have recognized (above) Owen's willingness to express the perfect human nature of Jesus in faculty psychology terms, he denies that original sin had any effects on Jesus's faculties as it does on the rest of humanity. This is what Owen means by making a distinction between internal and external temptations. Jesus's *internal* disposition resembles prelapsarian humanity rather than a corrupted postlapsarian disposition,

155. *Works* 17:567 (BE 16:499), emphasis added.
156. See *Works* 20:454–62 (BE 19:454–62). It is true, nonetheless, that while Owen uses this to draw attention to the true humanity of Jesus, he still stresses Jesus's relationship to the "spiritual" rather than the natural seed.
157. See *Works* 2:64. Here Owen is defending Christ's humanity as being free from all sin, yet he shows the unusual situation from which this occurs. See chap. 5, where we discuss this particular passage.
158. *Works* 20:422 (BE 19:422), emphasis added. Cf. Owen's claim noted above that Jesus is "obnoxious," liable to suffering and death, but on "our own account" rather than his own.

which naturally points away from God.[159] After the fall human nature suffers from the entrance of sin into the world: the mind becomes impotent and distorted, the will becomes opposed to the things of the Spirit, and the affections become confused and twisted.[160] Nevertheless, Jesus endured the effects that original sin has on the body (e.g., opening it up to disease and infirmities) as *external* consequences of original sin. Hence, when Owen argues against what he believes is the Arminian rejection of original sin, he concludes that humanity is thoroughly defiled, but that this defilement does not touch Christ: "All the distortures and distemperatures of the soul by lusts, concupiscence, passions, blindness of mind, perverseness of will, inordinateness of affects, wherewith we are pressed and turmoiled," are the result of original sin.[161] But these consequences of original sin do not extend to the human nature of Christ, who was "without sin." Although born of a fallen woman, Jesus possessed faculties uncorrupted by the fall. For this reason Jesus's virgin birth is important to Owen, who argues that "whereas the original contagion of sin is derived by natural procreation, had [Jesus] been by that means made partaker of human nature, how could he have been 'holy, harmless, undefiled, separate from sinners,' as it became our high priest to be?"[162] Owen affirms both the true humanity of Christ as well as his essential purity. He believes both are necessary for Jesus to qualify as the great high priest.[163]

Even as he goes on to argue that Jesus was familiar with all normal affections (e.g., love, joy, fear, sorrow, etc.) and that his body experienced normal physical sufferings (e.g., hunger, thirst, cold, pain, death), Owen maintains a fundamental difference between Jesus and his fellow humans. Fallen humanity experiences these things now with "irregular perturbations" whereas Jesus did not internally experience these "inordinate inclinations" that others do as a result of "their tempers and complexions."[164] Although "most of our temptations arise from within us, from our own unbelief and lusts," this cannot be the case for him

159. See *Works* 2:143: "There is something in all our temptations more than was in the temptation of Christ. There is something in ourselves to take part with every temptation; and there is enough in ourselves to tempt us, though nothing else should appear against us. With Christ it was not so, John xiv.30."

160. See chap. 2, "Created to Commune with God: Owen's Formulation of the *Imago Dei*."

161. Owen, *A Display of Arminianism*, in *Works* 10:79.

162. *Works* 20:467 (BE 19:467).

163. Significantly, Owen does acknowledge that one of the requirements of the high priest is that he "must be taken from among men"; see *Works* 20:469 (BE 19:469). For a developed discussion of the priesthood of Christ in Owen, see Robert K. M. Wright, "Owen's Great High Priest."

164. *Works* 20:467–68 (BE 19:467–68); cf. *Works* 3:167.

who knew no sin. Like pre-fallen humanity, Jesus's faculties were working correctly as his mind, will, and affections all pointed him toward the Father. While this should not be taken as implying that Jesus was not *truly and externally* tempted (cf. Adam and Eve in the garden, who were tempted even before the fall), it does mean that from *internal* temptations "he was absolutely free; for as he had no inward disposition or inclination unto the least evil, being perfect in all graces and all their operations at all times, so when the prince of this world came unto him, he had no part in him,—nothing to close with his suggestions or to entertain his terrors."[165]

Given the significant difference described above, the idea of a sinless Jesus calling believers his brothers becomes all the more significant, since such alliance between himself and the rest of humanity "cost him" by making him "instantly obnoxious unto all miseries and the guilt whereof we had contracted upon ourselves."[166] This is what makes justification so crucial. For on the cross the unique theanthropic Jesus could now take on the sin of the world.

Conclusion

The assumption of a human nature by the Second Person of the Trinity proves to be pivotal in Owen's theological anthropology. It paves the way for an understanding of the depth of God's redemptive love, which enables the reconciliation between fallen humanity and a holy God. As we already saw in chapter 2, although humanity was created to commune with God, the fall disrupted this communion. All of fallen humanity experiences the crushing weight of sin, and only by means of the incarnation does hope resurface: the chasm between the Creator and creature has been crossed in the Father's revelation of himself through his Son. Through the incarnation, humanity is uniquely confronted with the reality of a holy, transcendent God, whose loving immanence is set forth clearly in the Son. By the incarnation the Son experienced a perfect or complete human nature, which is like every other human nature—yet without sin, the only exception. As such, Jesus alone is able to take away the sin of the world. Through Christ alone does God clearly portray himself as "for us."

This background in Owen's Christology prepares us for discussing his theology of justification and renewed communion with the Triune

---

165. *Works* 20:468 (BE 19:468); cf. *Works* 10:85, describing humanity before the fall: "There was no inclination to sin, no concupiscence of that which is evil, no repugnancy to the law of God, in the pure nature of man." See also *Works* 3:167.

166. *Works* 20:422 (BE 19:422).

God. Without divine action, humanity would remain dead in their sins and without hope of ever enjoying fellowship with God. But Christ reveals the riches of divine love. Justification is not only a possibility but also an actuality for those who are found in Christ, and through Christ they are enabled to worship the Triune God, whose love made renewed communion a reality.

RECONCILING GOD AND HUMANITY

Looking at the Question of Justification

The great Work of them who are Embassadors for Christ, to beseech men in his stead, to be reconciled unto God, is to reveal the Will and Love of the Father, in making him to be sin for us, who knew no sin, that we might be made the Righteousness of God in him.

John Owen (1653)[1]

For all our rest in this world is from trust in God; and the especial object of this trust, so far as it belongs unto the nature of that faith whereby we are justified, is "God in Christ reconciling the world unto himself."

John Owen (1677)

Introduction

How one tries to explain the reconciliation between a morally compromised human being and a perfectly righteous God will expose many

---

1. From Owen's preface to William Eyre's *Vindiciæ justificationis gratuitæ* (London: Tho. Brewster, 1653). At this early date Owen adds a disclaimer, claiming ignorance regarding the persons and circumstances discussed in Eyre's work. In this context he also claims he is not yet ready nor does he desire to present his own thoughts on the topic of justification. He waits twenty-five years before he writes his own extensive treatise on the subject.

107

anthropological presuppositions of the writer. Writing a century and a half after Luther's "discovery" of God's righteousness in Romans 1:16–17, Owen entered a renewed debate surrounding the doctrine of justification. By 1640 many ministers expressed concern at the growing laxity and "coldness of heart" that they saw throughout England, and many of these reacted against those who appeared to minimize the role of good works in the believer's life.[2] Even leading orthodox theologians, such as William Twisse and Owen, found themselves labeled antinomian. In these turbulent seventeenth-century debates that supposed a tension between divine grace and human action, Owen represents an English Reformed "high orthodoxy" and adds to the countless treatises already written on this subject. By examining Owen's *The Doctrine of Justification by Faith* (1677; hereafter, *Justification*), written in the last decade of his life, we see how his methodology and conclusions reveal his underlying anthropology.[3] Here he will consistently move between the reality of human experience and the power of divine grace. This anthroposensitive dynamic contains a key to his view of relations between the divine and the human, seen particularly in the priesthood of Christ.

While a certain amount of historical background is necessary to appreciate Owen's emphases, this chapter—like the previous ones—will focus primarily upon theological rather than historical observations.

In his prefatory comments, Owen states that although justification is hotly contested, he desires to avoid those debates as much as possible. Instead, he seeks to give a "naked inquiry" into those things "revealed in scripture, and as evidencing themselves in their power and efficacy on the minds of them that do believe."[4] Though we now acknowledge various influences upon Owen's thought and recognize the impossibility of a "naked inquiry," our goal is to outline his own formulation.

Previous chapters have already discussed the foundational ideas of humanity made in the image of God and the centrality of the incarnation in redemption; this chapter will build upon these ideas by exploring

2. C. F. Allison, *The Rise of Moralism: The Proclamation of the Gospel from Hooker to Baxter* (London: SPCK, 1966) nicely traces this development, specifically focusing on the central debate about the "formal cause" of justification. For more on the historical context of Owen's work *The Doctrine of Justification by Faith* (1677), see L. G. Williams, "God and Nation," 299–300.

3. Clifford, in his *Atonement and Justification*, primarily discusses Owen's view of justification in light of his statements regarding limited atonement, drawing heavily upon Owen's work *The Death of Death in the Death of Christ* (1647). Given the title of Clifford's book, there is surprisingly little interaction with Owen's most complete and theologically mature statement on the subject in *Justification* (1677). For our purposes, we shall therefore focus on this neglected source, giving little attention to the much-discussed topic of the atonement's extent.

4. *Works* 5:4.

the justification of believers. Since being made in God's image primarily points to relations with God, our concern naturally moves to the theme of justification. This chapter will give particular attention to Owen's continued dual emphasis on Christology and praxis, for in this manner we observe how his anthropology affects the rest of his theological conclusions.

For our purposes we will highlight several relevant points from his work *Justification*. First, we shall observe how Owen conceives of the experiential situation, based in the objective reality of one's guilt, that gives birth to the question of justification. Second, Owen's handling of the topic of faith shows how he tries to weave together human responsiveness and Christology. This leads us to our third point, the significance of how Owen understands the priestly work of Christ as the key to justification. Fourth, we shall look into his discussion concerning "two justifications," which actually centers upon the relationship between faith and works. Finally, the vital role of imputation will be explored.

Approaching the Doctrine of Justification

While one might assume that Owen would begin his discussion of justification by outlining relevant attributes of God, he begins instead with *humanity*. Here we find the consistent anthroposensitive emphasis that arises throughout his corpus. Pointing to this *sensitivity* is considerably different from suggesting that he has an anthropocentric approach, as opposed to a theocentric one. Owen is not so easily categorized by this somewhat artificial juxtaposition. Rather, he appreciated the human, and more important, the christological implications of all theology; this allowed him to freely move between doing theology "from above" and "from below." Throughout our study we use the terms "above" and "below" as reference points: "below" stresses human and experiential questions; "above" focuses on revelation of the Divine Being. Though Owen never ultimately separates the two, especially as we have already seen in his conception of Christ, we use this distinction to show his emphasis.

Strongly believing that one must first rightly conceptualize oneself before properly comprehending and appreciating justification, Owen begins with the human catastrophe. Because of Adam's original sin, each subsequent human being is now born morally deformed. As we discussed in chapter 2, the image that once reflected the Creator has been shattered, with the result that all of creation no longer has a clear representation of God. When fallen humans look at themselves, they feel burdened by their sin, and until they find a way to be freed from their guilt, they remain in paralyzing despair. From this state of despair they can find hope only when their gaze turns away from self and toward Christ.[5] Only through the incarnate Christ, as we explained in chapter 3, does the image of God again become clearly apparent; in Christ's person and work the sinful human sees the Son of God in his humility and terrifying perfection. Christ provides hope for the hopeless both through forgiveness of sins *and* by the imputation of righteousness.

The above summary provides a rough map of how Owen understands the human journey from despair to hope, from guilt to righteousness. Owen begins his "General Considerations" (a 70-page introduction to *Justification*) by clearly stating his twofold aim: to reveal the "glory of God in Christ" and to aid in the "peace and furtherance of the obedience of believers."[6] After stating his general aim, he begins by assuming the universal sinfulness and guilt of humankind. Since Owen desires to penetrate the heart of his readers, he begins with *them* rather than diving into abstract concepts about God's nature. Owen's first "inquiry" concentrates on the person in need of justification; his second inquiry deals with the "God that justifieth."[7] In typical Calvinist fashion, he posits a reciprocal relationship between knowledge of God and knowledge of self.

Owen sets out to relieve the burdened conscience, which feels overcome by sin. To accomplish this, he first examines man's natural state. Using mostly Pauline vocabulary, Owen describes the human being in need of justification as "ungodly" (ἀσεβής), "guilty before God" (ὑπόδικος τῷ θεῷ), "liable to the righteousness of God" (τῷ δικαιώματι τοῦ θεοῦ), under "the curse" (ὑπὸ κατάραν), and finally "without plea, without excuse" (ἀναπολόγητος).[8] By employing this vocabulary, which stresses culpability, Owen urges the reader to ask, "What must I do to be saved?"[9] When Owen thus pushes the reader to self-application and away from detached abstraction, he enables the reader to face the next question: How will God forgive *my* sins? How can God ever consider a sinner righteous and no longer guilty? Could a sinner ever have a "right and title

5. See ibid., 2:189, for a vivid description of this psychological process.

6. Ibid., 5:7.

7. The first begins on ibid., 5:7, the second on 5:13. Section 3 (5:20) moves back to an anthropological discussion of man's sin and guilt under the law.

8. Ibid., 5:7. Cf. John 3:18, 36; Rom. 1:32; 2:1; 3:19; 4:5; Gal. 3:10, 22. In quoting the New Testament, Owen usually gives both the Greek and the verse reference; at other times he simply uses the Greek with the assumption that his reader will easily be able to locate the citation. Thus, when referring to the adjective ἀναπολόγητος, used only in Rom. 2:1, Owen either thinks a scriptural reference is unnecessary, or he simply neglects to include it.

9. Ibid., 5:8. He employs this technique elsewhere, as in *Works* 17:433–34 (*BT*, 628–30).

unto a blessed immortality"? After pointedly setting up the questions, Owen leads the reader through the answers.[10]

This manner of handling theology, by beginning with human concerns, moves Owen beyond his "General Considerations," to concrete pastoral theology. Common caricatures of Owen might lead one to think that he would start by examining God's nature with detached Aristotelian logic, but instead he begins with a discussion of *faith*, which is the "means of justification on our part."[11] This observation ought to give pause. Although exemplifying a premier seventeenth-century Reformed theologian who believes without compromise in God's sovereign election, Owen begins his discussion of justification with the *human's* role in faith, rather than God's role through predestination.[12] We shall therefore give significant attention to Owen's presentation of faith, since it illustrates how he brings together the interaction between a personal God and weakened humanity. Here again we find Owen seeking both faithfulness to his theological tradition and fidelity to human experience.

How to Understand Justifying Faith

According to Owen—who follows a common distinction often used by the early Reformers—the Scriptures display two kinds of faith, one justifying, the other not.[13] Some, like Simon the Magician in Acts 8, are said to have believed, but this was not a true faith that "purified the heart." Only the faith that has a "root in the heart" will justify.[14] Behind this discussion lies Owen's effort to make sense of a common sociologi-

10. Owen was not alone among Protestant scholastics in drawing practical applications from the doctrine of divine justice, since this doctrine was meant to ultimately bring people to doxology; Muller, *PRRD* 3:496–97.

11. *Works* 5:70.

12. Cf. Ames, *Marrow of Theology*, whose work moves quickly from the definition and divisions in theology to the question of faith, and only afterward moves to a discussion of God's essence and subsistence (77–94). Historically, this proves interesting in light of the development of Hyper-Calvinism in England, which often downplayed the significance of the individual out of concern for God's sovereignty: see, e.g., Curt D. Daniel, "Hyper-Calvinism and John Gill" (PhD diss., University of Edinburgh, 1983; privately published, 1983); Peter Toon, *The Emergence of Hyper-Calvinism in English Nonconformity, 1689–1765* (London: Olive Tree, 1967). Cf. the recent reassessment by George M. Ella, "John Gill and the Charge of Hyper-Calvinism," *BQ* 36, no. 4 (1995): 160–77.

13. See Philip E. Hughes, *Theology of the English Reformers*, new ed. as a Canterbury Book (1965; Grand Rapids: Baker Academic, 1980), 55. Cf. Johannes Wollebius, *Compendium theologiae christianae*, in *Reformed Dogmatics: Seventeenth-Century Reformed Theology through the Writings of Wollebius, Voetius, and Turretin*, ed. John W. Beardslee III (New York: Oxford University Press, 1965), 161–63.

14. *Works* 5:71; here he looks at Acts 8:13; 15:9; Rom. 10:10.

cal phenomenon witnessed in his day. Many men and women attended church, having made a profession of faith sometime in the past, but their attitudes and actions seemed to show the observer—at least to Owen's mind—that they did not love God. How can this be? Does not *any* faith bring justification? Does not every Christian love God and display that love through thankful obedience? For Owen, there is either genuine justifying faith or a powerless "temporary faith." True faith, by its very nature, manifests itself in the disposition and actions of the believer.[15] However, this idea raises serious questions for the anxious souls who desire to know if they have true faith.

Owen describes faith for his readers in a fourfold manner: faith's causes, a person's duty before faith, the object of justifying faith, and the nature of faith.[16] The fourth point is originally introduced by Owen as the "acts and effects of faith," but no such title resurfaces. Therefore, the following chapter in Owen's treatise, which discusses the "nature of faith" and reads as if completing the previous discussion, should be taken as his fourth point: he (or his publisher) appears to have neglected continuing with the numbering scheme. If this is not the case, then Owen must have left out his fourth proposed concern—unlikely for someone as systematic as this Oxford theologian. We shall consider each discussion of faith in turn.

Causes of Faith

Regarding the "causes of faith" in his work *Justification*, Owen simply states that he has discussed it elsewhere, likely referring to a section in his first book, *A Display of Arminianism* (1643).[17] The Remonstrance statement of 1610 had provided a strong endorsement of the theology of James Arminius, and it signified to Owen a rejection of orthodox Calvinism. In *A Display of Arminianism* Owen attacks what he believes is the Remonstrants' mistake of (1) undervaluing Christ, whose death is the "meritorious cause" of faith, grace, and righteousness; as well as (2) neglecting the efficacious role of God the Holy Spirit as the one who brings faith. He accuses them of making "fools of all the doctors of the church who ever opposed the Pelagian heresy."[18] During the next decade a few of Owen's writings reiterate his concern about this twofold mistake.[19]

15. Cf. ibid., 21:246 (BE 20:246).
16. This discussion can be followed in *Works* 5:73–107.
17. Ibid., 10:100–107.
18. Ibid., 10:103.
19. For similar arguments, see Owen's *Death of Death* (1647), in *Works* 10:249–58; and *Of the Death of Christ* (1650), in *Works* 10:468–70.

In this early context the point for Owen is that, while faith is often thought of as a human work, it must always have as its background the gracious movement of God. Throughout Scripture he sees a tension: *God commands* certain duties or responses by people; *God alone empowers* rebellious people to respond and obey him. So, for example, Deuteronomy 10:16 reports God's command for the people to circumcise their hearts and be stiff-necked no longer. Reading on to Deuteronomy 30:6, we learn that *God* is the one who "will circumcise their hearts" so that they will wholly love God. In Ezekiel 18:31 Israel is commanded to have a "new heart and a new spirit," for otherwise its people will die. As a command it demands obedience, and yet Ezekiel 36:26–27 explains that God is the one who will provide what is required by giving the people a new heart, taking "away the stony heart out of your flesh."[20] Examples like this, according to Owen, could be presented endlessly. Given this tension in Scripture, Owen concludes that "the same thing, in diverse respects, may be God's act in us and our duty towards him."[21] If this is denied, one ends up with Arminian moralism rather than gospel proclamation.

In his later book *Justification*, Owen simply states from the outset that justifying faith is unique and that this particular usage is different from a commonplace understanding of the word "faith." This faith has "its first original in the divine will."[22] Before Owen discusses a person's duty before faith, he makes certain that this underlying truth of divine gracious activity is seen as a nonnegotiable presupposition for all that follows.

A Person's Duty before Faith

Next Owen discusses at length what is required of men and women before belief: each individual must realize his or her own sinfulness. Sounding similar to Luther, he emphasizes the role of the law as the means to bring consciousness of sin. When effective, the law stirs the heart and causes "the conviction of sin, [which] is a necessary anteced-ent unto justifying faith."[23] Although humans must come to see their guilt under the law, which allows them to become *subjectum capax jus-tificationis*, this conviction does not necessitate their justification.[24] As

20. *Works* 10:105.
21. Ibid.
22. Ibid., 5:74.
23. Ibid. This is a standard Puritan pattern—humiliation precedes faith. Cf. Thomas Shepard, *The Sound Believer* . . . (London: Andrew Crooke, 1671), 66–68, 123–25.
24. Cf. *Works* 5:98; cf. Augustine's similar language in *Contra Julianum*, in PL 44, col. 690.

will be seen later, more is needed than a passing feeling of guilt or an intellectual assent.

While conviction of sin itself does not justify, it provides the necessary first step toward such a possibility. Before patients will go to the doctor, they must first recognize that they are sick.[25] Owen goes on to describe the qualities and manifestations—both internal and external—of true and lasting conviction. These include sorrow for sin, fear of punishment, fleeing from known sin, and involving oneself in the normal means of worshipping God. After discussing this, Owen stops to make sure he has not been misunderstood: none of these are "conditions of justification"![26] There are numerous dangers, according to Owen, which grow out of confusion at just this point; the Council of Trent's discussion of adult preparation for justification may be in his mind here.[27] He may also be thinking of others—including some Protestants—who had allowed this type of discussion to go too far when their idea of faith became loaded with requirements.[28] Without hesitation Owen therefore jumps "from below" to "from above" in his methodology, believing that a misunderstanding here would greatly obscure his overall goal of exalting Christ and encouraging believers in obedience.

Acknowledging his clear skepticism regarding human faithfulness to God, Owen calls the reader's attention to God's faithfulness, rather than to his own. If Christians do not recognize God's role as the giver and sustainer of their faith, they will quickly return to despair when their faith grows weak and their obedience wavers. Desiring to comfort the hearts of his readers, Owen reminds them of God's dealing with Adam and Eve after the fall.[29] He suggests that it was *God* who opened Adam and Eve's eyes so that they could see the reality of their sin. Once their blinders were fully removed, both of them felt ashamed and wanted to

25. *Works* 17:431 (Owen, *BT*, 625).

26. *Works* 5:78.

27. See *The Canons and Decrees of the Council of Trent*, trans. H. J. Schroeder (Rockford, IL: Tan Books, 1978), 31–34.

28. This occurs often in those theologians who argue for the "imputation of faith" rather than of Christ's righteousness. Two predominant figures of this position include John Goodwin (1594?–1665) and Richard Baxter (1615–91). Goodwin's main work in this area is aptly titled *Imputatio fidei* (London: Andrew Crooke, 1642). To understand Baxter's controversial and complex position on justification, see his *Aphorisms on Justification* (London: H. Hills, 1649) and *A Treatise of Justifying Righteousness* (London: Nevil Simons & Jonathan Robinson, 1676). The best treatment of Baxter's view of justification appears in H. Boersma, *A Hot Peppercorn: Richard Baxter's Doctrine of Justification in Its Seventeenth-Century Context of Controversy* (Zoetermeer: Boekencentrum, 1993). Cf. G. McGrath, "Puritans and the Human Will," esp. the appendix; and Ryken, *Thomas Boston*, 151–62. William Sherlock, *A Discourse*, 1st ed. (1674), 337–52, was also opposed to imputation of Christ's righteousness.

29. See *Works* 5:79–80.

conceal themselves: finding no escape from their sin, they tried to hide from God. Only through *God's* "act of sovereign grace" will sinners ever be able to enter again into God's presence. God's merciful intervention is the true cause of human faith. This caveat is Owen's attempt to place the individual's duty before faith within the cosmic context of God's gracious governance.

The Object of Faith

Primarily interacting with Robert Bellarmine's work (1542–1621) as representing "Rome,"[30] Owen claims that a significant difference surfaces between the two traditions regarding the object of faith.[31] Rome, Owen concludes, promotes nothing more than "an assent unto divine revelation."[32] This emphasis was common among medieval scholastics, going back most significantly to Thomas Aquinas.[33] For Roman theologians this revelation includes the teaching of the church in the apostolic tradition in addition to the biblical testimony. Bellarmine represents his tradition's emphasis, which tends to highlight the promises of God in revelation as the object of faith.[34] Although Owen's opponents would disagree with his shaping of the nuances, he nevertheless tries to make a clear distinction between the two positions. In our limited study we cannot fairly present the details of the complex debate between Owen

30. "Rome" will occasionally be used to represent Roman Catholicism. This is done for several reasons. First, this represents Owen's language. Second, we cannot fairly speak of "Catholic" in seventeenth-century debates, since Owen and his Puritan contemporaries would argue that their theology is catholic, and to attribute this exalted title to "Rome" biases any discussion from the beginning; G. S. Wakefield, *Puritan Devotion: Its Place in the Development of Christian Piety* (London: Epworth, 1957), 23. For the sake of reminding the reader of the historical context, we will occasionally employ Owen's shorthand.

31. For background on Bellarmine, see James Brodrick, *Robert Bellarmine: Saint and Scholar* (London: Burns & Oates, 1961). Possibly the most famous Protestant response to Bellarmine (and his *Apologia*) came from the pen of Lancelot Andrewes, who wrote *Responsio ad Apologiam Cardinalis Bellarmine* (London: printed by Robert Barker, 1610), seeking to answer Bellarmine point by point. Bellarmine's fullest discussion of justification comes from his massive tome *Disputationum . . . de controversiis christianae fidei adversus huius temporis haerticos*, 4 vols. (1581–93; repr., Coloniae Agrippineae [Cologne]: sumpt. hieratorum fratrum, 1628). Though Owen severely attacks Bellarmine's view of justification, he elsewhere was able to admit when Bellarmine was right, as on the topic of predestination; see *Works* 10:62.

32. *Works* 5:80–81. Elsewhere in this treatise *Justification*, Owen himself argues for the necessity of a "sincere assent unto all divine revelations," affirming the importance of revelation as pointing to the promises of Christ (5:99).

33. For Aquinas's discussion of the object of faith, begin with *ST* 2a–2ae.1–5.

34. This emphasis remains even today, as seen in the excellent work of the Catholic theologian Avery Dulles, *The Assurance of Things Hoped For: A Theology of Christian Faith* (Oxford: Oxford University Press, 1994), 185–203.

and his Roman opponents. Our interest lies not primarily in whether Owen creates a straw-man position to attack, but instead in how his attacks reveal his theological instincts, even if in the process he too easily dismisses his opponents.[35]

For Owen, one must encounter the object of faith, rather than simply assenting to historical realities. True faith communicates much more than mere assent; it requires a whole-souled response of the individual. It is an "act of the heart; which, in the Scripture, compriseth all the faculties of the soul."[36] He goes on to emphasize the particular importance of both the heart and the will. John von Rohr claims that among Puritan thinkers are three prominent positions regarding faith's relationship to justification.[37] The first stressed intellectual assent, as represented by George Downame and William Perkins. A second position, best represented by William Ames, held that the locus of faith is not in the intellect but rather in an act of the will. Out of these two emerges a via media propounded by the majority of Puritans, claiming that there must be a "significant place for both intellect and will in faith's act."[38] Owen falls into this third camp. His holistic anthropology

35. For more detailed analysis of the differences between "Rome" and early Protestant views of justification, which included their views of faith, begin with G. R. Evans, *Problems of Authority in the Reformation Debates* (Cambridge, UK: Cambridge University Press, 1992), esp. 119–36; Ricardo Franco, "Justification," in *Sacramentum Mundi: An Encyclopedia of Theology*, ed. Karl Rahner, vol. 3 (London: Burns & Oates, 1969), 239–41; J. P. Kenny, "Justification," in *A Catholic Dictionary of Theology*, ed. Monsignor H. Francis Davis, Ivo Thomas, and Joseph Crehan (London: Nelson, 1971), 172–82; Hans Küng, *Justification: The Doctrine of Karl Barth and a Catholic Reflection*, trans. Edmund Tolk, Thomas Collins, and David Grandskou (London: Burns & Oates, 1964); P. de Letter, "Justification: In Catholic Theology," in *New Catholic Encyclopedia* (New York: McGraw-Hill, 1967), 8:81–88; H. Edward Symonds, *The Council of Trent and Anglican Formularies* (London: Oxford University Press, 1933); Alister E. McGrath, "Justification," in *The Oxford Encyclopedia of the Reformation*, ed. Hans J. Hillerbrand, 4 vols. (Oxford: Oxford University Press, 1996), 2:360–68; idem, *Iustitia Dei: A History of the Christian Doctrine of Justification*, 2nd ed. (Cambridge, UK: Cambridge University Press, 1998). The recent Joint Declaration on the Doctrine of Justification states: "By justification we are unconditionally brought into communion with God"; in the "Official Common Statement by the Lutheran World Federation and the Catholic Church," *One in Christ* 36, no. 1 (2000): 89–92.

36. *Works* 5:83. Again, Owen's polemic tends to flatten out the complexity of his Roman opponents by adopting a view of faith different from the Catholic understanding of saving faith as faith formed by love. For a fair comparison between medieval scholastic views of "saving faith" and that of an English Reformer, see Ashley Null, *Thomas Cranmer's Doctrine of Repentance: Renewing the Power to Love* (Oxford: Oxford University Press, 2000), 116–212. I am grateful to Dr. Null for his countless hours of conversation with me regarding this thorny issue.

37. Von Rohr, *Covenant of Grace*, 68–72.

38. Ibid., 71. Von Rohr recognizes the difficulty in trying to create such divisions, for this third position still tends to stress the intellect over the will—a characteristic we find in Owen.

surfaces at this point and keeps him arguing for a concept of faith that touches the entire person.

As observed in our discussion regarding faculty psychology, Owen uses this paradigm to make sense of how believers respond to God.[39] Believers do not receive a supernatural faculty, as often portrayed in medieval scholasticism; instead, they respond with their natural faculties through faith. Faith must be "distinguished from opinion and moral certainty on the one hand, and science or demonstration on the other," which means that faith is an "act of that power of our souls . . . whereby we are able firmly to assent unto the truth upon testimony, in things not evident unto us by sense or reason."[40]

True faith requires not only the mind, but also a whole-souled response.[41] Consistently employing the language of *action* throughout this section, Owen stresses that faith is relational and holistic: faith is "a peculiar acting of the soul for deliverance," an "act of the heart," an "act of the will," an "act of our mind."[42] Danger arises when one tries to limit faith to only one of these. Justifying faith must be alive and relational, requiring a lively and personal response to its object. Assent is necessary for justifying faith; yet that is only part of the story, for one must assent unto the "testimony of God," who is "the revealer."[43] What Owen considers vital is not simply an ancient text known as revelation, but especially the one who is both the Reveal*er* and the Reveal*ed*.[44]

39. See chap. 2, "Created to Commune with God: Owen's Formulation of the *Imago Dei*."

40. *Works* 5:81; cf. Aquinas, *ST* 1a.46.2. Aquinas argues that the beginning of the world and the Trinity are matters of faith based on revelation "on which faith rests," rather than based on "demonstration or science." Cf. *ST* 3a.7.3.

41. Cf. Owen's statement from 1645: "Faith is in the understanding, in respect of its being and subsistence,—in the will and heart, in respect of its effectual working" (*Works* 1:486).

42. We have limited the examples, which could easily be expanded, by drawing only from ibid., 5:81–83.

43. Ibid., 5:81. See below for further discussion of faith as more than assent.

44. Owen is certainly not alone in seventeenth-century English theology in pointing to the *person* of Christ as the object of faith (this theme is more fully unpacked below), although his clarity on the subject remains noteworthy. George Downame's earlier argument proceeds in a similar style. While Christians should believe everything revealed or inferred from the Scriptures—though not the Apocrypha or the teaching of the "Church of Rome" (which Bellarmine includes in revelation)—Downame wants to narrow the discussion: "But howsoever by that faith, which justifieth, wee beleeve all and every truth revealed by God; yet the proper and formal Object of justifying faith, *quatenus justificat*, and by beleeving whereof it doth justifie, is not every truth, but that onely, which . . . is called the Truth, that is Christ with all his merits"; from *A Treatise of Iustification* (1633; London: Nicholas Bourne, 1639), 361. Turretin, *Elenctic Theology*, 2:558–631, esp. 571–80, offers a detailed account of the object of faith, but with a little less emphasis on Christ's "person" than is found in Owen's treatment of the subject.

Another misunderstanding is the claim that the "pardon of our sins" is the object of faith.[45] Some had borrowed this language from the Reformers, but in so doing had inappropriately—to Owen's mind—made the personal assurance of sins forgiven the great test for identifying true faith. This is problematic, however, because believers so commonly struggle with feeling assurance. Such a position reveals that believers are "neglective of their own experience," for if they knew themselves better, they would not make such unguarded claims. As recognized throughout our study, Owen's anthroposensitive approach considers Christian experience to be a legitimate and necessary tool for understanding and articulating correct doctrine. Obviously he does not want to deny the importance of having assurance that one's sins are pardoned, but even this is not the proper *object* of true faith. Later Owen will argue that assurance is better understood as an *effect* of God's love through Christ, rather than the actual *object* of faith.[46]

In this context Owen observes that many of the "great divines" of the Reformation "make the mercy of God in Christ, and thereby the forgiveness of our sins, to be the proper object of justifying faith."[47] Owen found the great divide between Rome and Protestant Reformers in how they answered the following question: Can one enjoy "a state of rest and assured peace with God" while "in this life?"[48] The Reformers addressed the grief and fear of their listeners and sought to free men and women burdened by Rome's apparent overemphasis on human merit. Distancing himself from those who fail to give compassionate pastoral help for Christian doubt, Owen claims the Reformers nowhere write that *every* Christian "always had a full assurance of the especial love of God in Christ."[49] In other words, a person with a wounded conscience often finds it difficult to believe that *their* sins are forgiven. Believers often place too much weight on their internal experiences rather than trusting the objective promises grounded in Christ.[50] Here Owen argues that his doctrine echoes the Reformers' concept of faith.

A brief look at John Calvin's discussion of the object of faith will demonstrate how close he and Owen are, especially in their christologi-

45. *Works* 5:83–85, 102.
46. Ibid., 5:88.
47. Ibid., 5:84–86; by using "our," Owen includes himself.
48. Ibid., 5:85.
49. Ibid.
50. Cf. Beeke, *Assurance of Faith*, 262, who rightly sees Owen as accepting levels of assurance. The higher level is full assurance—which includes both subjective and objective dimensions—and not of the essence of faith. The lower level is grounded solely in the objective truths of justification and the promises of God. To see how this issue surfaces throughout Puritan ministry, especially in the catechisms of the seventeenth century, see Green, *Christian's ABC*, 387–421.

cal approach to theology. According to Calvin, one should not simply speak of God as the object of faith, for Christ, the image of the invisible God, is the only proper sight of that object of faith.[51] The "schools" have incorrectly described the object of faith because "they call God simply the object of faith, and by fleeting speculations . . . lead miserable souls astray rather than direct them to a definite goal," which is to embrace Christ "our intermediary."[52] Likewise, Calvin stresses that God's glory is "visible to us in His person," adding later that "as God he [i.e., Christ] is the destination to which we move; as man, the path by which we go." Calvin's strong Christology requires the use of trinitarian language: the Son communicates the benefits of the Father, and the Spirit draws people to seek Christ. He furthermore emphasizes the role of "knowledge" in connection with faith, for people are called to receive Christ as "clothed with his gospel." Calvin ascribes a fundamental role to revelation, while still maintaining that the object of faith is Christ himself. Faith and the "Word" cannot be separated any more than one can "separate the rays from the sun from which they come." True faith is not about agreeing that God exists, nor is it about speculating on what God is "in himself." Instead, it is concerned with "what he wills to be toward us," and that is only understood in light of Christ. For Christ displays both the truth of God and God's mercy toward humanity.

After addressing many of the misconceptions, Owen restates his slightly altered twofold purpose for the book: "the advancement and glory of the grace of God in Christ, with the conduct of the souls of men unto rest and peace with him."[53] While acknowledging that various theologians disagree on the object of faith, Owen seems to think that most of the dissension stems from misunderstanding. As a remedy, he offers a formulation of the object of faith that he hopes others will find acceptable:

> The *Lord Jesus Christ himself*, as the ordinance of God, in his work of mediation for the recovery and salvation of lost sinners, and as unto that end proposed in the promise of the gospel, is the adequate, proper object of justifying faith, or of saving faith in its work and duty with respect unto our justification.[54]

---

51. Calvin, *Institutes*, 1:346–47 (2.6.4).

52. Ibid., 3.2.1. The rest of the quotations come from a section of Calvin's discussion of faith in 3.2.1–7. Calvin's examination of faith in a broader context continues throughout 3.2 and 3.3.

53. *Works* 5:85.

54. Ibid., 5:85–86, emphasis added; cf. 89. Cf. John Downe, who claims that "the object of faith" must be "the person of the Mediator" and not "present grace and future glory"; see *A Treatise of the True Nature and Definition of Justifying Faith* (Oxford: Edward Forrest, 1635), A2; cited by von Rohr, *Covenant of Grace*, 66.

This formulation emphasizes personal connections, concentrating primarily upon Christ's person and work, then moving to its beneficial consequences for believers.

Clearly the most significant element of the above quotation is how it begins, with the *"Lord Jesus Christ himself."* This functions as an umbrella under which the rest shelters. If Christ is the true object of faith, everything else naturally follows. Owen, like Calvin before him, believed that faith must ultimately rest on Christ rather than on speculations of an unknown divinity. Previous statements about the object of faith fail because they inadequately ground the discussion on a particular person, Jesus Christ. Later in the treatise Owen makes this point directly by saying that justifying faith means "the receiving of Christ, principally respect[ing] his person."[55] By making Christ's person the hinge for everything else, Owen tries to stop unnecessary disputes that often result from not focusing on the unifying truth of Christ's person.

This emphasis on Christ's person again reveals the high importance Owen assigns to the incarnation. Jesus as the Son of God represents the divine desire to redeem the lost. The Triune God did not merely present humanity with a proposition to believe, but rather, by the "ordinance of God" Christ came into the world. In doing so, the incarnate mediator becomes the sole person who can reconcile sinful people with the holy God, and as such he alone is the proper object of faith. Owen's language can be fluid, and elsewhere he speaks freely of "the blood of Christ" as the "object of faith."[56] Nevertheless, even here the object he is referring to remains ultimately Christ's person: the blood of Christ is shorthand for the priesthood of Christ, a theme we will again discuss below.

A christocentric definition of the object of faith only makes sense to Owen when it points to God the Father, who also becomes "the immediate object of faith as justifying."[57] Reflecting his fidelity to a trinitarian emphasis, Owen sees that faith without reference to the redeeming Triune God inevitably brings theological disaster. This disaster usually comes in the form of viewing the Father in a disposition of anger and Christ in one of love.[58] According to this pastoral theologian, nothing could be further from the truth, for it was the Father's love that first sent the Son

---

55. *Works* 5:116–17. In this context Owen unites faith in Christ's person with the promises of God. Additionally he argues that Christ's priestly office is more closely concerned with the believer's justification than is his role as prophet or king. In other words, we cannot ultimately understand Christ's person apart from his work. See below for how Owen develops this line of thought.

56. Ibid., 5:121. Here again, Owen may be following the lead of theologians like Downame, *Treatise of Iustification*, 361, who also speaks of "faith in the blood of Christ" in order to prove that Christ represents the object of faith.

57. *Works* 5:86.

58. Cf. ibid., 2:17–40.

as much as the Son's love in agreeing to accept the mission. So, to believe in Christ as the object of faith includes trusting in the loving disposition of the Father toward "lost sinners." As we will see later, the Spirit faithfully applies the work of Christ to the lives of believers, sustaining and preparing them for glory. In other words, Owen's christocentricism can never be rightly understood outside of this trinitarian structure of redemption, a theme we discuss at length in chapter 5.

Thus we see that Owen presents a *person* as the object of faith, rather than concepts, promises, or a set of beliefs. A ruined relationship caused the need for justification, which prompted God the Father to reach out to humanity through his Son, whose person and work guaranteed a restored relationship between God and his people, and this relationship is most clearly enjoyed in glory.[59] Sinners are not called to become academics who must learn a certain number of propositions in order to gain justifying faith. Instead, they are called to turn to a person, the living incarnate Christ, for justification.[60]

Scripture's purpose can be summed up as God's testimony to Christ as the proper object of faith. Beginning with "Moses and the prophets; the design of the whole Scripture [is] to direct the faith of the church unto the Lord Christ alone, for life and salvation."[61] Likewise, prayer testifies to Christ as the proper object of faith.[62] From his own practices, Owen points to the daily devotional experience of believers as a strong argument supporting his conclusions. The believer's connection with Christ enables him or her to have access to the "throne of grace." In a later work Owen claims that though prayer proceeds "from faith," it "must be fixed on the person so called on, . . . or that prayer is in vain."[63] Thus the object of faith can only be this *person* who establishes a communion between himself and his people. Take the object away, and all other Christian propositions become meaningless.

The Nature of Faith

Before we move beyond the topic of faith, we must conclude with the question of its nature. We shall limit our observations to Owen's view of the place of trust and then conclude with his use of biblical imagery.

---

59. Cf. ibid., 7:337.

60. W. Sherlock, *Union and Communion*, 3rd ed., corrected (1678), 22, 24, 38, and so on, believes Owen is too mystical and so opposes Christ's *person* as the object of faith, preferring to speak instead of "the Gospel" as the object of faith.

61. *Works* 5:90, citing Luke 24:25–27 to support his claim. Observe how Owen structures his work on the history of salvation in ΘΕΟΛΟΓΟΥΜΕΝΑ ΠΑΝΤΟΔΑΠΑ, in *Works* 17:27–480.

62. *Works* 5:92.

63. Ibid., 1:129.

The conviction of sin brings one into the state of *subjectum capax justificationis*, in which despair becomes the overriding emotion. From this position the subject must trust another since he himself has failed. Primarily through the reception of the preached word, faith responds with "a sincere renunciation of all other ways and means for the attaining of righteousness, life, and salvation." Likewise, the "will's consent" moves unto an "expectation of pardon of sin and righteousness before God."[64] Believers not only receive the forgiveness of sin; they also learn to trust continually that only through their connection to Christ can they be free of sin and be righteous before God.

The term *trust* best captures the essence of Owen's concerns at this point, where he appears to have the Reformers' term *fiducia* in mind.[65] He believes that the notion of trust surfaces throughout the Bible, especially in the Old Testament when it refers to the nature of faith. Yet again, we find Owen quick to qualify his assessment by denying that all believers will have full assurance that *their own personal sins* have been forgiven,[66] since he has learned from his own Christian experience and that of others: a stable "undeceiving belief" often eludes the believer this side of glory, even though such belief ought to be every Christian's desire and "privilege." Others—here he refers to the "Papists" and Socinians—unwisely include obedience as an "essential form of faith" concerning justification. Trust in Christ results from God's Spirit "transforming" the soul of an individual; this is the gracious gift of a "principle of spiritual life" that naturally ties together (1) the gift of faith with (2) the natural outworking of obedience. These, however, ought never to be collapsed into one another. Failure to keep this distinction, Owen argues, grows out of a naively optimistic anthropology rather than a biblical depiction of humanity crippled by the radical effects of sin.

Love and obedience are the *manifestations* of God's sovereign work rather than its cause. The Roman doctrine of faith as enlivened by charity appears to cause him much concern. Owen repeats the Reformation motto: "We are justified by faith alone, but not by that faith which is alone."[67] His following paragraphs include such things as repentance, baptism, and final perseverance under the second clause of the motto. Owen believes that many of the ancient Christian writers failed to make the necessary distinction between conditions, instruments, and results. Faith alone serves as the instrument, and those

64. Ibid., 5:100–101.
65. See ibid., 5:101–7.
66. Cf. ibid., 9:588.
67. Ibid., 5:104. Cf. John Calvin, *Short Treatise on the Lord's Supper* (1540), in *Tracts and Treatises on the Reformation of the Church*, trans. Henry Beveridge, annotated by Thomas F. Torrance (1849; repr., Grand Rapids: Eerdmans, 1958), 3:152.

who claim various aspects of Christian obedience (e.g., baptism) as conditional for salvation are gravely mistaken. Herein lies the problem with so many attempts at a definition of the "nature" of faith: ambiguous language creates a kind of theological chaos rather than Christian comfort.

Elsewhere in the book *Justification*, Owen addresses the growing debate regarding the language of "instrumentality." Not only Rome and the Socinians, but also many Protestants were claiming this terminology to be improper.[68] Referring to the Protestant scholar who wrestled most with this question, Owen states that "Dr. Jackson" offers a fair, "pious and sound" definition.[69] Owen nevertheless finds himself still unsatisfied and argues for a modified approach.

While often employing scholastic categories elsewhere, here Owen's pastoral sensitivity appears to move him to avoid continuing this type of debate.[70] Instead, he proposes that the most appropriate way to speak of true faith comes through "the lively scriptural expressions of faith, by *receiving* of Christ, *leaning* on him, *rolling* ourselves or our burden on him, *tasting* how gracious the Lord is, and the like," for these expressions "convey a better understanding of the nature, work, and object of justifying faith, unto the minds of men spiritually enlightened, than the most accurate definitions that many pretend unto."[71] Definitions can be ambiguous, formulaic, and are often sapped of all spiritual power. By employing biblical imagery, Owen moves the discussion from mental abstraction to spiritual awareness (cf. "enlightened mind").[72] Again, if one's theology does not both exalt Christ and promote Christian obedience, then the theology has somehow gone wrong; an inadequate or reductionist presentation can contribute to that failure.[73] Although he begins the chapter with a brief declaration—some might argue that it is a definition—of what he thinks

68. *Works* 5:108–11. Cf. also 5:114–15, where Owen reveals his frustration with the ambiguity regarding the language of "condition."

69. See Thomas Jackson, *Justifying Faith, or, The Faith by which the just do live* (London: John Clarke, 1631), esp. 48–81.

70. Early in his treatise *Justification* Owen argues against those who make justification into a speculative and abstract debate, "mixing evangelical revelation with philosophical notions . . . [which results in] the poison of religion" (*Works* 5:10).

71. *Works* 5:107, emphasis added.

72. See ibid., 17:430–31 (cf. *BT*, 624–25), where Owen argues that an emphasis on the Scriptures must be accompanied by an understanding of the Spirit's enlivening activity, making the Scriptures powerful in the heart of the reader.

73. Note Bobick's complaint ("Owen's Razor," 44) that Owen's "disinterest in a definition of justifying faith" hurts the Puritan, making it unclear if obedience is on par with faith. This seems to misunderstand Owen's reasons for avoiding such a definition.

describes the "exercise" of justifying faith,[74] he ends by pointing back to colorful and captivating images in Scripture. This is yet another example showing that while scholasticism is one of Owen's tools, he never allows it to drift into a formulaic rationalism; instead, he uses it to display his experimental biblicism more clearly. This conclusion goes against that propounded by Owen's nineteenth-century biographer Andrew Thomson. When discussing Owen's treatise *Justification*, Thomson concludes that Owen and other Puritan divines, "with their scholastic distinctions, were far inferior to the theologians of the Reformation. The great difficulty about faith is not a metaphysical but a moral one; and there is truth in the observation that elaborate attempts to describe it are like handling a beautiful transparency, whose lustre disappears whensoever it is touched."[75] In actuality, however, Owen apparently felt free to use both sophisticated scholastic language *and* imaginative biblical imagery; each served its own purpose and could be used in the appropriate context.

Christ's Priestly Importance

Acknowledging some debate among Reformed theologians on how the offices of Christ relate to justification, Owen allows that there is freedom for further inquiry. What he does not want to do is argue for the sake of "curiosity," as others have done, but rather with the goal of "edification."[76] Given this criterion, he begins by repeating that faith must be in Christ's person. Debate arises when the theologian unpacks this in terms of Christ's offices of king, prophet, and priest.

Believing in the unity of Christ's offices, Owen nevertheless argues that Christ's *priestly* office deserves the greatest attention in addressing the question of justification.[77] For Owen, justification chiefly concerns both the lack of individual righteousness and the guilt resulting from sin. Humanity's desperate position requires priestly activity that only the Son of God can accomplish. "Such was his incarnation, the whole course of his obedience, his resurrection, ascension, exaltation, and intercession;

74. See *Works* 5:93.
75. Andrew Thomson, in *Works* 1:xviv–cxxii, with xcvi quoted; also in *Life of Dr. Owen* (1850); repr. as *John Owen: Prince of Puritans* (Fearn, UK: Christian Focus Publications, 2004).
76. For this discussion, see *Works* 5:116–23.
77. This traditional Reformed emphasis continues into the twentieth century, as represented by Louis Berkhof, *Systematic Theology*, 4th ed. (1941; repr., Grand Rapids: Eerdmans, 1994), 356–411. Berkhof spends just over three pages on Christ's prophetic office, six pages on his kingly office, but forty-four pages on his priestly office, which covers the atonement and Christ's continued intercessory work.

for the consideration of all these things is inseparable from the discharge of his priestly office."[78] Behind Christ's earthly activities lie his priestly motivations. Functioning in his "sacerdotal office," Christ offers himself as the ultimate sacrifice.[79] The Bible speaks of "faith in his blood" (Rom. 3:25), but in priestly or cultic metaphors and never in kingly or prophetic ones. Without completely excluding the other offices, Owen still maintains that the priestly office best fits this particular aspect of redemption. Relying on biblical imagery about Christ, which so often consists of sacrificial representations, Owen is compelled to treat the priestly office as central. The other offices of Christ are not "towards God on our behalf," although they are all necessary for the salvation of sinners.[80] It is Christ's actions in his

> sacerdotal office alone, that respect God on our behalf. Whatever he did on earth with God for the church, in obedience, suffering, and offering up of himself; whatever he doth in heaven, in intercession and appearance in the presence of God, for us; it all entirely belongs unto his priestly office. And in these things alone doth the soul of a convinced sinner find relief, when he seeks after deliverance from the state of sin, and acceptance with God.[81]

While Owen does try to anticipate and answer objections, he concludes by stating that he does not want to "insist on the discussion of this inquiry," and so ends his argument.[82] Perhaps he worries that this type of discussion too easily turns to abstractions and abandons the relational aspect of Christology. The offices of Christ remain only a lens for seeing the *person* of Christ in his work for us. Trying to reconcile improper disputes, Owen concludes: "As it is granted that justifying faith is the receiving of Christ, so *whatever belongs unto the person of Christ*, or *any office of his*, or *any acts in the discharge of any office*, that may be reduced unto any cause of our justification, the meritorious, procuring, material, formal, or manifesting cause of it, is, so far as it doth so, freely admitted to *belong unto the object of justifying faith*."[83] In the end, Owen is most concerned to focus the eyes of faith on Christ rather than on impotent human "obedience," which others allow as a "condition" for justification. Justification must rely on Christ rather than on the believer; otherwise there would be no escape from perpetual fear and anxiety, an inevitable consequence of undervaluing the person and work of God incarnate.

78. *Works* 5:117. See also Owen's commentary on *Hebrews*, where he discusses the "sacerdotal office of Christ" at great length; in *Works* 19:3–259 (BE 18:3–259).

79. *Works* 5:117, 120.

80. Ibid., 5:121.

81. Ibid., 5:121–22.

82. Ibid., 5:122.

83. Ibid., 5:123, emphases added.

Again we see how Owen's scholastic training works with his pastoral sensitivity and how his anthroposensitive instincts affect the whole of his theological method. He uses a scholastic model as long as it displays the truth, but he also leaves scholastic terminology and method when they obscure theology and Christians' communion with God.

Justified Once or Twice?

In chapter 5 of his work *Justification*, Owen investigates the proposed distinction between a first and second justification. Historically, the concept of "double justice" surfaces in various forms in the thought of Augustine, Alexander of Hales, Aquinas, and sixteenth-century theologians like Erasmus, John Gropper, and Gaspar Contarini.[84] The 1541 Colloquy of Regensburg (Ratisbon), in which Contarini played a significant role, reveals an attempt to formulate a *duplicem iustitiam* in order to present an acceptable doctrine to both Catholic and Protestant leaders.[85] This effort ultimately yielded only frustration. Following Regensburg, the Council of Trent (1543–63) demonstrates that the theory of double justification becomes hotly contested even within Roman theology. Cardinal Girolamo Seripando, a papal legate, argues that a chapter *De duplici iustitia* ought to be included. In light of our discussion below, in which Owen clearly associates double justification with Rome, it seems ironic that Trent decided against the inclusion of the theory of double justice because it "sounded Lutheran" and they considered it a "novelty."[86] Trent consistently argued that "the *single* formal cause [of justification] is the justice of God, not that by which He Himself is just, but that by which He makes us just" (i.e., intrinsic righteousness).[87]

84. For an excellent survey of the complicated growth of this idea, see Edward Yarnold, "*Duplex iustitia*: The Sixteenth Century and the Twentieth," in *Christian Authority: Essays in Honour of Henry Chadwick*, ed. G. R. Evans (Oxford: Clarendon, 1988), 204–23. See also Frank James III, "The Complex of Justification: Vermigli versus Pighius," in *Peter Martyr Vermigli: Humanism, Republicanism, Reformation*, ed. Emidio Campi, Frank A. James III, and Peter-Joachim Opitz, Travaux d'humanisme et Renaissance (Geneva: Droz, 2002), 45–58.

85. Owen considers "Cardinal Contarinus" his ally on the question of justification. Owen then adds, in classic Protestant paranoia, that "upon the observation of what [Contarinus] had done [by writing his treatise on justification], some say he was shortly after poisoned; though I must confess I know not where they had the report." Owen also considered the pre-Trent Catholics Albertus Pighius and Antitagma Coloniense to hold similar supportive views of justification (*Works* 5:68). This again demonstrates how confusing the language of "double justification" is, for Pighius was one who employed such language in his effort to reconcile Luther's insights with the traditional Roman understanding.

86. Yarnold, "*Duplex iustitia*," 217.

87. *Council of Trent*, trans. Schroeder, 33: sixth session, chap. 7, emphasis added.

Moving into the seventeenth century, Robert Bellarmine's work becomes extremely important, especially since Owen bases much of his understanding of Roman theology upon it. Well into the late seventeenth century, Bellarmine's writings constituted arguably the most brilliant Roman Catholic presentation for Protestant interaction.[88] Bellarmine made some use of the twofold language of justification, specifically in his attempt to understand the apparent conflicting biblical data regarding this doctrine. Consequently, this idea commonly became associated with Roman theology in the eyes of seventeenth-century thinkers. Later orthodox Protestants like Owen associated this language with their opponents, whom they believed made works a conditional element for a believer's full and complete justification before God.

Not only did many Catholic theologians use this language, Protestants also occasionally employed it as well. For example, Martin Bucer (1491–1551) spoke of a double justification in which God both imputes and imparts righteousness: he distinguished between these two without separating them.[89] Confusingly, William Tyndale (1494?–1536) and other Henrician Reformers (1529–47) sometimes use expressions similar to a "twofold justification," but their meaning remains significantly different from the Roman conception.[90] What the early English Reformers tended to mean by the first justification was one's justification *before God*, having nothing to do with one's obedience; a second justification was *before one's fellow humans*, which included the believer's good works as a testimony to conversion. However, by the early part of the seventeenth century, when some later Protestant writers were using this language, they faced the accusation of advancing a Roman understanding of justification. In the controversy over Richard Montague's (Montagu/Mountagu, 1577–1641) books, his use and development of a first and second justification was

---

88. Jaroslav Pelikan, *The Christian Tradition*, vol. 4, *Reformation of Church and Dogma (1300–1700)* (Chicago: University of Chicago Press, 1984), calls Bellarmine "the most important theologian of the Counter-Reformation" (336).

89. W. P. Stephens, *The Holy Spirit in the Theology of Martin Bucer* (Cambridge, UK: Cambridge University Press, 1970), 48–70, esp. 49. Alister McGrath, *Iustitia Dei*, claims that for Bucer, "after a 'primary justification,' in which man's sins are forgiven and righteousness imputed to him, there follows a 'secondary justification,' in which man is made righteous" (221). Demonstrating the difficulty of interpreting this idea of double justification in Bucer, W. P. Stephens, "The Church in Bucer's Commentaries on the Epistle to the Ephesians," in *Martin Bucer: Reforming Church and Community*, ed. David F. Wright (Cambridge, UK: Cambridge University Press, 1994), 48, strongly disagrees with McGrath's representation of Bucer. Owen likewise recognizes the confusion caused in how Bucer "expressed" himself (*Works* 5:231–33).

90. Carl Trueman, *Luther's Legacy: Salvation and English Reformers, 1525–1556* (Oxford: Clarendon, 1994), 102–3, 140–42, 283; Trueman writes contra William A. Clebsch, *England's Earliest Protestants, 1520–1535* (New Haven: Yale University Press, 1964), 66–68, 87, 108–9, 166–68, 201–2.

severely attacked; others charged him with presenting a Roman rather than Protestant view of justification.[91] These debates, while only briefly outlined here, provide the background for Owen's concerns.

From the outset Owen identifies himself with the "evangelical" understanding of justification, which argues for one rather than two justifications: the "Roman church do ground their whole doctrine of justification upon a distinction of a double justification; which they call the first and the second."[92] While elsewhere Owen's language of "most of them" reveals his awareness of some diversity among Roman theologians, he considers the above-mentioned view most representative of the Roman Church as a whole.[93] Alister McGrath mentions the misunderstanding—even surfacing in twentieth-century scholarship—regarding how many Catholic theologians developed the idea of "double righteousness." He argues that this should not be understood as a doctrine of "double justification." Much of this confusion seems to date back to Bellarmine and his attempt to discredit the theologians at Regensburg.[94] Thankfully, recent scholarship has provided a more accurate historical assessment of the doctrine of "double righteousness." Yet for our purposes we must acknowledge that Owen—relying mostly upon Bellarmine—assumes that Roman teaching does in fact hold, implicitly or explicitly, a doctrine of double justification. Therefore we must use *Owen's* conception of the Roman position; otherwise we risk imposing our modern understanding upon him.

In Owen's understanding, Roman theologians contend that the first justification is the "infusion or the communication unto us of an inherent principle or habit of grace or charity."[95] With this infusion, they think "original sin is extinguished, and all habits of sin are expelled." To be justified in this way is to rely totally upon Christ and his merits. Although many of the medieval scholastics speak of preparation for salvation and of *meritum de congruo* (a half merit), Owen observes that the Council of Trent tried to avoid this language of merit when discussing the first justification.[96] For the most part, faith is needed as preparation, not as merit.

91. Montague's books include *A Gagg for the new Gospell? No: A New Gagg for an Old Goose* (London: Matthew Lownes & William Barret, 1624) and *Appello Caesarem* (London: Matthew Lownes, 1625). The attack against him comes from the anonymous work *A Dangerous Plot Discovered by A Discourse Wherein is proved, That, Mr Richard Montague . . . Laboureth to bring in the Faith of Rome, and Arminius; under the name and pretence of the doctrine and faith of the church of England* (London: Nicholas Bourne, 1626). For a history of this debate, see Allison, *Rise of Moralism*, 57–61.

92. To follow his arguments, see *Works* 5:137–62.

93. See ibid., 5:139.

94. McGrath, *Iustitia Dei*, 244–45.

95. *Works* 5:137.

96. Cf. ibid., 5:151, where Owen appreciates how some Roman Catholic theologians have tried to set aside "that ambiguous term *merit*."

Roman theologians principally see this justification by faith as "a habit of grace, expelling sin and making us acceptable to God." They believe that the Pauline literature refers to this justification. The second justification, as Owen constructs the Roman view, is the result of the first. In this second justification, the "proper formal cause" is "good works, proceeding from this principle [i.e., habit] of grace and love."[97] It is here that believers become righteous and therefore "merit eternal life." This justification is that to which the Epistle of James refers.[98] Using this concept of double justification, Roman theologians believe they have faithfully reconciled the apparent contradictions of Paul and James. Paul's language of being justified apart from the works of the law represents the first justification, whereas James's emphasis on being justified by one's works represents the second justification. At this point Owen argues primarily against Bellarmine and the conclusions of the Council of Trent.

So what does Owen see lying behind this twofold distinction? The problem with both Bellarmine and Trent is that they mistakenly allow human works to play a role in justification, even if it is only after one is initially justified. Thus, when Owen claims that Trent teaches a sort of "double justification," he refers to Session 6, chapter 10. This chapter deals with the "increase of the justification received."[99] Trent claims that those who have been "justified and made the friends and domestics of God . . . , through the observance of the commandments of God and of the Church, faith *cooperating with good works, increase* in that justice received through the grace of Christ and are *further justified*."[100] Between this section of Trent and Bellarmine's attempt to reconcile Paul and James, Owen seems convinced that Rome improperly combines justification and sanctification.[101] This is yet another example, he says, of unnecessary complication introduced into the simplicity of the message. The medievalists, he believes, unnecessarily multiplied theological distinctions, inevitably causing greater distortion. Distinguishing between a "first" and "second" justification similarly brought "confusion" rather than clarity. However, lest his reader form the wrong impression, Owen does not think that this debate centers simply upon a semantic difference—real theological consequences follow the Catholic presentation.

---

97. Ibid., 5:138.

98. Cf. Bellarmine, *Disputationum*, 1.17a; 3.33e; 3.309h; 3.266d; 4.204; 4.236–38; 4.267–68; etc. Cf. the controversial Protestant attempt to reconcile Paul and James in George Bull, *Harmonia Apostolica* . . . , trans. Thomas Wilkinson, 2nd ed. (repr., Oxford: John Henry Parker, 1844), esp. 43–220. Bull tends to elevate faith to the status of a work, a view strongly opposed by Owen.

99. See *Council of Trent*, trans. Schroeder, 36.

100. Ibid., emphasis added.

101. *Works* 5:138. This distinction primarily goes back to Melanchthon and the development of forensic justification.

Justification through the free grace of God, by faith in the blood of Christ, is evacuated by [Rome's view]. Sanctification is turned into a justification, and corrupted by making the fruits of it meritorious. The nature of evangelical justification, consisting in the gratuitous pardon of sin and the imputation of righteousness . . . and the declaration of a believing sinner to be righteous thereon . . . is utterly defeated.[102]

Owen believes that when the Roman position—as he understands it—is theologically applied, it causes the very core of Christ's atoning work to be without power or effect.[103] Consequently, believers depend more and more upon their own acts of obedience as the securing force by which they hope to lay claim to life eternal. From Owen's theological viewpoint, such a disastrous consequence must grow out of an overly confident perception of fallen humanity.

To be sure, Owen recognizes a "twofold" justification in Scripture, one by the works of the law, the other by grace through faith.[104] However, he believes that every reader of Scripture will see that these "ways" are obviously opposed: we must be justified by one or the other, but not by both.[105] In Owen's mind this biblical distinction differs from the one Rome makes, for one is justified either by the law or by grace through faith. There cannot be a mixture in which Christ does part of the work and the Christian does the rest. Either a person merits salvation himself, or he looks outside himself to another. To make his point clear, Owen argues that his opponents' view of a second justification "is no way applicable unto what the apostle James" is writing about: they have misunderstood and misapplied James, thus melding James's and Paul's teachings together inappropriately. Whereas Paul was primarily answering questions about how one might be accepted before God, James was addressing those who wrongly *presumed* justification, and so thought "there was nothing more needful unto them that they might be saved."[106]

---

102. Ibid.

103. Roman theology tends to make a distinction between sin and concupiscence. Accordingly, the justified still struggle with concupiscence, but technically "sin" is remitted while grace is infused. This doctrine makes little sense to a Protestant working with the presupposition that the believer can be *simul iustus et peccator*. Such confusion means that the theologians often talk past one another. See P. de Letter, "Justification," 81–88.

104. *Works* 5:139.

105. In his discussion on "Mosaic theology" and the rise of idolatry, Owen argues that this is what caused devastating consequences for Israel: they gave up the ideas of a gratuitous justification and eternal salvation based on the coming Messiah's merits and mediation ("Justificationem gratuitam et salutem aeternam Messiae meritis obtinendam et mediatione"), and instead sought a righteousness through works of the law and by observing ceremonially correct rituals; see *Works* 17:345 (*BT*, 487).

106. *Works* 5:387–88.

The confusion comes when people fail to realize that Paul and James are speaking of different kinds of *faith*: the one is alive (i.e., Paul), the other is dead (i.e., James). James is not writing about two kinds of justification; instead, he is focusing on a lifeless *faith* (i.e., the "one boasting of faith" is actually "dead"). Consequently, this Puritan believes that not even Rome can fairly understand James as supporting a second justification: "But he who hath the first justification, by the confession of our adversaries, hath a true, living faith, formed and enlivened by charity."[107] Owen also points out that both Paul and James, when discussing justification before God, refer to Abraham as their example of true faith.[108]

For Owen, Rome's mistake occurs when they mix their views of James and Paul together, creating a twofold justification that leaves the human with an insurmountable burden. If accepted, this view limits the value and effectiveness of Christ's work, making it only the basis for the infusion of a habit, after which humanity is left to rely on its own efforts to maintain and merit salvation.[109] The logical outcome of this construction of Roman theology is that the first justification is all of grace, but the second justification is all of human works. Christ's work is figured as incomplete, and human merit provides the necessary addition for final entrance into glory.

Making a more experiential argument, Owen contends that those who argue for a second justification, if they are truly led by the Spirit and are convinced of their own sin, will quickly see that their arguments cannot hold: "Their own personal righteousness will sink in their minds like water at the return of the tide, and leave nothing but mud and defilement behind them."[110] Ultimately, this distinction leaves people with no justification at all. Rome's difficulty is that their understanding of the first justification is weak and incomplete. It limits the efficacy of Christ's blood, and Owen contends that this does not do justice to Scripture's view of the atonement. Here we intentionally use the language of *limits* to show how traditionally negative presentations of Owen's view of the atonement fail to account for the positive nature of his argument.

We need briefly to review Owen's classic syllogism about the "limits" of the atonement. In 1647 Owen had written a treatise entitled *Salus Electorum, Sanguis Jesu, or The Death of Death in the Death of Christ*. Within this work Owen lays out a deceptively simple syllogism for the "Universalists" to answer:

107. Ibid., 5:142, 390–91.
108. Ibid., 5:142.
109. In fairness to their position, Roman theologians speak of "cooperation" with God rather than relying on oneself.
110. *Works* 5:141.

God imposed his wrath due unto, and Christ underwent the pains of hell
for, either
[A] all the sins of all . . . , or
[B] all the sins of some . . . , or
[C] some sins of all.[111]

Owen believes [C] means everyone would still have sins to answer for,
and the problem with [A] is that it implies everyone will be saved. Furthermore, Owen claims that one cannot look to the idea of "unbelief" as
a way out of this dilemma created by [A], since even unbelief, if a sin,
would itself be something for which Christ must have died, and thus no
punishment for unbelievers is possible. This leaves Owen opting for [B],
that Christ's death must cover all of the sins of whomever he died for,
and that must be understood as applying particularly to the elect.[112]

While Owen surely held a view of "limited atonement" as applied to
those for whom Christ died, he relentlessly argued for the *unlimited*
soteriological sufficiency of the atonement for believers. In other words,
Owen would never limit the atonement's effectiveness so that there were
still necessary requirements for believers to fulfill in order to enjoy eternal communion with God. Owen believed, as he explains in his work
Justification, that his Roman opponents had perpetuated such a "limit":
Christ's atonement pardoned sins initially and infused each of us with a
new habit, but this alone could not guarantee sinners a blessed eternal
life—a consequence that Owen thought greatly limited the atonement
in an unacceptable manner.

A correct understanding of the first justification would make a discussion of a second unnecessary. For the one true justification has many
consequences for believers:[113] (1) forgiveness of sin; (2) being made[114]
righteous; (3) being freed from condemnation, judgment, and death;
(4) being reconciled to God; (5) enjoying peace with God through his

111. For *The Death of Death*, see *Works* 10:139–428, and 10:173–74 for this quote.
112. For more on this debate, also see Owen's reply, primarily aimed at Richard Baxter,
in *Of the Death of Christ* (1650), in *Works* 10:429–79; cf. his later appendix from 1655, "Of
the Death of Christ, and of Justification," in *Works* 12:591–616; and *A Dissertation of Divine
Justice* (1653), in *Works* 10:481–624. For heated debate about Owen, and his relationship to
Calvin's view see, e.g., Clifford, *Atonement and Justification*, 82. Trueman, *Claims of Truth*,
has made a thorough response to Clifford's handling of Owen's view of the atonement. On
the debate about whether Calvin held to some version of "definite atonement," see Alan
C. Clifford, *Calvinus: Authentic Calvinism; A Clarification* (Norwich: Charenton Reformed
Publishing, 1996). For possibly the best study positing the opposing viewpoint, see Roger
Nicole, "John Calvin's View of the Extent of the Atonement," *WTJ* 47 (1985): 197–225.
113. See *Works* 5:142, for the list and Scripture references.
114. While the language "made" can sound Roman, Owen uses proof texts (Rom. 5:19;
10:4) that he believes clearly point to imputed, not inherent righteousness; see *Works* 5:57,
135, esp. 333–44.

love; (6) enjoying adoption and all of its privileges; (7) receiving a right and title unto the whole inheritance of glory; and (8) having eternal life as the consequence of all of the above.[115] If these are the results of justification, then there cannot be either a need or a possibility for a second justification. Thus Owen concludes: "Wherefore it is evident, that either the first justification overthrows the second, rendering it needless; or the second destroys the first, by taking away what essentially belongs unto it."[116]

Important anthropological questions regarding Christian experience arise from this view of two justifications. Both Roman and Protestant theologians agree that salvation without faith and the grace of God is impossible. Debate nevertheless arises, according to Owen, when the believer tries to live out his or her theology. How does one *remain* (or, in the language of the seventeenth century, *continue to be*) justified before God?

The Roman view asserts that justification initially occurs through the gift of a new *habitus* of *caritas*, whereby all of a person's sins are forgiven and that person is made holy. This initial justification occurs in baptism. Once in this state, the person must seek to maintain holiness through cooperation with God. Since believers sometimes yield to concupiscence or may commit a mortal sin, the sacraments serve as the means by which they are again renewed and made holy. Trent states: "Those who through sin have forfeited the received grace of justification, can *again be justified* when, moved by God, they exert themselves to obtain through the sacrament of penance the recovery, by the merits of Christ, of the grace lost."[117] To later Protestant readers like Owen, this seems to communicate that the burden ultimately remains upon believers to complete their justification lest they fall from the faith. We ought not to misunderstand Rome's view as asserting either that God does not assist believers to live without sin, or that God is unwilling to forgive sins.

---

115. In a private letter written by Thomas Barlow—the former tutor and friend of Owen—written in 1678 (one year after Owen's book appeared), an uncanny similarity is apparent. Thomas Barlow, *Two Letters . . . Concerning Justification by Faith Only* (London: Thomas Parkhurst, 1701), 33–34, writes:

> By Faith . . . we receive Christ, and are made the sons of God [cf. Owen #6].
> By Faith Christ lives in us, and we live [cf. #2?].
> By Faith we receive remission of all our sins [cf. #1]
> and freedom from condemnation [cf. #3]
> and justification [cf. #4].
> By faith we receive the Holy Spirit [cf. #7?]
> and peace with God [cf. #5]
> and eternal life [cf. #8].

116. *Works* 5:143.
117. *Council of Trent*, trans. Schroeder, 39: sixth session, chap. 14, emphasis added.

For this reason Christ instituted the church as the primary means for the Christian to experience forgiveness of sins and their continuation in justification (i.e., baptism and penance). Rome maintains, however, that the believer should never "boast of . . . [having] confidence and certainty of the remission of sins." Believers must recognize that "God does not forsake those who have been once justified by His grace, *unless He be first forsaken by them.*"[118]

Owen opposes what he perceives to be the erroneous conclusions of the Roman doctrine. The believer can only continue to be "justified" because of the person and work of Christ; at this point his Roman opponents would agree. In his life, death, and resurrection, the incarnate Christ has made the justified life imaginable. Significantly for Owen, Christ not only makes the forgiveness of sins possible, but also the imputation of righteousness. This forensic emphasis constructs justification as completely dependent upon God, which has implications for living out the Christian experience. Since God is the one who justifies, "the continuation of our justification is his act also."[119] The frail human finds security not in him- or herself, but in God's character (i.e., immutability and faithfulness), the "efficacy of his grace," in the complete satisfaction accomplished in the "propitiation of Christ," in Christ's continued heavenly intercession, and in the "irrevocable grant" of the Holy Spirit to believers. These objective realities ground a Christian's confidence that one will persevere to the end. It may be fair to summarize Owen's massive volume (over 650 pages) *The Doctrine of the Saints' Perseverance* (1654) as stressing that the Christian's ultimate comfort of assurance comes primarily from *God's* perseverance rather than his or her own.[120] Though Owen does not hesitate to call the Christian to righteous living, he nevertheless believes that the only means by which a person can continue to be acceptable before God must come from God alone. Owen is far too skeptical of human potential ever to trust in willpower as a path to righteous Christian living. Sanctification is as much an act of God's grace toward the sinner as is one's justification, a point sometimes confused by other Protestants.[121]

118. Ibid., 35, 37, emphasis added.
119. *Works* 5:147–48.
120. Ibid., 11. In this work Owen spends considerable time focusing his readers' attention on God's immutability, the significance of the mediation and intercession of Jesus Christ, and the reality of the indwelling of the Spirit.
121. Confusion at this point manifests itself in the preaching and writings of those who represent the "holy living" group, as represented by Jeremy Taylor (1613–1667). Cf. Allison, *Rise of Moralism*, 63–95. Taylor's doctrinal and devotional writings are compiled in *The Whole Works with a Life of the Author and a Critical Examination of His Writings*, 15 vols. (London: C. & J. Rivington, 1828).

Given the above background, Owen contends that continuing securely in the justified life comes solely through the person and work of Christ and not from personal holiness. Yet, how does the Christian deal with sins committed since original justification? This is the question that Owen thinks reveals a major difference between how Rome and the Protestants work out their doctrines of justification. According to Owen, we must never plead our own righteousness. On this point he believes the Catholic theologians appear weakest, since their theology seems inconsistent with their practice.

Although Owen may have oversimplified his opponents' position by imposing his Protestant model upon Roman theologians, for our purposes we must concentrate on the anthroposensitive method of Owen's work. Three arguments show how he uses this method to oppose Rome's claim that the believer's obedience plays even a minor role in securing and maintaining his or her justification before God.

First, Christian experience testifies against such claims of personal vindication. Owen wonders if any true believers would ask for their sins to be forgiven because of their own righteousness: "Do they [Roman theologians] leave the prayer of the publican, and betake themselves unto that of the Pharisee?"[122] For Owen, Christian experience strongly testifies against any hope for continuation in a justified state apart from the external righteousness of Christ received solely by faith.

Second, Owen appeals to Scripture, particularly to 1 John 2:1–2: "These things write I unto you, that ye sin not. And if any man sin, we have an advocate with the Father, Jesus Christ the righteous: and he is the propitiation for our sins." From this Owen deduces that believers are not to sin, while recognizing that tragically all Christians inevitably do. So how does the apostle John deal with this crisis? Again Owen emphasizes Christ's priestly office as both sacrifice and intercessor. Christ

---

122. *Works* 5:148. Earlier English Protestant writers often used this type of argument; obviously their Roman opponents would claim this as a gross misrepresentation of their view. E.g., John Davenant, *A Treatise on Justification, or, The Disputatio de Justinita habituali et actuali*, trans. Josiah Allport, 2 vols. (1631; repr., London: Hamilton, Adams, 1844), 1:228, argues that no Catholic theologian speaks "of their own inherent righteousness before the Divine tribunal, but fly full of fear to the mercy and acceptance of God in Christ. But if they were willing to stand by their doctrine, they must either depend upon this formal cause, or give up all hope of salvation. . . . Let us hear how little they attribute to this inherent righteousness, which they speak, not in a spirit of contention, but under a conviction of conscience." Barlow makes the same point to his fellow Anglican opponent: "Sir, whatever opinion we may have (at present) of justification by our good works, and our continuation of that justice by them; yet when we shall appear, (as one day we must) at the dreadful tribunal of our just god; we shall (I believe) be of Bellarmines opinion, (who had been earnest for justification by works) and say as (upon more serious and second thoughts) he did, Propter presentis vitæ incertitudinem, tutissimum est, in solo Christo recumbere, etc." (*Two Letters*, 76; cf. chap. 5n39).

not only offers himself in the believer's stead, but also empowers the believer through his continual heavenly prayers. Christ proves to be the right object of faith both initially and continually in the Christian's experience. "So our whole progress in our justified estate, in all the degrees of it, is ascribed unto faith alone."[123] "Duties" serve the Christian, not for justification, but to help keep him or her "preserved" from "those things which are contrary unto" justification. In other words, although the Christian's actions are a means for healthy spirituality, they never provide the grounding of one's initial or continued acceptance before God.[124] From here Owen cites abundant scriptural references that he thinks demonstrate how Christ's atonement secures one's justification, which is received through faith.[125]

Lest one think that Owen completely misrepresents his Roman opponents regarding the relationship between Christ and one's "second justification," we must clarify a few things regarding this second point. Owen recognizes that some theologians from the "Roman school" maintain a role for Christ's merits even beyond a person's first justification. These theologians would not claim that God first justifies a person, and then, once initially justified, abandons the believer to his or her own efforts. Referring to Gabriel Vásquez as an example, Owen points out how these theologians want to see God's grace and Christ's merit as having application on a person's second justification. Here the medieval idea of *facere quod in se est* (to do what is in one) manifests itself. Humanity's natural powers are never enough to achieve perfect righteousness while on earth, a fact that does not escape God's notice. Therefore each believer must simply do his or her best. Although the believer's merits, per se, are weak and imperfect, God's grace makes up the difference. Owen writes: "For it is on the account of the righteousness of Christ, they [the Roman school] say, that our own works, or imperfect obedience, is so accepted with God, as that the continuation of our justification depends thereon."[126] In other words, his opponents would think it unfair to claim that their position makes one's continual state of justification solely dependent upon works, for *God* makes a person's works acceptable—*Christ* makes up the deficiency. This distinction makes no substantial difference to Owen.

In Owen's doctrine, justification includes both "absolute justification" and the continuation of justification. To allow that the sinner's works

---

123. *Works* 5:149. Contra *Council of Trent*, trans. Schroeder, 37: "Wherefore, no one ought to flatter himself with faith alone thinking that by faith alone he is made an heir and will obtain the inheritance, even though he suffer not with Christ."

124. Cf. *Council of Trent*, trans. Schroeder, 39.

125. E.g., Rom. 1:17; Gal. 2:20–21; Heb. 10:38–39; see *Works* 5:150.

126. *Works* 5:151.

have *any* role in justification contradicts the biblical model and Christian experience. Thus, Paul in Romans 5:1–3 speaks of how the Christian gains access to God (absolute justification), how he or she remains standing in this experience of grace (continuation), and finally, how the believer "glories" in this position (with "assurance of that continuation"). Significantly, "all these [Paul] ascribeth equally unto faith, without the intermixture of any other cause or condition."[127]

Third, Owen appeals to the experience of believers in Scripture as representatives that testify to his claims regarding justification and faith. Abraham and David serve as his two examples. Just as Abraham is absolutely justified by his faith initially, his continued justification likewise results from his faith. Similarly, David's justification depends completely on his faith rather than on his works.[128]

Concluding this detailed discussion regarding "two justifications," Owen holds that there is "but one justification, . . . and that is the justification of an ungodly person by faith."[129] He believes that a biblical and experiential disaster results from holding any other causes for a second justification than that which caused the first. In his view, those who maintain a distinction between a first and second justification inevitably diminish the person and work of Christ. The complications introduced by such a distinction lead once again to confusion of the simple faith in Christ and a depreciation of his atoning work.

Imputation: Receiving the Benefits of Christ

Owen presents his view of imputation by carefully diagramming his position in contrast to the straw men presented by his opponents—who are sometimes Protestants.[130] First, he believes that imputation *does not* mean to judge or esteem people to be righteous "who truly and really

127. Ibid.
128. Noticeably Owen does not here refer to James 2:24, which seems to claim that Abraham was justified by works. The reader must wait for Owen's extensive analysis of this apparent contradiction in chap. 20 of *Justification*.
129. *Works* 5:152.
130. E.g., Thomas Hotchkis, *A Discourse concerning the Imputation of Christ's righteousness to us, and our sins to him* . . . (London: Walter Kettilby, 1675), 142. In this work Hotchkis attacks Owen's view of the imputation of Christ's righteousness and accuses Owen of antinomianism. Hotchkis is here attacking Owen's book *Of Communion* (in *Works* 2:1–274), published in 1657. After Owen's book *Justification* (in *Works* 5:1–400) was published in 1677, Hotchkis wrote *A Postscript, Containing the Authors Vindication of Himself and the Doctrine from the Imputations of Dr. John Owen* (London: Walter Kettilby, 1678), which reads as a feisty sample of seventeenth-century theological mudslinging.

are not so."[131] Here he is trying to counter the "Papists" who "cry out *'ad ravim'* [till they are hoarse] that we affirm God to esteem them to be righteous who are wicked, sinful, and polluted."[132] Second, Owen *does not* think that God can simply declare a person to be righteous, as if the words alone would change the actual state of affairs. Common caricatures occur at this point, especially with theologians less attentive than Owen. In carelessness they seem to present God as completely arbitrary, pronouncing the wicked to be holy for no reason other than the random whims of the Divine. According to Owen, "God declares no man to be righteous but him who is so." This statement begs the question of how the unrighteous can ever change their standing before God. If God cannot say the words and make it so, what hope is there for people, even repentant people, to escape their sinful lapses?

Before answering such questions, Owen makes one more clarification, specifically and carefully showing his disagreement with Rome. Imputation of righteousness, he believes, "is not the transmission or transfusion of the righteousness of another into them that are to be justified, that they should become perfectly and inherently righteous thereby; for it is impossible that the righteousness of one should be transfused into another, to *become his subjectively and inherently*."[133] Here Owen is resisting the scholastic conception of the infusion of habitual grace whereby believers become inherently righteous. Even so, he argues elsewhere that while forgiveness does allow a person to be "not guilty," that alone is insufficient grounds for entrance into eternal life: "We must also be actually righteous." Not only must sin be dealt with, but "all righteousness is to be fulfilled."[134] The negative imputation of sins is necessary, but the imputation of Christ's righteousness to believers is equally important.[135]

Given these clarifications, Owen presents a *positive* conception of imputation, and in so doing we see his guiding thesis for how he develops this doctrine through to the end of the book *Justification*.

> Imputation is an act of God "ex mea gratia,"—of his mere love and grace; whereby, on the consideration of the mediation of Christ, he makes an effectual grant and donation of a true, real, perfect righteousness, even

131. For this discussion, see *Works* 5:173.
132. Ibid.
133. Ibid., emphasis added.
134. Ibid., 2:104–5; cf. 2:170: "The old quarrel may be laid aside, and yet no new friendship begun; we may be not sinners, and yet not be so far righteous as to have a right to the kingdom of heaven."
135. Cf. ibid., 9:597–99, a unique sacramental discourse preached on this theme sometime in late 1675 or early 1676, the same period when Owen's work on justification is either being written, or had recently been completed and was at the publisher.

that of Christ himself, unto all that do believe; and accounting it as theirs, on his own gracious act, both absolves them from sin and granteth them right and title unto eternal life.[136]

To understand this statement, one needs to appreciate Owen's heightened view of the mystical union between the believer and Christ.[137] C. F. Allison rightly asserts that "Owen places more explicit emphasis on the union with Christ than even [George] Downame does, and perhaps more than anyone of the period with the exception of John Donne."[138] This union produces the imputation of believers' sins to Christ. As recognized throughout our study, Owen continually emphasizes the *person* of Christ since he is the means of reconciling the divine and human. When it comes to imputation, Owen again finds himself stressing Christ's person, only here he does so in terms of the mystical union that exists between Christ and his church. The means by which this union is accomplished is unquestionably the "uniting efficacy of the Holy Spirit."[139] First Corinthians 12:12–13 refers to Christ as the head and believers as the various members of that same person. Christ is not the head of one body while Christians are the limbs of another; rather, Christ and believers are inexplicably united.[140] Here we sense echoes of Calvin and Luther's conception of the "wondrous exchange" whereby, because of the union between Christ and believers, "Christ takes upon Himself what is ours, and transfers to us what is His own."[141]

Only this understanding of union with Christ can explain Owen's development of justification, both positively and negatively. Since believers are part of the very "body" of Christ, their sins can be imputed to him; likewise,

136. Ibid., 5:173.

137. For an excellent overview of Owen's understanding of "Union with Christ: The Channel of Grace," see Randall C. Gleason, *John Calvin and John Owen on Mortification: A Comparative Study in Reformed Spirituality*, Studies in Church History 3 (New York: Peter Lang, 1995), 89–95. For a wonderful survey of how Puritan theologians actively employ the idea of union with God to inform their devotional experiences, see Jean Dorothy Williams, "The Puritan Quest for Enjoyment of God: An Analysis of the Theological and Devotional Writings of Puritans in Seventeenth-Century England" (PhD diss., University of Melbourne, 1997), 65–75, 91.

138. Allison, *Rise of Moralism*, 175.

139. *Works* 5:176.

140. Ibid. In his LC and GC (1648), Owen claims that the first "privilege of believers" is "union with Christ," followed by five others, which include adoption, communion of saints, and so on. See *Works* 1:469, 489.

141. Ronald S. Wallace, *Calvin's Doctrine of the Word and Sacrament* (Edinburgh: Scottish Academic Press, 1995), 147. Cf. B. A. Gerrish's study of the "happy exchange" in Luther and Calvin, "Atonement and 'Saving Faith,'" *TT* 17, no. 2 (1960): 181–91. Gerrish claims that while the question of how the exchange takes place is unclear, what is clear for both is what is exchanged: "Christ's righteousness is exchanged for the believer's sin" (182).

his righteousness can be imputed to them. Having stated his position, Owen seeks historical validation. Although Reformers like Calvin—with their heavy emphasis on union—would be a rich source for arguing his point, Owen instead turns to patristic authors as his primary references.[142] In light of contemporary scholarship's tendency to argue that the doctrine of imputation largely grew out of the Reformation, Owen's use of the patristics is fascinating.[143] He quotes from a sermon of Leo, an epistle of Augustine, as well as further testimonies from Irenaeus, Origen, Cyprian, and Athanasius. Owen uses these quotations to investigate the special mystical connection between Christ and the church, whereby through the Spirit the two are "one mystical person." For example, Augustine writes: "We hear the voice of the body from the mouth of the head. The church suffered in him when he suffered for the church; as he suffers in the church when the church suffereth for him."[144] With the incarnation, Christ not only identifies with believers but also unites himself by his Spirit to them, thus making imputation possible.

Owen does not view this teaching (imputation) as new; rather, he believes the ancient authors affirm the implications of this doctrine, even if they did not clothe it in the sixteenth-century Reformation language of imputation. To demonstrate this, Owen looks to a time before Augustine to examine the Greek father Irenaeus's view of recapitulation: "Christ has summed up in himself all peoples scattered abroad since Adam, the source of human beings. Therefore, Paul called Adam himself a type of the one to come."[145] The quote from Origen, which Owen admits is

142. When debating the imputation of Christ's righteousness elsewhere, Owen clearly maintains that he has the "testimony of Scripture" and "the judgement of the catholic church of Christ on my side" (*Works* 2:361). Therefore he views his opponent, William Sherlock, as being the theological novice.

143. E.g., Alister McGrath, *Iustitia Dei*, argues that while the Reformation represents a rediscovery of Augustinian theology, the Reformers' *use* of Augustine is new: "The most accurate description of the doctrines of justification associated with the Reformed and Lutheran churches from 1530 onward is that they represent a radically new interpretation of the Pauline concept of 'imputed righteousness' set within an Augustinian soteriological framework" (189); cf. Peter Toon, *Justification and Sanctification* (London: Marshall Morgan & Scott, 1983). While Toon may recognize the nonimputation of sin in pre-Reformation thought (e.g., 50), he argues against any traces of a positive imputation of righteousness. For an approach which sees more continuity between the early fathers and the Reformation view, see Thomas C. Oden, ed. *The Justification Reader* (Grand Rapids: Eerdmans, 2002).

144. *Works* 5:176. Here Owen says he is quoting from Augustine, *Epistles* 120, "Ad Honoratum": "Audimus vocem corporis ex ore capitis. Ecclesia in illo patienbatur, quando pro ecclesia patiebatur, etc." However, this paraphrase is almost certainly coming from *De Gratia Novi Testamenti Liber, Seu Epistola CXL*, in *PL*, col. 0545.

145. "Christus omnes gentes exinde ab Adam dispersas, et generationem hominum in semet ipso recapitulatus est; unde a Paulo typus futuri dictus est ipse Adam" (*Works* 5:176).

enigmatic, claims that the soul of the first Adam was the soul of Christ: this enables one to deduce the idea of mystical relations. In Owen's mind, with mystical relations comes the possibility for imputation. The theme that develops from these chosen quotations is Christ's unique relationship to believers, especially in terms of suffering. So Cyprian adds, "He bare [= bore] us"—to which Owen interestingly adds a clarification for his readers, "or suffered in our *person*"—"when he bare our sins."[146]

Owen finds in Eusebius the best summation of what he himself wants to argue for. After quoting eighteen lines of Eusebius in Greek, Owen—in a somewhat unusual gesture—translates the entire selection for his reader. He does not want anyone to miss the essence of what this early father says, for Owen believes his "present discourse is declared fully therein." This type of argument and appeal was common among post-Reformation Reformed scholastics, who wanted to emphasize the catholicity of their teaching: theological novelty rarely motivates Owen.

In this selection, Eusebius reiterates the unique relationship between Christ and his body.[147] Christ is able to take on the sins of others because they are part of his body. Since our overarching concern remains anthropology, we especially stress the connection that Eusebius—and Owen through him—draws between the incarnation and the taking on of sin (imputation of sin according to Owen). Jesus took the form of a servant (cf. Phil. 2:7), in order to "be joined unto the common habitation of us all in the same nature." As God incarnate, Jesus was mysteriously able to take not only other humans' "sorrows," but also the "labors of the suffering members on him." God, it appears, could not have accomplished this if he did not first condescend through the incarnation. Again, this resembles Anselm's logic that humanity owed a debt, which only a God-Man could pay. Through his incarnation, Jesus shatters this difficulty by living "according to the laws of humanity," by which he "bare our sorrow and labour for us."[148] Owen goes so far as to say that this union makes Christ and his church one person, and that this must ground any discussion of the imputation of sins, and by implication, the imputation of righteousness.

Owen acknowledges that many will raise questions about the meaning of "person" as employed here.[149] Wanting to avoid disputes about

---

Owen refers to Irenaeus [*Against Heresies*] 3.33, but current editions show book 3 with only 25 chapters; more recent editions have the quoted passage in 3.22.3, as in *ANF* 1:455.

146. "Nos omnes portabat Christus; qui et peccata nostra portabat" (*Works* 5:176–77, emphasis added). See Cyprian, *Epistles* 62.13, in *ANF* 5:362. Owen cites Athanasius as simply saying, "We suffered in him."

147. For Eusebius, see his *Demonstratio evangelica* 10.1.

148. *Works* 5:177.

149. Ibid., 5:178–79.

personhood in the categories of his day (such as natural, legal, political, civil), he encourages his readers to accept mystical language. He relies on diverse biblical imagery that seems to support such usage (e.g., John 15:1–2; Rom. 5:12; 1 Cor. 12:12; Eph. 4:15; 5:25–32; Col. 2:19). These proof texts approach the idea from a variety of perspectives, including the relationship between a husband and wife, between the head and the rest of the body, and even between a vine and its branches. Difficulties arise when union with Christ becomes limited to one of the analogies. Thus, Owen guards the flexibility of this mystical language and spends considerable time developing the causes and grounds for such a union.[150]

While related, the imputation of human sins to Christ and the imputation of his righteousness to believers are not identical in nature. In fact, theological disaster results if one takes them to be so. According to Owen, the great difference between the two imputations is that Christ "cannot in the same manner be said to be made a sinner by the one as we are made righteous by the other."[151] This comes from Owen's concept of the holiness and justice of God. If Christ takes upon himself the sin of humanity forever, never actually ridding both the world and himself of it, then *he* could no longer enjoy communion with the Father since God cannot be in the presence of sin. To bar Christ from the presence of the Father is to divide the Triune God—an unthinkable proposition. While believers find security in the imputed righteousness of Christ, which remains theirs forever, "our sin was imputed unto him only for a season, not absolutely." Even as the incarnation was necessary for God to take the sins of humanity unto himself, it was by means of the cross (Owen uses Pauline language of becoming a "curse for us," Gal. 3:13) that sins were finally dealt with.[152] From this point one might expect Owen to move forward to how the resurrection and ascension affected the world, but this is not the case. Instead, he begins another chapter, once again maneuvering his way through the various views of justification.

150. For how Owen accomplishes this, see esp. ibid., 5:179–205. He highlights three causes: (1) The "spring" of this union is grounded in the "eternal compact" that took place between the Father and the Son and is made "effectual by the Holy Spirit" regarding the "recovery and salvation of mankind." (2) The human nature that Jesus thus had to assume was "predestined unto grace and glory." (3) This "grace and glory" included what was (a) "peculiar unto himself" and (b) "communicated, by and through him, unto the church." It is in this context that he becomes involved in a lengthy discussion of surety and covenant theology. See Wong, "Covenant Theology," 234ff., 373–76.

151. *Works* 5:203.

152. Ibid., 5:204, from Gal. 3:13–14. Cf. *Works* 20:410 (BE 19:410): God "hath found out to exercise grace and satisfy justice at the same time, in and by the same person. Sin shall be punished, all sin, yet grace exercised; sinners shall be saved, yet justice exalted;—all in the cross of Christ."

Since Owen's extended account of imputation (and all of the caveats that go with it) moves well beyond the scope of our study, we conclude by briefly identifying another way in which he relates the person of Christ to imputation.[153] Here he uses the language of "person" to speak less about mystical union and more about the individual person Jesus Christ, arguing that the imputation of Christ's righteousness to us depends on the union between the human and divine natures in Christ. This discussion occurs within the context of Owen's response to Socinus, who claims that Christ cannot impute his righteousness to others.[154] Socinus objects to the idea of imputation of righteousness on the grounds that all of Christ's obedience was necessary and obligatory for himself.[155] Consequently, Christ's personal obedience could not be imputed unto others.[156] Owen responds by arguing that Christ's obedience must be understood in terms of his role as the "mediator of the covenant," so that Christ's obedience was "of his person." Deciphering this somewhat strange language requires close analysis.

Owen's incarnational theology gives him categories with which he can address the problem raised by Socinus. Although Socinus denies the divine nature of Jesus before the resurrection, Owen fully affirms both the divine and human natures of Christ, and therefore that Jesus was both (1) fully obedient unto the law as required of all humanity and yet (2) still able to "communicate" his righteousness to others on account of the unique relationship between his two natures.[157] Thus, Jesus's obedience was "performed in the human nature; but the *person* of Christ was he that performed it." Owen says:

> As in the person of a man, some of his acts, as to the immediate principle of operation, are acts of the body, and some are so of the soul; yet, in their performance and accomplishment, are they the acts of the *person*: so the acts of Christ in his mediation, as to their ἐνεργήματα, or immediate

153. Owen spends the rest of the treatise *Justification* dealing with objections to imputation, providing a lengthy biblical exposition of every passage that he believes relates to this topic, and finally concluding with an attempt to explain the apparent differences between Paul and James regarding justification.

154. To follow the argument, see *Works* 5:251–75.

155. Cf. RC, 5.8; available in *The Racovian Catechism*, ed. Thomas Rees (1609; repr., London: Longman, Hurst, Rees, Orme & Brown, 1818), 315.

156. Cf. *Works* 19:196–97 (BE 18:196–97), where Owen succinctly compares his understanding of Christ's priestly work of oblation with that of Socinus, as in his *De Jesu Christo Servatore* (1594). See Alan W. Gomes, "*De Jesu Christo Servatore*: Faustus Socinus on the Satisfaction of Christ," *WTJ* 55 (1993): 209–31.

157. Ultimately, however, this argument would have meant little to Socinus since he denies the divine nature of the pre-risen Jesus. The chasm between Owen and Socinus can be traced to their different approaches to Scripture, with Socinus governed by the hermeneutics of rationalism and Owen by the boundaries of classic orthodoxy.

operation, were the actings of his distinct natures,—some of the divine and some of the human, immediately; but as unto their ἀποτελέσματα, and the perfecting efficacy of them, they were the acts of his *whole person*.[158]

Again we see that the *person* of Christ includes both his divine and human natures. Following classic orthodox formulations, Owen maintains unity while making distinctions. He answers Socinus by arguing both that the "obedience of Christ" was truly the "obedience of the Son of God," and also that "the Son of God was never absolutely made ὑπὸ νόμον" (under the law). In other words, because of the relationship between the divine and human natures, Jesus transcends the normal limitations assumed by personhood. Jesus's human nature was certainly under the law, but his divine nature was never "formally" under it, resulting in a technical need to clarify the distinction between *nature* and *person*. Jesus was obedient as one who "never was, nor ever could absolutely be, made under the law in his whole person; for the divine nature cannot be subjected unto the work of its own, such as the law is, nor can it have an authoritative, commanding power over it."[159] Affirming both the unity and distinctiveness of the natures in the one person, Owen claims that imputed righteousness is "not the obedience of the human nature abstractedly, however performed in and by the human nature; but the obedience of the person of the Son of God," whose "whole person was not obliged" under the law. The two natures of Christ make it impossible for his "whole person" to be made under the law. Therefore, since his person (having two natures) was not under the law and because he did not owe "obedience for himself," Jesus *alone* was able to uniquely apply his obedience to others in order to reconcile them to God.[160] Arguing in a very Anselmian fashion, Owen elsewhere concludes: "Had he not been man, he could not have suffered,—had he not been God, his suffering could not have availed either himself or us; . . . the suffering of a mere man could not bear any proportion to that which in any respect was infinite."[161] Additionally, Owen says the obedience of Jesus was not simply a "private" matter, for Christ functioned as a "public person."[162]

158. *Works* 5:255, emphasis added.

159. Ibid., 5:256.

160. This idea relates to Owen's conception of surety: he emphatically argues that God did not need a surety toward humanity, but humanity needed a surety with God. Christ alone voluntarily becomes that surety. Cf. Thomas Jacomb, *Several Sermons Preach'd on . . . the Epistle to the Romans . . .* (London: M. Pitt, R. Chiswell, & J. Robinson, 1672), 85: "You are in Christ, not only as the members in the head (which is your Mystical Union), but as the Debtor in the Surety (which is your Legal Union)." W. Sherlock, *Union and Communion*, 1st ed. (1674), 287–88, 290, rejects such language of surety.

161. *Works* 2:67.

162. Ibid., 5:260–61; cf. 2:177–80.

By this Owen means that Jesus's obedience needs to be viewed in light of his unique role as mediator between God and humanity. The federal theology of seventeenth-century Reformed thought manifests itself here. Whereas Socinus appears to believe that Jesus's atonement was for no one but himself, and thus a *private* matter, Owen argues that Jesus functions as the *public* mediator whose obedience was for others and not for himself.

All of Jesus's obedience takes place in "our human nature," and this was possible only by the voluntary act of Christ. The Second Person of the Trinity assumed human nature with a design to redeem the church. Humanity was loved by the Triune God, who made provision for fallen creation through the incarnation.[163]

Conclusion

Throughout this chapter we have displayed the anthroposensitivity in Owen's theological method and the realism of his results as he constructs his doctrine of justification in both its subjective and objective aspects.

On the subjective side, Owen continually acknowledges the reality of human guilt, anxiety, and faithlessness. Since he views the fall as a devastating event for human history, he is fundamentally a pessimist regarding postlapsarian human nature. Thus Owen concludes that faith and obedience are a human *response* to God, rather than human initiatives that affect God. Further, this human response is holistic, not merely willpower or mental assent, for God stirs the whole person and requires a whole-souled response. Since Owen is not afraid to address the subjective elements of human responses and experience throughout his work, the results are not simply academic: they are purposefully pastoral.

On the objective side, Owen stresses the implications of the person and work of Christ for believers. Christ assumed human nature; as the Son of God he functioned as the great high priest for humanity; and, ultimately, he alone made human reconciliation with God secure. Fallen people are unable to contribute to their justification, but they must rest solely on the accomplished work of Christ—a truth that Owen thinks will produce humble and grateful obedience to the Triune God.

These subjective and objective principles guide the whole of his discussion, whether he is addressing the question of double justification or the plausibility of imputation. This chapter serves to illustrate how

163. Here in ibid., 5:257, Owen addresses the old scholastic question about whether the incarnation would have occurred if humanity had not sinned.

two consistent concerns influence Owen's methodology: anthropological (how humanity can have communion with God) and christological (how Christ provides the bridge between God and humanity). This pattern continues throughout the rest of his corpus. With this background we are now in a position to turn our attention to Owen's concept of the believer's communion with the Triune God.

COMMUNION WITH THE TRIUNE GOD

God's Being and Action Informing Human Response

> Absolutely nothing worthwhile for the practical life can be made out of the doctrine of the Trinity.
>
> Immanuel Kant, *Der Streit der Facultäten*

> The infinite disparity that is between God and man, made the great philosopher [Aristotle] conclude that there could be no friendship between them. Some distance in the persons holding friendship he could allow, nor could [he] exactly determine the bounds and extent thereof; but that between God and man, in his apprehension, left no place for [friendship].
>
> John Owen[1]

> The LORD thy God in the midst of thee is mighty; he will save, he will rejoice over thee with joy; he will rest in his love, he will joy over thee with singing.
>
> Zephaniah 3:17

Introduction

It has always been a struggle for theologians to construct an orthodox conception of the Trinity that is anything other than a series of confus-

---

1. Cf. Aristotle *EN* 8.7 (p. 482): "When one party is removed to a great distance, as God is, the possibility of friendship ceases."

ing abstractions. If the Trinity is central to the Christian religion, why does it often appear irrelevant to the Christian life? In the latter half of the twentieth century, Karl Rahner (1904–84) represented a growing concern among contemporary theologians regarding the importance of the Trinity: "Its function in the whole dogmatic construction is not clearly perceived. It is as though this mystery has been revealed for its own sake, and that even after it has been made known to us, it remains, as a reality, locked up within itself. We make statements about it, but as a reality it has nothing to do with us at all."[2] He concludes that this leads to the common misunderstanding that the best we can do is to learn "something 'about it' through revelation," instead of grasping a connection between the Trinity and humanity, since after all the Trinity "is a mystery of salvation."[3] Colin E. Gunton has likewise observed that trinitarian theology understandably fell into disrepute because it failed "to be the living heart of worship and life." This disaster stems from a neglect of right theological reflection, which will necessarily yield practical implications.[4] Finally, in recent observations Thomas Weinandy looks further into why this problem has persisted. He asserts that theologians of the past often de-emphasized the distinct personalities and roles of the three persons. As a result, countless congregants received the common impression that Christians "simply worship and relate to the undifferentiated Godhead," a problem particularly apparent in the West with its tendency to stress the one substance while neglecting the Trinity of persons.[5]

Given this contemporary discussion, looking back to John Owen's insistent application of trinitarian theology to the believer's life may prove of interest not only to historians, but also to systematic theologians. Owen's description of communion with the Triune God offers insights into the relevance of trinitarian theology for the life of the church and human experience. By following the structure and argument of one of Owen's devotional works, we hope to demonstrate his anthroposensitivity and its theoretical and practical implications throughout his trinitarian reflections.

In 1657 Owen wrote a treatise exploring how a believer can have a positive and active relationship with the Triune God, titled *Of Communion with God the Father, Son, and Holy Ghost, Each Person Distinctly, In Love, Grace, and Consolation; or, The Saints' Fellowship with the Father,*

2. Karl Rahner, *The Trinity*, trans. Joseph Donceel (London: Burns & Oates, 1970), 14.

3. Ibid., 14, 21.

4. Gunton, *Trinitarian Theology*, 163.

5. Thomas Weinandy, *The Father's Spirit of Sonship: Reconceiving the Trinity* (Edinburgh: T&T Clark, 1995), 4, 56.

Son, and Holy Ghost Unfolded.[6] When other writers have discussed this work, it has usually been presented for a popular readership (e.g., Packer and Ferguson) or as a means to discuss a more narrowly defined topic (as briefly in Beeke's discussion of assurance). Although Trueman's recent study covers Owen's trinitarian theology extensively, he only mentions this work on two occasions, leaving ample room for further treatment.[7]

This treatise by Owen uniquely fills in the details of Owen's conception of renewed relations between God and humanity. After laying the groundwork for understanding Owen's interaction with philosophers regarding the possibility of relations between the divine and human, we will look at his definition of communion and its historical context. Since for Owen communion with God is distinctly trinitarian, we also outline his answer as to how a believer approaches the one Triune God. We then follow in detail Owen's development of distinct communion with the Father, Son, and Holy Spirit. In each section we observe what Owen highlights concerning the divine persons and how he encourages believers to respond appropriately. In the end we see that Owen's work resolutely tries to help his readers progress beyond the common human fears of divine anger and distance, and move into a peaceful and empowering relationship with their Triune God.

Laying the Groundwork

The Impossible Becomes Possible

How is any form of personal communion between God and humanity possible? By asking and answering this question yet again, and in some detail, Owen's anthroposensitive method combines deep theological reflection with personal affective application. Although discussions of the Trinity can become abstract and philosophical,[8] Owen gives his readers

6. *Works* 2:1–274. For a newly edited version of this classic work, see John Owen, *Communion with the Triune God*, ed. Kelly M. Kapic and Justin Taylor (Wheaton: Crossway Books, forthcoming).

7. Trueman, *Claims of Truth*, 98, 184. Despite its title, "Communion with Christ: An Exposition and Comparison of the Doctrine of Union and Communion with Christ in Calvin and the English Puritans," Won's study contains surprisingly little interaction with this particular text from Owen's corpus (266–69). Won is primarily interested in how Owen interprets the Song of Songs. For a brief survey of this work by Owen, see Kelly M. Kapic, "Communion with God by John Owen (1616–1683)," in *The Devoted Life: An Invitation to the Puritan Classics*, ed. Kelly M. Kapic and Randall C. Gleason (Downers Grove, IL: InterVarsity, 2004), 167–82.

8. By the end of the seventeenth century, this tendency becomes more apparent, especially among the many mathematicians who wrote about the Trinity. E.g., Isaac Bar-

practical insights for using these profound truths to inform their relations with the Triune God.

As we have recognized (in chap. 4) regarding his book *The Doctrine of Justification by Faith*, Owen's work commonly begins with his presuppositions regarding the fallen human condition. Persons who remain in the "natural" state into which they were born are at odds with God, not only alienated from God, but also showing enmity toward their Creator.[9] Because of the fall, each person lives in a state of impotency, unable—in fact, not even desiring—to please or even respond to God.[10] There is no aspect of humanity untouched by sin: each one, like the leper, receives the graphic label "unclean."[11] Owen's assertion of humanity's present condition pushes the reader to look beyond the self to God.

Such an understanding of one's plight often comes from self-exploration, which may pave the way for true self-knowledge. Owen shows the contradictory nature of self-exploration: it is only in the context of learning also about the God who created humanity that one can rightly learn about oneself. Those who do recognize that something is wrong with them often try to "disentangle the soul" through means like literature and learning—both of which emerged only after the fall.[12] Owen recognizes that God has given a conscience, the law, and ultimately Christ to expose humanity's condition.[13] Each of these divine gifts ought to drive people to despair of themselves and to rely on God. In Owen's thought, self-examination can serve as a way to turn people back to Christ, making the reestablishment of a positive relationship with the Triune God possible.[14] Even so, self-knowledge alone, without an appreciation of divine action, remains insufficient to establish communion.

Because of the vast distance between the two parties, no human in his or her natural condition can experience "walking with God." Even Aristotle believed that the obvious "infinite disparity" between God and humanity precludes any possibility of friendship. When another pagan philosopher

---

row (1630–77), *A Defense of the B. [Blessed] Trinity* (London: B. Aylmer, 1697); and the Unitarian John Wallis (1616–1703), *The Doctrine of the Blessed Trinity* (London: Thomas Parkhurst, 1693).

9. *Works* 2:6, 106.

10. Ibid., 2:101.

11. Ibid., 2:204.

12. Ibid., 2:80, 111–13.

13. Ibid., 2:94–96.

14. For a brief discussion of the role of self-examination within the Puritan experience, see Owen C. Watkins, *The Puritan Experience* (London: Routledge & Kegan Paul, 1972), 9ff. See also his discussion of the "Puritan Self" (226–39). He rightly claims that "one characteristic of the Puritan approach to these problems [referring to problems of the 'age'] was the way in which a personal identity was formulated primarily through its relationship with God" (227).

granted some form of communion, he was only able to conceive of it in abstract notions of providence, nothing ultimately testifying to personal relations between the divine and human.[15] Calvin makes a similar claim regarding the ancient philosophers, with Plato presented as the best of a darkened lot.[16] According to Owen, these things are "hid in Christ" and thus only discovered fully through him. In humanity's natural state outside of Christ, the idea of God's presence only brings "terror and apprehensions of death."[17] Furthermore, even Old Testament saints who did experience communion with God remained unable to enjoy its fullness: the incarnate Lord adds παρρησίαν ("boldness and confidence"; see Heb. 4:16; 10:19) and ἐλευθερίαν ("freedom and liberty in access to God"; see 2 Cor. 3:17) to the believer's fellowship with God.[18] Christ makes the impossible possible, establishing not only peace but also fellowship between God and believers, as we see in Owen's definition of communion.

Defining Communion

Since "communion" and "commune" can have various meanings, we need to explore Owen's somewhat complex formulation of these ideas. According to Owen, "communion" relates in general (1) to things and persons (cf. natures), (2) to a state and condition, or (3) to actions.[19] Communion with God cannot be restricted to any one of these, nor can it simply be said to include all of them without qualification. Since human persons share the same nature, they can engage one another in a way that a rock and a human cannot: this helps explain the incarnation, wherein the Son assumed the same "common nature with the rest of mankind."[20] Communion through sharing the same condition can be either internal or external. Owen gives the example of Christ with the thieves, all hanging on the crosses: they all shared the same external condition, which had them under a curse, yet one of the thieves came to share the same internal or spiritual condition with Christ in faith.[21]

15. *Works* 2:8. Owen seems to be referring to Cicero, *De natura deorum academica*, trans. H. Rackham, ed. T. E. Page et al., Loeb Classical Library 268 (1933; repr., Cambridge, MA: Harvard University Press, 1961), book 1. For the Aristotle reference, see note 1 (above).

16. Calvin, *Institutes*, 2:988 (3.25.2).

17. *Works* 2:8. Cf. a similar theme in Luther, who argued that the God "known by natural reason was an unapproachable God of wrath: his righteous judgments could only evoke man's hatred and rebellion"; from Christopher B. Kaiser, *The Doctrine of God: An Historical Study*, ed. Peter Toon, Foundations for Faith (London: Marshall Morgan & Scott, 1982), 96.

18. *Works* 2:6–7.

19. See ibid., 2:7–8.

20. Ibid., 2:7.

21. Ibid., see Luke 23:40.

Finally, a sort of communion occurs when two or more join together in action, which may be either good (e.g., worshipping God) or evil (e.g., plotting a murder).

This general discussion yields to Owen's particular concern for the wonder of human communion with God. To begin, this communion between divine and human persons is voluntary rather than something "natural," since their natures remain distinct. It also requires "consent," thus protecting the personal and purposeful foundation of the relationship. Communion with God cannot simply be thought of in terms of "state and conditions," but rather in terms of the action or responsiveness between two parties. Given the difference between the divine and human, interpersonal fellowship seems unlikely. Although Owen rejects pagan skepticism about the possibility of fellowship between God and men, he affirms the profundity of that fellowship. This is especially striking since he believes true communion involves the "mutual communication" of good between two persons, allowing each to delight in the other. Owen's conception of communion rules out unending monologue or isolated autonomy. Jonathan and David's intimate friendship as portrayed in 1 Samuel 20:17 serves as his positive example. Mutuality of love grounds Owen's formulation, testifying to his persistent unwillingness to speak in abstractions devoid of experiential content.

At this point we must observe a careful distinction between union and communion with God. Within the Calvinist Puritan tradition, union with God is unilateral in that it designates divine movement and action that prompts, secures, and preserves a person in the life of faith. Once united to Christ, there can be no final falling away: nothing is able to tear apart what God has brought together—clearly the underlying theology for the doctrine of perseverance. However, communion with God can be deeply affected by a believer's sin, unresponsiveness to God, and neglect of God's ordinary means of grace. Struggling believers are never at risk of losing their *union* with Christ, but they surely experience times when intimate *communion* with God feels blocked.[22] During the seventeenth century "to commune" became associated with spiritual communication, or to use the common language, it describes intercourse with God.[23]

22. Cf. Calvin's vision of "two communions": the first (i.e., justification) is "total" while the second (i.e., sanctification) "grows." See Dennis E. Tamburello, *Union with Christ: John Calvin and the Mysticism of St. Bernard*, Columbia Series in Reformed Theology (Louisville: Westminster John Knox, 1994), 86–87.

23. See C. T. Onions, ed., *The Oxford Dictionary of English Etymology* (Oxford: Clarendon, 1966), 196. An older usage of "commune" that was common between the sixteenth century and the nineteenth was "to hold intimate (chiefly mental or spiritual) intercourse" with another. Examples include the 1557 Geneva translation of Luke 24:15, "as they communed together and reasoned," or Milton, who in 1671 wrote in *Paradise Regained*, 2.261, "It was the hour of night, when thus the Son Commun'd in silent walk." By 1876 John

Obviously this imagery is not new: it has a long theological history that many Puritans drew from, especially in their use of allegorical readings of Canticles (Song of Songs).[24] Only when two people actively participate together can this imagery work. For example, distractions may cause a husband to neglect intimate relations with his spouse, just as a Christian may neglect fellowship with God. Although such neglect does not nullify the union between the parties, it deeply affects the level of intimacy experienced between them.

Although union and communion are related—one cannot have the latter without the former—they are not synonyms. Even though Puritan writers closely associate the terms "union" and "communion," in most (if not all) instances, union precedes communion. This is not a simple linguistic convention, but rather a theological expression of an underlying truth. When these terms are not carefully distinguished, grave misunderstanding can arise. This may partly explain why William Sherlock—the later dean of St. Paul's and certainly not of Owen's Calvinistic leanings—seemed to misread Owen so severely.[25] Attacking Owen's book *Of Communion* almost twenty years after its publication, Sherlock appears to see a different distinction: union should be understood within a political and ecclesiastical framework, while communion is viewed almost wholly in terms of fellowship between saints.[26] As Sherlock uses them, both of these terms point more directly to horizontal rather than vertical relationships. Behind his attack of Owen is his tendency toward rationalism and his reaction against elements of Puritan mysticism. Self-consciously taking a sideswipe at Puritan experimentalists, Sherlock complains: "Prayer and Meditation, and such-like Acts of Devotion, are no where called Communion with God, though a prevailing custom hath in our days almost wholly appropriated that name to them."[27] Sherlock

---

P. Norris in *Rudiments of Theology* (London: Rivingtons, 1876) acknowledges a common unwillingness to speak of spiritual "intercourse" even though it simply means "communion with God," although the latter appears to him more reverent. See J. A. Simpson and E. S. C. Weiner, eds., *The Oxford English Dictionary*, 2nd ed., vol. 3 (Oxford: Clarendon, 1989), 577, 580.

24. Examples of Puritan reflections on the Song of Songs include Richard Sibbes, J. Durham, D. Fenner, T. Wilcox, G. Gifford, T. Wilson, H. Ainsworth, J. Collinges, N. Homes, J. Cotton, and T. Brightman, and so on. See J. D. Williams, "The Puritan Quest," 177–203. Owen describes the design of Canticles as "a mystical, allegorical description of the graces and excellencies of the person of Christ, to render him desirable to the souls of believers" (*Works* 9:538).

25. For general background on Sherlock, see Muller, *PRRD* 4:123–29, although he focuses on Sherlock's later work (from 1690 and onward) rather than on this earlier material.

26. William Sherlock, *Union and Communion*, 3rd ed. (1678), 88–119. The first edition lacked corrections and was published in 1674. Both editions are used throughout.

27. W. Sherlock, *Union and Communion*, 3rd ed. (1678), 118–19.

fears that so much experiential language about "communing with God" and loving the "person of Christ" will ultimately lead people away from following Jesus's moral example, which helps to explain why he so freely accuses Owen of antinomianism.[28]

By redefining the Puritan distinction between union and communion, Sherlock becomes vulnerable to charges of Pelagianism and Socinianism from his opponents.[29] For example, when Sherlock objects to Owen's emphasis on gaining an "acquaintance with Christ's person," he does so because he believes this somehow lowers the gospel or adds something beyond what the Scriptures call for. Owen's conception of the gospel causes him to stress loving the person of Christ, who fulfilled all righteousness—Owen thus emphasizing personal relations; Sherlock conceives of the gospel more in terms of principles to live by.[30] "All that the Gospel tells us," explains Sherlock, "is that Christ loved sinners so as to dye for them, and that *he loves good men*, who believe and obey his Gospel so as to save them, and that *he continue to love them, while they continue to be good; but hates them, when they return to their old vices.*"[31] There is no perseverance of the saints in Sherlock's theology

28. For a general treatment on how heated rhetoric distorted debates regarding antinomianism, see Tim Cooper, *Fear and Polemic in Seventeenth-Century England: Richard Baxter and Antinomianism* (Aldershot: Ashgate, 2001).

29. W. Sherlock had numerous opponents. For example, Edward Polhill, *An Answer to the Discourse of Mr. William Sherlock, touching the Knowledge of Christ, and our Union and Communion with Him* (London: Ben Foster, 1675), attacks Sherlock's view of justification: "When I read it [Sherlock's book], I thought my self in a new Theological World; Believers appearing without their Head for want of a Mystical Union, strip'd and naked for lack of imputed Righteousness" ("To the Reader," unnumbered page). Cf. Henry Hickman, *Speculum Sherlockianum, or, A Looking Glass in which the Admirers of Mr. Sherlock may behold the Man, as to his Accuracy, Judgement, Orthodoxy* (London: Thomas Parkhurst, 1674), who argues against Sherlock: "A man's union to Christ, doth in order of Nature precede his union to the church" (11). He also thinks Sherlock is mistaken in his belief that union and communion are something easy to understand and not a mystery (36). See also Robert Ferguson, *The Interest of Reason in Religion* (London: Dorman Newman, 1675); Thomas Danson, *The Friendly Debate between Satan and Sherlock . . .* (London: 1676); Samuel Rolle, *Prodromus, or, The Character of Mr. Sherlock's book . . .* (London: 1674), and later *Justification Justified* (London: 1674).

Sherlock is not without his defenders, however, the most able being Thomas Hotchkis, *Imputation of Christ's righteousness to us* (1675); Hotchkis's main concern seems to arise from his fear of antinomianism, claiming that many of Owen's statements are guilty of this charge (142). See also Hotchkis's later response, *A Postscript* (1678). Sherlock personally responds to the specific attacks by Owen and Ferguson in his *A Defence and Continuation of the Discourse concerning the Knowledge of Jesus Christ* (London: Walter Kettilby, 1675).

30. Cf. *Works* 2:347, where Owen explicitly rejects W. Sherlock's rationalism, concluding that God does not simply present humans with "objective arguments."

31. W. Sherlock, *Union and Communion*, 1st ed. (1674), 210, emphasis added. For Sherlock, "the fundamental design of the Gospel" is clear: it "is to make men good and vertuous, and like to God" (432).

since union with Christ is grounded on a person's continual penitence and obedience rather than on the objective work of Christ.[32]

When Sherlock speaks of God's immutability, he means that God always loves the good: as long as a Christian does the good, God freely loves this person. However, since God remains immutable, when believers fail to live lives of obedience, they find themselves no longer under God's love, but under his hatred! An example of the logical conclusion of William Sherlock's theology is found in no better example than the later Bishop of London, Thomas Sherlock—William's son. In one of his discourses preached at Temple Church, Thomas argues that anyone who is a child of God "may *cease* to be a child of God."[33] This is the antithesis of Owen's view of adoption, as we will see later in this chapter, but it is theologically plausible when mystical union is disavowed and communion with God designates little more than fellowship with other saints.

Working within his anthroposensitive framework, Owen rejects claims like Sherlock's as theologically and pastorally disastrous. Although William Sherlock believes that the imputation of Christ's righteousness leads to antinomianism, Owen believes that imputation alone allows the believer to stand secure in God's immutable love.[34] Owen agrees that God's nature is consistent: because he is just, he must hate sin. Nevertheless, Owen finds hope for the believer, not in the sincerity of one's repentance and ability to sustain unblemished obedience, but rather in the satisfaction accomplished in the death of Christ, whereby "the greatest sins can do us no hurt."[35] Given that Christ's atonement was fully satisfying and complete, that God is immutable, and that the believer is united to Christ, no cessation of the love of God for his elect is possible. God's immutability and a believer's union to Christ were conceived in order to bring lasting freedom for open communion with God, rather than fearful obedience performed with the hope of remaining acceptable to God. Countering Sherlock's accusations, Owen contends that he does not deny the role of faith and repentance. While he takes holiness seriously, Owen rejects Sherlock's moralism because it makes election and redemption depend on a believer's holiness, rather than on Christ's.[36]

32. W. Sherlock, *Union and Communion*, 1st ed. (1674), 32.

33. Thomas Sherlock, *Several Discourses Preached at the Temple Church*, 1st ed., vol. 1, *Discourse 8* (London: J. Whiston et al., 1754); the quote and reference was brought to my attention by Howard Watkin-Jones, *The Holy Spirit from Arminius to Wesley* (London: Epworth, 1929), 312, emphasis added.

34. On divine immutability in the Protestant scholastics in general, see Muller, *PRRD* 3:308–25.

35. Owen, *A Vindication of Some Passages in a Discourse Concerning Communion with God, from the Exceptions of William Sherlock* (1674), in *Works* 2:295.

36. Owen, *Works* 2:296–97, 322.

Here Owen's distinction allows him to deal both with the theological question of God's commitment to his people and with the hard reality of every believer's continual battle with sin. Sherlock's almost exclusively horizontal emphasis deprives him of the resources to maintain an adequate distinction between justification and sanctification.[37] Defenders of Owen also thought Sherlock fell into this trap, as we see in Vincent Alsop's accusation that Sherlock borrowed from the Roman theologian Robert Bellarmine.[38] This may help explain why Owen's major treatment of justification, written just three years after Sherlock's book was first published, spends far more time attacking Bellarmine than Sherlock. As we observed in our last chapter discussing justification, Owen does not treat this as a new problem; he directs theologians to the doctrine of union with Christ as a necessary preparation for handling the doctrine of sanctification. Owen maintains his Reformed theology at this point by linking union and communion closely, yet without making them synonyms. Believers united to Christ are enabled and encouraged to commune with God.

We will add one further historical observation. In 1658 a meeting at the Savoy Palace produced "A Declaration of the Faith and Order," slightly revising the Westminster Confession for those within congregationalism. Owen was one of—if not *the*—leading figures at the conference and possibly the author of the preface. Several of the minor additions made to the Westminster text may have relevance for our study. One sentence added to the section on the Trinity links this doctrine with communion: "Which Doctrine of the Trinity is the foundation of all our Communion with God, and comfortable Dependence upon him."[39] Remembering that Owen's book *Of Communion* was published in 1657, it does not seem unreasonable to hear Owen's voice urging the need to make this formerly implicit connection explicit. In so doing, the necessary link between the Trinity and Christian experience becomes even more prominent. Another apparently insignificant addition to the Westminster text may also point to Owen. Chapter 13, on

37. Another critic of Owen, William Clagett, *A Discourse concerning the Operations of the Holy Spirit* (London: Henry Brome, 1680), likewise fails to distinguish between an initial justification and a progressive sanctification, thus also leaving little room to distinguish between union and communion. For a brief yet fair comparison between Owen and Clagett on related points, see Watkin-Jones, *Holy Spirit*, 264–66, 280–81.

38. N. N. (aka Vincent Alsop), *Anti-Sozzo, sive, Sherlocismus enervatus* . . . (London: Nathanael Ponder, 1675), 545. In his response to W. Sherlock, ironically, Owen only mentions Bellarmine to argue that at the end of his life even Bellarmine came to see that "the safest retreat" for the believer inevitably becomes "the merits and righteousness of Christ" (Owen, *Works* 2:321; cf. chap. 4n121).

39. A. G. Matthews, ed. *The Savoy Declaration of Faith and Order, 1658* (London: Independent Press, 1959), 2.3 (p. 79).

sanctification, includes the new words "united to Christ" in the first sentence, making it clearer for the reader that only from this starting point can one begin to speak properly of "the practice of all true holiness."[40] None at the Savoy Palace would have disagreed with this assertion, but Owen's sensitivity to the matter may be behind this minor adjustment. These observations fit Owen's handling of such ideas in his *Communion* book.

According to Owen, union with Christ is what makes the Christian life possible, allowing the believer to have communion with God, and only on this basis can the believer then express that communion through obedience. Communion between persons must be "bottomed upon some union between them," since union is the "foundation" of experiences of communion.[41] This distinction helps prevent many Puritan theologians from formulating a doctrine of justification by works, while allowing them to place a high value upon human responsiveness by those inside the house of faith. Within this historical background and theological framework, we now approach Owen's definition: "Our Communion . . . with God consisteth in his communication of himself unto us, with our returnal unto him of that which he requireth and accepteth, flowing from that union which in Jesus Christ we have with him."[42] Let us restate this in a chart:

God communicates of himself unto us. . . .

Union with Christ establishes our relationship to God.

The resulting overflow of union is our returning unto God what is both required and accepted by him (i.e., communion).

Divine action is first, union with Christ is the result, and human response is the desired consequence. Here Owen moves from the priority of God's self-revelation to the necessity of human response, the latter assumed to be possible based on a christological observation.

As we have seen throughout our study thus far, Owen is quick to apply a methodology that encompasses two approaches, one "from above" (i.e., beginning with God) and one "from below" (beginning with humanity). He accomplishes this by constantly moving between theology and anthropology, between Christology and praxis. Appreciating this dialectic in Owen's thinking helps explain his reflections on communion with the Triune God. Since Owen works from the presupposition that all truth about God necessarily has a means of exerting

40. Ibid., 13.1 (p. 92).
41. *Works* 2:8.
42. Ibid., 2:8–9.

power on the believer's life, he will not allow debate and discussion of the Trinity to remain within the academy. Instead, he uses his vast knowledge of Scripture and tradition, together with his pastoral sensitivity, to encourage his readers with a central truth of the Christian faith: the Triune God has not only established intimate fellowship with his people, but also desires the same. Examples of this integrated method will surface in our later discussion of distinct communion with each person of the Trinity.

Approaching the One Triune God

Having established Owen's view that human communion with God is not only possible, but also mutual and intimate, we now proceed to his discussion of the distinction and unity of the divine persons with whom the believer communes. Here we notice Owen's attempt to present a trinitarian conception of communion with God that avoids both tritheism and modalism.

Possibly the quickest way into Owen's trinitarian method comes through a succinct examination of his shorter work *A Brief Declaration and Vindication of the Doctrine of the Trinity* (1669). Owen makes three observations for those who seek to discuss trinitarian questions. First, he advises the inquirer to understand that this is no "ordinary controversy in religion," for the conclusions reached are "immediately and directly" relevant to the "the souls of men."[43] Second, the "majesty, and infinite, incomprehensible nature of God" requires reverence from the human questioner. Accordingly, this is not a subject "to be prostituted" before unbelievers for the sake of debate, but rather it should bring about humble worship before the revelation of God. Third, any inquirer who looks into the mystery of the Trinity and its importance for human life must willingly submit to whatever is found in Scripture. Clearly Owen thinks the traditional orthodox interpretation of debated texts will persuade all who earnestly seek God in his revelation. This is an example of the standard Reformed hermeneutic of *regula fidei et caritatis* (the rule of faith and love), the rule that ambiguous passages are dealt with in light of the apparently less ambiguous ones, ultimately leading those who love God to the truth of Scripture.[44] Just as Owen clearly trusts the testimony found in Scripture, he also recognizes the tendency within fallen humanity to self-deception. Therefore, the inquirer's humility and openness to God are as necessary for his understanding of this doctrine

43. Ibid., 2:368.
44. Cf. Heppe, *RD*, 34–35. See also Henry M. Knapp, "Understanding the Mind of God: John Owen and Seventeenth-Century Exegetical Methodology" (PhD diss., Calvin Theological Seminary, 2002), 63–80.

as are his hermeneutical skills—in fact, they are a crucial part of his hermeneutical skills.[45]

Owen's doctrine of the Trinity is a fairly standard orthodox position:[46]

> God is one;—that this one God is Father, Son, and Holy Ghost; that the Father is the Father of the Son; and the Son, the Son of the Father; and the Holy Ghost, the Spirit of the Father and the Son; and that, in respect of this their mutual relation, they are distinct from each other.[47]

Owen's doctrine has obvious social elements: the divine persons are "distinct among themselves, by certain peculiar relative properties."[48] Not only are they distinct regarding "internal acts one towards another," but also "in acts that outwardly respect the creation and the several parts of it."[49] Accordingly, Owen develops the root of the distinction between the persons in the traditional language of begetting, begotten, and proceeding. The three divine persons are distinct in their "mutual relation one to another" so that they act distinctly yet as triune—never acting alone, so to speak. Socially the divine persons "know each other, love each other, delight in each other," and consequently they are distinct and are "represented unto our faith" as such.[50] Owen's stress on distinction allows him to freely use the third-person plural pronoun "they"—as we shall see throughout—when referring to the Father, Son, and Spirit. However, at other times Owen may refer to the three by employing the third-person singular pronoun "he."[51] This is possible because Owen thinks Scripture clearly points to one God, Father, Son, and Holy Spirit, the three persons being "divine, distinct, intelligent, voluntary, omnipotent principles of operation and working."[52] In other words, Owen's language moves between the three persons and the one divine nature without hesitation.

45. See Kelly M. Kapic, "John Owen (1616–1683)," in *Historical Dictionary of Major Biblical Interpreters*, ed. Donald K. McKim (Downers Grove, IL: InterVarsity, forthcoming); cf. Carl R. Trueman, "Faith Seeking Understanding: Some Neglected Aspects of John Owen's Understanding of Scriptural Interpretation," in *Interpreting the Bible: Historical and Theological Studies in Honour of David F. Wright*, ed. A. N. S. Lane (Leicester: Apollos, 1997), 147–62.

46. For the best survey of Reformed and post-Reformation formulations of the doctrine of the Trinity, see Muller, *PRRD*, all of vol. 4.

47. *Works* 2:377.

48. Ibid., 2:405.

49. Ibid.

50. Ibid., 2:406.

51. E.g., ibid.: "concerning God the Father, Son, and Holy Ghost; so as that we may duly believe in *him*, yield obedience unto *him*, enjoy communion with *him*, walk in *his* love and fear, and so come at length to be blessed with *him* for evermore" (emphases added).

52. Ibid.

Does a strong emphasis on distinction endanger the unity of God? Owen unreservedly affirms the oneness of God when it comes to the "nature, being, substance, or essence" of the Godhead.[53] One may wonder if Owen is vulnerable to the recent charge leveled against Augustine and many following in his tradition, that he presents God as beyond the divine persons and either known outside of the economy of salvation or as being altogether unknowable.[54] Does Owen's comment that "this natural Godhead of God is his substance or essence" expose him to such an accusation? It would seem not. He escapes this danger by never opposing unity and distinction within the Godhead. The nature or substance of God is the nature or substance of Father, Son, and Holy Spirit, "one and the same absolutely in and unto each of them," which is simply another way of designating the unity of God. Distinction of the persons lies in their subsisting in the same divine nature:

> A divine person is nothing but the divine essence, upon the account of an especial property, subsisting in an especial manner. . . . Each person having the understanding, the will, and power of God, becomes a distinct principle of operation; and yet all their actings *ad extra* being the actings of God, they are undivided, and are all the works of one, of the self-same God.[55]

With this basic trinitarian framework in mind, we may now return to Owen's particular book *Of Communion* to see how he applies his understanding in more detail.

Building from a version of 1 John 5:7 that was still common in seventeenth-century scholarship,[56] Owen makes a case for distinct communion

---

53. Ibid., 2:407.

54. Gunton, *Trinitarian Theology*, 42; also see 31–57. For a recent defense of Augustine against such charges, see Lewis Ayres, "'Remember That You Are Catholic' (serm. 52.2): Augustine on the Unity of the Triune God," *JECS* 8, no. 1 (2000): 39–82.

55. *Works* 2:407. For helpful background on debate surrounding the order and distinction of the divine persons, see Muller, *PRRD* 4:207–14.

56. Here Owen follows the KJV of 1 John 5:7: "There are three that bear record in heaven, the Father, the Word, and the Holy Ghost: and these three are one" (*Works* 2:10). This textual gloss ("in heaven . . . in earth" in 5:7–8) is now considered to be a late addition into the Greek text, but in Owen's time the verse was still commonly accepted. In England, e.g., Thomas Watson, *Practical Divinity*, 108, freely used it; and later so did Edward Stillingfleet, *A Discourse in Vindication of the Doctrine of the Trinity* (London: Henry Mortlock, 1697), 120; on the Continent, Turretin, *Elenctic Theology*, 1:268–69, not only uses the full text, but also displays his knowledge of the controversy by arguing that it can be found in ancient manuscripts, such as in Jerome (*Prologus septem epistolarum canonicarum*, as in PL 29:870–74). Turretin blames the Arians for the occasions when the full text is missing in many of the ancient manuscripts. For a recent summary of the textual problems, see Bruce M. Metzger, *A Textual Commentary on the Greek New Testament*, 2nd ed. (London: United Bible Societies, 1994), 647–49.

with each person of the Trinity. This verse speaks of the Father, the Word, and the Spirit, all bearing testimony in heaven to Christ's sonship and believers' salvation. Owen's insight here hinges on the text's assertion that there are "three distinct witnesses." Believers are to receive God's testimony with the recognition of their distinction. "We are to receive their [referring to Father, Son, and Spirit] several testimonies: and in doing so we have communion with them severally; for in this giving and receiving of testimony consists no small part of our fellowship with God."[57] Scripture (e.g., 1 Cor. 12:4–6; Eph. 4:6) speaks of various gifts, administrations, and operations, each coming distinctly from Father, Son, or Spirit, but always from the same God: "So graces and gifts are bestowed, and so are they received."[58] Owen's point is simply that the one true God is the giver of all gifts, yet he gives them distinctly as Father, Son, and Spirit. Consequently, when believers approach God, they do so while mindful of such distinction, knowing that communion with God comes διὰ Χριστοῦ, ἐν πνεύματι, and πρὸς τὸν πατέρα (cf. Eph. 2:18)—"the persons being here considered as engaged distinctly unto the accomplishment of the counsel of the will of God revealed in the gospel."[59]

The doctrine of the economic Trinity informs believers how to commune with God, since this is how God has made himself known in special revelation. At times, only the Father and Son are mentioned in Scripture (e.g., 1 John 1:3; cf. John 14:23), joined by "the particle 'and,'" which "is both distinguishing and uniting."[60] Other times fellowship with God is mentioned with distinct reference to one person in particular, such as the Son or the Spirit (e.g., 1 Cor. 1:9). So, for example, while all three divine persons are mentioned in 2 Corinthians 13:14, the text nevertheless distinctly connects κοινωνία with the Holy Spirit. By receiving gifts from and returning worship to each divine person, the believer does not interact with abstractions, but with particular persons who are united in their being. Believers worship God, who is Father, Son, and Holy Spirit.

Thus all our encounters with God are encounters with the divine persons: we do not worship an undifferentiated Godhead. Every act of

57. *Works* 2:10, emphasis added.
58. Ibid. Cf. Owen's exegesis of 1 Cor. 12:3–6 in his work vindicating *The Doctrine of the Trinity* (1669), in *Works* 2:402.
59. *Works* 2:10. Given that Owen freely moves from 1 John 5:7 to this classic formulation, a recent comment on the textual gloss of 1 John 5:7 is challenging. The "gloss is not a very happy one, as the threefold testimony of verse 8 is to Christ; and the biblical teaching about testimony is not that Father, Son, and Holy Spirit bear witness together to the Son, but that the Father bears witness to the Son through the Spirit"; so says John R. W. Stott, *The Letters of John: An Introduction and Commentary*, 2nd ed. (Grand Rapids: Eerdmans, 1988), 183.
60. *Works* 2:11.

worship and obedience is necessarily and "distinctly directed unto Father, Son and Spirit."[61] Only in this way do believers have communion with God, which means it is necessarily and "distinctly" experienced with each person of the Trinity. Again, this is grounded in God's revelation of himself as triune. Yet, how can worship preserve both God's unity and diversity?

We now come to Owen's twofold defense of his thesis about the distinct communication of the Deity to the believer. First, he argues that "when the same thing is, at the same time, ascribed jointly and yet distinctly to all the persons in the Deity, and respectively to each of them," one cannot collapse the distinctions for the sake of unity.[62] Revelation 1:4–5, for example, asserts that each person of the Trinity (Father, Son, and Spirit) gives grace and peace unto the believer, yet the passage also proclaims that God alone gives such blessings. Owen cites this as a place to see at once both the threeness of the persons and the oneness of the Godhead without the reductionism that he warns against.

Second, Owen asserts that Scripture attributes the same thing "severally and singly unto each person" of the Trinity.[63] In so doing he remains faithful to the Augustinian dictum *Opera ad extra sunt indivisa* while allowing real distinction among the persons.[64] The divine persons are not divided, but they are certainly distinct: the alternative is a shift away from three persons, identities, energies, and so on, into a modalistic model that denies any real distinction between the three. The pattern in Scripture leads Owen to hold to a clear distinction within true unity, which we see him do in his description of God as our teacher. From the Father comes all spiritual teaching: "Him we hear, of him we learn, by him are we brought unto union and communion with Jesus Christ."[65] God the Father is the one who draws people to himself through his Spirit. Functioning as prophet and king, the Son's revelation is that of a "life-giving, a spirit-breathing teaching."[66] The close connection between the Father and Son moves Owen to the vital link between the Son and Spirit. These cannot be separated even though Owen acknowledges that Scripture distinguishes their respective activities of teaching the people of God. Finally, Owen portrays the Spirit as the Comforter, who makes all

61. Ibid., 2:15.
62. Ibid.
63. Ibid.
64. See ibid., 2:15, 18, 227, 269, 407. Cf. Wolfhart Pannenberg, *Systematic Theology*, 1:326: "We need not surrender the basic truth that the Father, Son, and Spirit work together in creation, reconciliation, and redemption because we accept the possibility of distinguishing the persons in these works."
65. *Works* 2:16.
66. Ibid.

things known to believers. In sum, God is the great teacher, yet he only teaches distinctly as Father, Son, and Spirit. Since God communicates grace distinctly "from the several persons of the Deity," the obvious implication for Owen is that "the saints must needs have distinct communion with them."[67] Such a pattern that we find in God's communication, Owen believes, would also appear in various other activities of God, including both the quickening and preserving of saints.

We may now ask again, how does one properly worship a Triune God? Is it inappropriate to worship each person of the Trinity distinctly, or is this even possible? Does this type of discussion drive a wedge between the divine persons, ultimately separating them? Owen's exploration of these mysteries brings him to the following conclusion: "The divine nature is the reason and cause of all worship; so that it is impossible to worship any one person, and not worship the whole Trinity."[68] He explains further:

> Our access in our worship is said to be "to the Father"; and this "through Christ," or his mediation; "by the Spirit," or his assistance. *Here is a distinction of the persons, as to their operations, but not at all as to their being the object of our worship.* For the Son and the Holy Ghost are no less worshipped in our access to God than the Father himself; only, the grace of the Father, which we obtain by the mediation of the Son and the assistance of the Spirit, is that which we draw nigh to God for. So that *when, by the distinct dispensation of the Trinity, and every person, we are led to worship . . . any person, we do herein worship the whole Trinity*; and *every person*, by what name soever, of Father, Son, or Holy Ghost, *we invocate him.*[69]

Owen's concept of prayer is deeply informed by the above statement. Since he believes that in worshipping any one divine person, the Chris-

---

67. Ibid. Cf. Ames, *Marrow of Theology*, 93: "The distinct manner of working consists in each [divine] person working according to the particular form [*ratio*] of his subsistence."

68. *Works* 2:268; cf. 12:380.

69. Ibid., 2:269, emphases added. In his work *ΧΡΙΣΤΟΛΟΓΙΑ*, Owen makes a similar observation: "1. That the divine nature, which is individually the same in each person of the holy Trinity, is the proper formal object of all divine worship, in adoration and invocation; wherefore, no one person is or can be worshipped, but in the same individual act of worship each person is equally worshipped and adored. 2. That it is lawful to direct divine honour, worship, and invocation unto any person, in the use of his peculiar name—the Father, Son, or Spirit—or unto them altogether; but to make any request unto one person, and immediately the same unto another, is not exemplified in the Scripture, nor among the ancient writers of the church" (ibid., 1:20–21). Owen sees this rule in many of the fathers, including Augustine in *Enchiridion* 38: "Quando unus trium in aliquo opere nominatur, universa operari trinitas intelligitur." ET: "When one person of the three is named in any work, the whole Trinity is to be understood to effect it" (in *NPNF*[1] 3:250).

tian is worshipping the whole Trinity, he does not hesitate to endorse the view that prayers may be made to each divine person, including the Holy Spirit.[70]

Along similar lines Owen's Continental contemporary Francis Turretin likewise argues that the distinction of the three does not take away from the One; rather, it ensures a full understanding of worship. Turretin stated that the worshipper is not thus dividing his worship between different Gods, but instead worshipping the one true God. The Christian "ought to be convinced that, on the ground of the unity and consubstantiality (*homoousia*) of the persons, the Son and the Holy Spirit are invoked by the same act of invocation that is addressed to the Father." At this point Turretin reminds the worshipper of Gregory of Nazianzus's statement: "I cannot think of one without being instantly surrounded with the splendor of three; nor can I discern the three without being suddenly attracted to one."[71] Owen also cites this particular comment of Gregory's, though he does so in an untranslated footnote, not indicating the particular work from which it comes.[72] Such historical observations remind the reader that, contrary to popular belief, twentieth-century theologians did not discover the insights of Gregory: the Protestant scholastics had long used them as a means to promote distinct worship of the Triune God.[73]

Underlying Owen's thought, and Turretin's, is the classic Western conception of the economic Trinity. Owen conceives of the grace of God as communicated distinctly from the Father through Christ in the power of the Spirit. The Father is viewed in terms of "original authority," the Son as the one who communicates this grace "from a purchased treasury," and the Spirit communicates "by immediate efficacy."[74] Given this presupposed framework, it is a mistake to accuse Owen of general heretical ideas. For example, he would not endorse any form of modalistic monarchianism. These are distinct persons, not mental abstractions produced by the believer, nor simply different masks worn by the hidden God: neither the Father nor the Spirit becomes incarnate and suffers

70. E.g., *Works* 2:229–30: "Now the Holy Ghost, being God, is no less to be invoked, prayed to, and called on, than the Father and Son." Owen is not alone in this assertion among his Puritan contemporaries, who built upon a tradition within the Reformation. See also ibid., 2:271–72. Cf. Philip Melanchthon, *Loci communes, 1555*, trans. Clyde L. Manschreck (New York: Oxford University Press, 1965), 37–38.

71. Turretin, *Elenctic Theology*, 1:272; quoting Gregory of Nazianzus, *On Holy Baptism* 40.41, in *NPNF*² 7:375; cf. Calvin, *Institutes*, 1:141–42 (1.13.17).

72. *Works* 2:10: "Οὐ φθάνω τὸ ἓν νοῆσαι, καὶ τοῖς τρισὶ περιλάμπομαι, οὐ φθάνω τὰ τρία διελεῖν, καὶ εἰς τὸ ἓν ἀναφέρομαι."

73. Such appreciation does not disappear even within later Reformed writers, such as George Smeaton, *The Doctrine of the Holy Spirit*, 2nd ed., Cunningham Lectures, 9th ser. (Edinburgh: T&T Clark, 1889), 6, who likewise quotes Gregory on this point.

74. See *Works* 2:16–17.

on the cross. Owen does not fall into the trap of tritheism either. While Sherlock and others would later attack elements of Owen's thought in this particular work, it is significant that tritheism is never a charge leveled against him.[75] Though these three (Father, Son, and Spirit) are distinct, they nevertheless remain one, "in that one divine essence" most clearly declared in the Shema.[76] Here plurality of persons is found within the unity of the Godhead.

Because Owen is so concerned for the believer's ability to commune fully with God, and in a way that appropriately corresponds to God's being and life, Scripture constrains the ministers of the gospel to speak as it does, in terms of both distinction and unity, and to lead their congregations in worship accordingly.

Communion with the Father

The Father and Human Psychological Hesitations

Some have claimed that the Puritan emphasis on sinful humanity, inherited largely from the line of Augustine and Calvin, lends itself to deep personal despair. Although this tradition allows God to receive all praise and glory for human salvation, it can also produce feelings of "unworthiness" and "a constant preoccupation with the need to assuage God's wrath."[77] Certain scholars have argued that those prone to obsessive analysis of their own unworthiness—a common phenomenon among many English Puritans—often ended in "deep depressions and extremes of self-loathing."[78] Such observations, however, did not first

75. During the trinitarian controversies at the end of the seventeenth century, W. Sherlock was the one who faced the charge of tritheism: Robert South strongly reacts against Sherlock's conception of three Minds with self-consciousness, understood as the Trinity in Unity. First William Sherlock published *A Vindication of the Doctrine of the Trinity and the Incarnation* (London: W. Rogers, 1690) and *A Defence of Dr. Sherlock's Notion of a Trinity in Unity* (London: William Rogers, 1694). Then Robert South attacked those two books in his *Animadversions upon Dr. Sherlock's Book, entitled A Vindication of the Holy and Ever-Blessed Trinity* (London: Randal Taylor, 1693) and *Tritheism charged upon Dr. Sherlock's New Notion of the Trinity, and the charge made good* (London: John Whitlock, 1694).

76. *Works* 2:381; for the Shema, see Deut. 6:4.

77. Christopher Durston and Jacqueline Eales, eds., *The Culture of English Puritanism, 1560–1700* (Basingstoke: Macmillan, 1996), 10, esp. 9–13. But see J. D. Williams, "The Puritan Quest," who complains: "Historians, far more obsessed with sin and salvation than the original Puritans, have generally concentrated on preparation, conversion and assurance rather than union and communion with God, resulting in an impoverished view of Puritan devotion" (90).

78. Durston and Eales, *Culture of English Puritanism*, 11. Cf. Patrick Collinson, *The Religion of Protestants: The Church in English Society, 1559–1625* (Oxford: Clarendon, 1982), 114.

appear in the writings of twentieth-century social historians: many Puritan pastors understood this problem in one form or another. Yet they usually viewed this phenomenon not as the result of an improper view of humanity, but arising from *an improper view of God*. Despair and anxiety arise in believers when they fail to perceive the true character of their heavenly Father.

Precisely along these lines Owen shows his concern for the psychological results of believers' improper views of God the Father. His involvement in pastoral care—as a congregational minister in Coggeshall, an army chaplain, and a spiritual mentor to Oxford students—informed him as to how saints often envisioned their heavenly Father. Apparently he did not simply learn these misconceptions from others, but they had been a part of his own life as well. As a younger man Owen had struggled with feeling God's acceptance and assurance of salvation even after being a chaplain and preaching for some time.[79] Thus Owen's treatise reflects his keen awareness of this widespread human experience.

People commonly view God as distant, wrathful, and angry about sin, "always angry" and so "implacable" that no creature would dare to draw near to him.[80] Though it is understandable that those outside the faith fear God in this way, these emotions often persist in the believer's conception of the Father. Owen assures the believer, "It is misapprehension of God that makes any run from him, who have the least breathing wrought in them after him."[81] He diagnoses that this "misapprehension" comes as a result of meditating solely on the Father's "terrible majesty, severity, and greatness," all of which overwhelm the soul seeking personal communion with the Father.[82] These images largely come from "natural expectations" of what God will be like, yet a believer's communion with God produces a loving "intercourse with him."[83]

If the believer ought not to view the Father as simply wrathful and angry, why is this so common among Christians? Owen argues that much of the problem stems from believers' uncertainty about the Father's attitude toward them. Believers may easily imagine Jesus's concern and the comforting work of the Spirit, but the Father seems distant and angry. An example of this may be seen in the disciples' response as they learn of Jesus's coming departure (see John 16:26–28). Although they are secure in Jesus's compassionate commitment to them, his coming ascension turns the disciples' thoughts toward the Father, and Jesus

---

79. See Beeke, *Assurance of Faith*, 239–40. Cf. *Works* 6:324. In chap. 1 we briefly discussed this struggle in Owen's life.

80. *Works* 2:19, 34.

81. Ibid., 2:32.

82. Ibid.

83. Ibid., 2:24.

perceives their uneasiness. Owen deduces that this is why when Jesus prays to the Father for his disciples, he adds the clarification, "for the Father himself loveth you."[84] Jesus is assuring his disciples that the Father does not need to be persuaded to love them, for indeed love is the Father's "peculiar respect towards you."[85] While Jesus does pray and the Spirit brings comfort, these are not the causes but the fruit of the Father's love. Since the idea of "love itself, free love, eternal love," comes from the Father, who is this fountain of love himself, "there is no need of any intercession for that."[86] However, Owen claims that until this truth is fully grasped, disciples in all ages will hesitate to hold communion with the Father.

Not only is the tendency to think negatively of the Father common to natural humanity; it is also stirred up by satanic powers. Satan uses "hard thoughts of God" to prevent and disrupt our communion with the Father, beginning in the garden by arguing that God threatens death to Adam and Eve for no good reason.[87] This kind of distortion, according to Owen, is still used effectively by the evil one against God's people. Only when believers remember the true love of God and his compassion toward them will they be psychologically free to commune with the Father. These "hard thoughts" are grievous to God since he knows "full well what fruit this bitter root is like to bear,—what alienations of heart,—what drawings back,—what unbelief and tergiversations in our walking with him."[88] Just as a child avoids an encounter with an angry father, so a believer will avoid the heavenly Father if his presence represents wrath and fear.

At this point Owen also makes an observation that he presumes is rather common among believers. He notices that while believers can imagine God as angry and willing to punish those who die in their sins, they fail to conceive of God's peculiar love for them, or as Owen writes, they "are afraid to have good thoughts of God."[89] Such thoughts of God's goodness, tenderness, and love seem difficult for saints to hold on to. This reaction is a result of "soul-deceit from Satan," who brings such fearful thoughts. In contradistinction, Owen argues that the Father is the fountain of love, and must be viewed as such for communion to take place between himself and the believer.

84. Ibid. 2:20; see John 16:26–27. Owen later restates this observation when discussing Christ's oblation in *Works* 2:198.

85. *Works* 2:20.

86. Ibid. Muller, *PRRD* 3:561–69, briefly explores the idea of God's love in the Reformers and Reformed orthodox.

87. *Works* 2:35.

88. Ibid.

89. Ibid.

The Reality of the Father's Love

Turning to the Father's attitude toward the saints, it seems appropriate to remember that in the twentieth century Owen was heavily attacked for presenting an angry and wrathful God void of compassion. R. G. Lloyd argues that the most significant problem in Owen's theology appears in his construction of a God who is simply "the embodiment of the Moral Law." Consequently, Owen's theology presents a Deity that "was bound by His own Nature to punish sin and to uphold righteousness, but that [God] possessed no inherent quality that compelled Him to be merciful."[90] A similar view espoused by James B. Torrance interprets Owen's doctrine of God and the atonement as driven primarily by Aristotelian logic and presuppositions (e.g., the divine as *actus purus*). Torrance argues that this inevitably led Owen to conclude "that justice is the essential attribute of God," whereas God's love is dismissed as secondary, arbitrary, or accidental.[91] Do such statements have merit?

As a Puritan preacher in the Reformed tradition of his day, Owen did not hesitate to speak about the holiness and justice of God, by which God in his purity could not simply dismiss sin as insignificant. In fact, writing against different arguments presented by Socinus, Twisse, and Rutherford, Owen's *A Dissertation on Divine Justice* (1653) makes the strong claim that God could not ignore or dismiss sin simply by means of his arbitrary will, for justice is of God's essence.[92] Owen believes that the cross of Christ, more than any other point, demonstrates that justice is not accidental to God.[93] However, to conclude that justice is more important or fundamental to God than love or mercy is to completely misunderstand Owen—and the Reformed scholasticism of the day.[94]

Although Owen believes in particular atonement, this does not place justice before love, since both love and justice are inseparable in God's being. Neither love nor justice is accidental, since both describe God in his essential being. Here Owen and his contemporary Reformed scholastics grow out of a long tradition that upholds divine simplicity: they reject the idea that some attributes of God are "accidental or incidental predicates," which can be lost or diminished.[95] Richard Muller rightly argues that divine simplicity "is among the normative assumptions of theology from the time of the church fathers, to the age of the great medieval scholastic

90. R. G. Lloyd, "Life and Work of John Owen," 333.
91. James B. Torrance, "The Incarnation and 'Limited Atonement,'" 33, 37. The same charge is leveled against Jonathan Edwards (37).
92. See *Works* 10:481–624.
93. E.g., ibid., 10:546–49, 556–60.
94. In ibid., 10:561–64, Owen deals with those who pit justice against love.
95. Muller, *PRRD* 3:278; although the topic appears throughout volume 3, see esp. 3:36–45, 70–76, 271–84.

systems, to the era of Reformation and post-Reformation theology, and indeed, on into the succeeding era of late orthodoxy and rationalism."[96] Although it is true that there are diverse and complex ways in which different Reformed theologians unpack divine simplicity in terms of distinguishing the attributes, there was a shared concern about making sure that God was not presented as divided or having internal conflict. Owen is counted among those who held that "the attributes are essentially one in God, but known to reason as distinct in their operation *ad extra*."[97] Versions of this position are held by the likes of Owen, Bucanus, Alting, Hottinger, Maccovius, and Heidanus.[98] According to Protestant scholastics working in this tradition, "The attributes are distinguished neither from the essence nor from each other but only by our conceiving."[99] Such division of attributes is a result of human limitation rather than a hierarchy within God's being. In his later work *ΧΡΙΣΤΟΛΟΓΙΑ* (1679), Owen places this discussion in the context of divine incomprehensibility, but there he goes on to point to Christ as the only way to ground one's representation of "the Divine Being and excellencies."[100] In Christ one does not choose between justice, mercy, and love, for in him they are embodied and perfectly upheld. Thus, contrary to how Owen is often portrayed, love is not accidental to his view of God. If love were not essential to God, then people would have been lost in their sins, never able to reestablish any right relationship with their Creator. Instead of this being the case, Owen portrays a God who, while perfectly holy and just, is a God of love and mercy, and this love is found particularly in his discussions of God the Father.

Throughout Owen's discussion of the Father, he often employs the specific imagery of a fountain.[101] This is not unusual: it has patristic roots and was employed freely among Protestant scholastics.[102] According to Owen, the "great discovery of the gospel" occurs in finding out that "the Father,

96. Ibid., 3:39.

97. Ibid., 3:289.

98. There is simply no better handling of the diverse ways in which Reformed scholastics worked out their view of divine simplicity and distinction of the attributes than that found in ibid., esp. 3:275–98.

99. Johann Henrich Hottinger, *Cursus theologicus: Methodo altingiana* (Duisburg: Wyngaerden, 1660); cited by Heppe, *RD*, 59; cf. 57–104. Heppe problematically presents the material on divine simplicity and distinction of attributes in the Protestant scholastics as if there were only one Reformed approach, which simply is not correct.

100. Cf. *Works* 1:65–79.

101. E.g., ibid., 2:19, 21–23, 28, 35–36, 38; cf. 20:99 (BE 19:99).

102. See Muller, *PRRD* 4:269–70. Cf. Muller, *DLGTT*, who notes that when the image "fountain" is applied to God the Father, it communicates the idea that "the First Person of the Trinity is the *fons totius divinitatis*, the source or ground of the whole Godhead" (44, cf. 123).

as the fountain of the Deity" is to be known not as wrathful, but as the One who has revealed himself "peculiarly as love."[103] As the fountain, the Father is the "spring of all gracious communications and fruits of love" revealed in Christ.[104] The analogy of the fountain unites the activities of the Father and the Son: "Though all our refreshment actually lie[s] in the streams, yet by them we are led up unto the fountain." The Father is the fountain of love, and though the worshipper sips from the stream (i.e., Jesus Christ), he or she is continually directed back to the source of "eternal love itself."[105]

This remarkable love coming from the divine fountain centers Owen's understanding of the Father. Love emerging from the Father is not limited, or liable to increase or decrease, nor is it based on whim; instead, it is "eternal," "unchangeable," "immutable," and "infinitely gracious."[106] Owen calls God an "infinite ocean of love" without beginning or end; such love does not "grow to eternity" but is "constant" and will not diminish.[107] Believers' actions cannot merit the Father's love, for it is a "compassionate" and "free love," and as such it is an "undeserved" love of "kindness."[108] In Owen's doctrine, justice does not exclude love, for "God is love" and has a "loving nature."[109] Owen encourages his readers to use their imagination by asking them to picture anything that appears to have "a loving and tender nature in the world," and after imagining away any imperfections or weaknesses, the love of the Father becomes easier to conceive: "He is as a father, a mother, a shepherd, a hen over chickens."[110] All these earthly manifestations of love serve as imperfect pointers to the source of love itself, the perfect love of the Father.

Owen examines divine love under two headings, namely, as *beneplaciti* (pleasing things) and as *amicitiae* (friendships). The former refers to a love of "good pleasure and destination," while the latter communicates a love "of friendship and approbation."[111] The *beneplacitum Dei* (good

103. *Works* 2:19.
104. Ibid., 2:23.
105. Ibid. Owen also uses his familiar analogy of the sun and its beams to make the same point.
106. Ibid., 2:19–20, 23, 29, 30, 36.
107. Ibid., 2:27, 30.
108. Ibid., 2:19–20, 23, 32, 34, 36.
109. Ibid., 2:19; cf. 1 John 4:8; Exod. 34:6–7.
110. Ibid., 2:22, citing Ps. 23:1; Ps. 103:13; Isa. 40:11; Isa. 63:16; Matt. 6:6; Matt. 23:37. Noticeably, Owen twice uses Isa. 66:13, 17, "'As one whom his mother comforteth, so will I comfort you,' . . . saith the Lord" (cf. *Works* 2:38), revealing a willingness to recognize motherly traits in the Father. For a similar use in Calvin, see William J. Bouwsma, "The Spirituality of John Calvin," in *Christian Spirituality*, vol. 2, *High Middle Ages and Reformation*, ed. Jill Raitt (London: Routledge & Kegan Paul, 1987), 323–24.
111. *Works* 2:21.

pleasure of God) was common language used by Reformed Protestant scholastics to convey the idea of God's voluntary, free, and sovereign plan.[112] This is the aspect of God's love where Owen grounds the incarnation, and by implication the reconciliation of the world to God, in the Father's eternal love. On the other hand, Owen speaks of divine love as that of friendship (*amicitiae*), hereby holding to Martin Bucer's paradigm and abandoning Aristotle's.[113] This is necessary because Owen's assumptions run contrary to Aristotle's regarding the friendship between parties who are truly unequal, especially in terms of "acts of justice."[114] Aristotle argues that when a great difference develops between parties (e.g., virtue, vice, wealth), "they are no longer friends, and do not even expect to be so. And this is most manifest in the case of the gods; for they surpass us most decisively in all good things."[115] The gods are far too distant from humanity to be considered friends for Aristotle. Owen must, of course, oppose speculations that are so alien from a Christian understanding of God, which sees the Father's love free to overcome that distance and establish friendship by sending his Son. Though Aristotle may speak of friendship normally restricted to equals, Owen's trinitarian theology drives him to a completely different conception of friendship, one that takes into account the friendship with the Triune God described in the Scriptures. Paraphrasing John 14:23, in which we learn of a reciprocal relationship between our loving Christ and the Father loving us, Owen further interprets Jesus's language of "we" as trinitarian, meaning that "even the Father and Son . . . by the Spirit" will come to dwell in believers. No divine person is excluded from the renewed relationship. Yet again, this promise and reality stems from the "peculiar prerogative" of the Father's love, though it is the undivided love of God.[116] Although Aristotle claims that the "better should be more loved than he loves," Owen claims that God's love for humanity far exceeds humanity's love for God.[117]

The Father's love is bounteous. While there may be some similarities between a believer's love for God and God's love for a believer, there

112. See Muller, *DLGTT*, 57.

113. In *Works* 2.21, Owen quotes Bucer: "Diligi a patre, recipi in amicitiam summi Dei; a Deo foveri, adeoque Deo esse in deliciis." ET: "To be loved by the Father, to be welcomed into the friendship of the most high God; to know God's favor, this is what it is to be in the delights of God." Friendship with God is a common theme among Puritans. Cf. Paul Blackham, "The Pneumatology of Thomas Goodwin" (PhD diss., King's College London, 1995), 210.

114. Aristotle, *EN* 8.7.

115. For Aristotle's full discussion on friendship, see *EN*, book 8.

116. *Works* 2:21.

117. Aristotle, *EN* 8.7.

are also significant dissimilarities. We may begin by looking at the parallels.

First, both God's love and the believer's are "love[s] of rest and complacency."[118] Although he cites both Augustine and Aquinas,[119] Owen turns primarily to Scripture, which displays God's rest as God's remarkable silence regarding believers' faults: he will not "complain of any thing in them whom he loves, but he is silent on the account thereof; . . . he will not seek farther for another object" for his love, but is satisfied. Regarding God's delight or complacency, Owen cites scriptural statements that portray both inward affections of God and outward demonstrations of that delight. God exceedingly delights in his church, rejoicing (i.e., *tripudiare*) in the same way "as men overcome with some joyful surprisal."[120] So overflowing is the Father's love that "He sings to his church."[121] Believers also discover God to be their rest and delight. While the soul has looked for a place to rest from its wanderings, nothing it has loved satisfies its longing until it embraces God, who alone fills the soul with "present and eternal rest."[122] We will pick up this theme in chapter 6 in our discussion of the Lord's day. Owen values communion with God as sweeter than life itself, the ultimate delight.

Second, Christ is the only means by which to communicate this love. "The Father communicates no issue of his love unto us but through Christ; and we make no return of love unto him but through Christ."[123] Although the Father's love is grounded in his grace and will, it is accomplished in and through his Son. Using the vivid image of an "infinite ocean of love" that is the Father, Owen says that believers "are not to look for one drop from him but what comes through Christ."[124] Since the Son uniquely

118. *Works* 2:25.
119. Aquinas, *ST* 1a–2ae.q.25.a.2. "Effectus amoris quando habetur amatum, est delectatio." ET: "But the effect of love, when the beloved one is possessed, is pleasure." Owen claims Augustine wrote (without reference): "Amore est complacentia amantis in amato. Amor est motus cordis, delectantis se in aliquo." ET: "The delight in love is that of the lover in the beloved. Love is the beat of the heart that delights itself in someone." The Latin definition of love, attributed to Aquinas by everyone else except Owen, is a favorite of Thomas Watson, see *A Divine cordial: Or, the transcendent priviledge of those that love God* . . . (London: Thomas Parkhurst, 1678), 85; *A body of practical divinity* . . . (London: Thomas Parkhurst, 1692), 245, 288; found also in Samuel Annesley, *Volume I. Containing the First Volume of the Exercise At Cripplegat* . . . (London: Thomas Tegg, 1884, first ed. 1661), 177. The actual wording is not clearly found in either Augustine or Aquinas.
120. *Works* 2:25.
121. Ibid., 2:25–26; he gets this idea from Ps. 147:11; 149:4; Isa. 27:2–3; Zeph. 3:17.
122. Ibid., 2:26.
123. Ibid., 2:27. Cf. Alsop, *Anti-Sozzo*, 718. For both Owen and Alsop, the covenant is the key.
124. *Works* 2:27. He also gives the image of the Father as the "honey in the flower;—it must be in the comb before it be for our use. Christ must extract and prepare this honey for us."

provides the way to understand the love of the Father—for the Father to work apart from his Son is unthinkable—the believer also approaches the Father only through Christ. Jesus is the sacrificial offering as well as the means through which prayers become pleasing incense to God. "Our love is fixed on the Father; but it is conveyed to him through the Son of his love. He is the only way for our graces as well as our persons to go unto God; through him passeth all our desire, our delight, our complacency, our obedience."[125] We will explore these ideas more fully in the section on communion with the Son.

The dissimilarities between the Father's love for us and ours for him may be summarized: (1) God's love is bounteous, ours is a duty; (2) the Father's love is antecedent, ours is consequent; and (3) the love of God is immutable, ours is mutable. Each of these differences highlights the supremacy of the Father's love. Like a fountain overflowing with water, or the clouds so full that they must pour forth rain, so the Father's love flows "out of its own fullness."[126] The Father's love is prior, whereas the believer's love follows out of response and gratitude. His love is not caused by anything outside of himself because, before there is anything "lovely" in people, God sets his affections on them. As a result, believers are captured by God's "excellency, loveliness, and desirableness," which causes their response of love to the Father. Furthermore, each party's love reflects his or her character. Since the Father is immutable, so is his love. Since we are mutable, so our love tends to waver. Using a favorite image, Owen claims the Father's love is like the sun, which is always full and does not change, whereas the changing "enlargements and straitenings" of the moon better reflect the unsteady love of believers. Thus, believers' behavior will not "heighten" nor "lessen" the Father's unchanging love. This does not mean that God never chastens his children, but rather that he only does so from a position of unflinching love and commitment to them.[127]

One final observation will shed a bit more light on how Owen understands the character of the Father's peculiar love. We have observed Owen's anthroposensitive method, which seeks to understand theological conclusions in light of anthropological observations. Such a concern extends to his views about God's nature. While fallen humans are called θεοστυγεῖς ("haters of God," Rom. 1:30), the word Owen chooses to describe the nature of God is φιλάνθρωπος (lover of humanity).[128] Although this term has only minor biblical attestation (esp. Titus 3:4; cf. Acts 27:3; 28:2), it has a rich theological history. For example, it was one of Athanasius's choice words used to describe God's active love, most

125. Ibid., 2:27–28.
126. Ibid., 2:28.
127. Ibid., 2:30.
128. Ibid., 2:29.

clearly seen in the incarnation.[129] Behind this idea one finds Owen's reading of 1 John 4:10, by which God loved his people before they loved him. This allows him to make a distinction: God loves "his people,—not their sinning"; if this were not the case, then salvation could never be secure.[130] Again, within a trinitarian context, this describes the manner and solidity of the eternal and free love by which the Father delights in his people together with the Son, who rejoices in the opportunity to fulfill the Father's desire. The Son is like a mirror of the Father, so that the Father looks to the Son and sees not only "the express image of his person and the brightness of his glory" (cf. Heb. 1:3), but also his "love and delight in the sons of men."[131] The Father and the Son are φιλάνθρωποι; God seeks true communion with his children. Later in his treatise Owen briefly explores the language in Titus 3:4–7 describing God's love.[132] The vocabulary in this passage appears below in chart form:

χρηστότης	God's goodness and desire to profit us
φιλανθρωπία	God's love, propensity to help, assist, and relieve those toward whom he is so affected
ἔλεος	God's mercy, forgiveness, compassion, and tenderness to those suffering
χάρις	God's free pardoning bounty, undeserved love

All of these attributes are ascribed to the Savior God (τοῦ Θεοῦ σωτῆρος). Owen's exposition follows an overtly trinitarian pattern that he derives from the biblical text: God's redemptive activities arise out of the love and kindness of the Father, procured by the Son, and communicated by the Holy Spirit, who is as water poured out abundantly on believers. The nature of God is one of love, mercy, compassion, and goodness; these are characteristics clearly seen in the Father, Son, and Holy Spirit.

Believers' Response to the Father

Given Owen's pastoral observations regarding common misconceptions that believers have of the Father, what direction can he give them to correct their understanding, their perceptions, and their practice? According to Owen, only by "eyeing" the Father's love will believers be able to rest from their fears in the midst of the storms of life.[133] Problematically, most Christians cannot "carry up their hearts and minds to

129. See T. F. Torrance, *Trinitarian Faith*, 74, 147–48.
130. *Works* 2:31.
131. Ibid., 2:33.
132. Ibid., 2:190.
133. Ibid., 2:23.

this height by faith," failing to see the Father's true love, and thus failing to find rest for their tired souls. By neglecting the Spirit's prompting to approach the Father through the Son, Christians who should be free feel heavy, and those who should rejoice find themselves anxious about the Father's disposition toward them.[134] Only when believers meditate on the kind of love displayed by the Father will they be prompted to commune with him.[135]

Owen reminds readers that the Triune God is self-sufficient, "infinitely satiated with himself and his own glorious excellencies and perfections." The Father has begotten the Son from all eternity and fully delighted in him, and yet, for some reason, the Father has shown that he freely and immutably "loves his saints also."[136] Such an observation aims to bring believers assurance that they can have confidence in the Father's love for them. Indeed, the most unkind reaction Owen imagines from believers is a failure to trust that the Father does desire communion with his people.

Nevertheless, communion is mutual, as recognized above, and so it requires two parties, not just one. Although the Father is the ground and source of all love and the believer's obedience thus "begins in the love of God," it "ends in our love to him."[137] Four characteristics summarize a believer's communion with the Father: rest, delight, reverence, and obedience.[138] Believers who have received the love of the Father are encouraged to make "returns," showing their love and delight in the Father.[139] In typical Owen fashion, the believer's response to God should be a holistic one, including the mind, will, and affections: "When the Lord is, by his word, presented as [loving] unto thee, let thy mind know it, and assent that it is so; and thy will embrace it, in its being so; and all thy affections be filled with it." He concludes, "Set thy whole heart to it; let it be bound with the cords of this love."[140] Every human faculty is involved in responding to God.[141] Any dialogue lacking the full atten-

---

134. Ibid., 2:32.
135. Ibid., 2:19, 33–34.
136. Ibid., 2:32–33.
137. Ibid., 2:24.
138. Ibid., 2:28–29.
139. Ibid., 2:19.
140. Ibid., 2:34. Here the imagery reflects Old Testament practice, using cords for binding sacrifices to the altar. See Susan Hardman Moore, "Sacrifice in Puritan Typology," in *Sacrifice and Redemption*, ed. Stephen W. Sykes (Cambridge, UK: Cambridge University Press, 1991), 182–202.
141. Cf. Henry Scougal, *Life of God in the Soul of Man* (London: Richard Baynes, 1677), 92: "Love is that powerful and prevalent passion, by *which all the faculties and inclinations of the soul are determined*, and on which both its perfection and its happiness depend" (emphasis added); cited by G. S. Wakefield, *Puritan Devotion*, 31.

tion of one participant fails to actualize Owen's conception of intimate communion.

Finally, Owen expects his opponents to ask: Does such an emphasis on God's love negate human responsibility? Antinomianism is not an issue because anyone who has truly tasted of the love of God would not support such a perversion of the gospel: "The doctrine of grace may be turned into wantonness; the principle cannot."[142] Rather, God's love endears the soul not only to delight in the Father, but also to abide in him. Here we see a direct correlation between Christians' views of God and their willingness to commune with him: "So much as we see of the love of God, so much shall we delight in him, and no more."[143] Therefore, Owen encourages his readers to return to the source of love and acceptance; in doing so he believes they will be transformed.

> Sit down a little at the fountain, and you will quickly have a farther discovery of the sweetness of the streams. You who have run from him, will not be able, after a while, to keep at a distance for a moment.[144]

Communion with the Son

While the Father is the fountain from which the believer drinks, he or she does so only through the Son, for though the Father and the Son cannot be separated, they can be distinguished. Significantly, this section on communion with the Son is more than twice as long as the sections on the Father and Spirit combined: clearly even Owen's trinitarian approach has a christocentric framework. To appreciate this emphasis, we will focus on three particular themes around which Owen structures this part of his work: first, the character of the Son, his excellencies and "personal grace"; second, the Son's affections for believers; and third, communion with the Son through "purchased grace." Throughout this exploration, and especially in the second and third points, Owen's anthroposensitive theology operates as a dialogue between truths discovered about the Son and how believers should respond to these discoveries. Here again, Owen's anthropological insights, relating humanity wholly to God, arise from reflection on God as portrayed concretely in the Scriptures, rather than through detached introspection.

142. *Works* 2:31.
143. Ibid., 2:36.
144. Ibid.

The Character of the Son

When describing communion with the Father, Owen stresses love as the dynamic and motive power of the communion. This does not deny the Son's or the Spirit's love, since elsewhere Owen clearly ascribes love to them.[145] But he does this to stress what believers ought to think specifically of the Father, without taking away from the Son or Spirit. Likewise, in his discussion of the Son, he highlights the idea of grace, which also consistently moves him back to observations about Christ's love. It is not that the Father and Spirit are without grace—for we remain speaking of the one God: nevertheless, we have this "peculiar communion" with the Son through grace. He cites John 1 as support: Jesus came in "grace and truth" and believers receive "grace for grace." Likewise, the apostolic benediction emphasizes the "grace of the Lord Jesus Christ."[146] This distinction is also sprinkled throughout Paul's salutations and prophetically in Old Testament texts that point to the uniqueness of Jesus. On the basis of these observations, Owen deduces that, while believers are to view the Father peculiarly in his love, they are peculiarly to "eye" in and receive from the Son grace "revealed in or exhibited by the gospel."[147]

Yet gospel grace makes sense for Owen only when it is grounded in the person of Christ—an emphasis we have seen consistently surfacing throughout our study.[148] The believer, looking to Jesus as truly God and truly man, encounters his excellencies. Contemplating these truths will inevitably excite believers and encourage them to "give up themselves to be wholly his."[149] First, one may consider Jesus's deity. Because he is not merely man—contrary to the Socinian description of him as *purus homo* (merely human)—Jesus is able to be an "endless, bottomless, boundless" source of grace and compassion.[150] Since Jesus as the Son of God does not have a beginning, his love and grace are based in eternity rather than in something that merely arose in first-century Palestine. Because this love is eternal and unchangeable, believers are comforted that Christ will not grow weary and abandon them. The love and grace of Jesus is

---

145. E.g., ibid., 2:35, 62, 63, 118, 342; 6:466; 9:522; etc.

146. Ibid., 2:47. The Scriptures he uses are John 1:14, 16–17; 2 Cor. 13:14.

147. Ibid. Just as believers are encouraged to keep an eye on the Father, so they should continually eye Jesus as well. See also ibid., 2:203–6.

148. W. Sherlock aggressively attacked Owen's emphasis on "person" as running the risk of divorcing Christ from the "gospel"; see his *Union and Communion*, 1st ed. (1674), passim ad nauseam. Owen defends himself throughout his response to Sherlock, as in *Works* 2:328–31.

149. *Works* 2:59.

150. Ibid., 2:61, 68. Cf. Lech Szczuchi, "Socinianism," in *Oxford Encyclopedia of the Reformation*, esp. 4:85–86.

based in his character, and this presents a sharp contrast between his love and that normally expressed by the rest of fallen humanity. "Our love is like ourselves; as we are, so are all our affections."[151] As Owen sees it, the common phenomenon among humanity is that their love is noticeably fickle and transient, one day running deep, the next day turning to hatred for the same person. Not so with Jesus, whose character, and thus his love, remains faithful (as we already noted with the Father), never having a beginning nor an ending.

As with his deity, Jesus's humanity quickens a believer's heart toward communion with the Son. As the Lamb of God, Jesus was free from sin, without spot or blemish. This is an amazing truth to Owen since, while morally Jesus appears like Adam, his earthly situation was entirely different from Adam's. Adam was created "immediately from the hand of God, without concurrence of any secondary cause," thus securing his purity.[152] As we saw in chapter 3, Jesus was not born in paradise; but as Owen here vividly argues, he was "a plant and root out of a dry ground, a blossom from the stem of Jesse, a bud from the loins of sinful man,—born of a sinner, after there had been no innocent flesh in the world for four thousand years, every one upon the roll of his genealogy being infected therewithal."[153] It is not a problem, he explains, to imagine a flower growing in paradise, but to have a "spotless bud" arise out of the woods or in the "wilderness of corrupted nature" is enough to cause angels to desire an understanding of this great mystery. All born after Adam were not only defiled, accursed, and unclean, but also guilty of his transgression, since all sinned in him: "That the human nature of Christ should be derived from hence free from guilt, free from pollution, this is to be adored."[154] Since Jesus was "never federally in Adam," he escapes the liability of the imputation of sin, which is reckoned to the rest of humanity; sin is only imputed to the one who "was made sin" by means of his voluntary covenant whereby he is the mediator.[155]

---

151. *Works* 2:62.

152. Ibid., 2:64.

153. Ibid. Throughout *ΘΕΟΛΟΓΟΥΜΕΝΑ ΠΑΝΤΟΔΑΠΑ*, as in *Works* 17:183 (*BT*, 247), Owen shows familiarity and general agreement with the dating of his contemporary James Ussher's (1581–1656) infamous "sacred chronology," as in *Chronologia sacra . . .* (Oxford: W. Hall, 1660). See Hugh Trevor-Roper, *Catholics, Anglicans, and Puritans: Seventeenth Century Essays* (London: Secker & Warburg, 1987), esp. 156–61. Owen would clearly have been familiar with Ussher's work, since the appendix added to it after Ussher's death was created by Thomas Barlow (Owen's former tutor), at that time the Bodleian Librarian, appointed to this position by Owen.

154. *Works* 2:64. Owen says that such pollution "was prevented in him from the instant of conception" (65).

155. Ibid., 2:65.

Not only was Jesus free from sin; in his human nature he also was full of grace. Such an observation is firmly established, for Owen, within a trinitarian structure. He claims that the incarnate Christ received from the "fountain of grace" the Holy Spirit without measure, since the Father was pleased so to fill the Son. As such, Jesus was full of grace and truth, enabling "a certainty of uninterrupted communion with God."[156] The Spirit was the guarantee of the relationship. This fullness allows Jesus uniquely to supply others with the grace and truth they need.

Most astonishing to Owen regarding the excellencies of Jesus's divine and human natures is that they are united in one person. Owen's reasoning on this topic resembles classic formulations, with his obvious indebtedness to Leo, whom he twice quotes at length. Owen, apparently trying to model his interpretation on early patristic (and one might also argue Anselmian) reasoning, concludes: "Had he not been man, he could not have suffered;—had he not been God, his suffering could not have availed either himself or us,—he had not satisfied; the suffering of a mere man could not bear any proportion to that which in any respect was infinite."[157] Given these reflections, Jesus is a fit mediator, for one cannot understand his grace apart from his person. It is not enough simply to think of his deity, or only to think of his humanity, but the "treasure of Christ's work" must always be marveled at in light of his *person*, which perfectly unites his divine and human natures.[158]

These reflections, under the heading "personal grace," have immediate implications for Owen's theological method and for his view of how one can know God or have any spiritual understanding. All true knowledge comes only through Christ, including (1) knowledge of God, (2) knowledge of ourselves, and (3) knowledge of how to walk in communion with God. This christologically based epistemology leads Owen to experiential application.

While creation itself does reveal and testify to many of God's "properties," only in Christ does one learn of God's pardon and mercy. Owen believes that to know the wisdom of God one must look to the crucified Christ.[159] God's particular "love unto sinners" is discovered only in the

---

156. Ibid., 2:66.

157. Ibid., 2:67. He cites Leo the Great: "Deus verus, et homo verus in unitatem Domini temperatur, ut, quod nostris remediis congruebat, unus atque idem Dei hominumque mediator et mori possit ex uno, et resurgere possit ex altero"; from *Sermon* 21.2 = *On the Feast of the Nativity* 1.2 (*NPNF²* 12:129). ET: "True God and true human meet in the unity of our Lord, so that, as befitting a remedy for us, one and the same mediator between God and humans was both able to die in virtue of the one nature, and able to rise again in virtue of the other."

158. See *Works* 2:48, 68.

159. Ibid., 2:79.

gospel.[160] The Spirit communicates this truth in Scripture (when referring to 1 John 4:8, 16, Owen claims "the Holy Ghost says") by revealing that God is love, so much so that he sent his Son to die on behalf of sinners.[161] Thus in Christ, sinners learn of God's love, and the Spirit of Christ continues to testify to this reality. Beyond simply the property of God's love, one sees more clearly and "savingly" God's vindicating justice[162] in the punishment of sin, his patience, wisdom, and all-sufficiency.[163] In sum, to have a true knowledge of God, one must look specifically to Jesus.

Similarly, only through Christ does a person gain a true knowledge of self, which includes a deeper knowledge of sin, righteousness, and judgment. The Christ who sends his Spirit convinces the world of sin in a way that surpasses the conviction caused by the law and conscience.[164] Human sin and rebellion against God is so serious that the death of Jesus Christ became necessary for fellowship between God and humanity to be reestablished. It should not be thought that the Father delighted in the blood, tears, and cries of his Son any more than he delights in the anguish of any one of his creatures (an idea Owen rejects outright). However, since God refuses to allow his creation to be unjust or unlawful, the Father, moved by his love, sends the Son, who voluntarily seeks to make atonement for a lost people.[165] Thus, by looking to Christ, sinners are confronted by their inability to make atonement for sin. Apart from Christ there can be no "true saving knowledge of sin," for "in him and his cross is discovered our universal impotency, either of atoning God's justice or living up to his will."[166]

160. Ibid., 2:81.

161. Ibid., 2:81–82. It is common for Owen to employ variations of this formula, "the Holy Spirit says," as for Heb. 3:7; 4:7 (esp. in *Works* 21:305 [BE 20:305]); Heb. 10:15–16; and with his reflections on these verses in his *Exposition of Hebrews*. Nevertheless, the contemporary commentator should not too quickly read back into Owen an unsophisticated dictation theory. Owen freely acknowledges the different personalities, styles, and emphases of the various authors of Scripture. Cf. Stanley N. Gundry, "John Owen on Authority and Scripture," in *Inerrancy and the Church*, ed. J. D. Hannah (Chicago: Moody, 1984), 189–221; idem, "John Owen's Doctrine of the Scriptures: An Original Study of His Approach to the Problem of Authority" (STM thesis, Union College of British Columbia, 1967); Donald K. McKim, "John Owen's Doctrine of Scripture in Historical Perspective," *EQ* 45, no. 4 (1973): 195–207.

162. See Trueman, "John Owen's *Dissertation on Divine Justice*," who rightly argues that Owen's mature understanding of vindictive justice is rooted in God's being rather than a free act of the divine will. "God's hatred of sin must manifest itself in an act of God's will to punish sin. Not to do so would involve a contradiction in God's being" (98). This is most clearly revealed in the atoning work of Christ.

163. See *Works* 2:83–91.

164. Ibid., 2:95.

165. Ibid., 2:96.

166. Ibid., 2:101, 105.

Through Christ's life, death, and resurrection sinners learn not only of their need to be freed from guilt, but also of their need to be "actually righteous." Just as clearly as Jesus on the cross demonstrates the reality of human sin, so through his life of obedience does he demonstrate true human righteousness. This righteousness, according to Owen, is made available to those who through faith enjoy the imputation of Christ's righteousness.

Reflecting on the knowledge of God and of oneself gained through Christ naturally leads Owen to consider how, in Christ, one gains a knowledge of "walking with God." Just as in any relationship, to walk with God requires an agreement between the two parties to walk together. Such agreement, however, would be impossible if Christ had not first taken away the cause and continuation of enmity, bringing reconciliation and establishing lasting peace with God. Since God remains wholly loving and just, one cannot approach the Father outside of the blood of Christ: to try such a thing would be to undervalue the incarnation and death of Jesus.[167]

Beyond simple agreement, there must be an acquaintance between the two who desire to walk together. Although William Sherlock thought Owen's ideas of "acquaintance" were suspect to abstract mysticism, Owen uses this language to protect the concrete connection between God and his people found in Christ. General revelation and even Scripture itself, apart from Christ opening it up, are insufficient: "All the world cannot, but by and in him, discover a path that a man may walk one step with God in."[168] Furthermore, since Christ is the "medium of all communication between God and us," he alone provides the way to walk with God.[169] Believers find strength and confidence to carry on this walking in Christ, keeping their aim the desire to bring glory to God.[170] Walking with God moves the believer's focus away from his or her own failings and the temptation of legalism, freeing one to the captivating affections the Son displays for believers.

The Son's Affections for Believers

A common misconception of Puritan theology has suggested that they focused on the believer's subjective internal disorders to the neglect of an assurance gained through the person and work of Christ. Such views usually contrast Calvin at this point with later Calvinism, claiming the former was christocentric while the latter was dangerously

167. See ibid., 2:107–8.
168. Ibid., 2:108–9.
169. Ibid., 2:109.
170. Ibid., 2:109–11.

anthropocentric.[171] While Owen highly valued Christian experience as a tool for his theology, he usually calls for the believer's attention to go *from* Christ *to* the self and then *back* to Christ, rather than remaining introspective. Indeed, introspection itself was normally encouraged only within a christocentric framework in order to avoid moralism. Owen clearly emphasizes the objective reality of the Son's affections for believers, which he believes liberates the believer.

He uses four particular expressions of the Son's love for believers: delight, valuation, pity and compassion, bounty. When believers realize how Christ graciously gives himself and his love, they naturally give and love in return—thus the communion is a genuine reciprocity, even though it is grounded in and secured by divine action.[172]

DELIGHT

The Son's delight in the believer is the basis of the believer's returned delight in the Son. Even as we recognized regarding the Father, Christ also sings and rejoices over the church.[173] Intimacy between the believer and Christ is possible because the Son of the Father so delights in the children of God. Thus, Christ reveals his "secrets" to his saints and enables them to reveal the "secrets of their hearts to him."[174] Christ calls believers his friends and reveals his mind and heart unto them by his Spirit in a way he does not do for those outside the fold. To believers, Christ reveals both himself and his kingdom, which is known through the "government of his Spirit in their hearts."[175]

While communion with the Son, in order to be communion at all, must be two-sided and have a reciprocal action, the participation of believers in their communion with the Son relies completely on divine aid: the work of the Spirit of Christ. When believers go to God expressing their desires, they must always approach with the Spirit's *assistance* and by *way* of the Son. This person, this great high priest, this Christ has worked and continues to work in and for believers, enabling them not only to approach God, but also to do so *boldly*—a theme Owen discusses at length in his *Hebrews* commentary.[176]

171. The classic statement expressing this line of argument is found in Kendall's work *Calvin and English Calvinism.* For particular accusations against Owen in this regard, see Stover, "The Pneumatology of John Owen." A recent and thoughtful response to such conclusions is found in Michael S. Horton, *"Of the Object and Acts of Justifying Faith* by Thomas Goodwin (1600–1680)," in *The Devoted Life,* ed. Kapic and Gleason, 108–22.

172. *Works* 2:118, 132.

173. Ibid., 2:118.

174. Ibid., 2:119.

175. Ibid., 2:120.

176. E.g., ibid., 21:428–38 (BE 20:428–38).

Although this sounds good theoretically, Owen's pastoral experience reminds him that such unhindered communion is the exception rather than the rule. So how should believers respond to his theology? Owen admits that sin will always try to disturb the rest that believers have when they commune with the Son. Nevertheless, the problem is not that *Christ's love* fades or lessens with the believer's struggle against sin, but rather that the soul becomes distracted or entangled in sin and thus avoids communion. Although God upholds communion, sin still attacks our side of the conversation. The relation ceases to be a communion when our response to God fails and we withdraw from him. Once the restless soul again allows itself to ponder and accept Christ's goodness toward it, the believer experiences a new level of rest and alertness, with a renewed obedience as the natural outflow. Christians tasting such communion seek to avoid temptations that can cause "disturbance of that rest and complacency" found in Christ, avoiding sin not out of fear, but out of a growing desire to have nothing between themselves and their Lord. "A believer that hath gotten Christ in his arms, is like one that hath found great spoils, or a pearl of price. He looks about him every way, and fears every thing that may deprive him of it."[177] The fear of the believer in this quotation is not that Christ may try to escape the believer's grasp and therefore he or she must tightly hold on to Christ—for this is the Son who delights in his people. Rather, believers fear their own waywardness, knowing how often they have been lured by the world and distracted from Christ, only to realize much later how far they have gone from the one they once held so dear.

We must not confuse this discussion of disrupted *communion* with that of undisturbed *union*. At no time is the believer's union with Christ at risk. However, the experiential communion with the Son does wax and wane, as commonly attested in Christian spirituality. Again, Owen's realism and practical concerns about human nature before the end-time glorification prompt him to encourage his readers to be careful, not because the Son will arbitrarily depart, but because the human heart so easily strays even from the one who most satisfies it. For the believer, neglecting communion with Christ is like the night, and even when one has tasted communion with the Son, one always longs for an even "nearer communion."[178] During times of darkness the believer must willingly engage in self-examination, seeking to discover where he or she may have gone wrong. Owen is here basing his reflections on the common allegorical reading of Canticles (i.e., Song of Songs). The woman of the story wanders about, seeking the cause of her spouse's

177. *Works* 2:126; cf. Song 3:4.
178. Ibid., 2:128, 126.

absence: "Have I demeaned myself, that I have lost my Beloved? Where have I been wandering after other lovers?"[179] Sometimes during this dry season the believer must show resolution and diligence in seeking Christ afresh. Going beyond private introspection, Owen encourages the believer to use the public means of grace (prayer, preaching, and the sacraments). Furthermore, since such dry periods are not a question of objective separation from God—God remains lovingly disposed toward and delighted in the believer who is united to Christ—but of subjective experience. The despairing soul may also turn to a "faithful watchman," who may advise the struggling believer.[180] This is a classic example of Puritan pastoral counseling, advising troubled believers to take their troubles to someone further along in the pilgrimage and thereby gain help and company through these difficulties. These are the ordinary means God employs to redirect his straying sheep.

VALUATION

The Son's delight in believers is no shallow amusement, but a matter of deeply valuing them. The simple fact of the incarnation, with all the pain and trouble that it involved, in particular the Son's "exinanition" (*exinanitio*, "emptying of the Son"), reveals his deep attachment.[181] Without this the Son would never have become a servant. Even less would he have done the unthinkable, of becoming obedient to death, which ultimately testified that "he valued them above his life."[182] While it appears throughout Owen's corpus that Christ particularly loves the church, that emphasis is strikingly clear in this section. The Son loves his "garden" far more than the "wilderness": "All the world is nothing to him in comparison to them."[183] Christ still prizes the weakest believer in the world "more than all the world besides." If believers grasped this, Owen explains, they would experience great consolation.

In response to Christ's valuing of believers, they are to value him. Quoting Luther's statement that Jesus is the most beautiful Lord (*pulcherrimus dominus Jesus*),[184] Owen argues that Christ should be valued above all else, including one's own life. When believers discover Christ and the value he has placed on them, they should willingly part with

179. Ibid., 2:129.

180. Ibid., 2:131. See Timothy J. Keller, "Puritan Resources for Biblical Counseling," *JPP* 9, no. 3 (1988): 11–43.

181. *Works* 2:134. See Heppe, *RD*, 488–94; Muller, *DLGTT*, 110.

182. *Works* 2:135. He concludes: "A death accompanied with the worst that God had ever threatened to sinners,—argues as high a valuation of us as the heart of Christ was capable of."

183. Ibid., 2:136.

184. Ibid., 2:137.

whatever brought inappropriate delight to them in former times: "Sin and lust, pleasure and profit, righteousness and duty, in their several conditions, all shall go, so they may have Christ."[185] One must be willing to give up everything to enjoy Christ, otherwise Christ is not one's highest value—a position only the Son of God deserves.

PITY AND COMPASSION

By looking to the incarnate Christ, we see the Son's affection of pity and compassion toward the believer. Sent by the Father, the Son assumed human nature and gained a "fellow feeling" with humanity, facing temptations and afflictions just as they do. This enables Jesus to have the heart of a sympathetic high priest, one who "grieves and labours with us."[186] Owen nevertheless does admit "there is something in all our temptations more than was in the temptation of Christ," a theme we have already discussed in chapter 3.

Because resisting temptation promotes communication with God, Owen describes ways in which he sees the Son aiding believers in their continuing struggle.[187] Christ gives them "a strong habitual bent against sin" and fortifies their hearts with his grace. Sometimes he will give a "strong impulse of actual grace" that will help protect them when they are on the edge of sin. At other times he will actually take away the temptation itself before it overwhelms the soul. When temptations grow, Christ will send "fresh supplies of grace" to bring strength to the weary. Wisdom is also often given in order to know how to combat temptation, usually by learning more about oneself. Finally, when the believer is overcome by temptation, Christ does not hesitate to be there "in his tenderness," bringing relief and pardon.

Not only did the incarnate Son face temptations; he also endured afflictions. From these experiences the Son is able to intercede to the Father on behalf of believers for their relief, "not only in respect of our sins, but also our sufferings."[188] Believers facing afflictions are to respond faithfully to God by not allowing their affections to cling to anything but Christ; during the difficulty they are to cherish the Spirit, whom Christ sent for believers' sanctification and consolation, themes we will discuss below. Therefore it makes sense that they should avoid grieving the Spirit through their unbelief, placing "comforts and joys in other things, and not being filled with joy in the Holy Ghost."[189]

185. Ibid., 2:140.
186. Ibid., 2:141.
187. See ibid., 2:143–45.
188. Ibid., 2:145.
189. Ibid., 2:149, 150.

BOUNTY

Finally, Christ's love and grace toward the saints is expressed in the rich bounty he provides for them. Owen considers it to be a great sin of believers that they do not make "use of Christ's bounty as they ought to."[190] Basing his conclusions on the character of God in Scripture, Owen argues that "whatever he gives us,—his grace to assist us, his presence to comfort us,—he doth it abundantly." For example, believers should not run from Christ, for his grace is like the oil that never runs out. Only from the perspective of the bounty of the Son's resources are believers in a position to seek holiness and obedience "unto Jesus Christ." Obedience is understood in light of the Son, not in order to gain justification, but because the Son has already secured the believer's good standing before God. Since God in Christ accepts believers, their obedience is pleasing to the Son, who honors the Father. There seems to be a peculiar relationship, however, between the believer's obedience and Christ. Thus the believer is encouraged in his or her obedience to view Christ in his bountiful love. As Philippians 1:29 and Hebrews 12:1–2 testify, Jesus is the author not only of faith but also of obedience, since he "adds incense to their prayers, gathers out all the weeds of their duties, and makes them acceptable to God." By obeying Christ, believers honor him and show the Son to be equal to the Father, "to whom all honour and obedience is due."[191] Such obedience is possible because of the bountiful resources made available in Christ. Only out of the bounty of Christ's love and grace can the believer seek the fruits of holiness, a quest that will not be fully satisfied until heaven.

Communion with Christ through Purchased Grace

Throughout Owen's writings one often comes across the terms "purchased" and "grace," but only in this book does he put them together as a unit. This phrase serves as a basic summation of the work of Christ, particularly his obedience, his suffering of death, and his continued heavenly intercession.[192] As the second Adam, Jesus lived a life of active obedience in order that he might take away believers' unclean robes and replace them with garments of righteousness. Understanding this as a voluntary and active work of Christ makes Owen wary of employing the classic division of active and passive obedience, for all "obeying is doing."[193] In this way, Jesus is truly the second Adam and not simply a puppet.

190. Ibid., 2:152.
191. Ibid., 2:153.
192. See ibid., 2:154–68.
193. Ibid., 2:163.

Purchased grace is subdivided into three graces. First, since outside of Christ there can be no communion with God, Owen believes that purchased grace removes the alienation caused by sin and provides the *grace of acceptance with God*. Second, the Son does not simply remove believers' sins, but through the *grace of sanctification* "He makes us not only accepted but acceptable."[194] Third, *the grace of privilege*—simply another way of speaking of *adoption*—is discovered by communion with the Son through purchased grace. Since sanctification and obedience are discussed in other sections, we may skip Owen's second point and focus on the graces of acceptance and adoption with God, especially since these two are integral to the theme of renewed communion with God.

ACCEPTANCE WITH GOD

Although Owen spends a great deal of time on acceptance before God, for our purposes we will concentrate on his trinitarian framework and the response he envisions for believers.

Even though only the Son assumed a human nature and suffered on behalf of God's people, Owen does not want believers to think that this means the Son loves believers more than does the Father or the Spirit. We have already recognized Owen's fear of this wrong thought in our discussion concerning communion with the Father. Given that the purpose of the "dispensation of grace" is to "glorify the whole Trinity," each divine person acts in a distinct and yet united way. Employing language of emanation, which might sound reminiscent of Neoplatonism but more likely comes from his studies of the early fathers, Owen pictures the overflow of love moving from the Father through the Son and Spirit. "The emanation of divine love to us begins with the Father, is carried on by the Son, and then [is] communicated by the Spirit; the Father designing, the Son purchasing, the Spirit effectually working: which is their order."[195] This reminds us of Owen's idea of the order of subsistence within the Trinity, which is how he explains that the Son became incarnate rather than the Father or the Spirit. Even as the love of God moves like a stream from the Father through the Son by the Spirit, so a believer returns to God by traveling back upstream, rather than

---

194. Ibid., 2:170.
195. Ibid., 2:180; cf. 20:35 (BE 19:35). Jonathan Edwards will later write along similar lines: "There is a natural decency or fitness in that order and oeconomy that is established. It is fit that the order of the acting of the Persons of the Trinity should be agreeable to the order of their subsisting. That as the Father is first in the order of subsisting, so He should be first in the order of acting. That as the other two Persons are from the Father in their subsistence, and as to their subsistence naturally originated from Him and are dependant on Him; so that in all that they act they should originate from Him, act from Him and in a dependence on Him" (*RR*, 71–72).

trying to jump straight into the river's source. Thus he explains, "Our participation is first by the work of the Spirit, to an actual interest in the blood of the Son; whence we have acceptation with the Father."[196] Quickening a person to faith, the Spirit creates an "interest" in the Son and the benefits he secures for believers.

The reader should not take this analysis as chronological because, even though the Spirit begins the movement in a person's heart, this does not occur outside a trinitarian structure: all work of the Spirit serves as "a fruit and part of the purchase of Christ."[197] The Spirit awakens believers to the benefits that Christ has already accomplished for them through his atoning work, and this ultimately leads to the Father's glory, with whom believers now experience true peace and acceptance. "And thus are both Father and Son and the Holy Spirit glorified in our justification and acceptation with God; the Father in his free love, the Son in his full purchase, and the Holy Spirit in his effectual working."[198] Although it is solely through Christ's death that God reconciles us with himself, he always affirms this within a trinitarian framework whereby the "whole Trinity" receives glory, and this affirmation is protected by acknowledging the Triune God's movement in terms of economic ordering. To neglect this structure will inevitably lead to a false conception of the Father and the Spirit—as if the Son were working alone. Such a misconception creates not only theological but also pastoral problems that can only be overcome by renewing one's view of "purchased grace" as the work of the entire Trinity.

In response to the Triune God's redeeming activity, believers are to yield obedience unto Father, Son, and Holy Spirit.[199] This is because obedience is not concerned primarily with an arbitrary set of rules established in nature; instead, obedience is the Triune God's will for his people, based on God's undivided being. Here Owen can speak of the one will of God without shying away from distinguishing between the divine persons. Each appoints and ordains the obedience of believers: Father by way of origin, Son as mediator, and Spirit as the one who calls believers. Out of his "electing love" the Father chooses some to be holy; from the Son's "exceeding love" some are purified to do good works; and "the very work of the love of the Holy Ghost" is to enable believers

196. *Works* 2:180.
197. Ibid.
198. Ibid. Cf. Wollebius, *Compendium*, 164: "The efficient cause of justification, that is, the agent that does it, is the entire Holy Trinity."
199. Cf. *Works* 17:418 (*BT*, 605): "Evangelium doctrina est de Deo Patre, Filio, et Spiritu Sancto ejusque cultu, nostraque obedientia ei debita." ET: "The gospel is the teaching about God [the] Father, Son, and Holy Spirit, and about the worship and our obedience due to God."

to bring forth fruit as he transforms them.[200] So while God does require obedience of his children, he personally makes such a response possible. Christian obedience

> is an eminent immediate end of the distinct dispensation of Father, Son, and Holy Ghost, in the work of our salvation. If God's sovereignty over us is to be owned, if his love towards us be to be regarded, if the whole work of the ever-blessed Trinity, for us, in us, be of any moment, our obedience is necessary.[201]

Obedience to God glorifies each person of the Godhead. Walking in obedience with God will show others a godly life and glorify the Father; the obedience offered to the Son is manifested by believing in him, so that others will learn that the Christ was sent by the Father; when one falls into disobedience, it grieves the Holy Spirit, but the Spirit is glorified when the fruits of obedience are displayed in a Christian's life.

This complex understanding of how believers relate to the Triune God illuminates Owen's thesis that we are created in the image of God. He stresses that "the Holy Ghost communicates unto us his own likeness; which is also the image of the Father and the Son."[202] Since humans reflect the image of the Triune God, they ought to relate to the different persons of the Trinity distinctly, yet as one (i.e., the triunity of God). Furthermore, all obedience must be considered "gospel obedience," lest it fall into legalistic moralism. No obedience may truly honor God outside of the purchased grace of Christ, the empowering of the Holy Spirit, and a knowledge of the Father's love. When obedience is sought in light of the gospel, the result is a renewal of the image of God in believers, whereby they are conformed to God. This transformation begins when one moves from hostility toward God and into God's family, a miraculous event explained in the doctrine of adoption.

ADOPTION

Communion with the Son includes adoption received through grace. Owen defines adoption as "the authoritative translation of a believer, by Jesus Christ, from the family of the world and Satan into the family of God, with his investiture in all the privileges and advantages of that family."[203] Here the paradigm shift is monumental: the person who once was bound in the chains of an oppressive family and existence is freed and brought into the caring household of God. Consequently the

200. *Works* 2:182–83.
201. Ibid., 2:183.
202. Ibid., 2:243.
203. Ibid., 2:207.

believer discovers God as Father and the Son as an elder brother, with other saints and even angels becoming fellow children in this kingdom family.[204] In light of this shift, the adoption is not only declared to Satan in a judicial manner, but experientially the Spirit of Christ moves in the believer's conscience and heart, testifying to a new familial position with a new name, which is "a child of God."[205]

With adoption comes not only freedom from previous bondage, but also a new sense of rights and privileges. Two significant ones are *liberty* and *title*.[206] Beginning with liberty, Owen bases his argument on Isaiah 41:1 and 2 Corinthians 3:17, connecting liberty with the Spirit's presence. Only by the anointing of the Spirit was Jesus able to proclaim freedom to the captives. Likewise, the Spirit of Christ is the Spirit of adoption: those formerly outside of God's family are not only engrafted, but also enabled to cry "Abba, Father."[207] The Son comes to set the captives free by the Spirit, which awakens the heart to sweet intimacy with the Father.

In light of this change, believers seek obedience not because they are servants, but because they enjoy the reality that "Sons are free."[208] Here Owen sees a difference—somewhat idealized—between slaves and children. Slaves obey from compulsion, whereas children enjoy freedom in obedience. While slaves may experience some outward freedom, children enjoy inward spiritual liberty toward God. Slaves might obey in order to avoid punishment; children desire obedience simply out of sheer love for God as Father. Here Owen describes Christians in terms of their response to the Triune God. They look at the Father and call out to him, "not in the form of words, but in the spirit of sons." This is possible because the Father always keeps the Son before the believer, knowing that his or her whole soul can endlessly delight in Christ.[209]

This picture of believers and their obedience to God does not fit the stereotyped legalism often alleged of Puritan thought. Children of God are enabled to obey and respond to God precisely because they have first encountered divine love: "From an apprehension of love, [believers] are effectually carried out by love to give up themselves unto him who is love. What a freedom is this!"[210] The movement is

204. Ibid., 2:209.

205. Ibid., 2:210. Owen's idea of a new name is based on Rev. 2:17.

206. Owen originally mentions four: liberty, title, boldness, and affliction; he fails to develop the final two of the list (ibid., 2:221).

207. Ibid., 2:211, based on Gal. 4:6–7. For a trinitarian emphasis on adoption, see 2:179.

208. Ibid., 2:213. He adds, "There is liberty in the family of God, as well as a liberty from the family of Satan."

209. Ibid., 2:215.

210. Ibid.

from God's love for them *to* their love for God and others. With willing and free obedience, they respond to God's love, manifested on the cross.

Adoption as God's children not only includes liberty, but also the privilege of a new title. This new title allows believers to partake and have an interest in the family of God. The primary purpose of the preached word is the gathering of the family of God "unto the enjoyment of that feast of fat things which he hath prepared for them in his house."[211] Believers obtain the title of membership in Abraham's family and thus are entitled to the future fulfillment of the inheritance. This title seals Christians as heirs to the promises of God, to righteousness by faith, and to final salvation.

Besides the "principal" rights noted above, there are also "consequential" rights for the children of God that pertain to the "things of this world." An Irenaean form of recapitulation appears in Owen's doctrine here, with Christ acting as the second Adam over creation. Sin's entrance into the world reversed the whole order of the original creation, and humanity forfeited its right and title to the land. This ushered in chaos and upset the primitive order. Hebrews 1:2, however, says that "Christ was the 'heir of all things,'" who has come to undo the curse to which the land was given over. Humanity's fall has deprived it of all title over the creation, and so it cannot "lay any claim" unto any part of the world. "But now the Lord, intending to take a portion to himself out of the lump of fallen mankind, whom he appointed heirs of salvation, he doth not immediately destroy the works of creation, but [doth] reserve them for their use in their pilgrimage."[212] The phrase "lump of fallen humanity" could have several patristic roots, although Owen gives no indication of his source.[213] Not only that, but whereas this language usually appears in discussions of the human nature assumed by the Son, Owen here uses it for the rest of creation. Now those who are adopted and find themselves "in Christ" become "fellow-heirs with Christ."[214] Christ is sovereign and supreme ruler over creation: believers have title to the things of creation, but are also accountable to their Lord.

Owen develops this reasoning in an interesting direction: only those who are in Christ have any title to creation, and those outside of the faith are *"malae fidei possessores*, invading a portion of the Lord's terri-

---

211. Ibid., 2:216.
212. Ibid., 2:219.
213. E.g., T. F. Torrance, *Trinitarian Faith*, 153, citing Basil, *Letter 261*, 2–3, in *NPNF*[2] 8:300; Weinandy, *In the Likeness of Sinful Flesh*, 32–33, citing Augustine, *Commentary on the Gospel of John* 4.10, in *NPNF*[1] 7:28–29. See also Kapic, "The Son's Assumption," 158.
214. *Works* 2:219.

tories, without grant or leave from him."[215] In God's patience, he allows those who are not adopted to enjoy the land, and they are protected in God's providence by civil government. Although believers have a *spiritual* right to the things of creation, they have no *civil* right except that which God has allowed them to acquire through normal means. There can be no seized property in the name of the Lord. Nevertheless, creation is redeemed in Christ, so it is the inheritance of believers who should in turn seek the greater welfare of society by their governance of it to the degree they have opportunity. Whatever God does give believers is theirs by right "as it is re-invested in Christ" and not as it is under the curse. Believers enjoying this privilege are "led unto a sanctified use of what thereby they do enjoy," since these things redeemed in Christ attest to the Father's love. On the other hand, Owen goes so far as to claim that unbelievers "have no true right unto any thing, of what kind soever, that they do possess."[216] Surely they have a civil right to their possessions, but no "sanctified right." Unbelievers will one day be asked to give account for how they used the gifts of God, and Owen sees little hope for their answer.

Owen concludes his reflections on communion with the Son by outlining the fullness of fellowship with the Son through adoption:[217]

Fellowship in name,	We are (as he is) sons of God.
in title and right,	We are heirs, coheirs with Christ.
in likeness and conformity,	We are predestinated to be like the firstborn of the family.
in honor,	He is not ashamed to call us brothers.
in sufferings,	He learned obedience by what he suffered; every received son is to be scoured.
in his kingdom	We shall reign with him.

This chart, capturing the consequences of adoption, illustrates the centrality of Christology as it informs Owen's overall approach to our communion with the Triune God. Apart from Christ, no union or communion can take place. In Christ, the believer has the privilege to commune with God and to be transformed into his image, preparing to reign with him. Understanding this transformation takes us to our next section, where our focus will be upon communion with the Holy Spirit.

215. Ibid., 2:220–21.
216. Ibid., 2:220: "They have a right and title that will hold plea in the courts of men, but not a right that will hold in the court of God, and in their own conscience."
217. Ibid., 2:222.

Communion with the Holy Spirit

Few in the twenty-first century would consider an emphasis on the Holy Spirit to be a particular strength of Reformed theology, but this has not always been the case. Calvin has been called the "Theologian of the Holy Spirit," a distinction that later Calvinists sought to maintain.[218] B. B. Warfield, the same author who gave Calvin this title, elsewhere uses inflated rhetoric in his claim that "the work of the Holy Spirit is an exclusively Reformation doctrine, and more particularly, a Reformed doctrine, and more particularly still a Puritan doctrine."[219] Writing before the expansive literature spurred on by the charismatic movement in the twentieth century, this Princeton theologian goes so far as to posit that Puritan thought and imagination, which were so captured by the person and work of the Spirit, possibly represent the doctrine's "highest expression in dogmatico-practical expositions."[220]

Warfield is not alone in his exalted assessment of the importance that Puritans placed on the Holy Spirit. Many have argued that a rediscovery, or at least a renewed zeal for exposition on the person and work of the Holy Spirit, took place in the seventeenth century.[221] In his lengthy essay on William Ames (1576–1633), John D. Eusden makes a similar observation, arguing that an insightful way to understand any major theologian or movement is to ask a key question: *Into which person of the Trinity do they pour most of their creative energies in explorative discussion?* For Augustine, one may think of the role of the Father; for Luther, the incarnate Son on the cross comes foremost to one's mind. But for Calvin and Puritan Reformed theologians, the "Holy Spirit was central; they were concerned especially with the present action of God in the lives of men; they were physicians of the soul, analyzing symptoms of spiritual decay and prescribing ways in which religious experience and renewal could take place."[222] While Eusden may rightly see William Ames as a significant figure within this tradition, arguably no other seventeenth-century Reformed theologian carries this pneumatological emphasis as far as John Owen does.

Many others in seventeenth-century England wrote on the Holy Spirit, but none so exhaustively as did the "Calvin of England." Owen penned

---

218. See B. B. Warfield, *Calvin and Augustine* (Philadelphia: P&R, 1980), 21.

219. B. B. Warfield, "Introduction," in A. Kuyper, *Work of the Holy Spirit*, xxxviii.

220. Ibid., xxviii.

221. E.g., Andrew A. Davies, "The Holy Spirit in Puritan Experience," in *"Faith and Ferment": Papers Read at the 1982 Westminster Conference* (London: Westminster Conference, 1982), 18–31; Roger Nicole, "New Dimensions in the Holy Spirit," in *New Dimensions in Evangelical Thought*, ed. David S. Dockery (Downers Grove, IL: InterVarsity, 1998), 331; Nuttall, *The Holy Spirit*, 1–19; Packer, *Quest for Godliness*, 179–89.

222. John D. Eusden, "Introduction," in Ames, *Marrow of Theology*, 36. Cf. *RR*, 239.

well over a thousand pages on different aspects of the person and work of the Holy Spirit. These are principally found in volumes 2–4 of the Goold edition of Owen's *Works*, although one cannot read *any* volume of his expansive writings without seeing his thoughts on pneumatology. For our purposes, we will look primarily at his treatise *Of Communion*, examining his view of the person and work of the Holy Spirit, and ending with a review of how believers are to respond to the Third Person of the Trinity.

God the Holy Spirit

Speaking of the Father and the Son as *persons* is hardly as conceptually difficult as referring to the Spirit in this fashion. During the seventeenth century a new skepticism was growing among many theologians regarding classical understandings of the Spirit. Some were opting for the old (fourth-century) Pneumatomachian heresy of a created Spirit, rather than the eternal Third Person of the Trinity.[223] Along similar lines, theologians like Episcopius believed that faithfully following biblical testimony pointed not only to an economic subordination but actually also to an ontological subordination of the Spirit; that view left the Spirit's position somewhat ambiguous.[224] Others reevaluated the biblical language and decided that πνεῦμα referred to a "virtue" of God, rather than to any sort of divine person. According to Owen, all of these conclusions were unacceptable and ultimately damaging to Christian experience.

The Holy Spirit is a person, and rightly acknowledged as such only within a proper trinitarian theology. Weak or mistaken understandings of the Triune God surface most often when discussions of the Spirit arise. To deny the person of the Spirit is actually a denial of the Triune God, and thus the end of positive theological reflection. Two exegetical examples from Owen will demonstrate his position on this point. First, Owen follows the classical reading of Acts 5:3–4, arguing that Ananias's lie was particularly to the Holy Spirit (not vaguely to the undifferentiated Godhead). Ananias lied to a distinct divine person, and in so doing, he lied to God.[225] We will discuss below the relation of the Spirit to the other

223. Cf. RC, 4.1 (p. 75n). In 1652 Owen and several other prominent ministers condemned the Racovian Catechism (published in England as the *Catechesis ecclesiarum . . . Poloniae* [Racoviae, 1607, 1609]) and sought to have it banned. In the end the catechism was recalled and burned (Toon, *God's Statesman*, 83–84). Owen also wrote *Vindiciae evangelicae* in 1655 (in *Works* 12:1–590), a lengthy treatise against the Socinian views of John Biddle.

224. Watkin-Jones, *The Holy Spirit*, 57–59. Episcopius's view was clearly not shared by most of the Remonstrants and is best considered as an extreme, rather than the norm, within early Arminianism.

225. *Works* 2:270.

divine persons, but for now we must simply record Owen's acknowledgment of the Spirit's distinct personhood.

Pronouns play an extremely important part in this discussion, especially since seventeenth-century Puritans' use of them varies widely when they are referring to the Holy Spirit. For example, Richard Hollinworth interchangeably refers to the Spirit as both "he" and "it."[226] Thomas Goodwin and John Howe normally refer to the Spirit as "him."[227] Geoffrey Nuttall similarly adds that Richard Sibbes also tends to refer "to the Holy Spirit as both 'it' and 'him'; Baxter appears usually to call the Spirit 'it'; Owen always 'him.' "[228] While we agree with Nuttall's assessment in general, there is an exception to this rule in Owen's writings. Even Owen's precise mind is open to slippage on this point. His frequent work with Greek texts, in which πνεῦμα is neuter rather than masculine, may explain the rare inconsistency. Within his discussion regarding Ananias, one reads: "The person of the Holy Ghost, revealing *itself*," but by the next sentence Owen jumps back into his modus operandi of referring again to the Spirit as "he." Applying a hermeneutic of generosity, it seems best to take Owen's standard phraseology (he/him) as his preferred manner of referring to the Spirit. As such, this slip is best read as an inadvertent inconsistency rather than a conscious restatement. Such an observation, however, highlights far more than Owen's standard vocabulary: it also signifies his insistence on always treating the Spirit as a *person* rather than a thing or vapor. Applying the personal pronoun seems useful in maintaining this distinction. Accordingly, when Ananias lied to the Holy Spirit, "he [Ananias] sinned peculiarly against him [Holy Spirit]."[229] By deduction, to sin against the Holy Spirit is to sin against a divine person, and to sin against a divine person is to sin against the Triune God.

This takes us to the second exegetical example: the unpardonable sin against the Holy Spirit (cf. Matt. 12:31–32; Mark 3:29; Luke 12:10). In this treatise Owen is less concerned with *what* this sin is, focusing instead on *why* it is unpardonable. His answer is simple: when you sin against the Spirit, you uniquely sin against the Triune God. Let us follow his logic. The Spirit does not come *only* by his own will or in his own name (though this is not to deny his will and name), but rather "in the

226. Richard Hollinworth, *The Holy Ghost on the Bench, Other Spirits at the Barre* (London: Luke Fawn, 1656). John Bunyan was also not particular about using personal and impersonal pronouns when referring to the Spirit; see Watkin-Jones, *The Holy Spirit*, 136.

227. E.g., Thomas Goodwin, *The Work of the Holy Ghost in Our Salvation*, in vol. 6 of *The Works of Thomas Goodwin*, ed. John C. Miller, 12 vols. (Edinburgh: James Nichol, 1861–66; repr., Eureka, CA: Tanski Publications, 1996); John Howe, *The Living Temple*, in vol. 3 of *The Works of John Howe*, 8 vols. (London: Religious Tract Society, 1862).

228. Nuttall, *The Holy Spirit*, 141.

229. *Works* 2:270.

name and authority of the Father and Son, from whom and by whom he is sent." Owen adds:

> To sin against him is to sin against all the authority of God, all the love of the Trinity, and the utmost condescension of each person to the work of salvation. It is, I say, from the authoritative mission of the Spirit that the sin against him is peculiarly unpardonable;—it is a sin against the recapitulation of the love of the Father, Son, and Spirit.[230]

In other words, to sin against the Holy Spirit is to deny God's loving movement toward fallen humanity. It is to accuse the Triune God of not caring enough for his creation, to deny the outward operations of the "whole Trinity," in the end demonstrating "contempt" toward "their [Father, Son, and Holy Spirit's] ineffable condescension to the work of grace."[231] In sum, it is to deny God's redemptive activity in reconciling the world to himself. Such a rejection of God seems not only unthinkable to Owen, but also unpardonable.

A brief look at the Spirit's relation to the Father and Son will lay the groundwork for Owen's particular concern about distinct communion with the Spirit. As we observed in the beginning of this chapter, even though Owen is seeking to explore "distinct" communion with the persons of the Trinity, he is theologically cautious in this endeavor. We see this caution arise most clearly at the beginning and end of the book. When discussing the Spirit, Owen recognizes the heightened opportunity for debate and misunderstanding; thus he tries to protect his work from objection by defining his parameters.

Owen affirms the Western conception of the *filioque*, since he believes the Spirit is sent from both the Father and the Son. The Father is the fountain of the Spirit's coming in a twofold procession: in respect to (1) the Spirit's personality or substance, and (2) the οἰκονομίκη concerning the work of grace.[232] In this context, Owen simply states rather than defends the first of these, which refers to the eternal procession of the Spirit from the Father and the Son. Moving to the topic of the Spirit's work in the economy of salvation, Owen adds some reflective remarks as he tries to hold together the Spirit's personality, his relationship to the Father and Son, and implications for the believer's view of the Spirit.

Christ promises to send the Spirit, which is thus commonly called the "Spirit of Christ." Coming from the Son, the Spirit's comforting presence among church members should be viewed as "better and more

230. Ibid., 2:229.
231. Ibid.
232. Ibid., 2:226.

profitable for believers than any corporeal presence of Christ," since the once-for-all sacrifice has been offered.[233] With this in mind, the Spirit moves to continue the work of the Triune God by testifying to the person and work of Christ. This testimony of the Spirit should not be viewed in terms of "his eternal procession, but of his actual dispensation."[234] Owen uses John 16:7—which speaks of Christ's coming departure to make room for the Spirit's descent—to show the connection between the ontological and economic Trinity: "This relation *ad extra* (as they call it) of the Spirit unto the Father and the Son, in respect of operation, proves his relation *ad intra*, in respect of personal procession."[235] Here Owen's logic moves backward, from the external works of God to the internal, establishing the Spirit's ontological relationship to the Father and Son. This connection allows for the believer's communion with the Spirit, since the only appropriate worship is worship of God.[236]

According to Owen, one danger in pneumatological discussions is the tendency to reduce the Spirit into something created, or inferior in divine essence, or simply "a mere servant." Such portrayals downplay the Spirit's "will" in the work of salvation. Owen does not hesitate to speak of the Spirit's will, just as elsewhere he speaks of the will of the Father and the will of the Son because he respects the freedom of God in redemptive activity. Just as the Father freely sends, so the Son is free even though he is sent, enabling him to voluntarily lay down his life for others. Likewise, "the Father's and Son's sending of the Spirit doth not derogate from his [the Spirit's] freedom in his workings, but he gives freely what he gives."[237] Does such a claim move Owen toward tritheism? He would certainly deny the charge. Although he mentions three wills, he grounds such language in the following presupposition: "The will of the Father, Son, and Holy Ghost is essentially the same; so that in the acting of one there is the counsel of all and each freely therein."[238] So the Spirit comes not reluctantly, but "he, of himself and of his own accord, proceedeth."[239] Like other Protestant scholastics, Owen is able

233. Ibid. Cf. Thomas Goodwin, *The Heart of Christ in Heaven, Towards Sinners on Earth . . .* , in *Works of Thomas Goodwin*, 4:101, who puts words into the mouth of Jesus and claims that the Spirit, "by reason of his office, will comfort you better than I should do with my bodily presence."

234. *Works* 2:227.

235. Ibid.

236. Cf. ibid., 2:270: "The formal reason of our worshipping the Holy Ghost is not his being our comforter, but his being God." He then adds that worship directed to the Holy Spirit "is no less directed, on that account, to the other persons than to him."

237. Ibid., 2:235.

238. Ibid.

239. Ibid., 2:227. One wonders if recent attempts to reformulate a basic trinitarian approach that more clearly accents the equality of the Spirit stems from previous theo-

to distinguish the Spirit from the Father and Son without fearing a trinitarian rupture.[240]

Working from within a covenant framework that extends into eternity, Owen says that the order of subsistence informs the economic workings of the Godhead: God's electing love springs from the Father's eternal purpose (πρόθεσις) and love, the Son's requesting (ἐρώτησις) that his death might benefit the church, and the Spirit's "willing proceeding" (ἐκπόρευσις) to apply the work of Christ to believers, bringing needed comfort to them until the day of glory. From this structure we can finally complete Owen's outline of distinct communion: "our peculiar communion with the Father in *love*, the Son in *grace*, and the Holy Ghost in *consolation*."[241]

The Work of the Spirit

When describing the work of the Holy Spirit, Owen discusses various aspects of that work at length.[242] We shall focus on how his presentation remains christologically grounded and experientially sensitive. Along the way we shall draw attention to Owen's guidance on how believers may "test the spirits."

While the Holy Spirit is distinct from the Son, this distinction does not mean a chasm between the two. When the Spirit came after the incarnate Son's departure, he came to enable the remembrance of the things of Christ, overcoming frail minds and disjointed memories.[243] Only by this testimony to the Son can the Spirit's role as Comforter be accomplished, for there is no true rest and consolation outside of Christ. Moving powerfully in believers' lives, the Spirit overcomes their despair when the "heavens are black over them, and the earth trembles under them," reminding them of the promises of Christ.[244] But there is no magic spell or incantation to guarantee the Spirit's movement, for as already stressed, the Spirit retains true freedom in consolation as in all his work. He freely brings comfort, even when it is not expected, which may partly explain the seasonal nature of Christian experience. Nevertheless, when comfort arrives, there is no mistaking it, for it will

---

logians' failure to emphasize divine freedom as Owen does. Cf. Weinandy, *The Father's Spirit of Sonship*.

240. Cf. Muller, *PRRD* 4:350–51.

241. *Works* 2:228.

242. Nine themes of the Spirit's activity, covering everything from the Spirit as Teacher to being anointed and sealed by the Spirit, are covered in Owen's exposition; see ibid., 2:236–49.

243. Ibid., 2:236.

244. Ibid., 2:238.

inevitably come in the form of the promises of Christ, which are the "breasts of all our consolation."[245]

Since the Spirit's work is *always* to glorify Christ, this provides a clear way to test the spirits. Does a spirit bring the person and work of Christ, as attested to in Scripture, to one's mind? Does he glorify Christ? If a spirit gives "new revelations" that subtly, or not so subtly, point away from Christ and the written word, then he is a false spirit.[246] The Spirit of God will *never* draw worship away from Christ; if a spirit does so, one may confidently assert that he is not the Holy Spirit: "We may see how far that spirit is from being the Comforter *who sets up himself in the room of Christ*."[247] Again, although Owen holds to distinct communion, he is grounded in the conviction of no *separation* within the Godhead. And if a spirit draws attention and worship away from Christ, he simply cannot be the true Spirit; as we stated in the beginning, any true worship of one divine person is worship of God: Father, Son, and Holy Spirit. One result would be to move toward tritheism and away from biblical monotheism, which explains Owen's uncompromising position regarding the relationship between the Spirit and the Son.

By persuading believers of God's love expressed in the promises of Christ, the Spirit convinces them of God's particular kindness toward them. Capturing all of one's "faculties and affections" with this revelation, the Spirit brings delight to the weary soul.[248] Again, the Christian is equipped to test the spirits. The result of the Spirit's movement of "shedding God's love abroad" in one's heart is *freedom* in Christ, whereas a false spirit only brings *bondage*. Here Owen is taking a sideswipe at the enthusiasts of his day, who "make men quake and tremble; casting them into an un-son-like frame of spirit, driving them up and down with horror and bondage, and drinking up their very natural spirits, and making their whole man wither away."[249] One must remember that William

245. Ibid., 2:239. Thomas Goodwin also uses this vivid expression when discussing communion with God; see *Of the Object and Acts of Justifying Faith*, in *Works of Thomas Goodwin*, 8:393. For an interesting exploration by a neo-Freudian who tries to make sense of such explicit language, see David Leverenz, *The Language of Puritan Feeling: An Exploration in Literature, Psychology, and Social History* (New Brunswick, NJ: Rutgers University Press, 1980).

246. *Works* 2:257.

247. Ibid., 3:239, emphasis added.

248. Ibid., 2:240.

249. Ibid., 2:258. For an excellent sampling of seventeenth-century enthusiasm, see Geoffrey F. Nuttall, *Studies in Christian Enthusiasm: Illustrated from Early Quakerism* (Wallingford, PA: Pendle Hill, 1948). The early Quakers are the most famous of the so-called enthusiasts. See also Hugh Barbour, *The Quakers in Puritan England* (New Haven: Yale University Press, 1964); Barry Reay, *The Quakers and the English Revolution* (London: Temple Smith, 1985), esp. 35–37.

Sherlock includes Owen in the enthusiasts' camp because of the personal and somewhat mystical language Owen uses to describe intimacy with God. But here is the fundamental difference: contrary to the tendency among so-called enthusiasts, Owen's mysticism affirms human faculties and sees communion only occurring by their proper operation. For Owen, the Holy Spirit engages all of a believer's natural faculties as created in the image of God, whereas false spirits move against them. This helps explain why Owen reacted so harshly against two Quaker women, Elizabeth Fletcher and Elizabeth Homes, who came and caused a major stir at Oxford while Owen was vice-chancellor. According to Owen, both women seemed to act completely irrationally; Fletcher even removed her clothing and "walked semi-naked through the streets, proclaiming the terrible day of the Lord."[250] These two Quaker women were publicly calling the students away from their books and learning, believing that all one really needed was the "inner light" of the Spirit.[251] Such behavior indicated to Owen, not a person acting like an Old Testament prophet,[252] but someone following a false spirit. Those who follow after false spirits are forced to deny their true humanity by suppressing their mind, will, and affections, showing little physical control, and therefore trying to commune with God in a manner outside of the created order. Part of the Spirit's sanctifying work in believers is to renew their damaged faculties so that they are restored in a Godward direction. Communication between God and the believer assumes the believer's active participation, which encompasses, rather than suppresses, the whole being. In Owen's mind, these false spirits inevitably bring cruelty and bondage rather than the freedom experienced when a believer is fully engaged—via his or her natural faculties—in communion with God.[253]

Before glorification believers experience their freedom in Christ because the Spirit is given as an earnest (ἀρραβών).[254] Owen defines an earnest, or a pledge, as something given to someone, assuring the full and final payment to come. Even as an earnest must be of the "same kind and nature" as the final promise, so believers receive the Spirit, who enables enjoyment of God even in the midst of continued battles

---

250. Toon, *God's Statesman*, 76.

251. Cf. the cobbler Samuel How, *The Sufficiency of the Spirit's Teaching without Humane Learning*, 1st ed. (London: William & Joseph Marshall, 1640 [1639?]), who energetically argues for dependence on the Spirit rather than the "education" learned at Oxford and Cambridge.

252. Cf. 1 Sam. 19:19–24; Isa. 20; Mic. 1:8.

253. Owen does write explicitly against key elements of Quaker doctrine in his treatise *Exercitationes adversus fanaticos* (1658), in *Works* 16:424–76 (*BT*, 769–856). By choosing to write this piece in Latin, Owen is making a statement about the value of a full education for the minister.

254. *Works* 2:245–46.

with sin. By receiving the Spirit, believers gain an "acquaintance with" both the love of God and their inheritance. Enjoyment of God is found in recognizing the Spirit's movement in one's life, preparing one for eternal and unhindered communion with God. Communion grows in intimacy through prayer, which helps explain why the Spirit stirs the heart in this devotional discipline. Consequently, another sign of a false spirit is that he does not show himself as the Spirit of supplication. Whereas the false spirit belittles "such low and contemptible means of communion with God," acting as if there is a higher avenue, the Holy Spirit helps one carry out the spiritual duty of prayer, "exalting all the faculties of the soul for the spiritual discharge" of this exercise.[255] Prayer is the appointed means of maintaining communion with God, whereby the soul receives God's love through the intimacy of being in the Father's bosom. "The soul is never more raised with the love of God than when by the Spirit taken into intimate communion with him in the discharge of this duty."[256] This passage clearly demonstrates Owen's conviction that the "mystical" experience of communion with God must be realized *in*—rather than *against*—the ordinary means of grace (e.g., prayer, preached word, and sacraments).

Owen does not deny human intimacy with the divine, but instead defines the parameters for experiencing true fellowship with God. He clearly writes to avoid what he thinks are the extremes that the church must always resist when discussing the Holy Spirit. Satan has consistently used excesses to steer the church away from the true Spirit. The first extreme Owen mentions concerns those who "decry" the "gifts and graces" of the Holy Spirit, especially in public worship, by employing "an operose [laborious] form of service."[257] In this way, dependence on the Spirit's ministry and gifting is lessened, leaving instead a sophisticated liturgy devoid of spiritual power. One result of this extreme is that the Spirit is neglected, and those who seek the Spirit or claim to be full of the Spirit are scorned. Apparently Owen believes that this was a significant temptation to previous generations of the church. Instead of responding with fear and mistrust toward the spiritual, Owen boldly proclaims, "Let us be zealous of the gifts of the Spirit, not envious at them."[258] On the other hand, Owen believes another extreme was growing rapidly in his own day, whereby Satan's tactic moved from outrightly opposing the Spirit to masquerading as him.[259] This is why Owen provides reflections on how to test the spirits, as we noted above. He wants Christians to

255. Ibid., 2:258, 249.
256. Ibid., 2:249.
257. Ibid., 2:255.
258. Ibid., 2:256.
259. Ibid.

be open to the Spirit without being drawn away by imposters. Looking at Owen's contrasting of the two approaches of Satan demonstrates his desire to acknowledge the continued active work of the Spirit without embracing seventeenth-century extremes of enthusiasm.[260]

Satan's working of extremes

In the past:	Now:
Cry up ordinances without the Spirit	Cry up a spirit without and against ordinances
A ministry without the Spirit	A spirit without a ministry
Reading of word enough, without preaching or praying by the Spirit	The Spirit is enough, without reading or studying the Word
Allowed a literal embracing of what Christ had done in the flesh	Talks of Christ in the Spirit only, denying he came in the flesh

Owen concludes, "Thus hath Satan passed from one extreme to another,—from a bitter, wretched opposition to the Spirit of Christ, unto a cursed pretending to the Spirit; still to the same end and purpose."[261] Believers must carefully avoid following Satan's extremes, instead relying on the Spirit of Christ, who draws his people into deeper fellowship with God.

Response to the Spirit

After spending this time in reflecting on the person and work of the Spirit, we ask, What implications does Owen draw for human experience? Just as one needs to make a distinction between union and communion with God, Owen calls on his readers to distinguish between receiving the Spirit of sanctification and the Spirit of consolation. While there is only one and the same Spirit, sanctification and consolation are distinct works. Using Ezekiel's imagery of the valley of dead bones, Owen claims that the "Spirit of sanctification" makes alive what was dead, and in doing so the recipient is necessarily and merely passive, "as a vessel receives water."[262] Once made alive in this manner, the Spirit acts for believers' consolation, but in so doing there is an "active power put forth in his reception."[263] What Owen means by this activity is an exercise or "power of faith," a believing in the Spirit promised in the covenant (cf. Eph. 1:13). Once enlivened, the believer cannot be a merely passive

260. See ibid., 2:257.
261. Ibid., 2:258.
262. Ibid., 2:231.
263. Ibid.

participant, but rather must actively seek the Spirit. Recognizing this dynamic of communion with the Spirit, one is now able to discuss the consequences of this relationship.

The primary characteristic of the Spirit's movement is consolation. Consolation from the Spirit should be *abiding* because it is based on God's everlasting faithfulness; *strong*, since it comes from the sovereign God, who overcomes all; *precious*, since it is experienced in relationship to Christ.[264] Therefore, while Christ is the Redeemer and Savior of the church, the Spirit is its Comforter. From this consolation comes peace and friendship with God: experiencing divine acceptance remains impossible without the Spirit. Peculiar communion with the Spirit comes when he comforts believers during their afflictions, grief over sin, and through their efforts toward obedience. Afflictions are unavoidable for everyone, and while people tend toward extremes when faced by them—either despising them as if they were not from God, or sinking under their weight—such times should, through the Spirit, drive each of us to the consolation of communion with God.[265] When one tries to "manage" situations apart from the Spirit, Owen believes there can be no true rest for the soul. Similarly, sin appears as an unbearable burden apart from the movement of the Spirit: "Our great and only refuge from the guilt of sin is the Lord Jesus Christ; in our flying to him, doth the Spirit administer consolation to us."[266] Here again, Owen's awareness of extremes is clear: apart from the Spirit, sin will either harden a person or cause one to neglect the means to resist temptation. In other words, with or without the Spirit, the same experiences come to all. The difference is whether one seeks the Spirit's consolation during these times.

Another consequence of communion with the Spirit is joy. The Spirit may work immediately or mediately to bring this about. *Immediately* signifies times when the Spirit himself comes with intensity, "without the consideration of any other acts or works of his, or the interposition of any reasonings, or deductions and conclusions."[267] These experiences, which usually arise unexpectedly and overwhelmingly, give renewed consideration to the love of God. On the other hand, the Spirit also works *mediately*, bringing a fresh sense of God's love through a renewed consideration of the believer's acceptance as a child of God. Even so, rational consideration of the promises of God apart from the Spirit's movement will fail to affect the heart, thus leaving it without joy and peace. Whether immediately or mediately, the action of the Spirit is the pivotal issue. The Spirit arouses hope in the heart of the believer

264. Ibid., 2:251.
265. Ibid., 2:259–60.
266. Ibid., 2:261.
267. Ibid., 2:252.

who expectantly waits in assurance, bringing a sense of boldness to an otherwise fearful soul.

Finally, Owen observes that Scripture uses negative commands to express communion with the Spirit, although always accompanied by positive duties. He refers to three pronounced warnings in the New Testament: do not grieve the Holy Spirit (Eph. 4:30), do not quench him (1 Thess. 5:19), and do not resist him (Acts 7:51).[268] "Grieving" refers to the Spirit's person, who dwells in believers, whereas "quenching" the Spirit refers more particularly to his "motions of grace." Similarly, "resisting" refers primarily to the Spirit's work through the word of God, and as such manifests itself in those who show contempt for the preached word. To avoid these obstacles to communion with the Spirit, one must seek "universal holiness" in response to the love of the Spirit, who "is striving with us"; the believer does this through growth in grace, since all movement in grace stems from the action of the Spirit.[269] Humbly placing oneself under the normal means of grace also promotes continued growth in communion with the Spirit.

Conclusion

In this chapter we have covered considerable ground by following Owen's attempt to employ trinitarian reflections for the encouragement of believers. In contradiction of the quotation from Kant, that "absolutely nothing worthwhile for the practical life can be made out of the doctrine of the Trinity," Owen's entire book shows how this doctrine speaks powerfully to the believer's relationship to God, both in understanding the structure of that relationship and in experiencing it. Since God has revealed himself, not as an undifferentiated Godhead but as triune, Owen calls believers to consider how they may commune with the three persons without abandoning the unity of God. We found him denying that God is a distant deity and unconcerned with the affairs of the world; instead, Owen presents God as triune, whose loving movement toward humanity brings about the communion between God and humans. Rather than being angry and arbitrary, the Father is the fountain or ocean of love, overflowing not simply to the other persons of the Trinity, but also to the world. As the Son delights in the Father, he willingly comes as the "sent one" whose unique person makes it possible for him to act as the mediator. Consequently the Son, out of his own delight, acceptance, and love for his people, is able to secure the redemption of the church.

268. Ibid., 2:264–68.
269. Ibid., 2:266–67.

The believer also communes with the Holy Spirit, who deserves equal honor and worship with the Father and the Son. The Third Person of the Trinity constantly draws believers to Christ, where they may find comfort during their earthly pilgrimage. In sum, we have displayed Owen's hope that believers equipped with a proper trinitarian appreciation of the love, grace, and consolation of God will find themselves in intimate communion with him. With this background we turn now to our final chapter, in which we explore the theme of signs that point to continuing communion with God.

SIGNS OF CONTINUING COMMUNION

Lord's Day and Lord's Supper

All duties proper and peculiar to this day are duties of communion with God. Everlasting, uninterrupted, immediate *communion with God is heaven.*

John Owen (1671)

There is, in the ordinance of the Lord's supper, an especial and peculiar communion with Christ, in his body and blood, to be obtained. One reason why we so little value the ordinance, and profit so little by it, may be, because we understand so little of the nature of that special communion with Christ which we have therein.

John Owen (1669)

Introduction

The topic of communion between God and believers naturally opens the question of the means of that communion. We have already addressed prayer as such a means in the previous chapter. Here we look at communion with God through ordained patterns of worship, specifically, a day of rest and the Lord's supper.[1] Each topic serves as a means for

1. Since Owen does not normally capitalize "supper" for Lord's supper and "day" for Lord's day, we will follow his style.

encouraging believers by emphasizing Christ, through whom communion with God is enjoyed. The Lord's day primarily reminds worshippers of the original goodness of creation and human rest, which is found in God and necessarily renewed through Christ. Similarly, the Lord's supper points believers to the goodness of the new creation in Christ, who unites his people with himself, enabling them to enjoy the intimate love of God. While covering both of these topics, which were and often still are considered highly controversial, we will keep our focus mostly on Owen's depiction of the interpersonal relations in this fellowship, and how he sees Christ as the reconciliation between God and his people, which enables this fellowship to take place.

Day of Sacred Rest

During the seventeenth century, many debates examined the Sabbath's remaining significance for the Christian community. These debates addressed both theological and social questions. What is the relationship between the Old and New Testaments? How are law and gospel related? When should corporate worship take place? Does this day of sacred rest belong to the church only, or to the entire world? Can one work and play on the day set aside for corporate worship? At the heart of the debate is a key question: If the fourth commandment was not absolutely abolished in Christ but rather points back—at least in part—to a creation ordinance, what are the implications for the church and society at large? Several significant studies have covered these questions, looking not only at Puritanism in general, but also at the predecessors who influenced their thought.[2] Among these examinations Owen receives little coverage.

2. See, e.g., the three historical chapters by Richard Bauckham in *From Sabbath to Lord's Day: A Biblical, Historical, and Theological Investigation*, ed. D. A. Carson (Grand Rapids: Zondervan, 1982), 251–341; James Dennison, *The Market Day of the Soul: The Puritan Doctrine of the Sabbath in England, 1532–1700* (Lanham, MD: University Press of America, 1983); Patrick Collinson, "The Beginnings of English Sabbatarianism," in *Papers Read at the First Winter and Summer Meetings of the Ecclesiastical History Society*, Studies in Church History 1, ed. C. W. Dugmore and Charles Duggan (London: Nelson, 1964), 207–21; Robert Cox, *The Literature of the Sabbath Question*, 2 vols. (Edinburgh: Maclachlan & Stewart, 1865); Richard Gaffin, *Calvin and the Sabbath* (Fearn: Mentor, 1998); R. L. Greaves, "The Origins of English Sabbatarian Thought," *HJ* 23 (1980): 17–35; Peter Heylyn, *The History of the Sabbath* (London: Henry Seile, 1636); Christopher Hill, *Society and Puritanism in Pre-Revolutionary England* (New York: Schocken Books, 1964), chap. 5; David S. Katz, *Sabbath and Sectarianism in Seventeenth-Century England* (Leiden: E. J. Brill, 1988); Kenneth L. Parker, *The English Sabbath: A Study of Doctrine and Discipline from the Reformation to the Civil War* (Cambridge, UK: Cambridge University Press, 1988); John Primus, "Calvin and the Puritan Sabbath," in *Exploring the Heritage of John Calvin*, ed. D. E. Holwerda (Grand Rapids: Baker Academic, 1976), 40–75; Winton U.

Since this section simply outlines how the day of rest fits into Owen's understanding of communion with God, we may avoid many of the more general questions mentioned above. Instead, we will quickly move through several of his key themes: his belief that this day of rest is a creation ordinance, that the church must view the idea of rest christologically within the history of redemption, and that this theological motif must necessarily highlight eschatological implications for struggling believers living in the present.[3] Our exploration of this material will demonstrate how Owen views the day of rest as part of his underlying concern for communion between God and humanity. This theme links Owen's anthropology and his doctrine of fellowship between God and humankind: the day of rest that represents communion with God begins with creation, is disrupted by the fall, redeemed in Christ, and continues until fully realized in heaven.

A Creation Ordinance

Readers familiar with the text of the creation narrative face the danger that, because of that familiarity, they easily overlook some striking features of it. According to Owen, possibly the most staggering of these features is the idea of *God's* rest on the seventh day. In fact, part of the goodness of creation includes this day of rest. Encompassing not only the idea of God's satisfaction with his creation, this rest also represents his original desire for humanity to enter into the "enjoyment of that rest . . . in and with God himself."[4] God not only rested on that day; he also was "refreshed," taking "great complacency" in his works (Exod. 31:17).[5]

Solberg, *Redeem the Time: The Puritan Sabbath in Early America* (Cambridge, UK: Cambridge University Press, 1977); Keith Sprunger, "English and Dutch Sabbatarianism and the Development of a Puritan Social Theology, 1600–1660," *CH* 51, no. 1 (1982): 24–38; W. B. Whitaker, *Sunday in Tudor and Stuart Times* (London: Houghton, 1933). Bobick, "Appendix A: Owen's Sabbath Argument," in "Owen's Razor," 249–63, is the most extensive on Owen and the Sabbath, but his stated concern is "not so much its content but Owen's method of establishing a theological position" (249). Bobick is looking for signs of Ramist bifurcations in Owen's argument and says nothing of real bearing on our study. See also Wong, "Covenant Theology," 157–62, 336–42.

3. While Owen discusses the idea of Sabbath in various places, the two most enlightening are in his seven-volume commentary on Hebrews. His work *Exercitations concerning the Name, Original, Nature, Use, and Continuance of a Day of Sacred Rest . . .* , in *Works* 19:261–460 (BE 18:261–460), serves as one of the preliminary treatises preceding his verse-by-verse commentary (two whole volumes, about 550 pages each, contain six "Preliminary Exercitations"). The second source is found in his verse-by-verse commentary, most clearly expounded in his exegesis of Heb. 4. See esp. *Works* 21:197–346 (BE 20:197–346).

4. *Works* 19:266 (BE 18:266).

5. *Works* 19:334 (BE 18:334). Even though there may be some "anthropopathy" allowed here, the language of "refreshment" should not be read as intending "weariness"

Similarly, interpreting Zephaniah 3:17, Owen believes that God rests "in his love," for he "rejoice[s] . . . with singing" over his work.[6]

Any discussion of *human* rest, let alone a day of sacred rest, must accordingly begin by examining *God's* rest.[7] While Owen believes the day of rest is a creation ordinance and not an ordinance imposed later—here he follows the basic position laid out by scholastic theologians, both Roman Catholic and Protestant[8]—its prominent place in the natural order comes from serving as an expression of divine perfection. God's rest provides the foundation for humanity's rest and true happiness.[9] A human, unlike angels, who have the capacity for "constant contemplation," is a "middle creature," which means he is "composed partly of an immortal soul, of a divine extract and heavenly original, and partly of a body made out of the earth."[10] According to Owen, this dual design naturally leads to the division of work partly "divine" and partly "terrene and earthly."

While humans are designed to work six days a week, they are also created to benefit from a Sabbath: a unique day of sacred rest was beneficial for humanity even before the fall. This does not place the day above humanity, but rather serves as part of the natural design by which humanity worships the God of creation.[11] Each person was made to be a relational as well as a rational creature in the image of God; each is likewise enabled to respond to God through worship.[12] Accordingly, the seventh day was given for all of creation—not simply Israel[13]—and exists as part of the natural order. Consequently, this day must be understood as a positive moral law.[14]

---

on God's part, but rather as describing God's cessation from his work of creation. See *Works* 21:284 (BE 20:284).

6. *Works* 19:334 (BE 18:334).

7. Cf. *Works* 21:273–74 (BE 20:273–74).

8. E.g., *Works* 19:287, 300, 308, etc. (BE 18:287, 300, 308, etc.). Bobick, "Owen's Razor," 254–56, argues that Owen departs from Calvin at this point. Cf. Gaffin, *Calvin and the Sabbath*, 25, 30–32, 127, 149–50. See Calvin, *Institutes*, 1:394–401 (2.8.28–34). Despite the long-standing myth that a doctrine of a morally binding Sabbath was a Puritan innovation, there is clearly a medieval tradition of general Sabbatarianism (e.g., Aquinas), which is quickly picked up again by many leaders of the post-Reformation era (e.g., Beza and Bullinger), who influenced much of Protestantism in general, and Puritanism in particular. Likewise, it is inaccurate to claim this as a Puritan innovation used to divide the conformists and nonconformists, much less a means employed by Puritans to undermine the established church's authority. Most helpfully, see Parker, *English Sabbath*. Cf. Collinson, "English Sabbatarianism."

9. *Works* 19:333, 301 (BE 18:333, 301).

10. *Works* 19:315 (BE 18:315).

11. *Works* 19:332, 263, 403 (BE 18:332, 263, 403).

12. *Works* 19:336–37 (BE 18:336–37).

13. *Works* 19:291 (BE 18:291).

14. Cf. *Works* 19:328, 347, etc. (BE 18:328, 347, etc.).

Confusion and debate over the distinctions between natural, moral, and positive laws have a long history. Here Owen follows an argument similar to that made by Daniel Cawdrey and Herbert Palmer. In their *Sabbatum redivivum* they modify the traditional categories and argue that positive and moral laws need not be exclusive;[15] Owen employs this line of argument. Using this combination of positive *and* moral, Owen constructs a space to make a crucial distinction about the Sabbath. He affirms *a* day to rest as part of the creation order (i.e., moral), while at the same time arguing that *the specific* day on which this should be practiced was dependent upon God's clear command (i.e., positive), and may therefore be changed. Employing these technical theological distinctions, Owen discusses the differences between moral and positive laws, and those which are mixed: "For there may be in a divine law a foundation in and respect unto somewhat that is moral, which yet may stand in need of the superaddition of a positive command for its due observation unto its proper end."[16] While a day of rest is part of moral law, the "precise observation of the seventh day" is not part of this natural law and thus is changeable.[17] Whether humanity sets aside Saturday, Sunday, or some other day of the week, what is fundamental to the design of creation is that a day be set apart to enter God's rest, primarily through corporate public worship.[18] This original rest included (1) "peace with God," (2) "satisfaction and acquiescency in God," and (3) "means of communion with God. All these were lost by the entrance of sin, and all mankind were brought thereby into an estate of trouble and disquietment."[19] For Owen, employing this general link to the natural order partly explains why people throughout history have expressed and acted on a need to set apart sacred days in a vague attempt to find peace with the divine.[20]

Humanity's need for work and a Sabbath rest did not change at the fall, but our "state or condition" did change.[21] Not only did the fall

15. Daniel Cawdrey and Herbert Palmer, *Sabbatum redivivum*, part 1 (London: Thomas Underhill, 1645) and parts 2–4 (London: Samuel Gellibrand & Thomas Underhill, 1652). See Bauckham, "Sabbath and Sunday in the Protestant Tradition," in *From Sabbath to Lord's Day*, 323–26. Cf. Jean Porter, *Natural and Divine Law: Reclaiming the Tradition for Christian Ethics* (Grand Rapids: Eerdmans, 1999), 159–60.

16. *Works* 19:329 (BE 18:329).

17. *Works* 19:436 (BE 18:436).

18. *Works* 19:426, 362–64 (BE 18:426, 362–64). Elsewhere Owen argues that the resurrection provides strong evidence for believing that the Lord's day properly belongs on the first day of the week, as in *Works* 19:409 (BE 18:409).

19. *Works* 21:261–62 (BE 20:261–62).

20. *Works* 19:356 (BE 18:356).

21. *Works* 19:316 (BE 18:316). Owen's Continental contemporary Joshua le Vasseur also argues that, even if there were no fall, humanity would have had a specific time set

make labor difficult and troublesome; it also disrupted the natural ability of human persons to find their rest in God. Idolatry and impiety corrupt or destroy humanity's enjoyment of God through the Sabbath rest.[22] Either of these two sins produces a break in communion between God and humanity: one because people replace the true God with a false one; the other by denying God's wisdom and guidance for human life.

Owen reasserts his belief that this rest is directly related to communion with God, for he denies that anyone can recognize the true Sabbath without first knowing God. In other words, the sin of neglecting the Sabbath is of secondary importance, a consequence of the greater problem that a person does not "know and own the true God, and him alone."[23] Elsewhere, Owen similarly argues that the questions concerning the "separation of time" are secondary, since the "first object of this law or command is the worship of God."[24] Thus, on the Lord's day we are encouraged to think primarily of communion with God, which is enjoyed by entering into God's rest.[25] In this sense Owen falls within the general Puritan consensus: "The Sabbath was the great, regular red-letter day of the Puritan calendar, which looked both backward to the Creation and forward to the consummation of Creation in the eternal delight and rest of God's elect in heaven."[26] Yet, while Owen would be fairly comfortable with this generalization, he also adds to it a stronger christological focus, which deserves our attention.

Christologically Transformed

Three points hold Owen's concept of a day of rest together: it is based in creation, christologically transformed, and eschatologically informed. Since we have examined the first point, we now focus on the latter two. Although Owen views the Sabbath as a creation ordinance and not just as a shadow realized and done away with in Christ,[27] his Christology shapes his doctrine of the Lord's day, as it does with all his doctrine, and he argues that any theology of the Sabbath not centered on its Lord

---

aside for reflecting upon and worshipping God. See Joshua le Vasseur et al., *Thesaurus disputationum theologicarum in Alma Sedanensi Academia* (Geneva: sumpt. Joan. Ant. & Samuelis de Tournes, 1661), 1066; as cited in Jochem Douma, *The Ten Commandments*, trans. Nelson D. Kloosterman (Phillipsburg, NJ: P&R, 1996), 125.

22. *Works* 19:324 (BE 18:324).

23. *Works* 19:325 (BE 18:325).

24. *Works* 19:348–49 (BE 18:348–49).

25. *Works* 19:354 (BE 18:354).

26. Horton Davies, *Worship and Theology in England*, vol. 2, *From Andrewes to Baxter and Fox, 1603–1690* (Grand Rapids: Eerdmans, 1996), 245.

27. *Works* 19:379–84 (BE 18:379–84).

effectively denies the risen Christ.[28] Building on his covenantal theology, which holds together his concept of redemptive history, Owen asserts that the gospel has been the same from the beginning: "From first to last the gospel is, and ever was, the only way of coming unto God."[29] While a weekly day set apart specifically for corporate worship was part of the creation order, there were also "additions made unto it or limitation given of it," which served as shadows of Christ.[30] Both the rest attested to in the law of nature as well as that rest established under the law of institutions "were designed to represent the rest of the gospel."[31] Thus, the specific requirement of the seventh day and the role that day performed as a sign between God and ancient Israel under the old covenant have been abolished in Christ.[32]

The "law of institutions" supplements the law of nature because of the fall and foreshadows the gospel.[33] From the beginning, the Sabbath pointed to God's pledge toward humanity: he would be their God and dwell with them, accepting their worship. After sin destroyed the original communion enjoyed between God and humanity under the law of nature, the "rest of Canaan" began to symbolize the rest possible under the law of institutions. During this period of redemptive history, God claims that the land of Canaan will represent the land where he dwells and is worshipped, and consequently the people are invited to enter God's rest anew by following after him in faith and obedience. As a result, a distinct day of rest is instituted. Although the day set apart is still the last day of the week, the law of institutions "re-established [it], upon new considerations and unto new ends and purposes."[34] It acted as "a token, sign, and pledge" of God's resting "in his instituted worship." In other words, believers were allowed to enter God's rest during this dispensation even though the Lamb of God had not yet come and offered himself as a sacrifice for sins. Worshippers were to hold on to the promises of God, observing in faith the institutions that embodied the promises pointing to the coming Messiah, waiting for their actualization in the future. As the people kept the creation ordinance of a correct proportion of time—one in seven days—given specifically for the corporate worship of God, this day also signified *God's* rest, not under the law of nature, but under the law of institutions. Here again, the people learned

28. *Works* 19:269, 393 (BE 18:269, 393).
29. *Works* 21:239, 232 (BE 20:239, 232).
30. *Works* 19:383 (BE 18:383); cf. *Works* 21:304 (BE 20:304).
31. *Works* 21:275 (BE 20:275).
32. *Works* 19:384 (BE 18:384).
33. For this discussion, see *Works* 21:275–76 (BE 20:275–76). Cf. *Works* 19:413–16 (BE 18:413–16).
34. *Works* 21:275 (BE 20:275). Cf. *Works* 19:402 (BE 18:402).

that "he was their God and that they were his people." Because of sin, the law of institutions follows the law of nature, but ultimately it was the gospel—even during this earlier period—that grounded the promise of rest for the people of faith.[35]

The relocation of the day from the end to the beginning of the week does not occur until Jesus's resurrection. Although Jesus observes the Sabbath throughout his earthly life,[36] all things are renovated in Christ, and the old Sabbath is no exception.[37] In Christ, "the old law, old covenant, old worship, old Sabbath, all that was peculiar unto the covenant of works as such, in the first institution of it [the law of nature] and its renewed declaration on mount Sinai [the law of institutions], are all antiquated and gone."[38] The old creation and covenant are fulfilled; the new creation renovates the image of God in humanity that was lost as a result of the fall; believers benefit from participating in the new covenant made, confirmed, and ratified in Christ.[39] Consequently, the chief cause of Christian obedience is Christ's authority and love, not the curse of the law.[40] Since, as Owen believes, the New Testament celebrates a day of rest in light of Jesus's resurrection, it is appropriate to change not only the day, but also the name. Now it is best to speak, not of the Sabbath, but of the "Lord's day": this expression emphasizes "its relation unto our Lord Jesus Christ, the sole author and immediate object of all gospel worship."[41] So what does this rest in Christ mean? How does this rest in Christ tie creation, redemption, and the eschaton together?

Hebrews 4: Emphasizing the Already Rather Than the Not Yet

We turn to Owen's exegesis of Hebrews, chapter 4, with specific attention on verse 10, which is structured around the theme of a new Sabbath rest.[42] Owen contrasts his own reading of the passage with the consensus

---

35. For a discussion of how Owen's view of sin encompasses not only the individual, but also church and society, see Steve Griffiths, *Redeem the Time: The Problem of Sin in the Writings of John Owen* (Fearn: Mentor, 2001).

36. *Works* 19:370 (BE 18:370).

37. One must keep in mind, however, *Works* 19:404–5 (BE 18:404–5), where Owen does limit the meaning of "renovation," fearing that those who apply this to the Sabbath without qualification will lose the idea of a day of sacred rest.

38. *Works* 19:404 (BE 18:404).

39. *Works* 19:405–6 (BE 18:405–6); cf. *Works* 21:280 (BE 20:280).

40. *Works* 19:446 (BE 18:446).

41. *Works* 19:286 (BE 18:286).

42. For hermeneutical discussions relating to Owen's approach to Hebrews, one may begin with Henry M. Knapp, "John Owen's Interpretation of Hebrews 6:4–6: Eternal Perseverance of the Saints in Puritan Exegesis," *Sixteenth Century Journal* 34, no. 1 (2003): 29–52; idem, "Understanding the Mind of God"; Craig A. Troxel, "'Cleansed Once for All': John Owen on the Glory of Gospel Worship in 'Hebrews,'" *CTJ* 32 (1997): 468–79.

interpretation. Of primary importance is his early disagreement with "expositors generally," who interpret the rest spoken of in this passage as referring only to a future glory.[43]

Owen provides six reasons for his disagreement with this common reading. First, the principle of "rest" in Hebrews 4 cannot refer to eternal life, since the gospel is the same for both Old Testament believers and contemporary Christians: *all* who believe(d) will enter into eternal glory. Rather, this rest draws attention to what is "peculiar to the gospel and the times thereof," and therefore, this cannot be heaven.[44] Second, the author of Hebrews, whom Owen believes to be the apostle Paul,[45] proceeds in his argument by way of antithesis: the discussion contrasts Old Testament promise with New Testament fulfillment. Moses and Joshua pointed to the rest in Canaan, with Joshua even leading the people into the land where they could experience hints of church-state peace for the worship of God. But Jesus, as the true Joshua, leads believers into unlimited rest in himself.[46] Third, the intention of the author is for believers to enter this rest *now*, not simply in the future. Just as some of the people under Joshua entered into the land of rest during their lifetimes, so under Christ one may experience the present reality of rest. Fourth, Old Testament believers held on to the promises as "means" to enter into the promised rest, and these promises principally pointed to the person of Christ, not simply to the hope of eternity.

Fifth, expositors have failed by not properly recognizing the realized aspect of the eschatology in this passage. The promise, which one is encouraged to enter into, must be interpreted as the preached gospel. Heaven is only part of the gospel promises, while the primary object of faith remains "Christ himself" and "the benefits of his mediation."[47] Thus, rest in Christ is not for some future period, but presently experienced and enjoyed by believers.

Sixth, the design of this passage is *not* to argue that eternal life is greater than life under the law and the temporary rest experienced by the Israelites who entered Canaan, because none of the Hebrews doubted this

43. *Works* 21:215 (BE 20:215). Owen does not list any names, but the clear consensus was that this rest described believers' experience in heaven. E.g., William Bates, *The Everlasting Rest of the Saints in Heaven*, in *The Works of the Late Reverend and Learned William Bates*, 2nd ed. (London: James Knapton et al., 1723); and Richard Baxter, *The Saints' Everlasting Rest, or, A Treatise of the Blessed State of the Saints in Their Enjoyment of God in Glory*, 2nd ed. (London: Thomas Underhill & Francis Tyton, 1651); both build on Heb. 4.

44. *Works* 21:215 (BE 20:215).

45. For Owen's argument for Pauline authorship, see *Works* 18:65–92 (BE 17:65–92).

46. *Works* 21:216 (BE 20:216).

47. *Works* 21:217 (BE 20:217).

obvious observation. Rather, the argument here is to show the "excellency of the gospel" as realized in Jesus Christ over and above "the privileges and advantages" that the Jews enjoyed under the Mosaic law.[48] In other words, the rest referred to throughout Hebrews 4 is "that rest which believers have an entrance into by Jesus Christ *in this world*."[49] This point is central, not only to chapter 4, but also to the entire epistle, and any exposition of Hebrews that misses it will be accordingly distorted.

If the rest mentioned in Hebrews 4 does not refer to heaven, what does it refer to? Let us first mention some general observations and then conclude by observing Owen's exegesis of Hebrews 4:10, which adds an unexpected twist to the conclusions often made regarding this verse.

This new rest signifies peace with God achieved through the blood of Christ. Believers need not wait for heaven to experience this rest; it is already accomplished: "Justification, and peace with God thereon, are properly and directly ours."[50] Those who are in Christ worship God in the present, not with the "spirit of servants," but in the spirit of being sons and daughters. Although Old Testament believers were sons and daughters, they were also infants unable to guide themselves, which means they differed little from servants. But now, believers may enjoy the knowledge of being children of God: where the Spirit of Christ is, there is liberty to cry out to the Father, "Abba."[51] Since the yoke of the Mosaic law and institutions is broken, believers may rest in Christ rather than in the things that simply pointed to him. This rest calls believers to enter immediately into gospel worship and not to wait for glory. Owen's pneumatological emphasis causes him to see the Spirit as the means through which believers are now freed to worship God through the Son, and in the Spirit of Christ they find strength for every duty they face. Consequently, worship of God is easy, not burdensome. As we will see below, this easiness may be misunderstood if not grasped christologically. Consistent with his previously stated view, Owen finally asserts that we must first understand this rest as God's rest, which believers may *enter into*. "God resteth ultimately and absolutely, as to all the ends of his glory, in Christ, as exhibited in the gospel,—that is, he in whom his 'soul delighteth.'"[52] In his Son, God ultimately "rests in his love towards believers," and thus the worship of Christ is fully and finally what is required from people in this world. In our concluding remarks on the Lord's supper, we will discuss how God and humanity meet in the love

48. Ibid.
49. Ibid., emphasis added.
50. *Works* 21:218 (BE 20:218).
51. *Works* 21:218–19 (BE 20:218–19). Also see the discussion of adoption in chap. 5.
52. *Works* 21:220 (BE 20:220).

of Christ; for now it is sufficient to state that those who worship Christ enter into God's rest even in the present.

So how does this work out in his exegesis of Hebrews 4:10? The immediate passage (4:8–11) embedding this verse reads:

> For if Jesus [i.e., Joshua] had given them rest, then would he not afterward have spoken of another day. There remaineth therefore a rest to the people of God. For *he* that is *entered into his rest, he* also hath *ceased from his own works, as God did from his*. Let us labour therefore to enter into that rest, lest any man fall after the same example of unbelief. (Emphasis added.)

Most commentators, both then and now, read Hebrews 4:10 as applying to believers and their entrance into God's rest.[53] However, Owen is not satisfied with this interpretation. His arguments influence his formulation of how believers enjoy communion with God before glory.

Owen asks, What rest does verse 10 intend for the person? Some commentators argue that this verse refers to believers and conclude that this rest is from "sins," or from "their sorrows, and sufferings."[54] Problematically, the idea of rest is here contrasted with God's rest at creation (cf. Heb. 4:3–4, 10), wherein God "so rested from them as that *he rested in them*, and blessed them, and blessed and sanctified the time wherein they were finished."[55] In other words, the rest described here must be like God's rest at creation; this person does not find rest *from* his or her own evil deeds, but rather *rests in the good of God's finished labor*. Again, Owen asks, When do believers rest from their sins, sorrows, and labors? Given the realism that permeates his view of the continuous Christian struggle, Owen does not think believers can rest from temptation or sorrows, much less from the mortification of sin, before glorification.[56] This type of rest awaits them in heaven.

---

53. For Owen's handling of this verse, see esp. *Works* 21:331–36 (BE 20:331–36) and 19:417–21 (BE 18:417–21). Cf. William L. Lane, *Hebrews 1–8*, ed. Ralph P. Martin, Word Biblical Commentary 47A (Dallas: Word Books, 1991), 101–2.

54. *Works* 21:332 (BE 20:332).

55. Ibid., emphasis added.

56. Cf. *Works* 21:323 (BE 20:323). For Owen's classic expositions of the ongoing struggle Christians have with sin, begin by reading his shorter treatises: *Of the Mortification of Sin in Believers*, in *Works* 6:1–86; *Of Temptation: The Nature and Power of It*, in *Works* 6:87–151; and *The Nature, Power, Deceit, and Prevalency of the Remainders of Indwelling Sin in Believers*, in *Works* 6:153–322. For a new edition of the above three treatises, see John Owen, *Overcoming Sin and Temptation: Three Classic Works*, ed. Kelly M. Kapic and Justin Taylor (Wheaton: Crossway Books, 2006). See also Gleason, *Calvin and Owen on Mortification*; Steve Griffiths, *Redeem the Time: The Problem of Sin in the Writings of John Owen* (Fearn: Mentor, 2001); J. H. Yoon, "The Significance of John Owen's Theology on Mortification for Contemporary Christianity" (PhD diss., University of Wales, Lampeter, 2003).

Here we may find a subtle attack on Calvin's influential handling of this passage. The Swiss Reformer argues that from Hebrews 4:10 believers learn to "rest from our works."[57] To be fair, Calvin is arguing for a present experience of rest and goes on to connect the idea of resting from works with the practice of self-denial and mortification. But since Calvin is committed to seeing the rest in verse 10 as applying to believers in general, he asserts that this rest *"cannot be attained in this life,* yet we ought ever to strive for it. Thus *believers* enter it but on this condition,—that by running they may continually go forward."[58] While Calvin presupposes that the subject of the verse is believers, Owen wants to move from the general to the particular. Since Owen, like Calvin, believes that the argument of the epistle refers not to heaven but to the rest "in and of the gospel," the rest in verse 10, which is "entered into," must for Owen refer to the present experience of *someone besides a believer.*

Owen continues with the observation that, although Hebrews 4 has been using the plural (e.g., "us/we," vv. 1–3; "people of God," v. 9), in verse 10 it suddenly jumps to the singular: *"He* that is entered" (ὁ εἰσελθών).[59] Believers in general cannot be referred to here, but rather a particular person. Not only this, but the rest itself also is significantly described as *"his* rest." Whenever believers enter rest, it is never described as "their rest" or "our rest," but rather as "God's rest," "my [referring to God] rest," or "rest absolutely." As mentioned above, the foundation for human rest must always be God's rest, and so this verse—given Owen's theological presuppositions—cannot refer principally to a believer's rest. Again, there is a distinct parallel between the creation narrative and this passage, between the old and the new creation, but there is no comparison between God's works and the works of sinful humanity.[60] God is the author of both the old and new works of creation. These works of creation and building the church "must be *good* and *complete* in their kind and such as rest and refreshment may be taken in as well as upon. To compare the sins or the sufferings of men with the works of God, our apostle did not intend."[61]

The parallel between the old and new creation is illuminating. Forasmuch as God, at the foundation of the world, ceased from creating and took refreshment in his work, so also the Son ceases from his work of suffering—not facing death ever again—and delights with satisfaction in his works. "As our Lord Jesus Christ, as the eternal Son and

57. John Calvin, *Commentaries on the Epistle of Paul the Apostle to the Hebrews*, trans. John Owen (Edinburgh: Calvin Translation Society, 1853), 98.
58. Calvin, *Hebrews*, 99, emphasis added.
59. *Works* 21:333 (BE 20:333), emphasis added.
60. *Works* 19:417 (BE 18:417).
61. *Works* 21:333 (BE 20:333), emphasis added.

Wisdom of the Father, was the immediate cause and author of the old creation, . . . so as Mediator he was the author of this new creation."[62] This is not to say that, after the old or new creation, God ceases to care for and preserve his work and people in the Spirit; but it does affirm that God looks on these works as not only complete, but also good. Consequently, Owen argues the "he" must refer to Jesus. Joshua could not provide ultimate rest, and thus the people awaited another day and another person (Heb. 4:8–9). Every rest of God is preceded by his work.[63] Only Christ resting from his work in the incarnation can rightly be compared with God resting from his work at creation. While from the beginning the world observed a rest based on God's work of creation, now the church may enter into God's rest based on the person and work of Christ.

This brings us to Owen's eschatological emphasis. What does Owen mean by speaking of Christ resting from his work, and when does this rest begin? Owen defines the scope of Christ's works thus: "In brief, all that he [Jesus Christ] did and suffered, in and from his incarnation to his resurrection, as the mediator of the covenant, with all the fruits, effects, and consequences of what he so did and suffered, whereby the church was built and the new creation finished, belongs unto these works."[64] Although some might say that Christ rests from his work either at his death or his ascension, Owen looks instead to the resurrection. On the one hand, death cannot be his rest, for Owen believed that "this separation of body and soul under the power of death was penal, a part of the sentence of the law which he underwent."[65] On the other hand, the ascension describes not Christ's rest, but his taking possession of glory, which he considers a different thing from rest.

Instead, "in, by, and at his resurrection" Christ rests from his works. The reasons are fourfold: (1) at that moment, Jesus was freed from the power of death and the law; (2) all types, shadows, prophecies, and such that relate to the work of redemption are here fulfilled; (3) his work of fulfilling the law, subduing Satan, making peace with God, paying the price for redemption, and such were all finished; and (4) at that time he was declared to be the Son of God with power (Rom. 1:4; Acts 13:33).[66] Owen concludes that the author of the new creation enters into his rest on the first day of the week. Here we see the clear link between our background discussion of the Sabbath based in creation and its transformation as the Lord's day.

62. *Works* 19:409 (BE 18:409).
63. Cf. *Works* 21:278 (BE 20:278).
64. *Works* 19:419 (BE 18:419).
65. *Works* 19:420 (BE 18:420).
66. *Works* 19:420 (BE 18:420).

The consequences are clear: a new work of God has been completed, and *Christ* enters into his rest. Believers are invited to enter into God's rest. In this way, those in Christ are secure in the communion enjoyed by their head, who has already ascended into the heavens as their forerunner.[67] Additionally, the first day of the week, which celebrates the resurrection of Christ, becomes the new day wherein the community of God should gather together for worship.[68] This community rests not *in* their own works, nor even *from* them, but rather *in the person and work of Christ*. Believers will continue to struggle in their own experience of communion with God, but they gain assurance because the Son has entered into his rest, having accomplished his work of redeeming his people. Christians need not wait for heaven to know with confidence that God has entered the rest of his new work, and that he is satisfied with the work of the Son, rejoicing over it with singing. While living in a fallen world, believers still struggle; but through the resurrection of Jesus, they have a foretaste of what is still to come: "full and eternal enjoyment" of communion with God in heaven.[69]

This clarifies Owen's idea of easiness in worship mentioned above. Hebrews 4:11 moves back to the plural, "us," calling believers to labor "to enter into that rest." But what is this labor? It is belief. "To know God in Christ is 'life eternal'; . . . to believe, is to enter into the rest of God."[70] Again, this is not simply a future rest, but a present participation in the rest of Christ.[71] The day of sacred rest fosters human communion with God both in the present and in the future. This follows Owen's repeated pattern in which divine action always precedes and gives a basis for human response. In Christ, God has entered his rest, and believers, by being united to Christ, are called to enter into *his* rest. Because of this, the church considers this weekly event a celebration rather than a day for fasting and sadness.[72] It is a day in which all are called to enter the communion with God for which they were originally created. All may enter into God's rest by faith in Christ, the forerunner who has completed his work, declared that it is good, and rested from and in it. On this day the church celebrates renewed fellowship with God, looking forward expectantly to a time of "everlasting, uninterrupted, immediate communion with God [which] is heaven."[73]

---

67. Cf. Wallace, *Word and Sacrament*, 156; Heppe, *RD*, 637.

68. *Works* 19:410, 416 (BE 18:410, 416).

69. *Works* 21:325 (BE 20:325).

70. *Works* 21:338 (BE 20:338). This is why Owen believes that unbelievers shall never enter into the rest of God; see *Works* 21:204 (BE 20:204).

71. *Works* 21:344 (BE 20:344).

72. *Works* 19:459 (BE 18:459).

73. *Works* 19:452 (BE 18:452).

The Lord's Supper

Just as God gives us the Lord's day as an opportunity for intimate communion with him, the Lord's supper functions as a special ordinance in which communion between the divine and human may be enjoyed. Whereas the Lord's day is wrapped in the imagery of creation, the Lord's supper primarily points to redemption. Owen develops both divine appointments christologically. Although Owen's work on this subject is rarely examined, his discussion of the "peculiar communion" found in the Lord's supper ties this sacrament to the themes we have been exploring.[74] While baptism is the sacrament, according to Owen, of the believer's new birth, the Lord's supper is about "our further growth in Christ," and thus we repeat the sacrament.[75] The supper connects to our discussion because of its regular and repeated role in the life of the believer, who is being renewed in the image of God. This ordinance must be celebrated until the "end of the world" because it serves as one crucial means by which Christ is present with his people until the consummation.[76] In this ordinance, God and humanity meet in a most intimate way. Owen connects Christ's presence in the supper with the enjoyment of God's love and acceptance experienced therein.

A Peculiar Communion

In the words of Owen, the believer experiences a "peculiar communion" with Christ in the Lord's supper.[77] Modern readers familiar with the Puritans' emphasis on the written and preached word may be surprised to discover the elevated position Owen gives to this sacrament. Without doubt he wholeheartedly affirms that God represents Christ through Scripture as written and preached.[78] Yet Owen does not follow the growing tendency among late seventeenth-century nonconformists to devalue the Lord's supper.[79] The written and preached word are consid-

74. One exception to the neglect is Jon D. Payne, who provides a thoughtful introductory essay in a recent reprint of Owen's "Discourses" on the Lord's supper, in his *John Owen on the Lord's Supper* (Edinburgh: Banner of Truth, 2004), esp. 18–75.

75. *Works* 1:491; GC, 24, q. A, n. 3.

76. See *Works* 9:571–75.

77. Ibid., 9:523.

78. Ibid., 9:538–40.

79. Nuttall, *The Holy Spirit*, 90–101, sees a logical connection between Puritan attitudes toward the sacraments and their eventual disuse by the Quakers; Stephen Mayor, *The Lord's Supper in Early English Dissent* (London: Epworth, 1972), traces the eventual decline in appreciation for the Lord's supper among nonconformists. See also Christopher J. Cocksworth, *Evangelical Eucharistic Thought in the Church of England* (Cambridge, UK: Cambridge University Press, 1993), 54, 58–59; Horton Davies, *The Worship of the English Puritans* (1948; repr., Morgan: Soli Deo Gloria, 1997), 204–16; Darwell Stone, *A History of*

ered general representations of Christ, whereas in the Lord's supper the particular is discovered.[80] At this point there is great similarity between Owen and his elder friend Thomas Goodwin.

Goodwin argues that the supper is the "most immediate and expressive" representation of Christ in comparison with the "word read or heard."[81] While these other ordinances point to Christ as the "author and deliverer" of some truth being considered, the Lord's supper focuses believers on the *person* of Christ. "The word preached is termed the word of Christ, Col. iii [v. 16] and elsewhere, *but it is nowhere termed Christ*; no, nor is prayer or any other ordinance so named, but the rock was Christ, the bread is Christ, of which says, 'This is my body,' and of the wine, 'This is my blood'; yea, and it is Christ entire, whole Christ."[82] Notice the change in tense: whereas the rock *was* Christ, the bread *is* Christ, a move from past tense to the continuing present. Goodwin's overall reasoning in this section parallels Owen's thought on the closeness to Christ enjoyed by the believer in this sacrament.

In one discourse given before administering the Lord's supper, Owen claims that Christ in two ways draws people to himself. Preaching serves as the first way by calling all sinners to repentance. The sacramental meal is the second way, where believers are drawn "into actual communion with him" through their participation in this ordinance.[83] Owen places high value on the role of the supper in the experience of the Christian life: to lose this sacrament is to sacrifice much comfort and strength for the believer. It should not be surprising that, in one of his catechisms, Owen advocates the supper as part of the weekly worship service, or "at least as often as opportunity and conveniency may be obtained."[84] He goes so far as to argue that "we have in no other ordinance" the same communion enjoyed with Christ as is found in the supper.[85] Through this great mystery a believer receives Christ by eating and drinking: this is something not done in prayer, the hearing of God's word, nor "in any other part of divine worship whatsoever."[86] Only by maintaining the link between faith, the elements, and God's movement can this unique experience be fully appreciated.

---

the Doctrine of the Holy Eucharist, 2 vols. (New York: Longmans, 1909), with vol. 2 serving as a rare yet helpful resource, essentially offering selections from primary sources; Watkin-Jones, *The Holy Spirit*, 243–55.

80. *Works* 9:540.

81. Thomas Goodwin, *Of Gospel Holiness in the Heart and Life*, in *Works of Thomas Goodwin*, 7:312.

82. Ibid., emphasis added.

83. *Works* 9:595.

84. Ibid., 15:512; SC, q. 40.

85. *Works* 9:620.

86. Ibid.

The Presence of Christ

As we have already recognized in earlier chapters, Owen is well aware of the tendency among Christians to move toward extremes. For example, when he wrote his treatise on the Holy Spirit, Owen self-consciously argued against the Socinian rationalists on the one side and the enthusiasts on the other.[87] Approaches to the Lord's supper similarly move between two polar opposites and these extremes lose a proper understanding of the believer's experience of communion with God. Owen sees the two extremes as the medieval view of transubstantiation and the opposite view of empty symbolism.

Transubstantiation emerges, according to Owen, from a failure to uphold the role of faith in relation to the supper.[88] No other than the devil himself has used the idea of transubstantiation to "overthrow" faith.[89] Reading history with this in mind, Owen believes that the error of seeing the carnal presence of Christ in the elements arises directly from those who have not enjoyed the "spiritual experience" through faith, which gives rise to "sensible experience."[90] Those not having such legitimate experiences thought they could "do that with their mouths and teeth which they could not do with their souls."[91] With the loss of mystery comes the rise of transubstantiation.[92] This observation compels Owen to uphold some degree of mystery in his own references to the supper.[93]

For several commonly accepted reasons, Owen rejects transubstantiation. These include his view that Rome's position cannot be reconciled with common sense and reason, much less with faith.[94] Turning

87. See ibid., vols. 3–4, passim.

88. Ibid., 17:597 (BE 16:529). The Benedictine monk Paschasius Radbertus, writing in the ninth century, is commonly considered as the first to clearly teach the position that later became known as transubstantiation. Though opposed by the more Augustinian thinker Ratramnus, who argued for Christ's spiritual presence, Radbertus won the day, with transubstantiation later becoming the official Roman Church dogma under Innocent III at the Fourth Lateran Council (1215). See Philip Schaff, *History of the Christian Church*, 8 vols. (1910; repr., Grand Rapids: Eerdmans, 1985), 4: §§125–30; 5: §§41, 115–16. The Council of Trent (1545–63) later expounded on the church's more developed view of the supper (in sessions 13 and 22). For how English Protestant theologians respond to transubstantiation, see Peter Newman Brooks, *Thomas Cranmer's Doctrine of the Eucharist: An Essay in Historical Development*, 2nd ed. (London: Macmillan Academic, 1992), esp. 3–36; Clifford W. Dugmore, *Eucharistic Doctrine in England from Hooker to Waterland* (London: SPCK, 1942).

89. *Works* 9:572.

90. Ibid., 9:591; cf. 9:563.

91. Ibid., 9:591.

92. Ibid., 9:563.

93. E.g., ibid., 9:540, 583, 620, 621, etc.

94. See ibid., 9:572. Cf. Zwingli's similar link with "the reason of faith," explained by W. P. Stephens, *The Theology of Huldrych Zwingli* (Oxford: Clarendon, 1986), 244.

to biblical evidence, Owen believes that the idea of Christ's corporeal presence in the bread and wine undermines the New Testament view of the Holy Spirit. Owen's pneumatology stresses that the Third Person of the Trinity is the Spirit of Christ, and as the Comforter, the Spirit only comes afresh with Christ's physical departure. Maintaining the presence of Christ's corporeal body on earth (in the elements) rather than in heaven is "inconsistent" with his reading of John 16:7, which tells of the Comforter who will come *after* Jesus's ascension. In a sarcastic aside, Owen muses that the promise of the Spirit cannot be reconciled with the idea that Jesus *must* return bodily as often as the priests call him.[95] Agreeing with the Reformed, who saw their position as protecting the true humanity of Jesus even after his resurrection, Owen believes that Christ is present through his Spirit, but not bodily present in the elements.[96] Here Owen also seeks to avoid the Eutychian temptation of maintaining that Christ's divine nature absorbed his human nature, an idea he consistently rejects.

On the other hand, these "adversaries" (i.e., Roman theologians) charge their Protestant opponents with falling into mere symbolism, a charge Owen believes he escapes. The argument against Protestants like Owen was that, by rejecting transubstantiation, they failed to maintain any real difference between the communion with Christ in the preached word and that experienced in the supper. The Roman critics argued that unless one affirms a "real presence"—by which is meant a "real substantial transmutation of the elements into the substance of the body and blood of Christ"—there is nothing special about this ordinance.[97] In response, Owen argues that there is a peculiar communion with Christ in the Lord's supper: by faith, there is more in this ordinance than mere bread and wine, yet there is less than the carnal flesh and blood of Christ. Therefore, while Christ is present in the supper, believers cannot properly understand this reality in a corporeal manner.

Having rejected transubstantiation, Owen also refuses to see the supper as "naked" symbolism. Although Zwingli's reconsideration of the Lord's supper, with its stress on faith, symbolism, and thanksgiving, had a widespread impact upon many thinkers who followed, it was common among Reformed theologians to adopt a more mediated position, often attributed to Calvin, though similar to Peter Martyr Vermigli.[98] One sees

95. *Works* 9:572.
96. Wilhelm Niesel, *Reformed Symbolics: A Comparison of Catholicism, Orthodoxy, and Protestantism*, trans. David Lewis (London: Oliver & Boyd, 1962), 273–74.
97. *Works* 9:622; cf. *Council of Trent*, trans. Schroeder, 72–76.
98. For Peter Martyr Vermigli's influential writings on the subject, see Pietro Martire Vermigli, *The Oxford Treatise and Disputation on the Eucharist, 1549*, ed. and trans.

this supposed mediated view most clearly demonstrated in the Reformed confessions from the sixteenth and seventeenth centuries.[99]

While not entering the continuing debate about how best to understand the particularities of Zwingli's and Calvin's views of the supper,[100] we must affirm that many of the later Reformed thinkers tried to stress the real or true presence of Christ in the sacrament, and not simply their opposition to transubstantiation. B. A. Gerrish, muddying the waters a bit, argues that there are actually three doctrines of the Eucharist found in Reformed confessions: *symbolic memorialism* (cf. Zwingli), *symbolic parallelism* (cf. Bullinger), and *symbolic instrumentalism* (cf. Calvin).[101] The difficulty is that these positions are not necessarily mutually exclusive, and the shared language used by all only adds to the confusion. This is clearly seen, for example, in the difference between how Zwingli and Calvin understand symbolism: "For Zwingli symbolism is what enables him to use realistic language without meaning it realistically. For Calvin symbolism is what assures him that he receives the body of Christ without believing in a localized presence of the Body in the elements."[102] Such enduring ambiguity illustrates the danger of trying to categorize Owen in a particular eucharistic camp.

Although Owen often avoids stating the particulars of his own position, instead resorting to general and commonly accepted categories, he firmly holds that the elements are more than "a naked figure" or "bare" representation: "There is something in the figure, something

---

Joseph C. McLelland, Sixteenth Century Essays and Studies 56 (Kirksville, MO: Truman State University Press, 2000).

99. Jan Rohls argues along these lines in *Reformed Confessions: Theology from Zurich to Barmen*, trans. John Hoffmeyer, Columbia Series in Reformed Theology (Louisville: Westminster John Knox, 1998), 177–88, 219–37.

100. In deciding whether Owen's own views more closely resemble Zwingli, Calvin, or for that matter Bucer, what positions these theologians actually held would need to be generally agreed upon; no final voice has settled the heated debates. For one of the fairest treatments of Zwingli that takes into account how his thought develops, see Stephens, *Theology of Zwingli*, 218–59; on Bucer, see idem, *The Holy Spirit* (Cambridge, UK: Cambridge University Press, 1970), 245–50. Calvin remains the most disputed figure, being characterized as everything from a "crypto-catholic" to a "subtle sacramentarian"; see B. A. Gerrish, *Grace and Gratitude: The Eucharistic Theology of John Calvin* (Edinburgh: T&T Clark, 1993), 2–9. Besides the recent study of Gerrish, see also Wallace, *Word and Sacrament*, 133–74, 197–233. To understand how Luther fits into this discussion, see Hermann Sasse, *This Is My Body: Luther's Contention for the Real Presence in the Sacrament of the Altar* (Minneapolis: Augsburg, 1959).

101. B. A. Gerrish, "The Lord's Supper in the Reformed Confessions," *TT* 23 (1966): 224–43.

102. Ibid., 231. He adds that for Calvin, "because sacraments are divinely appointed signs, and God does not lie, therefore the Spirit uses them to confer what they symbolize."

in the representation; but there is not all in it."[103] Owen affirms God's omnipresence, but he also argues for a special divine presence in the ordinances.[104] Pagan idolatry used images to represent an *absent* god, but in the Christian ordinances believers encounter their *present* God.

Seeing that God is not absent from anywhere in his world, he nevertheless has chosen to show his presence in extraordinary ways at particular times and places. The Old Testament records numerous examples, such as the burning bush, in which God's appearance is clear and intense. Even so, Owen muses, sheep fed upon the same ground on the following day. Here he indirectly attacks Rome's view of the "permanence of Christ's eucharistic presence."[105] Owen argues that God may choose to make a specific space and time the locality of his special presence, but that it is holy only as long as "God's appearance made it so."[106] Similar examples include the tabernacle and the temple. In these, God's presence was instituted by no other than God himself. Wherever God may appear, there is his special presence. As these Old Testament revelations pass away with the coming of Christ, Owen knows that many have declared Christ's special presence no longer to be found in any ordinance. He flatly rejects such a position. Although his congregation may claim that it was easier for Old Testament saints to go to a designated place (e.g., the temple) and expect God's presence, Owen thinks the case is no different for the faithful living in the present. He emphatically proclaims, "It is no harder matter for us to go and expect God's presence in his instituted ordinances now than for them to go to the temple; considering [that] God, as the object of our worship, is no less present with us."[107] In the New Testament as in the Old, God meets with his people and blesses them through his presence in the ordinances.

The Lord's supper manifests Christ's special presence. There is, and must be, something real communicated in the supper, and here Owen affirms the vital role of faith and sacramental union:

> If there was no more in this ordinance exhibited but only the outward elements, and not, by virtue of sacramental relation upon God's institution, the body and blood of Christ, his life, and death, and merits, exhibited unto us, we should come to the Lord's table like men in a dream, eating

103. *Works* 9:563; cf. 17:597 (BE 16:529): "There is, indeed, a figure or representation in this ordinance; but that is not all."
104. *Works* 9:548.
105. Niesel, *Reformed Symbolics*, 105.
106. *Works* 9:549.
107. Ibid.

and drinking and be quite empty when we have done; for this bread and wine will not satisfy our souls.[108]

Unless believers enjoy a "real communication" in the Lord's supper, their actions are empty.[109] Through faith, believers see the connection between the signs and the things signified in the sacramental relationship.[110]

Not only is Christ's death set before the worshipper in the supper; it also is "an holy action" that "communicate[s] unto us spiritually his body and blood by faith."[111] Yet again, Owen tries to hold together divine action and human response: in this sacrament God's act is primarily to exhibit Christ to his people, and their primary act is to receive him by faith.[112] Christ is present in this sacrament, but without faith the participant does not benefit from that presence. E. Brooks Holifield, when discussing the misconception that Independents always held an "antisacramental spiritualism," turns to Owen as a counterexample: "Owen stressed even more than Calvin himself the uniqueness of the sacramental presence."[113] Certainly Holifield is correct insofar as Owen does argue for a communion with Christ that is "special and peculiar" to the supper. Faith sees in the supper the death of Christ, and it causes what is past to be "present to the soul. It is to realize it and bring it before us. It is not a bare remembrance of it, but such a one as makes it present."[114] Owen goes on to claim that, by faith, participation in the supper brings the same advantage "as there would have been if we had stood by the cross."[115] This image takes one to the heart of Owen's view of

108. Ibid., 9:617. This serves as an excellent example of how Owen's language is saturated with biblical imagery, even when—as is the case here—he does not directly cite a biblical reference. His imagery clearly comes from Isa. 29:8.

109. Ibid.; cf. Rohls, *Reformed Confessions*, 237.

110. This union, according to Owen's Continental contemporary Petrus van Mastricht (1630–1706), is not corporeal, nor imaginary, nor strictly spiritual, but "sacramental," by which "although the thing signified is not contained in the sign or, much less, is the sign by nature; but in virtue of the divine institution and promise there is such a moral nexus between thing and thing signified, that he who accepts the signs in the way appropriate to the divine institution, at the same time receives the thing signified" (cited in Heppe, *RD*, 598).

111. *Works* 1:491; GC, 24.1.

112. *Works* 17:599 (BE 16:531).

113. E. Brooks Holifield, *The Covenant Sealed: The Development of Puritan Sacramental Theology in Old and New England, 1570–1720* (New Haven: Yale University Press, 1974), 131. Cf. Charles E. Whiting, *Studies in English Puritanism from the Restoration to the Revolution, 1660–1688* (New York: Macmillan, 1931), 75–81.

114. *Works* 17:596 (BE 16:528).

115. *Works* 17:596 (BE 16:528). This imagery is similar to Zwingli's, who argues that "everything Christ did in the flesh becomes as if (*verlut*) present to them" (Gerrish, "Lord's Supper," 227).

the supper. To stand at the foot of the cross is not to eat Christ's physical body and blood, but to stand in the actuality of God's gracious presence. In his mind, Christ hanging on the cross is not primarily a gruesome picture, but rather the most colorful and rich tapestry of God's love. Bread and wine represent the person of Christ, who wholly identified with humanity and gave himself up as a sacrifice. Thus, in the person of Christ hanging on the cross, one encounters the depth of God's love and acceptance.

God's Love and Acceptance

Owen describes the Lord's supper under several headings, most commonly commemorative, profession, eucharistic, federal, exhibition, and incorporation.[116] These categories often overlap, and rarely does Owen use all of this language in any one setting. Nevertheless, through these various categories and diverse language, Owen weaves together a fairly consistent presentation. He regularly stresses God's love in Christ, who alone restores fellowship with God. By participating in the supper, believers taste their union with Christ by the power of the Holy Spirit, and the Spirit nourishes them in this renewed experience and remembrance of God's abiding love for those who are found in the Son.

As we have seen throughout his writings, when Owen stresses God's love, he often begins by reminding his audience that cosmic reconciliation is needed. Employing Aristotelian categories to understand why Christ was given up as the great sacrifice, Owen believes the *moving cause* was the eternal love of God, the *procuring cause* was human sinfulness—without sin there would be no need for Christ's suffering, the *efficient cause* was the justice and righteousness of God, and the *final cause* was the glory of God.[117] Although in Christ believers enjoy the forgiveness of sins, they should not forget the depth of the sinfulness out of which Christ has brought them by his sacrifice as remembered in the supper. Therefore, one way to prepare for the supper is by gaining a "deep sense of the infinite distance that is between God and us," not in order to keep believers away, but paradoxically, to bring them closer to their God. He adds: "Nothing brings God and man so near together as a due sense of our infinite distance."[118] Acknowledging the gap that

116. E.g., *Works* 9:538–44; 9:572–75; 9:594; 17:595–96, 598 (BE 16:527–28, 530); etc.
117. *Works* 9:525–26, 579.
118. Ibid., 9:551–52. Cf. 5:4: "It is required that [the theologian or minister] weigh every thing he asserts in his own mind and experience, and not dare to propose that unto others which he doth not abide by himself, in the most intimate recesses of his mind, under his nearest approaches unto God . . . and [his] humble contemplations of the *infinite distance between God and him*" (emphasis added). See also ibid., 24:40–41 (BE 23:40–41).

God has spanned enables worshippers to see the depths of God's love and to respond to him with gratitude.

Here again, faith plays a central role, for it allows "us to sit down at God's table as those that are the Lord's friends,—as those that are invited to feast upon the sacrifice. . . . God makes a feast upon it, and invites his friends to sit down at his table, there being now *no difference between him and us*."[119] In this supper believers are invited to the table for a feast, not to an altar for a sacrifice. There are no further sacrifices, nothing for those in Christ to fear. In the Lord's supper, Christ "hath perfectly made an end of all differences between God and us," embodying the grace found "in the heart of God."[120] Elsewhere Owen also describes Christ, who erects "a spiritual house," which is his church, "wherein he makes provision for the entertainment of those guests whom he so freely invites."[121] Those who enter this house eat of the bread and drink the wine "so graciously prepared," and by doing so they enjoy a special fellowship with God: "For in what ways or things is there nearer communion than in such?"[122]

This material indicates the weakness of Stephen Mayor's claim that Owen does not have a significant place for thanksgiving and joy in the Lord's supper.[123] Owen consistently upholds the eucharistic nature of the supper, not with reference to Christ's resurrection—as he does in his view of the Lord's day—but rather in view of Christ's atoning work on the cross.[124] Christ's suffering and believers' thanksgiving are intimately connected, for without the former the latter proves to be impossible.[125] The incarnate Lord approached his suffering with joy because of his love toward those for whom he endured the pain.[126] Thus, the act of remembering and showing forth Christ's death in the supper *is celebration*, for by participating in the meal, believers "profess and plead our interest therein" and receive the benefits from Christ's work.[127]

According to Owen, the Lord's supper uniquely highlights the particularity of the gospel. The promises of the gospel go out "indefinitely" to all who believe, but the supper moves from the universal to the particular. In the supper, "by God's institution, Christ is tendered and given to me and to thee,—to every one in particular; for it is by his institution that

119. *Works* 9:566, emphasis added.
120. Ibid., 9:565.
121. Ibid., 2:46.
122. Ibid.
123. Mayor, *Early English Dissent*, 121; idem, "The Teaching of John Owen concerning the Lord's Supper," *SJT* 18 (1965): 180–81.
124. E.g., *Works* 9:528, 537, 544, 589, 612; 17:596 (BE 16:528).
125. *Works* 9:569.
126. Ibid., 9:577.
127. Ibid., 9:579; cf. 1:469, 492; GC, 24.6.

the elements in this ordinance are distributed to every particular person, to show that there is a tender [consideration] and communication of Christ to particular persons."[128] In other words, whereas in preaching the word goes out generally to all who will hear, the supper makes the general more particular. In this sense, the Protestant scholastics speak of the "visible word," which applies only to Christians who may benefit from the sacraments.[129] "Now every one knows, that whatever feasts be prepared in the world, unless every one in particular takes his own portion, and eats and digests it, it will not turn to nourishment unto him."[130] "Christ had a special love, not only to the church in general, but the truth is, Christ had a special love for me in particular."[131] What baffles Owen is that he can see nothing in any believer, including himself, that would make Christ love them, and yet Christ does. This is how Owen expresses the Reformers idea of *pro nobis*: Christ gave himself "for us both collectively and individually."[132] While the proclamation of the gospel goes out universally and generally, in this ordinance Christ becomes most immediate to each believer. Functionally this particularity does not promote pride or intolerance of others, but rather, it inspires wonder at the undeserved grace bestowed upon individual sinners.

Central to Owen's entire conception of the Lord's supper is his view of God's love. As stressed above, we discover the clearest manifestation of God's love by looking to Christ, and especially to Christ crucified. While the procuring cause of the atonement is sin, the moving cause is God's eternal love.[133] Here Owen's strong trinitarian framework informs his understanding of the workings of this love and the place of the Lord's supper in it.

In a brief discourse on Matthew 3:17, which he preached before celebrating the Lord's supper, Owen connects God's intratrinitarian love with his love for his people.[134] Preached in 1676, six years before his death, this sermon reflects Owen's mature thinking on the subject and shows his logic: In the Lord's supper, believers are called principally to think

128. *Works* 9:600–601.

129. Heppe, *RD*, 595: "The word proclaims salvation to all who hear it, the sacrament appropriates it only to believers. The word is meant to arouse faith in itself, the sacrament is meant to fortify faith in the word"; cf. 601–4, 650–54. Cf. the Reformed Thomistic approach of Peter Martyr, who influences the direction of sacramental theology as it develops in England: Joseph C. McLelland, *The Visible Words of God: An Exposition of the Sacramental Theology of Peter Martyr Vermigli* (Edinburgh: Oliver & Boyd, 1957).

130. *Works* 9:601.

131. Ibid.

132. Ibid., 9:602.

133. Ibid., 9:525.

134. I.e., "This is my beloved Son, in whom I am well pleased" (Matt. 3:17; 17:5). For this short discourse, see *Works* 9:612–15.

of Christ's death; thinking of his death makes them remember his love; and reflecting on Christ's love leads them back to the fullest expression of love found in the Trinity. Only the person of Christ may be the "first complete object of the love of God the Father."

Here Owen makes a brief and rare comment regarding the immanent Trinity: "A great part . . . of the essential blessedness of the holy Trinity consists in the mutual love of the Father and the Son, by the Holy Ghost; which is the love of them both."[135] Thus it is the Son's divine nature alone that provides the "full, resting, complete object of the love of God the Father."[136] From eternity, this was the delight of the Father, and so Owen deduces that it was before the incarnation. From eternity the Son was begotten of the Father, for he comes from the bosom of the Father. God's love, therefore, cannot be rightly understood without seeing it first and foremost as an intratrinitarian love, wherein "every thing else of love is but a free act of the will of God,—a free emanation from this eternal love between the Father and the Son." Then Owen adds, "God never did any thing without himself, but the end of it was to manifest what is in himself."[137] Through his old and new creation God makes known his own power, wisdom, grace, and love. All love is but a reflection or shadow of *intratrinitarian* love.[138] People throughout the ages have contemplated both the idea and manifestations of love, but found it impossible to locate the source of that love; Owen sees the origin of all love in that "God necessarily loved himself."[139]

Next, Owen moves from immanent to economic trinitarian action and links it to the Lord's supper. For while this first love of God reflects intratrinitarian love among the divine persons and is what "we call *ad intra*," Owen makes the profound jump to God the Father's first act of love "*ad extra*." God's first loving action *ad extra* is focused on "the person of Christ considered as invested with our nature."[140] The humanity first loved by God is the human nature assumed by the Son, for God finds great pleasure in this union of the divine and human in the person of Christ. Without such love expressed in this union, there could be no "communication of

135. Ibid., 9:613.

136. Ibid.

137. Ibid.

138. Ibid.: "The sole reason why there is such a thing as love in the world among the creatures, angels or men,—that God ever implanted it in the nature of rational creatures,—was, that it might shadow and represent the ineffable, eternal love that the Father had unto the Son, and the Son unto the Father, by the Spirit."

139. Ibid. Cf. 9:613–14: "God's loving of himself absolutely as God, is nothing but his eternal blessed acquiescence in the holy, self-sufficing properties of his nature." Cf. Augustine, *The Trinity*, in *The Works of Saint Augustine: A Translation for the 21st Century*, trans. Edmund Hill (Brooklyn, NY: New City, 1991), 6:7.

140. *Works* 9:614.

love unto us."[141] Drawing from a series of divine declarations throughout the New Testament, Owen distills a consistent pattern: whether looking at Jesus's baptism, his personal testimony about the Father, or the transfiguration, all of these provide clear statements of the Father's distinct pleasure, delight, and particular love for his Son. Here Owen puts words into God's mouth, inferring God's heart from the events: "Let the sons of men (I speak it from heaven again and again) take notice of this, that the infinite love of my whole soul is fixed on the person of Jesus Christ *as incarnate*."[142] Without this christological connection, Owen can see no way for fallen human beings to be recipients of God's love.

In his work ΧΡΙΣΤΟΛΟΓΙΑ Owen similarly emphasizes that it is the "human nature of Christ, in his divine person and together with it," which is the "object of all divine adoration and worship." Consequently he warns that "no other creature," whether a saint or angel, should receive "divine honour," for this would be to "rob Christ of the principal flower of his imperial crown."[143] Thus, crucial to the believer's response in the supper is Christ's person as the object of faith, with Owen drawing particular attention to Christ's humanity.[144]

This takes our study full circle, connecting Owen's doctrine of the Lord's supper with his concept of the *imago Dei*, with which we began. Owen connects our renovation *into the image of God* with our *love for Christ*, claiming that God's work is organic, dynamic, and personal, rather than mechanistic, static, or impersonal. "Proportional to the renovation of the image and likeness of God upon any of our souls, is our love to Jesus Christ. *He that knows Jesus Christ most, is most like unto God*; for there the soul of God rests,—there is the complacency of God."[145] For Owen, growing in one's knowledge and love of God must be understood in a christological framework. Human communion with God occurs in, with, and through the incarnate Christ. The person who seeks renewal in God's image must "exercise" his love for Christ. Quoting Owen at length shows his logic, and the rhythms of his anthroposensitive movement:

> And pray let me observe it to you, the world, that is full of enmity to God, doth not exercise its enmity against God immediately under the first notion

141. Ibid. He adds, "From the first eternal love of God proceeds all love that was in the first creation; and from this second love of God, to the person of Christ as incarnate, proceeds all the love in the second creation."

142. Ibid., 9:614–15, emphasis added. He later adds: "The great satisfaction of the soul of God, wherein he rests and delights, consists in love to Christ as incarnate."

143. Ibid., 1:241.

144. E.g., ibid., 8:560; 9:522, 524, 560, 586–89, 590, 595, etc. Cf. Calvin's emphasis on participation in Christ's humanity: John Calvin, "Short Treatise on the Lord's Supper" (1540), in *Tracts and Treatises* (trans. Beveridge), 2:170–72; repr. in *RR*, 317.

145. *Works* 9:615, emphasis added.

of God, but exerciseth its enmity against God in Christ: and if we return to God by the renovation of his image, we do not exercise our love to God immediately as God, but our love to God by and in Christ. . . .

Here is a trial, brethren, of our return to God, and of the renovation of his image in us,—namely, in *our love to Jesus Christ. There God and man do meet,*—there God and his church above and below centre. The Lord grant that this ordinance may be the means to stir up our hearts more to the exercise of this grace![146]

Humans reflect God to the degree that they love Jesus Christ since Christ is the great object of the Father's love. A person never images God more clearly than when he or she is loving Jesus Christ.

To love Christ is to love God; to oppose Christ is to oppose God. For Christ is the one "adequate, complete object of the love of God, and of the whole creation that bears the image of God."[147] In the supper, the believing participant is reminded of God's love in Christ and is invited to share in God's love for his Son. To the believer, the reception of the supper visually displays God's redemptive action in Christ. In Christ alone, "God and man meet," and therefore relations between the divine and human occur only in Christ. To love Christ is to love God, and to be loved by Christ is to be loved by God. As our entire study has shown, *to be fully human as originally created is to be in communion with God, and that fellowship can only be centered upon Christ, where God and humanity meet.*

Conclusion

In this chapter we have observed how Owen exhibits the Lord's day and the Lord's supper as signs of continuing communion with God. The Lord's day not only points back to the original goodness of creation wherein humanity enjoyed fellowship with God, but also to the new creation discovered in the person and work of Christ. In Christ alone is fallen humanity able once again to enter into God's rest and delight, for "in, by, and at" the resurrection Christ rests from his work. Owen shows that Christ has accomplished and provided a rest for us, which will be fully realized in the world to come, but in which we may abide now. Believers enjoy the gospel in the present, knowing that the future holds out promise of perfect communion. Although believers still struggle with sin in this world, they can by faith enter into Christ's rest, since he has secured their "full and eternal enjoyment of God," which is fully

146. Ibid., emphasis added.
147. Ibid., 9:612–13.

actualized in the uninterrupted communion-with-God experienced in heaven.

Similarly, the "peculiar communion" with Christ obtained in the Lord's supper repeatedly encourages believers by faith. The supper is neither naked symbolism nor the material flesh and blood of Christ. Rather, in the supper the special presence of God is presented to believers, just as throughout redemptive history God has revealed his willingness to meet with his people and to bless them in the ordinances. Again, while divine action is given primacy in this "holy action" as Christ is exhibited, it still calls for human response through faith. The supper reminds believers not simply of God's general love, but of his love for them particularly. Love is pivotal to Owen's whole concept of the supper, and by implication, to his whole doctrine of human communion with God. As we discovered in Owen's mature reflections on the subject, the clearest display of a person's renewal into the image of God is seen in his or her response to Christ. The Triune God's love is embodied in the Son, who was sent by the Father and empowered by the Spirit. *In the love of Christ, God and humanity meet: in Christ, God and humanity commune.* This is what best defines being made in God's image. For Owen, anthropology only makes sense when developed within the framework of relations with God.

EPILOGUE

John Owen, often called the prince of Puritan theologians, clearly does not fit the dismissive stereotype too often given to Puritans. If his logic sometimes appears cold and crisp, its goal is warm and human. His anthropology has as its objective the pastoral concern of promoting his readers' and parishoners' communion with God, and it cannot be understood apart from the framework of that communion. We have studied a Puritan theologian who presents an early modern attempt at a holistic understanding of human existence grounded in a trinitarian and incarnational theology, informed by his own spiritual struggles, and aiming at the spiritual health of believers.

Scholars have been divided in their reading of Owen: some argue that he has an anthropocentric theology, while others describe it as theocentric. We contend that, while Owen is theocentric, this works hand in hand with his profound results in anthropological concerns. Throughout our study we have seen that Owen is best described as presenting an *anthroposensitive* theology: he avoids divorcing his theology from practical human applications, always weaving his theological reflections through with anthropological concerns. He achieves this primarily through his acknowledgment that humanity's alienation from and restoration to communion with God can only be understood by a christological analysis performed within a trinitarian framework. Whether he is discussing the Son's assumption of a human nature, how to approach the topic of justification, or the doctrine of the Trinity, Owen shows how the topic bears on the fellowship of believers with God.

Our investigation demonstrates that this Puritan theologian deserves further study, especially for his historical, theological, and pastoral significance. Although one should not romanticize the past or naively wish

235

to return to a previous century, there is great wisdom in listening to voices of the past, for they tend to foster fresh reflection and analysis among those willing to listen.[1] Renewed and fruitful efforts to better understand Owen in his historical situation have already begun (e.g., Trueman, Rehnman, et al.), with many more studies now in the works. Beyond historical investigations, however, two other groups may find Owen's writings worthy of renewed attention: those engaged in some form of pastoral ministry and those interested in contemporary theological discussions. A few suggestive comments growing out of our study will point down paths that appear inviting for future rambles.

First, Owen's concept of humanity, defined in terms of its created purpose for communion, deserves further attention. F. LeRon Shults's recent study traces the shift in contemporary theological thinking about personhood, which occurred in light of the relatively recent "philosophical turn to relationality."[2] Along similar lines Stanley Grenz's stimulating study *The Social God and the Relational Self* tries to bring together trinitarian theology and anthropology. Grenz reaches a common conclusion: Theologians after Calvin and Luther tried to "replace the concept of the divine image as a static structure of human nature . . . with a thoroughgoing dynamic understanding of the *imago Dei* as the human person standing in right relationship with God and thereby mirroring the divine." Nevertheless, they were not able to "expound fully an explicitly relational understanding of the divine image."[3] It is disappointing that Grenz does not even mention Owen, since this Puritan does provide an approach to anthropology that highlights relationality in terms of communion with the Triune God. While not abandoning concern for the "structure of human nature," Owen with his conception of the *imago Dei* tries to hold together both relationality and structure, thus moving beyond the problematic labels of "dynamic" versus "static." Though there is much to commend in the recent focus on relationality as a guiding light in anthropological discussions, we may wonder if the very term "relationality" is in danger of becoming meaningless, especially when it is cut off from classical conceptions of the human person. What or who relates to

1. For more detailed reflections on why twenty-first-century Christians would benefit from reading the Puritans in particular, see Gleason and Kapic, "Who Were the Puritans?" in *The Devoted Life*, 15–37, esp. 32–34.

2. Shults, *Reforming Theological Anthropology*. Cf. Alistair I. McFadyen, *The Call to Personhood: A Christian Theory of the Individual in Social Relationships* (New York: Cambridge University Press, 1990); Wolfhart Pannenberg, *Anthropology in Theological Perspective* (Philadelphia: Westminster, 1985); Gunton and Schwöbel, eds., *Persons, Divine and Human*; John D. Zizioulas, *Being as Communion: Studies in Personhood and the Church* (Crestwood, NY: St. Vladimir's Seminary Press, 1985).

3. Stanley Grenz, *The Social God and the Relational Self: A Trinitarian Theology of the Imago Dei* (Louisville: Westminster John Knox, 2001), 170.

what? How does such relationality occur? One does not need to return to an unreconstructed faculty psychology to learn from Owen's creative maneuvering through difficulties of this kind in his own day.

Second, current renewed discussions about the humanity of Christ would likewise benefit from more detailed interaction with Owen's views. For example, most contemporary theologians have tended to assume that only by the Son's assumption of a "fallen" nature can one maintain the full humanity of the Savior, while others fear that such an affirmation compromises Jesus's freedom from personal sin. Recent research is demonstrating, however, that the simple categories of "fallen" and "unfallen" may be insufficient to articulate nuanced views of the incarnation.[4] Furthermore, while it has been assumed that the "fallen" perspective offers more pastoral promise for bringing sympathy and comfort to the struggling believer, a fresh round of questions about such a presupposition may now be appropriate. Owen provides an older model that tries to affirm both the true humanity of Jesus in solidarity with others and the sinlessness of the Lamb: the path forward, according to Owen, is by an unflinching emphasis on the Spirit that is not limited to the virginal conception. Current discussions about the anhypostasis-enhypostasis formula, Spirit Christology, Jesus's self-understanding and vocation, the priesthood of Christ, and the atonement—all these would benefit from a richer appreciation of Owen's view of the Savior's humanity.

Third, the topic of justification is currently receiving more attention now than it has in centuries.[5] Although one positive result has been a fresh attempt to evaluate the doctrine in light of Scripture, one negative consequence has been proliferating caricatures of past doctrinal formulations. Too frequently Luther is portrayed as a navel-gazing, existentially

4. For further bibliographical data, see Kapic, "The Son's Assumption of a Human Nature." Cf. Crisp, "Did Christ Have a *Fallen* Human Nature?" Also, Hastings, "'Honouring the Spirit,'" 279–99, esp. 285–99; McFarlane, *Christ and the Spirit*.

5. A brief sampling of different perspectives covering both biblical and historical studies (not already mentioned in chap. 4) is all that can fit here: Carl E. Braaten and Robert W. Jenson, *Union with Christ: The New Finnish Interpretation of Luther* (Grand Rapids: Eerdmans, 1998); D. A. Carson, Peter Thomas O'Brien, and Mark A. Seifrid, *Justification and Variegated Nomism*, 2 vols. (Grand Rapids: Baker Academic, 2001); James D. G. Dunn and Alan M. Suggate, *The Justice of God: A Fresh Look at the Old Doctrine of Justification by Faith* (Carlisle: Paternoster, 1993); Mark Husbands and Daniel J. Treier, *Justification: What's at Stake in the Current Debates* (Downers Grove, IL: InterVarsity, 2004); Eberhard Jüngel, *Justification: The Heart of the Christian Faith* (Edinburgh: T&T Clark, 2001); Thomas C. Oden, *The Justification Reader* (Grand Rapids: Eerdmans, 2002); Mark A. Seifrid, *Christ, Our Righteousness: Paul's Theology of Justification* (Downers Grove, IL: InterVarsity, 2000); Pietro Martire Vermigli, *Predestination and Justification: Two Theological Loci*, ed. Frank A. James, Sixteenth Century Essays and Studies 68 (Kirksville, MO: Truman State University Press, 2003); N. T. Wright, *What Saint Paul Really Said: Was Paul of Tarsus the Real Founder of Christianity?* (Grand Rapids: Eerdmans, 1997), 113–33.

challenged monk who simply created a doctrine to satisfy a personal need. Protestant scholastics are trivialized as more influenced by Aristotelian logic than the Bible. Rather than dismissing the past, we hope that contemporary biblical scholars and theologians will treat historical achievements in doctrine that grew out of the Reformation, like Owen's understanding of justification, with the care they deserve, even if they do not completely approve of the results. Owen makes his way through difficulties such as union with Christ, imputation, guilt, assurance, and objective and subjective aspects of justification. He thereby provides an example of a classic Reformed theologian's attempt to formulate an exegetically faithful portrait, incorporating the wisdom of past orthodox theologians with his developed anthroposensitive method.

Fourth, in light of the renaissance in trinitarian theology, it seems that Owen's contributions should no longer be neglected.[6] As the likes of Irenaeus, the Cappadocian fathers, Calvin, Edwards, and Barth have proved to be most fruitful resources for furthering contemporary trinitarian discussions, Owen's voice also deserves renewed attention. Karl Rahner once expressed his concern that "Christians, for all their orthodox profession of faith in the Trinity, are almost just 'monotheist' in their actual religious existence. One might almost dare to affirm that if the

6. The recent literature on trinitarian theology is enormous, but some representative studies are Boris Bobrinskoy, *The Mystery of the Trinity: Trinitarian Experience and Vision in the Biblical and Patristic Tradition* (Crestwood, NY: St. Vladimir's Seminary Press, 1999); Leonardo Boff, *Holy Trinity, Perfect Community* (Maryknoll, NY: Orbis Books, 2000); David Coffey, *Deus Trinitas: The Doctrine of the Triune God* (New York: Oxford University Press, 1999); Stephen T. Davis, Daniel Kendall, and Gerald O'Collins, *The Trinity: An Interdisciplinary Symposium on the Trinity* (New York: Oxford University Press, 1999); Colin E. Gunton, *The One, the Three, and the Many: God, Creation, and the Culture of Modernity*, Bampton Lectures 1992 (Cambridge, UK: Cambridge University Press, 1993); idem, *The Promise of Trinitarian Theology*, 2nd ed. (Edinburgh: T&T Clark, 1997); Eberhard Jüngel, *God's Being Is in Becoming: The Trinitarian Being of God in the Theology of Karl Barth: A Paraphrase* (Grand Rapids: Eerdmans, 2001); Catherine Mowry LaCugna, *God for Us: The Trinity and Christian Life* (San Francisco: HarperSanFrancisco, 1991); Paul Louis Metzger, ed., *Trinitarian Soundings in Systematic Theology* (New York: T&T Clark, 2005); Jürgen Moltmann, *The Trinity and the Kingdom: The Doctrine of God* (San Francisco: Harper & Row, 1981); Lesslie Newbigin, *Trinitarian Faith and Today's Mission* (Carlisle: Paternoster, 1998); Ted Peters, *God as Trinity: Relationality and Temporality in Divine Life* (Louisville: Westminster/John Knox, 1993); Christoph Schwöbel, ed., *Trinitarian Theology Today: Essays on Divine Being and Act* (Edinburgh: T&T Clark, 1995); Kathryn Tanner, *Jesus, Humanity and the Trinity: A Brief Systematic Theology*, 1st Fortress Press ed. (Minneapolis: Fortress, 2001); John Thompson, *Modern Trinitarian Perspectives* (New York: Oxford University Press, 1994); T. F. Torrance, *Trinitarian Perspectives: Toward Doctrinal Agreement* (Edinburgh: T&T Clark, 1994); Kevin J. Vanhoozer, ed., *The Trinity in a Pluralistic Age: Theological Essays on Culture and Religion* (Grand Rapids: Eerdmans, 1997); Miroslav Volf, *After Our Likeness: The Church as the Image of the Trinity* (Grand Rapids: Eerdmans, 1998).

doctrine of the Trinity were to be erased as false, most religious literature could be preserved almost unchanged throughout the process."[7] Not so with Owen. His anthroposensitivity shows many practical, pastoral applications achieved by developing an incarnational theology with a trinitarian basis. In other words, Owen rejects any divorce between the doctrines of God and humans, or between dogmatics and ethics, for all theological reflections inevitably have practical implications. Owen provides a promising trinitarian spirituality, centering his formulation for understanding human beings on the idea of communion with God. H. Richard Niebuhr long ago warned about the danger of "three unitarianisms in Christianity," in which various traditions (and often distinct denominations) crudely focus on one divine person, but fail to be robustly trinitarian.[8] Drawing from his pastoral experience and theological reflections, Owen's extended argument for peculiar communion with the divine persons affirms both the unity and distinctness of God. In this case his method may be as stimulating as his content. Amid a fragmented church, might Owen's deliberations provide some possibilities for envisioning how a biblical trinitarianism could inform Christian experience and worship?

Finally, Owen's explorations of the Lord's day and Lord's supper provide useful tools for a contemporary assessment of how the worshipping community experiences the reality of God's presence, grace, and call to be light in a chaotic world. During the past fifty years there has been widespread interest in the idea of the Sabbath, as represented by the Jewish scholar Abraham Heschel's book *The Sabbath: Its Meaning for Modern Man*, which has had over twenty-two printings since its original publication in 1951.[9] Similarly, a recent surge in publications has promoted the idea of a day of rest among evangelicals.[10] But such volumes, even those written by Christians, do not always have the christological centering that Owen rightly requires. He thus would provide a rich resource for envisioning the importance of a day of rest understood in

7. Karl Rahner, *Theological Investigations*, trans. Kevin Smyth (Baltimore: Helicon, 1966), 4:79.

8. H. Richard Niebuhr, "The Doctrine of the Trinity and the Unity of the Church," *TT* 3 (1946): 371–84.

9. Abraham Joshua Heschel, *The Sabbath*, rev. ed. (New York: Farrar, Straus & Giroux, 2005).

10. E.g., Lynne M. Baab, *Sabbath Keeping: Finding Freedom in the Rhythms of Rest* (Downers Grove, IL: InterVarsity, 2005); Marva J. Dawn, *Keeping the Sabbath Wholly: Ceasing, Resting, Embracing, Feasting* (Grand Rapids: Eerdmans, 1989); Tony Jones, *Soul Shaper: Exploring Spirituality and Contemplative Practices in Youth Ministry* (Grand Rapids: Zondervan, 2003), 208–21; Eugene H. Peterson, *Christ Plays in Ten Thousand Places: A Conversation in Spiritual Theology* (Grand Rapids: Eerdmans, 2005), especially 108–18.

light of the life, death, resurrection, and ascension of Jesus.[11] Instead of focusing solely on creation as the context for understanding the Lord's day, a Christian doctrine of the day should move from creation to re-creation, and always in the light of the resurrection.

Although the Lord's supper is perpetually of interest among Christian theologians, evangelicals have tended to have an underdeveloped view of it. Again, there are signs of renewed interest covering both the theology and practice of the supper.[12] Owen's voice may be helpful because he places his discussion within a trinitarian matrix: the Father's eternal love for his Son, the centrality of the incarnation, and the promise of the presence of the Spirit. In this way Owen believes that these consid-erations uphold the significance of the supper for the worshipping com-munity without either compromising the continuing humanity of Jesus or reducing the supper to empty ritual. Such emphases are welcome if those who count Owen as part of their Protestant heritage are going to appreciate the richness of their tradition.

Throughout this book our goal has been twofold. Specifically, the aim has been to represent John Owen's anthropology in light of his view of communion with God, and more generally, to introduce a wider audience to this neglected theologian. It would be a great joy to learn that others from a variety of traditions find that reading Owen is a profitable use of their time. Understanding this Puritan divine will certainly enrich their view of classic Protestant Reformed theology, and carefully wrestling with his thought may even provide fresh insights into contemporary challenges and discussions.

It is fitting to close with an extract from Owen's tombstone, located in evocative Bunhill Fields, London:

> And, having set aside other pursuits, he cultivated and experienced the blessed communion with God of which he wrote. In this world he was a pilgrim who drew very near to grasping the full glory of heaven.[13]

---

11. E.g., Randy Reynolds and David Lynn, *Stress Relief: Overcoming Exhaustion, Re-lapse, and Burnout* (Grand Rapids: Zondervan, 1992), employ what is labeled "Sabbath Psychology," exemplifying a position almost lacking christological import.

12. E.g., Gordon T. Smith, *A Holy Meal: The Lord's Supper in the Life of the Church* (Grand Rapids: Baker Academic, 2005); Leonard J. Vander Zee, *Christ, Baptism, and the Lord's Supper: Recovering the Sacraments for Evangelical Worship* (Downers Grove, IL: InterVarsity, 2004); N. T. Wright, *The Meal Jesus Gave Us* (Louisville: Westminster John Knox, 2002).

13. "Et, missis Caeteris, Coluit ipse, Sensitque, Beatam quam scripsit, cum Deo Commu-nionem, in terris Viator comprehensori in caelis proximus." Toon, *God's Statesman*, 182–83, provides this Latin epitaph by Thomas Gilbert, along with his own English translation.

APPENDIX

Comparing Westminster Standards and John Owen on Humanity (Jesus's and Ours)

This appendix serves to illustrate points made in chapters 2 and 3. Here we have selectively gathered the most relevant statements concerning human nature in general, and Christ's humanity in particular (with emphasis added). The chart presents the closest parallels from Owen for the sake of comparison. As used in quotations throughout, "man" reflects the original language and the seventeenth-century's tendency to include both genders in the category of "man."

Westminster Confession of Faith	Westminster Larger Catechism	Westminster Shorter Catechism	Owen's Greater Catechism
Chap. 5.2 on creation: God "created man, male and female, with reasonable and immortal souls, endued with knowledge, righteousness, and true holiness, after His own image."	*Q. 17 on creation:* "God created man male and female; formed the body of the man of the dust of the ground, . . . [and] endued them with living, reasonable, and immortal souls."	*Q. 10 on creation:* God created "male and female, after his own image, in knowledge, righteousness, and holiness, with dominion over the creatures."	*Chap. 5.4 on creation:* Man was originally able to worship and serve God "to the uppermost, being created upright in the image of God, in purity, innocency, righteousness, and holiness."
Chap. 6.2 on the fall: Humanity became "wholly defiled in all the *faculties and parts of soul and body*."	*Q. 28 on punishments for sin:* The penalties are "either inward, as blindness of *mind*, a reprobate sense, strong delusions, hardness of heart, horror of conscience, and vile *affections*; or outward, . . . [including] all other evils that befall us in our *bodies*, names, estates, relations, and employments; together with death itself."	*Q. 18 on man's estate after the fall:* Man suffered "the corruption of his *whole nature*, which is commonly called Original Sin."	*Chap. 8.2 on the effects of the fall:* His list includes the idea that "our *souls* with [Adam's fall] were deprived of that holiness, innocency, and righteousness wherein they were at first created." Also, "pollution and defilement of nature came upon us." And finally came "an extreme disability of doing any thing that is well-pleasing unto God."

Chap. 8.2 on Christ the mediator: The Son took "upon Him man's nature, with all the *essential properties* and common *infirmities* thereof."	*Q. 37 on Christ becoming man:* He became man "by taking to himself a true *body, and a reasonable soul.*"	*Q. 22 on Christ becoming man:* He became man "by taking to himself a true *body, and a reasonable soul.*"	*Chap. 9.2 on God's means of redemption:* God worked redemption "by sending his own Son Jesus Christ in the likeness of sinful flesh, condemning sin in the flesh. —Rom. viii. 3" *Chap. 10.6 on why the Redeemer needed to be human:* Christ needed to be human so "that the nature which had offended might suffer, make satisfaction, and so he might be every way a fit and sufficient Saviour for men."
Chap. 8.4 on Christ the mediator: Jesus "endured most grievous torments *immediately in His soul,* and most *painful sufferings in His body.*" The biblical references here include feelings of "sorrow," "agony," and experiencing being "forsaken."	*Q. 39 on why the mediator had to be man (human):* "That he might *advance our nature,* perform obedience to the law, suffer and make intercession for us in our nature, *have a fellow-feeling of our infirmities.*" (Cf. also WLC, Q. 28.)	*Q. 27 on Christ's humiliation:* It "consisted in his being born, and that in a low condition, made under the law, undergoing the miseries of this life, the wrath of God."	*Chap. 10.5 on proving that Jesus was a "perfect man":* His proofs include noting how the Scriptures assign to Jesus "those things which are required to a perfect man; as first, a *body; . . . secondly, a soul . . . ; and therein [within the soul], first, a will . . . ; secondly, affections . . . ; thirdly, endowments."* He also includes *"general infirmities of nature."*

BIBLIOGRAPHY

Primary Sources

Alsop, Vincent. *Anti-Sozzo, sive, Sherlocismus enervatus: In Vindication of Some Great Truths Opposed, and Opposition to Some Great Errors Maintained by Mr. William Sherlock*. London: Nathanael Ponder, 1675.

Ames, William. *The Marrow of Theology*. Translated by John Dykstra Eusden. Boston: Pilgrim, 1968.

Andrewes, Lancelot. *Responsio ad Apologiam Cardinalis Bellarmini*. London: printed by Robert Barker, 1610.

Annesley, Samuel. *Volume I. Containing the First Volume Of The Exercise At Cripplegat*. 1661. Repr., London: Thomas Tegg, 1844.

Anselm. *Cur Deus homo*. In *A Scholastic Miscellany: Anselm to Ockham*, translated and edited by Eugene R. Fairweather, Library of Christian Classics 10:100–183. Ichthus ed., 1956. Repr., Philadelphia: Westminster, 1981.

Aquinas, Thomas. *Summa theologiae*. 60 vols. London: Blackfriars, 1963–75. Vol. 61, *Index*. 1981.

Aristotle. *De anima (On the Soul)*. In *Introduction to Aristotle*, edited by Richard McKeon, 145–235. New York: Modern Library, 1947.

———. *Ethica nicomachea (Nicomachean Ethics)*. In *Introduction to Aristotle*, edited by Richard McKeon, 298–543. New York: Modern Library, 1947.

Asty, John. "Memoirs of the Life of John Owen." In *A Complete Collection of the Sermons of John Owen*, edited by John Asty. London: John Clark, 1721.

Augustine. *Commentary on the Gospel of John*. Translated by John Gibb and James Innes. In *Nicene and Post-Nicene Fathers*, 1st ser., edited by Philip Schaff, 7:7–452. 1896. Repr., Peabody, MA: Hendrickson, 1994.

———. *De correptione et gratia*. Translated by Peter Holmes and Robert E. Wallis. In PL 44. Also in *Nicene and Post-Nicene Fathers*, 1st ser., edited by Philip Schaff, 5:471–92. 1896. Repr., Peabody, MA: Hendrickson, 2004.

245

———. *Enchiridion*. Translated by J. F. Shaw. In PL 40. Also in *Nicene and Post-Nicene Fathers*, 1st ser., edited by Philip Schaff, 3:237–76. 1887. Repr., Peabody, MA: Hendrickson, 2004.

———. *The Literal Meaning of Genesis*. Translated and edited by John Hammond Taylor. 2 vols. Ancient Christian Writers 41–42. New York: Newman, 1982.

———. "The Trinity." In *The Works of St. Augustine: A Translation for the 21st Century*, translated by Edmund Hill. Brooklyn: New City, 1991.

Barker, Matthew. *A Continuation of Morning-Exercise: Sermon 19*. London: John Dunton, 1683.

Barlow, Thomas. *Two Letters Written by the Right Reverend Dr. Thomas Barlow . . . concerning Justification by Faith Only*. London: Thomas Parkhurst, 1701.

Barrow, Isaac. *A Defence of the B. [Blessed] Trinity*. London: B. Aylmer, 1697.

Basil. *The Letters*. Translated by Blomfield Jackson. In *Nicene and Post-Nicene Fathers*, 2nd ser., edited by Philip Schaff and Henry Wace, 8:109–327. 1895. Repr., Peabody, MA: Hendrickson, 1994.

Bates, William. *The Everlasting Rest of the Saints in Heaven*. In *The Works of the Late Reverend and Learned William Bates*, 823–74. 2nd ed. London: James Knapton et al., 1723.

Baxter, Richard. *Aphorisms on Justification*. London: H. Hills, 1649.

———. *Methodus theologiae christianae*. London: typis M. White & T. Snowden, etc., 1681.

———. *The Saints' Everlasting Rest, or, A Treatise of the Blessed State of the Saints in Their Enjoyment of God in Glory*. 2nd ed. London: Thomas Underhill & Francis Tyton, 1651.

———. *A Treatise of Justifying Righteousness*. London: Nevil Simons & Jonathan Robinson, 1676.

Beardslee, John W., III, ed. *Reformed Dogmatics: Seventeenth-Century Reformed Theology through the Writings of Wollebius, Voetius, and Turretin*. New York: Oxford University Press, 1965.

Bellarmine, Robert Francis. *Disputationum . . . de controversiis christianae fidei adversus huius temporis haereticos*. 4 vols. 1581–93. Repr., Coloniae Agrippinae [Cologne]: sumpt. hieratorum fratrum, 1628.

Beza, Theodore. *Epistolarum theologicarum Theodori Bezae Vezelii, liber unus: Secunda editio, ab ipso auctore recognita*. Geneva: apud Eustathium Vignon, 1575.

Bibliotheca Oweniana, sive, Catalogus librorum. London: Edward Millington, 1684.

Boston, Thomas. *Human Nature in Its Fourfold State*. 1720. Repr., Edinburgh: Banner of Truth, 1997.

Bull, George. *Harmonia Apostolica, or, Two Dissertations: in the Former of Which the Doctrine of St. James on Justification by Works Is Explained and Defended; in the Later, the Agreement of St. Paul with St. James Is Clearly Shewn*. Translated by Thomas Wilkinson. 2nd ed. Repr., Oxford: John Henry Parker, 1844.

Calvin, John. *Commentaries on the Epistle of Paul the Apostle to the Hebrews*. Translated by John Owen. Edinburgh: Calvin Translation Society, 1853.

———. *The Institutes of the Christian Religion*. Translated by Ford Lewis Battles. Edited by John T. McNeill. 2 vols. Library of Christian Classics 20–21. Philadelphia: Westminster, 1960.

———. *Short Treatise on the Lord's Supper* (1540). In *Tracts and Treatises on the Reformation of the Church*, translated by Henry Beveridge, annotated by Thomas F. Torrance, 3:140–66. 1849. Repr., Grand Rapids: Eerdmans, 1958.

The Canons and Decrees of the Council of Trent. Translated by H. J. Schroeder. Rockford, IL: Tan Books, 1978.

Cawdrey, Daniel, and Herbert Palmer. *Sabbatum redivivum*. Part 1, London: Thomas Underhill, 1645. Parts 2–4, London: Samuel Gellibrand and Thomas Underhill, 1652.

Chemnitz, Martin. *De duabus naturis in Christo: De hypostatica earum unione; De communicatione idiomatum, et aliis quaestionibus inde dependentibus libellus*. Jena: typis Tobiae Steinmanni, 1591.

Cicero. *De natura deorum academica*. Translated by H. Rackham. Edited by T. E. Page et al. Loeb Classical Library 268. 1933. Repr., Cambridge, MA: Harvard University Press, 1961.

Clagett, William. *A Discourse concerning the Operations of the Holy Spirit*. London: Henry Brome, 1680.

Cocceius, Johannes. *Summa doctrinæ de fœdere et testamentis Dei*. Lugduni Batavorum [Leiden]: Elsevirorum, 1648.

Coleridge, Samuel Taylor. *Notes on English Divines*. Edited by Derwent Coleridge. Vol. 2. London: Edward Moxon, 1853.

Council of Trent, The. See *Canons and Decrees* (above).

Cox, Robert. *The Literature of the Sabbath Question*. 2 vols. Edinburgh: Maclachlan & Stewart, 1865.

Cyprian. *The Epistles of Cyprian*. Translated by Ernest Wallis. In *Ante-Nicene Fathers*, edited by Alexander Roberts and James Donaldson, 5:275–409. 1896. Repr., Peabody, MA: Hendrickson, 1994.

Cyril of Alexandria. *On the Unity of Christ*. Orig., 438. Translated by John Anthony McGuckin. Crestwood, NY: St. Vladimir's Seminary Press, 1995.

A Dangerous Plot Discovered by a Discourse Wherein is proved, That, Mr Richard Montague . . . Laboureth to bring in the Faith of Rome, and Arminius; under the name and pretence of the doctrine and faith of the church of England. London: Nicholas Bourne, 1626.

Danson, Thomas. *The Friendly Debate between Satan and Sherlock. . . .* London, 1676.

Davenant, John. *A Treatise on Justification, or, The Disputatio de Justinita habituali et actuali*. Translated by Josiah Allport. 2 vols. 1631. Repr., London: Hamilton, Adams, 1844.

Downame, George. *A Treatise of Iustification*. 1633. London: Nicholas Bourne, 1639.

Downe, John. *A Treatise of the True Nature and Definition of Justifying Faith*. Oxford: Edward Forrest, 1635.

Edwards, Jonathan. *Religious Affections*. Edited by John E. Smith. 1746. Repr., New Haven: Yale University Press, 1959.

Eusebius of Caesarea. *Demonstratio evangelica*. Translated by W. J. Ferrar as *The Proof of the Gospel*. Translations of Christian Literature, 1st ser., Greek Texts. 1920. Repr., Grand Rapids: Baker Academic, 1981; Eugene, OR: Wipf & Stock, 2001.

Fenner, William. *A Treatise of the Affections*. 1641. London: I. Rothwell, 1642.

Ferguson, Robert. *The Interest of Reason in Religion*. London: Dorman Newman, 1675.

Goodwin, John. *Imputatio fidei*. London: Andrew Crooke, 1642.

Goodwin, Thomas. *The Works of Thomas Goodwin*. Edited by John C. Miller. 12 vols. Edinburgh: James Nichol, 1861–66. Repr., Eureka, CA: Tanski Publications, 1996.

Goold, W. H. "John Owen." In *The Evangelical Succession*, 3rd ser., printed lecture. Edinburgh: MacNiven & Wallace, 1883.

Gregory of Nazianzus. *Orations* and *Letters*. Translated by Charles Gordon Browne and James Edward Swallow. In *Nicene and Post-Nicene Fathers*, 2nd ser., edited by Philip Schaff and Henry Wace, 7:203–434, 437–82. 1894. Repr., Peabody, MA: Hendrickson, 1994.

Heppe, Heinrich. *Reformed Dogmatics: Set Out and Illustrated from the Sources*. Translated by G. T. Thomson. Edited by Ernst Bizer. Grand Rapids: Baker, 1978.

Heylyn, Peter. *The History of the Sabbath*. London: Henry Seile, 1636.

Hickman, Henry. *Speculum Sherlockianum, or, A Looking Glass in which the Admirers of Mr. Sherlock may behold the Man, as to his Accuracy, Judgement, Orthodoxy*. London: Thomas Parkhurst, 1674.

Hollinworth, Richard. *The Holy Ghost on the Bench, Other Spirits at the Barre, or, The Judgment of the Holy Spirit of God upon the Saints of the Times*. London: Luke Fawn, 1656.

Hooker, Richard. *Of the Laws of Ecclesiastical Polity*. Edited by Georges Edeln. 6 vols. 1639. Cambridge, MA: Harvard University Press, Belknap, 1977–83.

Hooker, Thomas. *The Application of Redemption*. London: printed by Peter Cole, 1657 (1656?).

Hotchkis, Thomas. *A Discourse concerning the Imputation of Christ's righteousness to us, and our sins to him: With many useful questions, thereunto pertaining, resolved; Together with Reflections more at large upon what hath been published concerning that subject by Mr. Robert Ferguson in his Interest of Reason in Religion, and by Dr. John Owen in his Book styled Communion with God*. London: Walter Kettilby, 1675.

———. *A Postscript, Containing the Authors Vindication of Himself and the Doctrine from the Imputations of Dr. John Owen*. London: Walter Kettilby, 1678.

Hottinger, Johann Henrich. *Cursus theologicus: Methodo altingiana*. Duisburg: Wyngaerden, 1660.

How, Samuel. *The Sufficiency of the Spirit's Teaching without Humane Learning*. London: William & Joseph Marshall, 1640 (1639?).

Howe, John. *The Living Temple*. 8 vols. In *The Works of John Howe*, vol. 3. London: Religious Tract Society, 1862.

Hughes, Philip E., ed. *Faith and Works: Cranmer and Hooker on Justification*. Wilton, CT: Morehouse-Barlow, 1982.

Irenaeus. *Against Heresies*. Translated by Alexander Roberts and W. H. Rambaut. In *Ante-Nicene Fathers*, edited by Philip Schaff, 1:315–567. 1896. Repr., Peabody, MA: Hendrickson, 1994.

Irving, Edward. *The Collected Writings of Edward Irving*. Edited by G. Carlyle. 5 vols. London: Alexander Strahan, 1865.

Jackson, Thomas. *Justifying Faith, or, The Faith by which the just do live*. London: printed by John Beale, 1615. Repr., London: John Clarke, 1631.

Jacombe, Thomas. *Several Sermons Preach'd on the Whole Eighth Chapter of the Epistle to the Romans. . . .* London: M. Pitt, R. Chiswell, & J. Robinson, 1672.

John of Damascus. *Exposition of the Orthodox Faith*. Translated by S. D. F. Salmond. In *Nicene and Post-Nicene Fathers*, 2nd ser., edited by Philip Schaff and Henry Wace, 9:1–101 (separate pagination). 1899. Repr., Peabody, MA: Hendrickson, 1994.

Johnson, William Stacy, and John H. Leith, eds. *Reformed Reader: A Sourcebook in Christian Theology*. Vol. 1, *Classical Beginnings, 1519–1799*. Louisville: Westminster John Knox, 1993.

Kuyper, Abraham. *Het werk van den Heiligen Geest*. Amsterdam: J. A. Wormser, 1888.

———. *The Work of the Holy Spirit*. Translated by Henri De Vries. New York: Funk & Wagnalls, 1900.

Leo I. "Letter to Flavian of Constantinople." In *The Christological Controversy: Sources of Early Christian Thought*, edited by Richard A. Norris, 145–55. Philadelphia: Fortress, 1980.

Leo the Great. *Sermons*. Translated by Charles Lett Feltoe. In *Nicene and Post-Nicene Fathers*, 2nd ser., edited by Philip Schaff and Henry Wace, 12:115–205. 1895. Repr., Peabody, MA: Hendrickson, 1994.

Locke, John. *Locke: Political Essays*. Edited by Mark Goldie. Cambridge, UK: Cambridge University Press, 1997.

Matthews, A. G., ed. *The Savoy Declaration of Faith and Order, 1658*. London: Independent Press, 1959.

Melanchthon, Philip. *Loci communes, 1555*. Translated by Clyde L. Manschreck. New York: Oxford University Press, 1965.

Moffatt, James, ed. *The Golden Book of John Owen*. London: Hodder & Stoughton, 1904.

Montague [Mountagu/Montagu?], Richard. *Appello Caesarem*. London: Matthew Lownes, 1625.

———. *A Gagg for the new Gospell? No: A New Gagg for an Old Goose*. London: Matthew Lownes & William Barret, 1624.

Novatian. *Treatise concerning the Trinity*. Translated by Robert Ernest Wallis. In *The Ante-Nicene Fathers*, edited by Philip Schaff, 5:611–44. 1896. Repr., Peabody, MA: Hendrickson, 1994.

"Official Common Statement by the Lutheran World Federation and the Catholic Church." *One in Christ* 36, no. 1 (2000): 89–92.

Owen, John. *Biblical Theology, or, The Nature, Origin, Development, and Study of Theological Truth, in Six Books*. Translated by Stephen P. Westcott. Morgan, PA: Soli Deo Gloria, 1994.

———. *Communion with the Triune God*. Edited by Kelly M. Kapic and Justin Taylor. Wheaton: Crossway Books, forthcoming.

———. *Overcoming Sin and Temptation: Three Classic Works*. Edited by Kelly M. Kapic and Justin Taylor. Wheaton: Crossway Books, 2006.

———. *The Oxford Orations of Dr. John Owen*. Edited and translated by Peter Toon. Cornwall: Gospel Communication, 1971.

———. "Preface." In *Vindiciæ justificationis gratuitæ*, edited by W. Eyre. London: Edward Forrest, 1654.

———. *The Works of John Owen*. Rio, WI: Ages Software, 2000.

———. *The Works of John Owen*. Edited by William H. Goold. 24 vols. Edinburgh and London: Johnstone & Hunter, 1850–55. Repr., Edinburgh: Banner of Truth, vols. 1–16 in 1965; and the 7 vols. of *An Exposition of the Epistle to the Hebrews* in 1991.

Polhill, Edward. *An Answer to the Discourse of Mr. William Sherlock, touching the Knowledge of Christ, and our Union and Communion with Him*. London: Ben Foster, 1675.

The Racovian Catechism. Edited by Thomas Rees. 1609. Repr., London: Longman, Hurst, Rees, Orme & Brown, 1818.

Rogers, Henry. *The Life and Character of John Howe, M.A.: With an Analysis of His Writings*. New ed., London: Religious Tract Society, 1862.

Rolle, Samuel. *Justification justified: or, The great doctrine of justification . . .* London: 1674.

———. *Prodromus, or, The Character of Mr. Sherlock's book . . .* London: 1674.

Russell, Thomas, ed., *The Works of John Owen*. 21 vols. London: Richard Baynes, 1826.

Scougal, Henry. *Life of God in the Soul of Man*. London: Charles Smith & William Jacob, 1677.

Shepard, Thomas. *The Sound Believer: A Treatise of Evangelical Conversion; Discovering the Work of Christs Spirit, in Reconciling of a Sinner to God*. London: Andrew Crooke, 1671.

Sherlock, Thomas. *Several Discourses Preached at the Temple Church*. Vol. 1, *Discourse 8*. 1st ed. London: J. Whiston et al., 1754.

Sherlock, William. *A Defence and Continuation of the Discourse concerning the Knowledge of Jesus Christ*. London: Walter Kettilby, 1675.

———. *A Defence of Dr. Sherlock's Notion of a Trinity in Unity*. London: William Rogers, 1694.

———. *A Discourse concerning the Knowledge of Jesus Christ, and our Union and Communion with him. . . .* London: Walter Kettilby, 1674. 3rd ed., corrected. London: Walter Kettilby, 1678.

———. *A Vindication of the Doctrine of the Trinity and the Incarnation*. London: W. Rogers, 1690.

Smeaton, George. *The Doctrine of the Holy Spirit*. Cunningham Lectures, 9th ser., 2nd ed. Edinburgh: T&T Clark, 1889.

South, Robert. *Animadversions upon Dr. Sherlock's Book, entitled A Vindication of the Holy and Ever-Blessed Trinity*. London: Randal Taylor, 1693.

———. *Tritheism charged upon Dr. Sherlock's New Notion of the Trinity: And the charge made good*. London: John Whitlock, 1695.

Spurgeon, Charles H. *Commenting and Commentaries*. London: Passmore & Alabaster, 1876.

Stillingfleet, Edward. *A Discourse in Vindication of the Doctrine of the Trinity*. London: Henry Mortlock, 1697.

Stone, Darwell. *A History of the Doctrine of the Holy Eucharist*. 2 vols. New York: Longmans, Green, 1909.

Taylor, Jeremy. *The Whole Works with a Life of the Author and a Critical Examination of His Writings*. 15 vols. London: C. & J. Rivington, 1828.

Thomson, Andrew. *The Life of Dr. Owen*. Edinburgh, 1850. Repr. as *John Owen: Prince of Puritans*. History Makers. Fearn, Tain, UK: Christian Focus Publications, 2004.

Toon, Peter, ed. *The Correspondence of John Owen (1616–1683)*. Cambridge, UK: James Clarke, 1970.

———, ed. *The Oxford Orations of Dr. John Owen*. Cornwall: Gospel Communications, 1971.

Turretin, Francis [François Turretini]. *Institutes of Elenctic Theology*. Translated by George Musgrave Giger. Edited by James T. Dennison Jr. 3 vols. Phillipsburg, NJ: P&R, 1992–97.

Under Calvin's Yoke: Dr. Owen's Three Invincible Questions [regarding universal redemption] Answered by Bereana [a pseudonym]. London: Elliot Stock, 1930.

Vasseur, Joshua le, et al. *Thesaurus disputationum theologicarum in Alma Sedanensi Academia*. 2 vols. Geneva: sumpt. Joan. Ant. & Samuelis de Tournes, 1661.

Vernon, George. *A Letter to a Friend*. London: printed by J. Redmayne, 1670.

Wallis, John. *The Doctrine of the Blessed Trinity*. London: Thomas Parkhurst, 1690.

Watson, Thomas. *A Body of Practical Divinity*. London: Thomas Parkhurst, 1692. Rev. ed. as *A Body of Divinity*. Edinburgh: Banner of Truth, 1983.

———. *A divine cordial: Or, the transcendent priviledge of those that love God*. London: Thomas Parkhurst, 1678.

The Westminster Confession of Faith. Glasgow: Free Presbyterian Publications, 1994 (also containing the Catechisms, Directories for Worship, etc.).

Wilberforce, William. *A Practical View of the Prevailing Religious System of Professed Christians, in the Higher and Middle Classes in this Country, Contrasted with Real Christianity*. 18th ed. London: T. Cadell, 1830.

Wilson, W., ed. *Selections from the Works of John Owen*. London, 1826.

Witsius, Herman. *The Oeconomy of the Covenants between God and Man*. Translated by William Crookshank. 3 vols. London: Edward Dilly, 1763.

Wollebius, Johannes. *Compendium theologiae christianae*. In *Reformed Dogmatics: Seventeenth-Century Reformed Theology through the Writings of Wollebius, Voetius, and Turretin*, edited by John W. Beardslee III, 27–262. New York: Oxford University Press, 1965.

Secondary Sources

Abbott, John. "John Owen and the Basis of Christian Unity." In *"Out of Bondage": Papers Read at the 1983 Conference*, 52–69. London: Westminster Conference, 1984.

Acheson, R. J. *Radical Puritans in England, 1550–1660*. Seminar Studies in History. London: Longman, 1990.

Ackrill, J. L. "Aristotle on Action." In *Essays on Aristotle's Ethics*, edited by Amélie Oksenberg Rorty, 93–101. Berkeley: University of California Press, 1980.

Allison, C. F. *The Rise of Moralism: The Proclamation of the Gospel from Hooker to Baxter*. London: SPCK, 1966.

Anderson, Ruth L. *Elizabethan Psychology and Shakespeare's Plays*. University of Iowa Humanistic Studies 3. Iowa City: University of Iowa Press, 1927.

Armstrong, A. H. *An Introduction to Ancient Philosophy*. University Paperbacks. London: Methuen, 1965.

Asselt, Willem J. van, and Eef Dekker. *Reformation and Scholasticism: An Ecumenical Enterprise*. Grand Rapids: Baker Academic, 2001.

Ayres, Lewis. "'Remember That You Are Catholic' (serm. 52.2): Augustine on the Unity of the Triune God." *Journal of Early Christian Studies* 8, no. 1 (2000): 39–82.

Ayto, John. *Dictionary of Word Origins: The Histories of More Than 8,000 English-Language Words*. New York: Arcade, 1990.

Baab, Lynne M. *Sabbath Keeping: Finding Freedom in the Rhythms of Rest*. Downers Grove, IL: InterVarsity, 2005.

Baker, J. Wayne. "Church, State, and Toleration: John Locke and Calvin's Heirs in England, 1644–1689." In *Later Calvinism: International Perspectives*, edited by W. Fred Graham, 525–43. Kirksville: Sixteenth Century Journal Publishers, 1994.

Barbour, Hugh. *The Quakers in Puritan England*. New Haven: Yale University Press, 1964.

Barr, James. "The Image of God in the Book of Genesis—A Study in Terminology." *Bulletin of the John Rylands Library* 51 (1968–69): 11–26.

Barraclough, Peter. *John Owen (1616–1683)*. London: Independent Press, 1961.

Barth, Karl. *Church Dogmatics*. Edited by G. W. Bromiley and T. F. Torrance. Translated by T. H. L. Parker et al. 5 vols. in 14. Edinburgh: T&T Clark, 1956–77.

Bass, William Ward. "Platonic Influences on Seventeenth-Century English Puritan Theology as Expressed in the Thinking of John Owen, Richard Baxter, and John Howe." PhD diss., University of Southern California, 1958.

Bauckham, Richard. "Sabbath and Sunday in the Medieval Church in the West." In *From Sabbath to Lord's Day: A Biblical, Historical, and Theological Investigation*, edited by D. A. Carson, 299–309. Grand Rapids: Zondervan, 1982.

———. "Sabbath and Sunday in the Post-Apostolic Church." In *From Sabbath to Lord's Day: A Biblical, Historical, and Theological Investigation*, edited by D. A. Carson, 251–98. Grand Rapids: Zondervan, 1982.

———. "Sabbath and Sunday in the Protestant Tradition." In *From Sabbath to Lord's Day: A Biblical, Historical, and Theological Investigation*, edited by D. A. Carson, 311–41. Grand Rapids: Zondervan, 1982.

Beeke, Joel R. *Assurance of Faith: Calvin, English Puritanism, and the Dutch Second Reformation*. New York: Peter Lang, 1991.

———. "Personal Assurance of Faith: Calvin, English Puritanism, and the Dutch 'Nadere Reformatie' from Westminster to Alexander Comrie (1640–1760)." PhD diss., Westminster Theological Seminary, 1988.

———. "Personal Assurance of Faith: The Puritans and Chapter 18:2 of the Westminster Confession." *Westminster Theological Journal* 55 (1993): 1–30.

Beeke, Joel R., and Viliet, Jan van. "*The Marrow of Theology* by William Ames (1576–1633)." In *The Devoted Life: An Invitation to the Puritan Classics*, edited by Kelly M. Kapic and Randall C. Gleason, 52–65. Downers Grove, IL: InterVarsity, 2004.

Berkhof, Louis. *Systematic Theology*. 4th ed. 1941. Repr., Grand Rapids: Eerdmans, 1994.

Bierma, Lyle D. "Federal Theology in the Sixteenth Century: Two Traditions?" *Westminster Theological Journal* 45 (1983): 304–21.

———. "Law and Grace in Ursinus' Doctrine of the Natural Covenant: A Reappraisal." In *Protestant Scholasticism: Essays in Reassessment*, edited by Carl Trueman and R. S. Clark, 96–110. Carlisle: Paternoster, 1999.

Blackham, Paul. "The Pneumatology of Thomas Goodwin." PhD diss., King's College London, 1995.

Blight, James G. "Solomon Stoddard's *Safety of Appearing* and the Dissolution of the Puritan Faculty Psychology." *Journal of the History of the Behavioral Sciences* 10 (1974): 238–50.

Bloom, Harold. *Shakespeare: The Invention of the Human*. London: Fourth Estate, 1998.

Bobick, Michael W. "Owen's Razor: The Role of Ramist Logic in the Covenant Theology of John Owen." PhD diss., Drew University, 1996.

Bobrinskoy, Boris. *The Mystery of the Trinity: Trinitarian Experience and Vision in the Biblical and Patristic Tradition*. Crestwood, NY: St. Vladimir's Seminary Press, 1999.

Boersma, H. *A Hot Peppercorn: Richard Baxter's Doctrine of Justification in Its Seventeenth-Century Context of Controversy*. Zoetermeer: Boekencentrum, 1993.

Boff, Leonardo. *Holy Trinity, Perfect Community*. Maryknoll, NY: Orbis Books, 2000.

Bouwsma, William J. "The Spirituality of John Calvin." In *Christian Spirituality*, vol. 2, *High Middle Ages and Reformation*, edited by Jill Raitt, 318–33. London: Routledge & Kegan Paul, 1987.

Braaten, Carl E., and Robert W. Jenson. *Union with Christ: The New Finnish Interpretation of Luther*. Grand Rapids: Eerdmans, 1998.

The British Museum General Catalogue of Printed Books. London: Trustees of the British Museum, 1959.

Brodrick, James. *Robert Bellarmine: Saint and Scholar*. London: Burns & Oates, 1961.

Brooks, Peter Newman. *Thomas Cranmer's Doctrine of the Eucharist: An Essay in Historical Development*. 2nd ed. London: Macmillan Academic, 1992.

Buescher, G. N. "Dispositions for Justification." In *New Catholic Encyclopedia*, 4:92–93. New York: McGraw-Hill, 1967–89.

Cairns, David. *The Image of God in Man*. New York: Philosophical Library, 1953.

Cameron, Nigel M. de S. *Complete in Christ: Discovering Jesus and Ourselves*. Carlisle: Paternoster, 1989; repr., 1997.

———. *Dictionary of Scottish Church History and Theology*. Downers Grove, IL: InterVarsity, 1993.

Carson, D. A., ed. *From Sabbath to Lord's Day: A Biblical, Historical, and Theological Investigation*. Grand Rapids: Zondervan, 1982.

Carson, D. A., Peter T. O'Brien, and Mark A. Seifrid. *Justification and Variegated Nomism*. 2 vols. Grand Rapids: Baker Academic, 2001.

Chalker, William H. "Calvin and Some Seventeenth-Century English Calvinists—A Comparison of their Doctrines of the Knowledge of God, Faith, and Assurance." PhD diss., Duke University, 1961.

Chan, Simon K. H. "The Puritan Meditative Tradition, 1599–1691: A Study of Ascetical Piety." PhD diss., University of Cambridge, 1986.

Clark, Stephen R. L. *Aristotle's Man: Speculations upon Aristotelian Anthropology*. Oxford: Clarendon, 1975.

Clebsch, William A. *England's Earliest Protestants, 1520–1535*. New Haven: Yale University Press, 1964.

Clements, R. E., et al., eds. *Eucharistic Theology Then and Now*. Theological Collections 9. London: SPCK, 1968.

Clifford, Alan C. *Atonement and Justification: English Evangelical Theology, 1640–1790: An Evaluation*. Oxford: Clarendon, 1990.

———. *Calvinus: Authentic Calvinism; A Clarification*. Norwich: Charenton Reformed Publishing, 1996.

———. "John Calvin and the Confessio Fidei Fallicana." *Evangelical Quarterly* 58 (1986): 195–206.

Cocksworth, Christopher J. *Evangelical Eucharistic Thought in the Church of England*. Cambridge, UK: Cambridge University Press, 1993.

Coffey, David. *Deus Trinitas: The Doctrine of the Triune God*. New York: Oxford University Press, 1999.

Cohen, Charles L. *God's Caress: The Psychology of Puritan Religious Experience*. Oxford: Oxford University Press, 1986.

Collinson, Patrick. "The Beginnings of English Sabbatarianism." In *Papers Read at the First Winter and Summer Meetings of the Ecclesiastical History Society*, edited by C. W. Dugmore and Charles Duggan, Studies in Church History 1:207–21. London: Nelson, 1964.

———. *The Religion of Protestants: The Church in English Society, 1559–1625*. Oxford: Clarendon, 1982.

Cook, Sarah Gibbard. "Congregational Independents and the Cromwellian Constitution." *Church History* 44 (1977): 335–57.

———. "A Political Biography of a Religious Independent: John Owen, 1616–83." PhD diss., Harvard University, 1972.

Cooper, Tim. *Fear and Polemic in Seventeenth-Century England: Richard Baxter and Antinomianism*. Aldershot: Ashgate, 2001.

Copleston, Frederick. *Augustine to Scotus*. Vol. 2, *A History of Philosophy*. New York: Image Books, 1985.

———. *Greece and Rome*. Vol. 1, *A History of Philosophy*. New York: Image Books, 1985.

Crisp, Oliver. "Did Christ Have a *Fallen* Human Nature?" *International Journal of Systematic Theology* 6 (2004): 270–88.

Daley, B. E. "'A Richer Union': Leontius of Byzantium and the Relationship of Human and Divine in Christ." *Studia patristica* 24 (1993): 239–65.

Daniel, Curt D. "Hyper-Calvinism and John Gill." PhD diss., University of Edinburgh, 1983; privately published, 1983.

Daniels, Richard W. *The Christology of John Owen*. Grand Rapids: Reformation Heritage Books, 2004.

Davidson, Ivor. "Theologizing the Human Jesus: An Ancient (and Modern) Approach to Christology Reassessed." *International Journal of Systematic Theology* 3, no. 2 (2001): 129–53.

Davies, Andrew A. "The Holy Spirit in Puritan Experience." In *"Faith and Ferment": Papers Read at the 1982 Westminster Conference*, 18–31. London: Westminster Conference, 1982.

Davies, Horton. *Worship and Theology in England*. Vol. 2, *From Andrewes to Baxter and Fox, 1603–1690*. Grand Rapids: Eerdmans, 1996.

————. *The Worship of the English Puritans*. 1948. Repr., Morgan, PA: Soli Deo Gloria, 1997.

Davis, Stephen T., Daniel Kendall, and Gerald O'Collins. *The Trinity: An Interdisciplinary Symposium on the Trinity*. New York: Oxford University Press, 1999.

Dawn, Marva J. *Keeping the Sabbath Wholly: Ceasing, Resting, Embracing, Feasting*. Grand Rapids: Eerdmans, 1989.

DeKoeyer, R. W. "Pneumatologia: Een onderzoek naar de leer van de Heilige Geest bij de puritein John Owen (1616–1683)" PhD diss., Utrecht, 1990.

————. "Pneumatologia: Enkel aspecten van de leer van de heilige Geest bji de puritein John Owen (1616–1683)." *Theologia reformata* 34 (1991): 226–46.

Del Colle, Ralph. "The Holy Spirit: Presence, Power, Person." *Theological Studies* 62 (2001): 322–40.

Dennison, James. *The Market Day of the Soul: The Puritan Doctrine of the Sabbath in England, 1532–1700*. Lanham, MD: University Press of America, 1983.

Douma, Jochem. *The Ten Commandments*. Translated by Nelson D. Kloosterman. Phillipsburg, NJ: P&R, 1996.

Dugmore, Clifford W. *Eucharistic Doctrine in England from Hooker to Waterland*. London: SPCK, 1942.

Dulles, Avery. *The Assurance of Things Hoped For: A Theology of Christian Faith*. Oxford: Oxford University Press, 1994.

Dunn, James D. G., and Alan M. Suggate. *The Justice of God: A Fresh Look at the Old Doctrine of Justification by Faith*. Carlisle: Paternoster, 1993.

Dupré, Louis, and Don Saliers, eds. *Christian Spirituality*. Vol. 3, *Post-Reformation and Modern*. London: SCM, 1990.

Durston, Christopher, and Jacqueline Eales, eds. *The Culture of English Puritanism, 1560–1700*. Basingstoke: Macmillan, 1996.

Ella, George M. "John Gill and the Charge of Hyper-Calvinism." *The Baptist Quarterly* 36, no. 4 (1995): 160–77.

Entwistle, F. R. "Some Aspects of John Owen's Doctrine of the Person and Work of Christ." In *Faith and a Good Conscience*, 47–63. 1963. Repr., London: Westminster Conference, 1992.

Evans, G. R. *Problems of Authority in the Reformation Debates*. Cambridge, UK: Cambridge University Press, 1992.

Everson, Don M. "The Puritan Theology of John Owen." ThD diss., Southern Baptist Theological Seminary, 1959.

Feenstra, Ronald J., and Cornelius Plantinga Jr., eds. *Trinity, Incarnation, and Atonement: Philosophical and Theological Essays*. Edited by Thomas V. Morris. Library of Religious Philosophy 1. Notre Dame, IN: University of Notre Dame Press, 1989.

Ferguson, Sinclair. "The Doctrine of the Christian Life in the Teaching of Dr. John Owen (1616–1683): Chaplain to Oliver Cromwell and Sometime Vice-Chancellor of the University of Oxford." PhD diss., University of Aberdeen, 1979.

———. "John Owen on Conversion." *Banner of Truth* 186 (1979): 1–9.

———. *John Owen on the Christian Life*. Edinburgh: Banner of Truth, 1987.

Fiering, Norman. *Moral Philosophy at Seventeenth-Century Harvard*. Chapel Hill: University of North Carolina Press, 1981.

Fortenbaugh, W. W. *Aristotle on Emotion*. London: Duckworth, 1975.

Franco, Ricardo. "Justification." In *Sacramentum Mundi: An Encyclopedia of Theology*, edited by Karl Rahner, 3:239–41. London: Burns & Oates, 1969.

Franks, Robert S. *The Work of Christ: A Historical Study of Christian Doctrine*. 1918. Repr., New York: T. Nelson & Sons, 1962.

Fulcher, J. Rodney. "Puritans and the Passions: The Faculty Psychology in American Puritanism." *Journal of the History of the Behavioral Sciences* 9 (1973): 123–39.

Gaffin, Richard. *Calvin and the Sabbath*. Fearn: Mentor, 1998.

Gerrish, B. A. "Atonement and 'Saving Faith.'" *Theology Today* 17, no. 2 (1960): 181–91.

———. *Grace and Gratitude: The Eucharistic Theology of John Calvin*. Edinburgh: T&T Clark, 1993.

———. "The Lord's Supper in the Reformed Confessions." *Theology Today* 23 (1966): 224–43.

Gleason, Randall C. *John Calvin and John Owen on Mortification: A Comparative Study in Reformed Spirituality*. Studies in Church History 3. New York: Peter Lang, 1995.

Gockel, M. "A Dubious Christological Formula? Leontius of Byzantium and the Anhypostasis-Enhypostasis Theory." *Journal of Theological Studies*, 51 no. 2 (2000): 515–32.

Gomes, Alan W. "*De Jesu Christo Servatore*: Faustus Socinus on the Satisfaction of Christ." *Westminster Theological Journal* 55 (Fall 1993): 209–31.

Greaves, R. L. "The Origins of English Sabbatarian Thought." *Historical Journal* 23 (1980): 17–35.

Green, Ian. *The Christian's ABC: Catechisms and Catechizing in England c. 1530–1740*. Oxford: Clarendon, 1996.

Grenz, Stanley. *The Social God and the Relational Self: A Trinitarian Theology of the Imago Dei*. Louisville: Westminster John Knox, 2001.

Griffiths, Steve. *Redeem the Time: The Problem of Sin in the Writings of John Owen*. Fearn: Mentor, 2001.

Grillmeier, Aloys. *Christ in Christian Tradition*. Vol. 1, *From the Apostolic Age to Chalcedon (451)*. Translated by John S. Bowden. London: Mowbray, 1965. 2nd, rev. ed., 1976. Vol. 2, *From the Council of Chalcedon (451) to Gregory the Great (590–604)*. Translated by Pauline Allen and John Cawte. Part 1, *Reception and Contradiction*. London: Mobray, 1987.

Guelzo, Allen C. "John Owen, Puritan Pacesetter." *Christianity Today* 20 (May 21, 1976): 14–16.

Gundry, Stanley N. "John Owen on Authority and Scripture." In *Inerrancy and the Church*, edited by J. D. Hannah, 189–221. Chicago: Moody, 1984.

————. "John Owen's Doctrine of the Scriptures: An Original Study of His Approach to the Problem of Authority." STM thesis, Union College of British Columbia, 1967.

Gunton, Colin E. "God the Holy Spirit: Augustine and His Successors." In *Theology through the Theologians*, 105–28. Edinburgh: T&T Clark, 1996.

————. *The One, the Three, and the Many: God, Creation, and the Culture of Modernity*. Bampton Lectures 1992. Cambridge, UK: Cambridge University Press, 1993.

————. *The Promise of Trinitarian Theology*. Edinburgh: T&T Clark, 1991.

Gunton, Colin E., and Christoph Schwöbel, eds. *Persons, Divine and Human: King's College Essays in Theological Anthropology*. Edinburgh: T&T Clark, 1991.

Hannah, John D. "Insights into Pastoral Counseling from John Owen." In *Integrity of Heart, Skillfulness of Hands*, edited by Charles Dyer and Roy Zuck, 348–60. Grand Rapids: Baker Academic, 1994.

Hastings, W. Ross. "'Honouring the Spirit': Analysis and Evaluation of Jonathan Edwards' Pneumatological Doctrine of the Incarnation." *International Journal of Systematic Theology* 7 (2005): 279–99.

Hawkes, Richard Mitchell. "The Logic of Grace in John Owen, D.D.: An Analysis, Exposition, and Defense of John Owen's Puritan Theology of Grace." PhD diss., Westminster Theological Seminary, 1987.

Helm, Paul. "Article Review: Calvin, English Calvinism and the Logic of Doctrinal Development." *Scottish Journal of Theology*, no. 34 (1981): 179–85.

————. *Calvin and the Calvinists*. Edinburgh: Banner of Truth, 1982.

Heppe, Heinrich. "Die Föderaltheologie der reformierten Kirche." In *Geschichte des Pietismus und der Mystik in der reformierten Kirche namentlich der Niederlande*, 204–40. Leiden: E. J. Brill, 1879.

Heschel, Abraham Joshua. *The Sabbath*. Rev. ed. New York: Farrar, Straus & Giroux, 2005.

Hill, Christopher. *The English Bible and the Seventeenth-Century Revolution*. London: Penguin, 1993.

————. *The Experience of Defeat: Milton and Some Contemporaries*. London: Faber & Faber, 1984.

————. *God's Englishman: Oliver Cromwell and the English Revolution*. London: Weidenfeld & Nicholson, 1970.

———. *Society and Puritanism in Pre-Revolutionary England*. New York: Schocken Books, 1964.

Hillerbrand, Hans J., ed. *The Oxford Encyclopedia of the Reformation*. 4 vols. Oxford: Oxford University Press, 1996.

Hinson, E. Glenn. "Baptist and Quaker Spirituality." In *Christian Spirituality*, vol. 3, *Post-Reformation and Modern*, edited by Louis Depré and Don Saliers, 324–38. London: SCM, 1990.

Holifield, E. Brooks. *The Covenant Sealed: The Development of Puritan Sacramental Theology in Old and New England, 1570–1720*. New Haven: Yale University Press, 1974.

Horton, Michael S. "*Of the Object and Acts of Justifying Faith* by Thomas Goodwin (1600–1680)." In *The Devoted Life: An Invitation to the Puritan Classics*, edited by Kelly M. Kapic and Randall C. Gleason, 108–22. Downers Grove, IL: InterVarsity, 2004.

Houston, James M., ed. *Sin and Temptation: The Challenge of Personal Godliness*. Minneapolis: Bethany House, 1996.

Hughes, Philip E. *Theology of the English Reformers*. New ed. as a Canterbury Book. Grand Rapids: Baker Academic, 1980.

———. *The True Image: The Origin and Destiny of Man in Christ*. Grand Rapids: Eerdmans, 1989.

Husbands, Mark, and Daniel J. Treier. *Justification: What's at Stake in the Current Debates*. Downers Grove, IL: InterVarsity, 2004.

Irwin, T. H. "The Metaphysical and Psychological Basis of Aristotle's Ethics." In *Essays on Aristotle's Ethics*, edited by Amélie Oksenberg Rorty, 35–53. Berkeley: University of California Press, 1980.

James, Frank, III. "The Complex of Justification: Vermigli versus Pighius." In *Peter Martyr Vermigli: Humanism, Republicanism, Reformation*, edited by Emidio Campi, Frank A. James III, and Peter Opitz, Travaux d'humanisme et Renaissance, 45–58. Geneva: Droz, 2002.

Jones, M. Lloyd. "John Owen on Schism." In *Diversity in Unity*, 59–80. London: Westminster Conference, 1963.

Jones, R. Tudor. *Congregationalism in England, 1662–1962*. London: Independent Press, 1962.

———. "Union with Christ: The Existential Nerve of Puritan Piety." *Tyndale Bulletin* 41, no. 2 (November 1990): 186–208.

Jüngel, Eberhard. *God's Being Is in Becoming: The Trinitarian Being of God in the Theology of Karl Barth: A Paraphrase*. Grand Rapids: Eerdmans, 2001.

———. *Justification: The Heart of the Christian Faith*. Edinburgh: T&T Clark, 2001.

Kaiser, Christopher B. *The Doctrine of God: An Historical Study*. Edited by Peter Toon. Foundations for Faith. London: Marshall Morgan & Scott, 1982.

Kapic, Kelly M. "Communion with God: Relations between the Divine and the Human in the Theology of John Owen." PhD diss., King's College London, 2001.

———. "John Owen (1616–1683)." In *Historical Dictionary of Major Biblical Interpreters*, edited by Donald K. McKim. Downers Grove, IL: InterVarsity, forthcoming.

———. "The Son's Assumption of a Human Nature: A Call for Clarity." *International Journal of Systematic Theology* 3, no. 2 (2001): 154–66.

Kapic, Kelly M., and Randall C. Gleason. *The Devoted Life: An Invitation to the Puritan Classics*. Downers Grove, IL: InterVarsity, 2004.

Katz, David S. *Sabbath and Sectarianism in Seventeenth-Century England*. Leiden: E. J. Brill, 1988.

Keller, Timothy J. "Puritan Resources for Biblical Counseling." *Journal of Pastoral Practice* 9, no. 3 (1988): 11–43.

Kelly, J. N. D. *Early Christian Doctrines*. San Francisco: Harper & Row, 1978.

Kendall, R. T. *Calvin and English Calvinism to 1649*. 1979. Repr., Carlisle: Paternoster, 1997.

Kenny, J. P. "Justification." In *A Catholic Dictionary of Theology*, edited by Monsignor H. Francis Davis, Ivo Thomas, and Joseph Crehan, 3:172–82. London: Nelson, 1971.

King, David M. "The Affective Spirituality of John Owen." *Evangelical Quarterly* 63, no. 3 (1996): 222–33.

Knapp, Henry M. "John Owen's Interpretation of Hebrews 6:4–6: Eternal Perseverance of the Saints in Puritan Exegesis." *Sixteenth Century Journal* 34 (2003): 29–52.

———. "Understanding the Mind of God: John Owen and Seventeenth-Century Exegetical Methodology." PhD diss., Calvin Theological Seminary, 2000.

Kosman, L. A. "Being Properly Affected: Virtues and Feelings in Aristotle's Ethics." In *Essays on Aristotle's Ethics*, edited by Amélie Oksenberg Rorty, 103–16. Berkeley: University of California Press, 1980.

Kot, Stanislas. *Socinianism in Poland*. Translated by Earl Morse Wilbur. Boston: Starr King, 1957.

Küng, Hans. *Justification: The Doctrine of Karl Barth and a Catholic Reflection*. Translated by Edmund Tolk, Thomas Collins, and David Grandskou. London: Burns & Oates, 1964.

LaCugna, Catherine Mowry. *God for Us: The Trinity and Christian Life*. San Francisco: HarperSanFrancisco, 1991.

Lane, William L. *Hebrews 1–8*. Edited by Ralph P. Martin. Word Biblical Commentary 47A. Dallas: Word Books, 1991.

Lang, U. M. "Anhypostatos-Enhypostatos: Church Fathers, Protestant Orthodoxy and Karl Barth." *Journal of Theological Studies* 49 (1998): 630–57.

Law, R. J. K. ed. *The Treasures of John Owen for Today's Readers*. Edinburgh: Banner of Truth, 1991 to present.

Letis, Theodore P. "John Owen versus Brian Walton: A Reformed Response to the Birth of Textual Criticism." In *The Majority Text: Essays and Reviews in the Continuing Debate*, edited by Theodore P. Letis, 145–90. Grand Rapids: Institute for Biblical Textual Studies, 1987.

Letter, P. de. "Justification: In Catholic Theology." In *New Catholic Encyclopedia*, 8:81–88. New York: McGraw-Hill, 1967–89.

Leverenz, David. *The Language of Puritan Feeling: An Exploration in Literature, Psychology, and Social History*. New Brunswick, NJ: Rutgers University Press, 1980.

Lloyd, R. Glynne. *John Owen—Commonwealth Puritan*. Liverpool: Modern Welsh Publications, 1972.

———. "The Life and Work of John Owen with Special Reference to the Socinian Controversies of the Seventeenth Century." PhD diss., Edinburgh University, 1942.

Lovelace, Richard C. "The Anatomy of Puritan Piety: English Puritan Devotional Literature, 1600–1640." In *Christian Spirituality*, vol. 3, *Post-Reformation and Modern*, edited by Louis Depré and Don Saliers, 294–323. London: SCM, 1990.

Lund, Eric. "Second Age of the Reformation: Lutheran and Reformed Spirituality, 1550–1700." In *Christian Spirituality*, vol. 3, *Post-Reformation and Modern*, edited by Louis Depré and Don Saliers, 213–39. London: SCM, 1990.

Lundgaard, Kris. *The Enemy Within: Straight Talk about the Power and Defeat of Sin*. Phillipsburg, NJ: P&R, 1998.

Macleod, Donald. *The Person of Christ*. Downers Grove, IL: InterVarsity, 1998.

Macleod, Jack N. "John Owen and the Death of Death." In *"Out of Bondage": Papers Read at the 1983 Conference*, 70–87. London: Westminster Conference, 1984.

Macquarrie, John. "Christology without Incarnation? Some Critical Comments." In *The Truth of God Incarnate*, edited by Michael Green. London: Hodder & Stoughton, 1977.

Matthews, A. G. "The Puritans." In *Christian Worship: Studies in its History and Meaning*, edited by Nathaniel Micklem, 172–88. Oxford: Clarendon, 1936.

Mayor, Stephen. *The Lord's Supper in Early English Dissent*. London: Epworth, 1972.

———. "The Teaching of John Owen concerning the Lord's Supper." *Scottish Journal of Theology* 18 (1965): 170–81.

McCormack, Bruce. *Karl Barth's Critically Realistic Dialectical Theology: Its Genesis and Development, 1909–1936*. Oxford: Oxford University Press, 1995.

McCoy, C. S. "Johannes Cocceius: Federal Theologian." *Scottish Journal of Theology* 16 (1963): 352–70.

McFadyen, Alistair I. *The Call to Personhood: A Christian Theory of the Individual in Social Relationships*. New York: Cambridge University Press, 1990.

McFarlane, Graham W. P. *Christ and the Spirit: The Doctrine of the Incarnation according to Edward Irving*. Carlisle: Paternoster, 1996.

McGowan, A. T. B. *The Federal Theology of Thomas Boston*. Edited by David F. Wright and Donald Macleod. Rutherford Studies in Historical Theology. Edinburgh: published for Rutherford House by Paternoster, 1997.

McGrath, Alister E. *Iustitia Dei: A History of the Christian Doctrine of Justification*. 2nd ed. Cambridge, UK: Cambridge University Press, 1998.

———. "Justification." In *The Oxford Encyclopedia of the Reformation*, edited by Hans J. Hillerbrand, 2:360–68. Oxford: Oxford University Press, 1996.

———. "Justification in Earlier Evangelicalism." *Churchman* 98, no. 3 (1984): 217–28.

———. *The Making of Modern German Christology: From the Enlightenment to Pannenberg*. Oxford: Blackwell, 1986.

McGrath, Gavin. "'But We Preach Christ Crucified': The Cross of Christ in the Pastoral Theology of John Owen, 1616–1683." St. Antholin's Lectureship Charity Lecture, 1994. London: Latimer Trust, 1994.

———. "Puritans and the Human Will: Voluntarism within Mid-Seventeenth Century English Puritanism as Seen in the Works of Richard Baxter and John Owen." PhD diss., University of Durham, 1989.

McKim, Donald K. "John Owen's Doctrine of Scripture in Historical Perspective." *Evangelical Quarterly* 45, no. 4 (1973): 195–207.

McKinley, D. J. "John Owen's View of Illumination: An Alternative to the Fuller-Erickson Dialogue." *Bibliotheca Sacra* 154 (1997): 93–104.

———. "John Owen's View of Illumination and Its Contemporary Relevance." ThD diss., University of Santo Tomas, 1995.

McLachlan, John H. *Socinianism in Seventeenth-Century England*. London: Oxford University Press, 1951.

McLelland, Joseph C. *The Visible Words of God: An Exposition of the Sacramental Theology of Peter Martyr Vermigli*. Edinburgh: Oliver & Boyd, 1957.

Metzger, Bruce M. *A Textual Commentary on the Greek New Testament*. London: United Bible Societies, 1971.

Metzger, Paul Louis, ed. *Trinitarian Soundings in Systematic Theology*. New York: T&T Clark, 2005.

Meyer, Susan Sauvé. *Aristotle on Moral Responsibility: Character and Cause*. Oxford: Blackwell, 1993.

Middlekauff, Robert. "Piety and Intellect in Puritanism." *William and Mary Quarterly*, 3rd ser., 2, no. 3 (July 1965): 457–70.

Miller, Perry. "The Marrow of Puritan Divinity." In *Errand into the Wilderness*, 48–98. Cambridge, MA: Harvard University Press, Belknap, 1956.

———. *The New England Mind: The Seventeenth Century*. Cambridge, MA: Harvard University Press, 1939.

Moffatt, James. *The Life of John Owen, Puritan Scholar, Some Time Vice-Chancellor of the University of Oxford and Dean of Christ Church*. Congregational Worthies 6. 1908. London: Congregational Union of England and Wales, 1911.

Møller, Jens G. "The Beginnings of Puritan Covenant Theology." *Journal of Ecclesiastical History* 14 (1963): 46–67.

Moltmann, Jürgen. *The Trinity and the Kingdom: The Doctrine of God*. San Francisco: Harper & Row, 1981.

Moore, Susan Hardman. "Sacrifice in Puritan Typology." In *Sacrifice and Redemption*, edited by Stephen W. Sykes, 182–202. Cambridge, UK: Cambridge University Press, 1991.

Muller, Richard A. "Calvin and the 'Calvinists': Assessing the Continuities and Discontinuities between the Reformation and Orthodoxy." *Calvin Theological Journal* 30 (1995): 345–75; 31 (1996): 125–60.

———. *Christ and the Decree: Christology and Predestination in Reformed Theology from Calvin to Perkins*. Grand Rapids: Baker Academic, 1988.

———. *Dictionary of Latin and Greek Theological Terms: Drawn Principally from Protestant Scholastic Theology*. Grand Rapids: Baker Academic, 1985.

———. *God, Creation, and Providence in the Thought of Jacob Arminius: Sources and Directions of Scholastic Protestantism in the Era of Early Orthodoxy*. Grand Rapids: Baker Academic, 1991.

———. *Post-Reformation Reformed Dogmatics: The Rise and Development of Reformed Orthodoxy, ca. 1520 to ca. 1725*. 2nd ed. 4 vols. Grand Rapids: Baker Academic, 2003.

———. *The Unaccommodated Calvin: Studies in the Theology of a Theological Tradition*. Oxford Studies in Historical Theology. Oxford: Oxford University Press, 2000.

The National Union Catalogue, Pre-1956 Imprints. Chicago: Mansell, 1972.

Newbigin, Lesslie. *Trinitarian Faith and Today's Mission*. Carlisle: Paternoster, 1998.

Nicole, Roger. "John Calvin's View of the Extent of the Atonement." *Westminster Theological Journal* 47 (1985): 197–225.

———. "New Dimensions in the Holy Spirit." In *New Dimensions in Evangelical Thought: Essays in Honor of Millard J. Erickson*, edited by David S. Dockery, 330–37. Downers Grove, IL: InterVarsity, 1998.

———. "Particular Redemption." In *Our Savior God: Man, Christ, and the Atonement; Addresses Presented to the Philadelphia Conference on Reformed Theology, 1977–1979*, edited by James M. Boice, 165–78. Grand Rapids: Baker Academic, 1980.

Niebuhr, H. Richard. "The Doctrine of the Trinity and the Unity of the Church." *TT* 3 (1946): 371–84.

Niesel, Wilhelm. *Reformed Symbolics: A Comparison of Catholicism, Orthodoxy, and Protestantism*. Translated by David Lewis. London: Oliver & Boyd, 1962.

Null, Ashley. *Thomas Cranmer's Doctrine of Repentance: Renewing the Power to Love*. Oxford: Oxford University Press, 2000.

Nuttall, Geoffrey F. *The Holy Spirit in Puritan Faith and Experience*. 2nd ed. 1947. Repr., Chicago: University of Chicago Press, 1992.

———. *Studies in Christian Enthusiasm: Illustrated from Early Quakerism*. Wallingford, PA: Pendle Hill, 1948.

Oden, Thomas C., ed. *The Justification Reader*. Grand Rapids: Eerdmans, 2002.

———. *Systematic Theology*. Vol. 2, *The Word of Life*. San Francisco: HarperSanFrancisco, 1989.

Oki, Hideo. "Ethics in Seventeenth-Century English Puritanism." ThD diss., Union Theological Seminary, New York, 1960.

Onions, C. T., ed. *The Oxford Dictionary of English Etymology*. Oxford: Clarendon, 1966.

Packer, J. I. *A Quest for Godliness: The Puritan Vision of the Christian Life*. Wheaton: Crossway, 1990.

Pannenberg, Wolfhart. *Anthropology in Theological Perspective*. Philadelphia: Westminster, 1985.

———. *Systematic Theology*. Translated by Geoffrey W. Bromiley. 2 vols. Grand Rapids: Eerdmans, 1991–94.

Parker, Kenneth L. *The English Sabbath: A Study of Doctrine and Discipline from the Reformation to the Civil War*. Cambridge, UK: Cambridge University Press, 1988.

Payne, Jon D. *John Owen on the Lord's Supper*. Edinburgh: Banner of Truth, 2004.

Pelikan, Jaroslav. *The Christian Tradition*. Vol. 4, *Reformation of Church and Dogma (1300–1700)*. Chicago: University of Chicago Press, 1984.

Peters, Ted. *God as Trinity: Relationality and Temporality in Divine Life*. Louisville: Westminster John Knox, 1993.

Peterson, Eugene H. *Christ Plays in Ten Thousand Places: A Conversation in Spiritual Theology*. Grand Rapids: Eerdmans, 2005.

Peterson, Mark A. *The Price of Redemption: The Spiritual Economy of Puritan New England*. Stanford, CA: Stanford University Press, 1997.

Plantinga, Alvin. *Warranted Christian Belief*. New York: Oxford University Press, 2000.

Poole, David N. J. *The Covenant Approach to the Ordo Salutis*. Lewiston, NY: Mellen, 1995.

Porter, Jean. *Natural and Divine Law: Reclaiming the Tradition for Christian Ethics*. Grand Rapids: Eerdmans, 1999.

Preus, Robert D. *The Theology of Post-Reformation Lutheranism*. Vol. 1, *A Study of Theological Prolegomena*. Saint Louis: Concordia, 1970.

Primus, John. "Calvin and the Puritan Sabbath." In *Exploring the Heritage of John Calvin*, edited by D. E. Holwerda, 40–75. Grand Rapids: Baker Academic, 1976.

Quasten, Johannes. *Patrology*. Vol. 3, *The Golden Age of Greek Patristic Literature from the Council of Nicaea to the Council of Chalcedon*. Westminster, MD: Newman, 1960.

Rahner, Karl. *Theological Investigations*. Vol. 4. Translated by Kevin Smyth. Baltimore: Helicon, 1966.

———. *The Trinity*. Translated by Joseph Donceel. London: Burns & Oates, 1970.

Reay, Barry. *The Quakers and the English Revolution*. London: Temple Smith, 1985.

Reedy, Gerard. "Socinians, John Toland, and the Anglican Rationalists." *Harvard Theological Review* 70 (1977): 285–304.

Rehnman, Sebastian. *Divine Discourse: The Theological Methodology of John Owen*. Texts and Studies in Reformation and Post-Reformation Thought. Grand Rapids: Baker Academic, 2002.

———. "John Owen: A Reformed Scholastic at Oxford." In *Reformation and Scholasticism: An Ecumenical Enterprise*, edited by W. J. van Asselt and E. Dekker, 181–203. Grand Rapids: Baker Academic, 2001.

———. "Theologia Tradita: A Study in the Prolegomenous Discourse of John Owen (1616–1683)." DPhil diss., Oxford University, 1997.

Rohls, Jan. *Reformed Confessions: Theology from Zurich to Barmen*. Translated by John Hoffmeyer. Columbia Series in Reformed Theology. Louisville: Westminster John Knox, 1998.

Ross, Sir William David. *Aristotle*. 6th ed. New York: Routledge, 1995.

Ryken, Philip Graham. *Thomas Boston as Preacher of the Fourfold State*. Edited by David F. Wright and Donald Macleod. Rutherford Studies in Historical Theology. Edinburgh: Rutherford House, 1999.

Santos, Valdeci dos. "O 'Crente Carnal' à Luz do ensino de John Owen sobre a Mortificação." *Fides reformata* 4, no. 1 (1999): 57–68.

Sasse, Hermann. *This Is My Body: Luther's Contention for the Real Presence in the Sacrament of the Altar*. Minneapolis: Augsburg, 1959.

Schaff, Philip. "The Canons and Decrees of the Council of Trent." In *The Creeds of Christendom*, vol. 2, *The Greek and Latin Creeds*. 4th, rev. and enlarged ed. 1877. Repr., Grand Rapids: Baker Academic, 1996.

———. *History of the Christian Church*. 8 vols. 1910. Repr., Grand Rapids: Eerdmans, 1985.

Schreiner, Susan. *The Theater of His Glory: Nature and the Natural Order in the Thought of John Calvin*. Durham: Labyrinth, 1991.

Schwarz, Hans. *Christology*. Grand Rapids: Eerdmans, 1998.

Schwemmer, Oswald. "Habitus." In *Sacramentum Mundi: An Encyclopedia of Theology*, edited by Karl Rahner, 3:1–3. London: Burns & Oates, 1969.

Schwöbel, Christoph, ed. *Trinitarian Theology Today: Essays on Divine Being and Act*. Edinburgh: T&T Clark, 1995.

Seifrid, Mark A. *Christ, Our Righteousness: Paul's Theology of Justification*. Downers Grove, IL: InterVarsity, 2000.

Shields, James Leroy. "The Doctrine of Regeneration in English Puritan Theology, 1604–1689." PhD diss., Southwestern Baptist Theological Seminary, 1965.

Shults, F. LeRon. *Reforming Theological Anthropology: After the Philosophical Turn to Relationality*. Grand Rapids: Eerdmans, 2003.

Simpson, J. A., and E. S. C. Weiner, eds. *The Oxford English Dictionary*. 2nd ed. Vol. 3, *Cham–Creeky*. Oxford: Clarendon, 1989.

Smith, Christopher R. "'Up and Be Doing': The Pragmatic Puritan Eschatology of John Owen." *Evangelical Quarterly* 61, no. 4 (1989): 335–49.

Smith, Gordon T. *A Holy Meal: The Lord's Supper in the Life of the Church*. Grand Rapids: Baker Academic, 2005.

Solberg, Winton U. *Redeem the Time: The Puritan Sabbath in Early America*. Cambridge, UK: Cambridge University Press, 1977.

Spence, Alan J. "Christ's Humanity and Ours: John Owen." In *Persons, Divine and Human*, edited by C. Schwöbel and Colin E. Gunton, 74–97. Edinburgh: T&T Clark, 1991.

———. "Incarnation and Inspiration: John Owen and the Coherence of Christology." PhD diss., King's College London, 1989.

———. "Inspiration and Incarnation: John Owen and the Coherence of Christology." *King's Theological Review* 12 (1989): 52–55.

———. "John Owen and Trinitarian Agency." *Scottish Journal of Theology* 43 (1990): 157–73.

Sprunger, Keith. "English and Dutch Sabbatarianism and the Development of a Puritan Social Theology, 1600–1660." *Church History* 51, no. 1 (1982): 24–38.

Stephens, W. P. "The Church in Bucer's Commentaries on the Epistle to the Ephesians." In *Martin Bucer: Reforming Church and Community*, edited by David F. Wright, 45–60. Cambridge, UK: Cambridge University Press, 1994.

———. *The Holy Spirit in the Theology of Martin Bucer*. Cambridge, UK: Cambridge University Press, 1970.

———. *The Theology of Huldrych Zwingli*. Oxford: Clarendon, 1986.

Stevenson, Kenneth. *Covenant of Grace Renewed: A Vision of the Eucharist in the Seventeenth Century*. London: Darton, Longman & Todd, 1994.

Stoever, William K. B. *"A Faire and Easie Way to Heaven": Covenant Theology and Antinomianism in Early Massachusetts*. Middletown, CT: Wesleyan University Press, 1978.

Stott, John R. W. *The Letters of John: An Introduction and Commentary*. Edited by Leon Morris. 2nd ed. Tyndale New Testament Commentaries 19. Grand Rapids: Eerdmans, 1988.

Stover, Dale Arden. "The Pneumatology of John Owen: A Study of the Role of the Holy Spirit in Relation to the Shape of a Theology." PhD diss., McGill University, Montreal, 1967.

Strehle, Stephen. *Calvinism, Federalism, and Scholasticism: A Study of the Reformed Doctrine of the Covenant*. Basler und Berner Studien zur historischen und systematischen Theologie 58. Bern: Peter Lang, 1988.

Stumpf, Samuel Enoch. *Socrates to Sartre: A History of Philosophy*. 5th ed. New York: McGraw-Hill, 1993.

Symonds, H. Edward. *The Council of Trent and Anglican Formularies*. London: Oxford University Press, 1933.

Szczuchi, Lech. "Socinianism." In *The Oxford Encyclopedia of the Reformation*, edited by Hans J. Hillerbrand, 4:83–87. Oxford: Oxford University Press, 1996.

Tamburello, Dennis E. *Union with Christ: John Calvin and the Mysticism of St. Bernard*. Columbia Series in Reformed Theology. Louisville: Westminster John Knox, 1994.

Tanner, Kathryn. *Jesus, Humanity and the Trinity: A Brief Systematic Theology*. 1st Fortress Press edition. Minneapolis: Fortress, 2001.

Thompson, John. *Modern Trinitarian Perspectives*. New York: Oxford University Press, 1994.

Toon, Peter. *The Emergence of Hyper-Calvinism in English Nonconformity, 1689–1765*. London: Olive Tree, 1967.

———. *God's Statesman: The Life and Work of John Owen; Pastor, Educator, Theologian*. Exeter: Paternoster, 1971.

———. *Justification and Sanctification*. Foundations of Faith. London: Marshall Morgan & Scott, 1983.

———. "The Latter-Day Glory." In *Puritans, the Millennium and the Future of Israel: Puritan Eschatology, 1600 to 1660*, 23–41. Cambridge, UK: James Clarke, 1970.

———. "A Message of Hope for the Rump Parliament." *Evangelical Quarterly* 43 (1971): 82–96.

———. "Puritan Eschatology: 1600–1648." In *The Manifold Grace of God: Papers Read at the Puritan and Reformed Studies Conference, 1968*, 49–60. London: Evangelical Magazine; Hartshill, Stoke-on-Trent: Tentmaker Publications, 1968.

Torrance, James B. "The Incarnation and 'Limited Atonement.'" *The Scottish Bulletin of Evangelical Theology* 2 (1984): 32–40.

———. "The Vicarious Humanity of Christ." In *The Incarnation*, edited by T. F. Torrance, 127–47. Edinburgh: Handsel, 1981.

———. *Worship, Community, and the Triune God of Grace*. Downers Grove, IL: InterVarsity, 1996.

Torrance, T. F. *Calvin's Doctrine of Man*. London: Lutterworth, 1949.

———. *The Trinitarian Faith: The Evangelical Theology of the Ancient Catholic Church*. Edinburgh: T&T Clark, 1988.

———. *Trinitarian Perspectives: Toward Doctrinal Agreement*. Edinburgh: T&T Clark, 1994.

Trevor-Roper, Hugh. *Catholics, Anglicans, and Puritans: Seventeenth Century Essays*. London: Secker & Warburg, 1987.

Troxel, Craig A. "'Cleansed Once for All': John Owen on the Glory of Gospel Worship in 'Hebrews.'" *Calvin Theological Journal* 32 (1997): 468–79.

Trueman, Carl R. *The Claims of Truth: John Owen's Trinitarian Theology*. Carlisle: Paternoster, 1998.

———. "Faith Seeking Understanding: Some Neglected Aspects of John Owen's Understanding of Scriptural Interpretation." In *Interpreting the Bible: Historical and Theological Studies in Honour of David F. Wright*, edited by A. N. S. Lane, 147–62. Leicester: Apollos, 1997.

———. "John Owen's *Dissertation on Divine Justice*: An Exercise in Christocentric Scholasticism." *Calvin Theological Journal* 33 (1998): 87–103.

———. *Luther's Legacy: Salvation and English Reformers, 1525–1556*. Oxford: Clarendon, 1994.

———. "A Small Step towards Rationalism: The Impact of the Metaphysics of Tommaso Campanella on the Theology of Richard Baxter." In *Protestant Scholasticism: Essays in Reassessment*, edited by Carl R. Trueman and R. S. Clark, 181–95. Carlisle: Paternoster, 1999.

Trueman, Carl R., and R. S. Clark, eds. *Protestant Scholasticism: Essays in Reassessment*. Carlisle: Paternoster, 1999.

Vander Zee, Leonard J. *Christ, Baptism, and the Lord's Supper: Recovering the Sacraments for Evangelical Worship*. Downers Grove, IL: InterVarsity, 2004.

Vanhoozer, Kevin J., ed. *The Trinity in a Pluralistic Age: Theological Essays on Culture and Religion*. Grand Rapids: Eerdmans, 1997.

Vermigli, Pietro Martire. *The Oxford Treatise and Disputation on the Eucharist, 1549*. Edited and translated by Joseph C. McLelland, Sixteenth Century Essays and Studies 56. Kirksville, MO: Truman State University Press, 2000.

———. *Predestination and Justification: Two Theological Loci*. Edited by Frank A. James. Sixteenth Century Essays and Studies 68. Kirksville, MO: Truman State University Press, 2003.

Volf, Miroslav. *After Our Likeness: The Church as the Image of the Trinity*. Grand Rapids: Eerdmans, 1998.

Von Rohr, John. *The Covenant of Grace in Puritan Thought*. Edited by Charley Harkwick and James O. Duke. AAR Studies in Religion 45. Atlanta: Scholars Press, 1986.

Vose, Godfrey Noel. "Profile of a Puritan: John Owen, 1616–1683." PhD diss., State University of Iowa, Iowa City, 1963.

Wakefield, G. S. *Puritan Devotion: Its Place in the Development of Christian Piety*. London: Epworth, 1957.

Wallace, Dewey D. "The Life and Thought of John Owen to 1660: A Study of the Significance of Calvinist Theology in English Puritanism." PhD diss., Princeton University, 1965.

———. *Puritans and Predestination: Grace in English Protestant Theology, 1525–1695*. Chapel Hill: University of North Carolina, 1982.

Wallace, Ronald S. *Calvin's Doctrine of the Christian Life*. Edinburgh: Oliver & Boyd, 1959.

———. *Calvin's Doctrine of the Word and Sacrament*. Edinburgh: Scottish Academic Press, 1995.

Ware, Kallistos [Bishop of Diokleia]. "The Humanity of Christ: The Fourth Constantinople Lecture." Paper presented at the Anglican and Eastern Churches Association, 1985. *Eastern Churches Newsletter: The Journal of the Anglican and Eastern Churches Association* 21 (1985).

Warfield, B. B. *Calvin and Augustine*. Philadelphia: P&R, 1980.

Watkin-Jones, Howard. *The Holy Spirit from Arminius to Wesley*. London: Epworth, 1929.

Watkins, Owen C. *The Puritan Experience*. London: Routledge & Kegan Paul, 1972.

Weinandy, Thomas G. *Does God Suffer?* Notre Dame, IN: University of Notre Dame Press, 2000.

———. *The Father's Spirit of Sonship: Reconceiving the Trinity*. Edinburgh: T&T Clark, 1995.

———. *In the Likeness of Sinful Flesh: An Essay on the Humanity of Christ*. Edinburgh: T&T Clark, 1993.

Weir, David A. *The Origins of the Federal Theology in Sixteenth-Century Reformation Thought*. Oxford: Clarendon, 1990.

Whitaker, W. B. *Sunday in Tudor and Stuart Times*. London: Houghton, 1933.

Whiting, Charles E. *Studies in English Puritanism from the Restoration to the Revolution, 1660–1688*. New York: Macmillan, 1931.

Wilbur, Earl Morse. *A History of Unitarianism: In Transylvania, England, and America*. Boston: Beacon, 1952.

———. *A History of Unitarianism: Socinianism and Its Antecedents*. Cambridge, MA: Harvard University Press, 1947.

Williams, George H. *The Radical Reformation*. 3rd, rev. and enlarged ed. Kirksville, MO: Sixteenth Century Journal Publishers, 1992.

Williams, Jean Dorothy. "The Puritan Quest for Enjoyment of God: An Analysis of the Theological and Devotional Writings of Puritans in Seventeenth-Century England." PhD diss., University of Melbourne, 1997.

Williams, Lloyd G. "'Digitus Dei': God and Nation in the Thought of John Owen; A Study in English Puritanism and Nonconformity, 1653–1683." PhD diss., Drew University, 1981.

Willis, David E. *Calvin's Catholic Christology: The Function of the So-Called Extra-Calvinisticum in Calvin's Theology*. Leiden: E. J. Brill, 1966.

Wingren, Gustaf. *Man and the Incarnation: A Study of the Biblical Theology of Irenaeus*. Translated by Ross Mackenzie. London: Oliver & Boyd, 1959.

Won, Jonathan Jong-Chun. "Communion with Christ: An Exposition and Comparison of the Doctrine of Union and Communion with Christ in Calvin and the English Puritans." PhD diss., Westminster Theological Seminary, 1989.

Wong, David Wai-Sing. "The Covenant Theology of John Owen." PhD diss., Westminster Theological Seminary, 1998.

Wright, N. T. *The Challenge of Jesus: Rediscovering Who Jesus Was and Is*. Downers Grove, IL: InterVarsity, 1999.

———. *The Meal Jesus Gave Us*. Louisville: Westminster John Knox, 2002.

———. *What Saint Paul Really Said: Was Paul of Tarsus the Real Founder of Christianity?* Grand Rapids: Eerdmans, 1997.

Wright, Robert K. M. "John Owen's Great High Priest: The Highpriesthood of Christ in the Theology of John Owen (1616–1683)." PhD diss., Iliff School of Theology and University of Denver, 1989.

Yarnold, Edward. "*Duplex iustitia*: The Sixteenth Century and the Twentieth." In *Christian Authority: Essays in Honour of Henry Chadwick*, edited by G. R. Evans, 204–23. Oxford: Clarendon, 1988.

Yoon, J. H. "The Significance of John Owen's Theology on Mortification for Contemporary Christianity." PhD diss., University of Wales, Lampeter, 2003.

NAME INDEX

Ainsworth, H., 153n24
Alexander of Hales, 126
Allen, Pauline, 83n66
Allison, C. F., 108n2, 128n91, 134n121, 139, 139n138
Allport, Josiah, 135n122
Alsop, Vincent, 156, 156n38, 172n123
Alsted, Johann Henrich, 74n26
Alting, Jacob, 169
Ambrose, 41, 41n27
Ames, William, 43n38, 50n74, 62n133, 74n27, 111n12, 116, 163n67, 193, 193n222
Anderson, Ruth L., 45n49
Andrewes, Lancelot, 115n31
Anselm, 69, 69n5, 70, 70n7, 70n10, 100n144, 141
Aristotle, 30, 36, 43, 43n35, 45, 45n48, 47n59, 48, 48n65, 49, 49n66, 49n72, 52, 52n86, 52n88, 54, 54n97, 55, 58, 60, 62, 63, 65, 147n1, 150, 151n15, 171, 171n114, 171n115, 171n117
Arminius, James, 30n51, 37n7, 112
Asty, John, 18n13, 23n28
Athanasius, 37n4, 140, 141n146
Augustine, 50, 50n77, 56, 56n104, 75n33, 113n24, 126, 140, 140n144, 160n54, 163n69, 165, 172, 172n119, 191n213, 193, 231n139
Ayres, Lewis, 160n54
Ayto, John, 62n135

Baab, Lynne M., 239n10
Baker, J. Wayne, 25n33

Barbour, Hugh, 199n249
Barker, Matthew, 61n129
Barlow, Thomas, 133n115, 135n122, 178n153
Barr, James, 37n6
Barraclough, Peter, 21n25
Barth, Karl, 37n6, 84, 98n137, 99n141, 238
Basil, 191n213
Bass, William Ward, 32n62, 56n106
Bates, William, 215n43
Battles, Ford Lewis, 56n105
Bauckham, Richard, 208n2, 211n15
Baxter, Richard, 9, 25, 30, 30n55, 114n28, 132n112, 195, 215n43
Beardslee, John W. III, 111n13
Beeke, Joel R., 32, 32n65, 51n80, 118n50, 149, 166n79
Bellarmine, Robert, 115, 115n31, 117n44, 127, 127n88, 128, 129, 129n98, 135n122, 156
Berkhof, Louis, 124n77
Beveridge, Henry, 46n54, 122n67, 232n144
Beza, Theodore, 78n46, 210n8
Biddle, John, 37, 194n223
Bierma, Lyle D., 98n137
Bizer, Ernst, 41n26
Blackham, Paul, 171n113
Blight, James G., 45n49
Bloom, Harold, 21n26
Bobick, Michael W., 36n1, 98n137, 123n73, 209n2, 210n8
Bobrinskoy, Boris, 238n6

271

SUBJECT INDEX

Abraham, 137
absolute justification, 136–37
acceptance with God, 187–89
acquaintance, 181
Adam, 43, 58, 98, 101, 109, 178
Adam and Eve, 37, 58, 69
adoption, 155, 189–92
adoptionism, 82
affections, 53–55
afflictions, 185, 203
Alexander of Hales, 126
Alexandrian school, 78
Allison, C. F., 108n2, 139
Alsop, Vincent, 156
Alsted, Johann Henrich, 74n26
Alting, Jacob, 169
Ambrose, 41
Ames, William, 50n74, 111n12, 116, 193
amicitiae, 170–71
angels, 100, 210
anhypostasis, 83–84, 237
Anselm, 69–71, 89, 100, 141, 144, 179
anthropocentric theology, 31–32, 235
anthropology, 31–32
  and Christology, 68, 78, 146
  and justification, 133
  and theology, 157
anthroposensitivity, 33, 53, 68, 78, 88, 108, 235
  and assurance, 118
  and communion with God, 149
  and communion with the Son, 176
  and justification, 109, 145

antinomianism, 108, 137n130, 154, 155, 176
Antiochene school, 78
Apollinarianism, 84
Arians, 91, 160n56
Aristotle, 29–30, 43, 52
  on affections, 54
  on character, 58
  on contemplation, 49
  epistemology, 47
  faculty psychology, 35–36, 45–46, 48, 65
  on friendship, 150, 171
  on habits, 62–63
  logic, 168, 228, 238
  on mind, 49
  on passions, 59
Arminians, Arminianism, 21, 23, 60, 112–13, 194n224
Arminius, James, 30n51, 37n7, 112
assent, 116, 117
assumption, of human nature (incarnation), 78–83, 88, 89, 100
assurance, 118, 134, 166, 204
Athanasius, 140, 173
"Atlas of Independency," 20
atonement, 30, 131–32, 145, 155, 180
Augustine, 50, 53, 126, 140
  on body, 56
  on the Father, 193
  on love of God, 172
  on Trinity, 75n33, 160, 162, 163n69
Augustinianism, 28–29